THE COLD WAR AS COOPERATION

The Cold War as Cooperation

Edited by
Roger E. Kanet

and
Edward A. Kolodziej

The Johns Hopkins University Press
Baltimore

First published, 1991, by
The Johns Hopkins University Press
701 West 40th Street
Baltimore, Maryland 21211

Library of Congress Cataloging-in-Publication Data

The cold war as cooperation / edited by Roger E. Kanet and Edward A.
Kolodziej.
    p. cm.
Includes papers presented at a workshop held at the University of
Illinois at Urbana-Champaign, 4–6 May 1989.
Includes bibliographical references and index.
ISBN 0–8018–4206–9
1. Cold War—Congresses.   2. World politics—1945–   —Congresses.
I. Kanet, Roger E., 1936–   . II. Kolodziej. Edward A.
D842.C59   1991
909.82′5—dc20   90–21345

Contents

Acknowledgements

The editors wish to express their sincere appreciation to all of those who made the project and this resulting study possible. The original idea of a study of superpower cooperation emerged out of an earlier project in which many of the contributors to this book were also involved. In the course of carrying out the research included in *The Limits of Soviet Power in the Developing World: Thermidor in the Revolutionary Struggle* (Macmillan and Johns Hopkins, 1989), it became evident that superpower conflict and competition were accompanied by persistent cooperation. As the editors traced US–Soviet competition in regional conflicts since World War II, the concept of cooperation based on a game-theoretic understanding of that term provided one important key to explaining the dilemma of why a cold war could arise *and* why it is is now coming to an end. This volume is one attempt to relax, if not resolve, this dilemma.

A key element in the preparation and emergence of the present study was a major workshop on the cooperative aspects of the superpower relationship throughout the entire postwar period. This workshop was held at the University of Illinois at Urbana-Champaign on 4–6 May 1989. Contributors and invited guests, most of whom had already met in smaller groups to work out the details of the theoretical framework of the project, came together to address the issue of cooperation within the context of conflict in the postwar US–Soviet relationship. In addition to the primary contributors who presented the initial drafts of the papers included here, Frederick S. Pearson of the Wayne State University in Detroit and David W. Tarr of the University of Wisconsin, Madison, served as formal commentators and provided detailed written comments on the papers. Terry D. Clark and James M. Finlay, both of the University of Illinois at Urbana-Champaign, served as rapporteurs.

The editors wish to express their appreciation to all the participants whose perceptive criticisms and suggestions resulted in greater clarity and precision in the final drafts of the individual papers. They also wish to thank James Finlay for the index of cases of superpower cooperation that he prepared. This index is drawn from the regional chapters and is designed to assist scholars and analysts who, like the authors of the volume, wish to pursue further and test the thesis that the Cold War can be understood as an epic effort to decide the political order and socio-economic welfare system of the emerging world society and the principles of legitimacy on which it should rest.

The editors are also grateful for the support provided for the workshop by the Program in Arms Control, Disarmament and International Security and the Department of Political Science, both of the University of Illinois at Urbana-Champaign. Moreover, without the substantial financial backing of the Midwest Consortium for International Security Studies (a program managed by the Midwest Center of the American Academy of Arts and Sciences and funded by the MacArthur Foundation) and the National Defense University, the workshop would not have been possible. The editors wish to give special thanks to Russell Hardin and Marian Rice of the former organization, and to Robert Butterworth of the latter for their role in providing that support. Of course, the views, opinions, and findings contained in this book are those of the authors and should not be construed as an official position of either the Midwest Consortium or the National Defense University.

The editors also wish to thank all of the other authors for their willingness to revise their chapters, taking into account the recommendations from workshop participants and the sometimes stringent demands of the editors; thanks are also due to Barbara Cohen for preparing the subject index. Finally they wish to acknowledge the essential role of the secretarial staff in the Department of Political Science – especially Janie Carroll, Mary Anne Heiderscheit, and Peggy Currid – who dealt effectively and patiently with 'incompatible' computer programs, illegible handwriting, and related problems.

ROGER E. KANET
EDWARD A. KOLODZIEJ

Notes on the Contributors

Stephen P. Cohen is Professor of Political Science at the University of Illinois at Urbana-Champaign and director of the University's Program in Regional Security Studies. He served as a member of the Policy Planning Staff of the US Department of State during 1985–7. Dr Cohen is the author or co-author of numerous books and articles on security questions in South Asia, including *The Indian Army* (1971), *The Pakistan Army* (1984), and (ed.) *The Security of South Asia: Asian and American Perspectives* (1987). He also contributed to *The Limits of Soviet Power in the Developing World* (1989).

W. Raymond Duncan is Distinguished Teaching Professor of Political Science at the State University of New York, College at Brockport. During 1984–6 he was Scholar-in-Residence with the Central Intelligence Agency, where he worked on Soviet–Third World relations. Included among his many publications are his most recent books, *The Soviet Union and Cuba: Interests and Influence* (1985) and with Carolyn McGiffert Ekidahl *Moscow and the Third World Under Gorbachev* (1990). He also contributed to *The Limits of Soviet Power in the Developing World* (1989).

Galia Golan is Jay and Leonie Darwin Professor of Social Studies and Chair of the Department of Political Science at the Hebrew University, Jerusalem. Among her numerous publications on aspects of Soviet foreign policy are *The Soviet Union and the Palestine Liberation Organization* (1980), *Yom Kippur and After: The Soviet Union and the Middle East Crisis* (1977), *The Soviet Union and National Liberation Movements in the Third World* (1988), *Gorbachev's 'New Thinking' on Terrorism* (1990), and *Soviet Policies in the Middle East since World War Two* (1990).

Roger E. Kanet is Associate Vice Chancellor for Academic Affairs and Director of International Programs and Studies, as well as Professor of Political Science, at the University of Illinois at Urbana-Champaign. Included among his publications are: (ed.) *Soviet Foreign Policy and East–West Relations* (1982), (ed.) *Soviet Foreign Policy in the 1980s* (1982), (ed.) *The Soviet Union, Eastern Europe and the Third World* (1987), and (ed.) *The Limits of Soviet Power in* *the Developing World: Thermidor in the Revolutionary Struggle* (1989).

Daniel R. Kempton is Assistant Professor of Political Science at Northern Illinois University. Included among his publications is *Soviet Strategy Toward Southern Africa: The National Liberation Movement Connection* (1989). He also contributed a bibliography on Soviet foreign policy to *The Limits of Soviet Power in the Developing World* (1989).

Samuel S. Kim is a member of the faculty of the Woodrow Wilson School of Public and International Affairs of Princeton University. He has written widely on Chinese foreign policy, US policy in East Asia, and the international relations of East Asia. Included among his publications are *China, the United Nations, and World Order* (1979), *China in the Global Community* (1980), *The Quest for a Just World Order* (1984), and *China and the World* (1989).

Edward A. Kolodziej is Research Professor of Political Science at the University of Illinois at Urbana-Champaign. His research and teaching interests focus on two related concerns: the role of military force and threats in international relations and the arms control and security problems in Europe. Among his major publications are: *The Uncommon Defense and Congress: 1945–1963* (1966), *French International Policy under De Gaulle and Pompidou: The Politics of Grandeur* (1974), and *Making and Marketing Arms: The French Experience and Its Implications for the International System* (1987). He was co-editor of *The Limits of Soviet Power in the Developing World: Thermidor in the Revolutionary Struggle* (1989).

Victor A. Kremenyuk has been Associate Director of the Institute for the Study of the USA and Canada of the Academy of Sciences of the USSR since 1989, and Department Head at the Institute since 1978. He is author of numerous studies of US foreign policy, in particular on US policy toward the developing world. These include, in Russian, *US Foreign Policy in the Third World* (1977), *US Policy Toward National Liberation Movements, 1945–1980* (1983), *Problems of Non-Alignment* (1986) and, in English, *USA and Dependent Regimes* (1981), *International Conflict Resolution* (1988), and four contributions to Graham T. Allison and William L. Ury (eds),

Windows of Opportunity: From Cold War to Peaceful Competition in US–Soviet Relations (1989).

Sheldon W. Simon is Professor of Political Science and Faculty Associate of Arizona State University's Center for Asian Studies. He also serves as a consultant with the US Information Agency and the Department of Defense. He has written extensively on Asian foreign and security policies and is the author or editor of six books, including *The ASEAN States and Regional Security* (1982) and *The Future of Asian-Pacific, Security Collaboration* (1988). He also contributed to *The Limits of Soviet Power in the Developing World* (1989).

Marvin G. Weinbaum is Professor of Political Science and Director of the Program in South and West Asian Studies at the University of Illinois at Urbana-Champaign. He has written widely about Afghan domestic and foreign politics. Among his recent publications are also *Food, Development and Politics in the Middle East* (1982) and *Egypt and the Politics of US Economic Aid* (1986). He spent spring semester 1990 in Peshawar, Pakistan, where he conducted research on prospects for Afghan postwar reconstruction. He contributed to *The Limits of Soviet Power in the Developing World* (1989).

Howard J. Wiarda is Professor of Political Science and of Comparative Labor Relations at the University of Massachusetts/Amherst, and Research Associate of the Center for International Studies, Harvard University. Until 1988 he served as Resident Scholar and Director of the Center for Hemispheric Studies at the American Enterprise Institute for Public Policy Research. He is the author or editor of fifteen books, including (with Harvey Kline) *Latin American Politics and Development* (3rd edn, 1990), (ed.) *Rift and Revolution: The Central American Imbroglio* (1984), *New Directions in Comparative Politics* (1985), and (with Mark Falcoff and others) *The Communist Challenge in the Caribbean and Central America* (1987), *Foreign Policy without Illusions* (1990), *The Democratic Revolution in Latin America* (1990). He also contributed to *The Limits of Soviet Power in the Developing World* (1989).

Crawford Young is Professor of Political Science at the University of Wisconsin, Madison, where he has served as chair of both the

Department of Political Science and the African Studies Program. His many publications on domestic and international politics in Africa include *The Politics of Cultural Pluralism* (1976), *Cooperatives and Development* (1982), *Ideology and Development in Africa* (1982), and *The Rise and Decline of the Zairian State* (1985). He also served as a formal commentator on the project that resulted in *The Limits of Soviet Power in the Developing World* (1989).

I. William Zartman is Jacob Baustein Professor of International Organization and Conflict Resolution and Director of the African Studies Program at the Johns Hopkins School of Advanced International Studies. He is the author and editor of a number of books on North Africa, including *Man, State and Society in the Contemporary Maghreb* (1974), *Elites in the Middle East* (1980), and *The Political Economy of Morocco* (1987). Professor Zartman has also written extensively on African politics and relations, with his latest work including *Ripe for Resolution: Conflict and Intervention in Africa* (1985), and, as editor, *The Political Economy of Nigeria* (1983), and *The OAU after Twenty Years* (1984). He also contributed to *The Limits of Soviet Power in the Developing World* (1989).

Preface

Measured by the blood and treasure marshalled and directed in its pursuit, the Cold War must be reckoned among the great epics in human history. Unprecedented quantities of wealth and hundreds of millions of people from nations around the world were absorbed in this endeavor. Unlike Homer's *Iliad* and *Odyssey*, it was not limited to two peoples washed by common waters. It spread and sprawled to the far reaches of the globe, sparking wars – Korea and Vietnam most notably – and stirring civil strife along its path.

Among the many puzzles that the superpower struggle prompts, quite aside from its causes and consequences, is the question why the Cold War did not result in a global conflagration similar to the great power conflicts that led to the Napoleonic wars and to two world wars in this century. This volume attempts to supply a partial answer to this question. By that token it also contributes to an explanation of why the Cold War is rapidly drawing to a close and why the Cold War experience may be viewed as a necessary bridge between a lamentably devastating war-ridden past to a more productive or, at least, less destructive future.

Following the principle that the simplest solution to a problem is the best, this volume argues that the Cold War was cooperative from start to finish. Chapter 1 explains this paradoxical proposition. Situating the superpower struggle in a historical setting created by over four centuries of nation-state competition, this volume portrays the Soviet–American competition as the last in a line of Big Power attempts to define the structures of world political order and economy to suit their preferences and to base those structures, putatively, on principles of authority of universal worth and legitimacy. The Cold War served the aims and interests of the superpowers and for a long time those of many nations and peoples in the developed and developing world. It catalyzed, for example, the process that culminated in the globalization of the nation-state as the principal unit of authority in the world society. Except for close calls, like the Cuban Missile crisis and a series of Berlin crises, the leadership of each superpower was careful to signal to its rival-partner that their regional conflicts could be managed short of general war, the traditional international instrument to settle profound national clashes over interests and values. Even in these crises, superpower diplomacy was marked by a prudence and restraint that was some-times belied by the bombast and threats issuing from leadership circles.

In the logic of game theory, each superpower has had to learn to cooperate – mostly implicitly, sometimes explicitly – with its adver-sary to coordinate their mutually contingent behavior to avoid the worst consequences of their competition and to maximize the dif-ferential gains of compromises. They also had to develop rules of engagement and disengagement to regulate their conflict, as well as those of their allies and clients. These implicit and explicit comprom-ises on outcomes and conflict processes essentially formed an institu-tional structure on which the superpowers could provisionally rely in pursuing their discord within an evolving and enlarging set of understandings, and of tolerable and legitimate practices in pressing their respective national and systemic claims.

The regional chapters below attempt to apply this conceptual framework to the superpower struggle since World War II. Each author is a specialist who has an intimate knowledge not only of the politics and local cleavages but also of superpower behaviour and stakes in his or her region. The editors charged each contributor to draw on his or her knowledge and experience and, speaking *ex cathedra*, to identify the lines of superpower cooperative behavior within the meaning of the term used in this volume.

As a collaborative exercise, the editors and contributors trust that the final product will be greater than the sum of the individual parts. Dr Victor Kremenyuk's important contribution encourages this view. Across the barriers of language, culture, and a bitter and costly Cold War, Dr Kremenyuk and the other authors struck an immediate rapport when we first met in a conference on the campus of the University of Illinois in May 1989. Dr Kremenyuk, who has been honored by the Soviet Academy of Sciences for his contribution to conflict resolution and mediation theory and practice, assumed a leading role in the vigorous and sometimes heated discussions leading to adoption of a common conceptual framework and to the game theoretic notion of cooperation underlying this volume. Cooperation is understood in broad enough terms to encompass, paradoxically, the surface phenomena of superpower conflict as well as the coordin-ated choices of otherwise apparently irreconcilable foes.

The final chapter echoes and elaborates on Dr Kremenyuk's view that the past, i.e. the Cold War, has to be understood as cooperation, if it is to be successfully surmounted by the United States, the Soviet

Union, and other leading nations of the world. The regional chapters furnish prima facie evidence for the proposition that there has been more superpower cooperation than may initially strike the eye of the untutored observer. This experience and the expectations that it has generated among ruling elites in the United States and the Soviet Union provide a foundation on which to build toward a more peaceful and prosperous world and to define principles of political authority that apply across national boundaries and that approach system-wide acceptance to guide international conduct.

The volume is one attempt to get below the surface appearance of seemingly irremediable conflict to reveal the ill-formed, loose, and unsymmetrical cooperative webbing that underlay the Cold War. Chapter 1 differentiates the approach of this volume from several other parallel efforts. Unlike Penelope's tapestry, unraveled daily to await a better future, the fabric of superpower cooperation promises to be more durable and lasting cloth than the conflict that instigated the chain of decisions and actions that, not always wittingly designed, now comprise its warp and woof. As the Cold War recedes as a force, the remembrance of those cooperative experiences and of the limited but mutually beneficial results of superpower cooperation can be projected into the future to inform expectations in foreign capitals about the risks and likelihood of multiplying the frequency and scope of cooperation not only between the superpowers but also among the other nation-states of the globe. The shadow of the future can be seen, however dimly, in light of the past.

ROGER E. KANET
EDWARD A. KOLODZIEJ
Urbana-Champaign, Illinois

Part I
The Cold War
as Cooperation

1 The Cold War as Cooperation
Edward A. Kolodziej

The Cold War may be viewed as cooperation. Less than a decade ago, during the first years of the Reagan administration and the last years of the Brezhnev era, such a suggestion would have appeared naively sanguine – even absurd. Now the reverse appears true, even to the casual observer. As we all sense and as this chapter and those that follow detail, the Cold War is no longer a driving force in world politics, nor is it as central a problem as before in addressing the problems facing the world community, including the superpowers.

Signs of the Cold War's demise are everywhere: the sweeping changes introduced by *glasnost*, *perestroika*, and democratization in the Soviet Union; the collapse of the Berlin Wall, symbol of the ideological division between the East and the West as well as the two-bloc military confrontation in the heart of Europe; the creation of pluralistic governments in Eastern Europe and a turn to market practices to spur lagging socialist command economies; the enlarging expression of human freedoms – speech, association, petition, movement, and assembly – throughout the Eastern bloc; unilateral cutbacks in armed forces and military spending by the superpowers and their allies; widening arms control agreements in the form of the 1986 Stockholm accord and the 1987 treaty banning nuclear missiles between 500 to 5,500 kilometers; arms talks to cut strategic nuclear weapons, to reduce conventional forces in Europe, and to end nuclear testing; and the gradual expansion of superpower cooperation in southwest Asia, the Persian Gulf, southern Africa, the Middle East, and Central America.

While these changes are welcome, it is not particularly satisfying just to observe that something new is abroad in superpower relations. We still need to explain why these changes have occurred if gains are to be consolidated and if further progress is to be made. Otherwise, and despite the best intentions, governmental policy aims and instruments will be defined by hunches or guesses, chance, or biased preferences, rooted in ideology or personal and bureaucratic interests, with scant regard for their relevance or efficacy in broadening

3

and deepening superpower cooperation.

Can the relaxation of superpower tensions be attributed to the West's military strength, to the magnetic attractiveness of its open political processes and pluralism, or to its economic and technological superiority – to all three – or are there yet other factors at work, deep within the domestic political structures of these states or within international society, that are generating incentives and pressures on superpower governments and ruling elites to seek a respite in their global struggle and to explore new areas of accord and avenues for cooperation? Using a regional approach in tracing the superpower conflict since World War II, this volume attempts to provide some answers to these complex questions.

The volume argues that cooperation marks superpower relations throughout the Cold War period. The Grand Coalition to defeat Nazi Germany was its initial, and remains its most dramatic and sweeping, expression. Since then, despite profound differences of ideology and interest, the superpowers have learned to cooperate with each other, however reluctantly, in regulating their arms races and in adjusting to each other's conflicting demands and claims in their regional struggles around the globe. A critical part of the explanation for their cooperative behavior, hidden below more visible signs of conflict and obscured by threatening, confrontational behavior, is rooted simply enough – ideology aside – in the differences in interest and value that each attached to a region and in the evolving and shifting calculations of cost, risk, and benefit that each made in allocating its resources and commitments to a particular region to gets its way.

Whether a region was of interest or not has depended not only on its intrinsic, geopolitical importance – Eastern Europe, for example, has always weighed heavily on Soviet thinking whereas the Caribbean and Central America occupy a similar priority in US thinking – but also, and critically, on the varied limits on the expansion of super-power influence at play at regional levels. In other words, the conditions for superpower cooperation arise then from two principal sources: from their nuclear stalemate at a global level in which neither side can impose its will on the other and from the constraints confronted by the United States and the Soviet Union in the form, alternately, of resistance to superpower pressures and of the assertion of regional interests by local states and peoples in pursuit of their own interests. These limits on superpower intervention and influence lie deep within an international system divided against itself by differ-

ences of nationality, race, ethnic origin, communal loyalties, and
socio-economic class and status.

This line of analysis may become clearer if the notion of cooperation underlying this volume is first sketched and then related to the
assumptions animating the analysis below and succeeding chapters
about the nature of international relations today and the role that the
superpowers have played within them. Once these conceptual matters have been addressed, the stage will be set to assess the strengths
and weaknesses of a regional approach and the need to supplement
this partial explanation of the Cold War with other approaches if we
are to understand why the Cold War arose, what sustained it and
how, and why it is now waning. Conversely, we are also interested in
defining those conditions which might prompt its re-emergence.

COOPERATION AND THE IMPERATIVES OF THE GLOBAL SOCIETY

Mixed motive cooperation

Cooperation is used in two principal senses in this volume. In its
purest form, it essentially means co-valuation by individuals, groups,
or states of their mutual aims and interests as well as the strategies
chosen by each to pursue them. Not surprisingly, such unadulterated
instances of cooperation as co-valuation are not easily found in
superpower relations. This is no less the case in most human affairs.
Even instances of cooperation that appear self-evident by any test –
say the Grand Coalition against the axis powers – can be shown to
obscure underlying intractable differences.[1]

In the case of the wartime coalition major rifts erupted over how to
win the war and, with the Cold War as evidence, over how to win the
peace.[2] Regime differences and war aims were obviously incompatible if one compares the Atlantic Charter with Soviet territorial and
political claims against its eastern neighbors. Similarly, the military
strategies preferred by each of the Big Three contrasted sharply:
Moscow wanted a second front as soon as possible to relieve pressure
on its forces; London favored an indirect strategy to dissipate
German resources across Europe, to reduce allied casualties, and to
widen as large as possible Western influence in postwar Europe; and
Washington pressed for a build-up of allied forces to defeat the

German army in a frontal assault, largely leaving political matters to be finally settled once Germany was defeated.

The sense in which cooperation will be primarily used by the contributors to this volume departs from the everyday meaning of the term as co-valuation. It is based on Thomas Schelling's notion of cooperation.[3] Drawn from game theory it refers to situations in which players – in this case the superpowers – are engaged in a continuous series of interdependent exchanges, in which the stakes, i.e. payoffs, and the moves of players are defined by their mutually expected behavior in pursuit of shared and conflicting values and interests. These exchanges or games are not necessarily zero-sum, although the players may indeed conceive them to be so at different times over specific clashes, say Berlin or Cuba. Most will be shown to have variable payoffs, depending on the values, expectations, and moves of the players. What is particularly critical in the bargaining over differences is the ability and willingness of the actors, despite their differences under conditions of imperfect communication, to coordinate their moves for mutual, if not equal, advantage. Whereas Schelling focused primarily on nuclear deterrence and coercive diplomacy, this volume adapts his special notion of cooperation to regional areas of superpower exchange. Moreover, this conceptual approach is used as a device to understand and to explain the principal axes of superpower cooperation and conflict within the special limits set to their struggle in each region by local actors. This perspective contrasts with Schelling's prescriptive aim, which was to define moves and commitment strategies to win in the bargaining process.[4] The contributors to this volume seek first to understand how superpower games were played regionally and, drawing on that experience, to suggest how both might widen the scope of their cooperation and increase the benefits of their exchanges as partners and rivals.

For the authors of this study, cooperation does not imply congruent values or similar strategies. Nor does it mean that in pursuing an overlapping common interest in a context of conflict and competition that each superpower will employ the same policy instruments. In this second sense, cooperation refers primarily to convergent superpower acceptance of results, conditions, rules, and precedents, arising from their interactions, including most particularly (and paradoxically) from their conflictual relations.[5] These outcomes – say the Berlin Quadripartite Accord of 1971 – are conceived as constraints on the behavior of each superpower and the basis for mutual expectations about its future actions or reactions with respect to what Raymond Aron characterized as its superpower 'brother enemy'.[6] As one examines superpower regional relations, the analyst is struck by the number, variety, and accumulation of understandings, some explicit but more frequently tacit, that have been relied upon by elites in Moscow and Washington in shaping their initiatives and responses to the behavior and policies of their rivals and in managing their mutual conflicts. In a theoretical sense, these cooperative understandings or constraints can be transgressed at any time as a response to new opportunities or a re-calculation of national interests. Witness the North Korean attack across the 38th parallel and the subsequent extension of the war to the Yalu River by the United States, or the unexpected extension of the Brezhnev Doctrine from East Europe to southwest Asia in Afghanistan. But, as the discussion below suggests, superpower cooperation in accepting – rarely freely and almost always reluctantly – the outcomes and rules of engagement for its future pursuit gradually acquired a life of its own. The constraints arising from their rivalry have not been abandoned or overturned lightly by either superpower. For example, both respect Austrian and Finnish neutrality. Similarly, the United States accepts Soviet troops and advisors in Cuba, but Moscow agrees not to station nuclear missiles on the island. Their cooperation on such matters was a precondition for sustaining their rivalry at tolerable levels, short of mutually catastrophic war.

Acceptance and toleration of these outcomes, rules, or constraints do not imply that they are the dominant preference of the ruling coalitions of either superpower at any particular point in time. They are the grudging crystallization of compromises between the two superpowers because neither can fully get its way in a region, for whatever reason, nor can either impose its particular solutions on the superpower adversary or its regional clients at an acceptable cost or risk. The superpowers have also discovered – witness Egyptian–Soviet or Israeli–American relations – that they often have not been able to control their client. At the point of initial toleration and adjustment, compromised regional outcomes represent secondary or tertiary preferences for one or both superpowers. The division of Germany until the fall of the Berlin Wall illustrated a cooperative superpower acquiescence in an outcome – Germany's division – that neither ostensibly preferred. As the Cold War regime in Europe suggests, some of these compromised outcomes acquired the status of dominant preferences over forty years. Whether as compromised

results or as an unrequited expectation to which the superpowers
have had to adjust, cooperation will be treated in the following
chapters as the outcome of fundamental differences between the
superpowers that did not admit to a final solution through a test of
arms or nuclear war. More generally, the superpowers were compelled to cooperate because the alternative – unilateral pursuit of a
superpower's preferences and strategies to impose a coercive solution
– was perceived to be too risky or costly whether calculated in terms
of real losses or of lost opportunities under conditions of scarce
resources and competing foreign and domestic policy priorities and
commitments.

Specifically, contributors accept the assumption, which their chapters attempt to explicate, that superpower regional cooperation can
be identified largely, though not necessarily exclusively, as the result
of the following specific calculations of cost and risks: the estimates
made by each superpower over time of the variable value or priority
of a region to its interests and aims (e.g. Europe high, North Africa
low); the geopolitical and economic impediments hampering the
projection of national power; the means and will of its superpower
rival to check its initiatives; the capacity of regional states to frustrate
the superpowers and to assert their own preferences (e.g. India in
South Asia or China in East Asia); and the costs of non-cooperation
to other desired aims and interests (e.g. regional linkages, strategic
arms control accords and economic growth).

Forms of superpower cooperation

Superpower coordination of shared (if not equal and symmetrical)
interests has assumed two forms. The most frequent and significant,
until now, has been the implicit cooperative coordination by the
superpowers of their unilaterally taken decisions and initiatives.
Under this rubric of coordinated, unilateral decisions and initiatives,
one can identify for illustrative purposes several, by no means fully
inclusive, lines of cooperative action. First, there are those instances
limiting or precluding a superpower's direct military intervention into
a region. These are illustrated by US forbearance in the East
European crises of 1953 (East Germany), 1956 (Hungary), 1968
(Czechoslovakia) and 1980–1 (Poland) and by Soviet restraint in the
Korean and Vietnam Wars.

Second, there are those cases associated with managing regional conflicts to prevent escalation, to staunch or cut losses, or to focus resources and priorities elsewhere. The instruments used have varied, including limits on economic and military assistance to clients (Soviet shipments to Egypt before the Yom Kippur war); diplomatic restraints to check a client's efforts to widen or aggravate a conflict (US pressures on Israel to desist in its 1982 invasion of Lebanon); pressures and compensations for allies to induce accords (Soviet good offices with the Luanda government and US efforts with Pretoria to facilitate the withdrawal of Cuban troops from Angola); or toleration or encouragement of a superpower's presence or its mediating role in a region (the Soviet Union's arbitration of the 1965 Pakistan–Indian war).

Third, unilaterally coordinated superpower cooperation can be associated with postures of coercive diplomacy or economic advantage rather than with a striving for strategic ascendancy (Latin America). These cases also extend to reliance on third parties (the Organization of African Unity) or international bodies to end or lower regional conflicts (the use of UN peacekeeping forces in the Suez crisis of 1956).

One can also identify a second form of cooperation, namely instances of joint superpower coordination of their shared interests. In Europe, the creation of the Conference on Security and Cooperation in Europe (CSCE) at Helsinki has proved to be a durable (if sometimes contention-prone) vehicle for the negotiation of East–West and superpower differences over security, human rights, and the exchange of peoples and ideas across frontiers. It has now been extended to conventional arms talks between the blocs which for the first time have been framed within this larger European setting, including neutral states and non-bloc members. The non-proliferation treaty has also furnished a mechanism for the joint intervention of the superpowers into a region. Witness parallel superpower pressures on South Africa to desist from testing any nuclear devices.

The systemic framework eliciting cooperation and conflict

The adoption of game theoretic insights to illuminate and partially to explain the superpower struggle at a regional level reveals in simplest light the formal structure of the mixed cooperation–conflict incentives (payoffs) confronting leaders in both states, quite apart from the substantive stakes at issue. On the other hand, the limitations of such an approach should be recognized at the outset to sober expectations about what this volume purports to show. If this volume can show a discernible inclination over time toward superpower cooperation, it makes no claim to a full explanation of the fundamental reasons why the superpowers have been engaged in the Cold War struggle; why they attach shifting and differential significance and salience to a region; why they chose or court certain allies and adversaries; why they prefer some policy instruments over others – military force or arms sales or economic assistance – or assign varying priorities and resources to a region in pursuing their aims and interests; or why, after much effort, they either unexpectedly disengage from a region (the US in Vietnam and the Soviet Union in Afghanistan) or reverse previously held policy aims and relax seemingly unalterable commitments (Soviet rejection of the Brezhnev Doctrine in Eastern Europe). Fuller, if not final, answers to these specific questions appear to lie, alternately, *outside* immediate regional superpower struggles – the latter, the central focus for our analysis in the chapters below – and *within* the political cultures, histories, socio-economic structures, and policy processes of superpowers themselves.

While this volume does not – nor can it – explore all these intriguing questions, it is guided by several assumptions about the principal factors, operating throughout the international community, albeit with differential impact on the superpowers, on the nation-states composing the present global political order, and on the elites in control of state policy. This volume is based on the systemic assumption, for which superpower regional struggles since World War II furnish a vast evidentiary base and prima facie case, that the Cold War between the United States and the Soviet Union, understood in its broadest terms, is but the latest iteration of a series of failed attempts by major powers to create an international environment congenial to their national interests and values. This modern quest commenced with the rise of nation-states five centuries ago and their subsequent struggle to dominate European and overseas territories. The salient imperative has been the nation's security and the corresponding requirement that, alone or in alliance, it be able to protect itself from opponents and to define the international order in preferred ways. What analysts now term the security dilemma arises from this condition of uncertainty and the limited power of states to define their security function. None has enjoyed the luxury of the United States which, throughout much of the nineteenth century in expanding westward, was essentially free from external threat.[7] Today, not even the United States enjoys so boundless a measure of control over its security.

The superpower Cold War is heir to the titanic rivalries that can be traced to the division of the world between Portugal and Spain in 1492, and to the competition among the newly emerging national states of Austria, France, England, Russia, and Prussia to become the dominant power in Europe or to establish a favorable balance of power in support of their divergent national interests. The penultimate phase of the nation-state struggle for regional and international ascendancy encompasses the creation of the German, Italian, and Japanese nations and empires, joining those already organized under the aegis of France and England. World Wars I and II were the crucible of these national and imperial struggles to organize the European and world order in congenial ways. The United States and the Soviet Union are then the latest of a line of Big Powers that have been induced, both by the opportunities presented by their immense power and by the postwar chaos and the uncertainties of the international political order, to define and control the kind of order that best suited the real and perceived security interests of each state and its ruling elites.

But the Cold War cannot be fully understood by exclusive appeal to external or system-wide security imperatives. The phenomenon is too complex and the relations of Soviet and American states, and those of the states and peoples of the global society, are too interdependent to be confined to a procrustean bed of security concerns, however compelling these urgencies may be. Co-equal in force are two other imperatives that overlie the ceaseless effort to satisfy the need for security and control. This struggle to prevail and to impose a preferred order on other states and peoples joins two other imperatives of ever expanding contemporary force and moment. There is, first, the demand of peoples everywhere for more material wealth, comfort, and freedom from want. This welfare function can be traced to the rise of nationally based capitalist market economies and the gradual emergence of mass consumer societies. It was expanded by the Industrial Revolution that promised to end poverty and famine as intrinsic limitations of the human condition.[8] This socio-economic transformation of the global society also promised unlimited progress in meeting the ever-expanding demands of peoples everywhere for increasingly higher and expanded welfare levels.[9] The Marxist critique of capitalism was not aimed at undoing the Industrial Revolution. Marxism sought, instead, to share its promise with the greatest number – the working masses and peasants – by applying socialist principles of distribution and public ownership of the means of production.

The demands of populations everywhere for ever enlarging welfare are persistent and pervasive throughout the international community and a ceaseless concern of governments if they are to survive. These welfare pressures are obviously expressed in multiple forms and with varying insistence by different peoples, depending on their stage of socio-economic development and knowledge of their comparative advantages with respect to perceived peers whose material conditions furnish standards to measure relative progress. These demands represent the incessant operation of what might be termed Sait's law within the global community. Demands for material welfare appear to be limitless. Certainly their parameters are not clear today. These demands create a chronic global and national crisis. Current national and world modes of private and public-based production and distribution – capitalist, socialist, or mixed – have proved incapable of fully satisfying these demands, whatever might be the claims made by partisans of one system or another about their relative ability to meet the rising expectations and resulting claims of mass populations for greater material wealth and comfort. Socialist models are clearly defunct by the admission of their once most ardent advocates; but capitalist and market solutions, currently in the ascendancy as responses to welfare imperatives, are not assured solutions to global or national welfare, notwithstanding their relative success when Western and socialist bloc economic development is compared. The endemic poverty and deprivation of the developing world, where eighty per cent of the world's population commands only twenty per cent of its wealth, raises into question whether either command or market solutions can cope with the needs and welfare demands of the global population.[10] This is not to mention the structured political tensions within developed societies arising from endemic economic and social stratification.

To this perpetual revolution within the world community for more *now* must be added a third: the search for universally applicable principles of economic and political legitimacy. This quest assumes several, not fully compatible, forms. No global economic system today can be judged legitimate by competing national elites and national peoples unless it responds to its nationally defined welfare function. So also, no international political regime – e.g. Cold War bipolarity – can fully pass the test of legitimacy unless it permits the expression of national self-determination. How else to explain decolonization, French resistance to US leadership in Western Europe, or the re-emergent nationalism sweeping Eastern Europe today?[11] To these international standards of legitimacy must now be added those that extend to internal governmental arrangements defining the powers, rights, and duties of individual citizens and officeholders as well as the diverse social compacts regulating the varying relations between society and the state within different nations.

Solutions to these internal tests of legitimacy range from Western-style open and pluralistic systems to authoritarian rule based on secular one-party or army domination or on religious and communal principles. These prevailing, if not universally accepted, tests of legitimacy are obviously neither internally coherent nor reconcilable. Regimes, like that in Cuba, may control domestic crime and ensure more equal access to public goods and services than some open systems, but their denial of personal liberties and the right to own and use property for private gain run counter to liberal democratic principles. Or, if the principle of national self-determination doomed empires, its spread did not automatically ensure democratic rule, defined by competing parties for office and by guarantees of personal liberty. The Communist victory in China and the Stalinist regime illustrate the troubling point that mass mobilization is possible, a requirement of popular democracy, but meeting one test or condition of legitimacy ensures neither personal liberty nor long-term economic security and welfare.[12] As de Tocqueville observed over a century and a half ago, in attempting to understand the compelling force and attraction of mass democracy, the drive for equality was as powerful as freedom in mobilizing public allegiances. In the absence of intermediary groups, representing divergent interests, national societies could be reduced to a mass of impotent individuals content to consign their participatory rights in governing themselves to ruling elites, mass parties, or pervasively controlling governments.[13]

The Cold War is then a more profound conflict than those of interstate competitors before the French and Industrial Revolutions. It was framed by a contest over what order should prevail between nation-states, the principles of regime governance within them, and the welfare system best calculated to produce and distribute wealth. The Cold War can be understood as a history of conflicting superpower attempts to impose, or to elicit support for, their rival solutions to the unresolved problems of order, welfare, and legitimacy characterizing the relations of states and peoples of the emerging international society.[14] That the superpowers were induced to respond to these external imperatives arises from the inability of their governing elites and peoples to satisfy them solely within a national framework.

With respect to order, each superpower has sought ascendancy in their military competition, primarily through the sustained nuclear arms races that they have pursued, with varying intensity and scope, since the dawn of the atomic age. The warfighting strategies that both states adopted testify to the serious and deadly intent of each power to get its way.[15] Each has also sought to create favorable military balances at regional levels to suit its aims and interests. The European theater, where the two military blocs directly confront each other, remains the primary zone of competition. Neither was able to have its way fully in Europe, but each enjoyed, until recently with the collapse of the Warsaw Pact, a dominant strategic position within its respective sphere of influence. The complex and shifting sets of alliance and alignment strategies followed by Moscow and Washington since World War II in other regions of the world were parts of this systemic struggle to define favorable global and regional balances. The incentive for dominion, alluring to Big Powers which appear to have some hope of realizing this objective, arises from the very decentralization and disorder of the international system, composed of nation-states of varying power to resist the claims of others to assert their own interests.[16]

The superpowers have been no less engaged in attempting to define the socio-economic principles on which the world economy will rest and the political regimes that will rule nation-states. The United States created an open and liberal world economic system, built on market principles and institutionalized in such organizations as the International Monetary Fund, the World Bank, and the General Agreement on Tariffs and Trade. This liberal regime was underwritten by the enormous productivity of the American economy; fueled by American grants, loans, and investments as prime investor and banker for the world; and guaranteed by the dollar as the dominant international currency tied to gold. The Soviet Union opted instead for a closed, autarchic system based on central planning, a command economy, and cumbersome barter arrangements between states because Communist currencies were non-convertible. Both expanded their models to other parts of the globe: the United States through an international market system over which its unquestioned hegemony prevailed until the 1970s; the Soviet Union, primarily through military and political assistance to its allies in East Europe and in the developing world.[17] The Cold War was also marked by different superpower solutions to the problem of how power should be organized and what principles of legitimacy should govern the authority and power of the state and its citizens. The United States advanced the ideal of a pluralist democracy and an open economic system. For its part, the Soviet Union sided with socialist or communist parties and movements in the developing world and with so-called progressive political elements, defined principally as nationalist-minded 'bourgeois' groups opposed to Western and US influence. Neither, however, consistently pursued their regime preferences when national security interests, political power, or economic concerns proved compelling. Witness, for example, the contradictions in US and Soviet behavior in their support, respectively, for authoritarian regimes in Central America and for national and anti-communist regimes in the Middle East.

We have now entered a new period when both superpowers, for different but converging reasons, are retreating from the Cold War struggle. Both have expended incalculably vast amounts of human and material treasure in this global struggle with mixed results. Their nuclear and conventional arms races produced stalemate; internal economic growth and technological development, particularly acute for the Soviet Union, has been stifled; and their stature as global powers is now seriously challenged, partly as a consequence of their mutual exhaustion in mounting and sustaining their rivalry. If the Soviet Union is currently a military superpower, its long-term prospects as a major power are, by the admission of its leadership, under serious socio-economic siege.[18] Growing concern for US budget and balance of payments deficits and slipping competitiveness abroad, as the result of a variety of factors, including underinvestment in civilian research and development and the erosion of US cities, industries, transport systems, and educational facilities, also advises retrenchment, if the United States is to maintain its present share of world power and influence.[19] If by 'superpower' one means that either the United States or the Soviet Union can dictate the policies of other states to suit its will, neither can claim that title today in its dealings with most states. While it would be an exaggeration to assert that they are ordinary powers – Big Powers they remain[20] – it no longer makes sense to view global political and economic systems as bipolar despite the relative military superiority of the United States and the Soviet Union *vis-à-vis* third parties.[21] This volume retains the term 'superpower' as a shorthand convenience to signify the United States and the Soviet Union. It is not used to designate a measure of their relative power in global affairs today where their former hegemonic status no longer reflects their real influence of significance in a progressively multipolar world.

As Chapter 3 delineates, reform is especially pervasive and discernible in the Soviet Union. Aside from the long-term concerns of a receding power that underlie the drive for internal change, the socio-economic and political revolution under way in the Soviet Union is propelled by a genuine commitment to democratize at least some features of authoritarian state and one-party rule and to liberalize and decentralize economic planning and decisions. To the degree that these values are shared and implemented by the Gorbachev government in the Soviet Union, they will begin to approximate the pure meaning of cooperation as the co-valuation of shared ends and strategies to achieve them between the United States and the Soviet Union. This is not to argue that the competition for power and influence between the United States and the Soviet Union will cease. The point to stress is that this ongoing condition of international conflict will be counterbalanced by considerations of common interest that will inevitably change the value of the stakes of the superpower relations for both sides, i.e. the payoff functions defined by the elites in both states, upgrading the values for cooperation as co-valuation over those for cooperation as conflict.

But whereas Soviet reforms have been launched by a disaffected elite within the Soviet ruling class, it is impelled by mass sentiment in Eastern Europe over the resistance of discredited communist parties throughout the bloc. In the Soviet Union, reform approaches a legalized *coup d'état* where the transfer for power was accomplished within the rules of the old regime but against its continued maintenance.[22] The revolt has been initiated from the top – much like Bismarck's reforms of Prussian society and the state – to match the nation's power with that of its foreign competitors. The success of these reforms and the ability of the Gorbachev regime to hold on to power is by no means assured at this writing. There are those who want reforms to go faster and farther and those, principally within the party and governmental bureaucracies, who resist what reforms have been attempted. There is also a perplexed population anxious about the possible losses of privilege and welfare guarantees, however modest by Western standards, that the old regime assured in the absence of compensating assurances that reforms will make their lives better.[23] There is also the problem of economic mismanagement ushered in by well-intentioned but ill-considered or misapplied reforms. It is always awkward and no mean feat to change the tire of a moving car. On the other hand, the East European masses have totally rejected the Stalinist–Brezhnev political and economic model. Its delegitimization flowed inexorably from its economic failures, political oppression, and corruption. Reform in the Eastern bloc has been generated from the bottom up. Nevertheless, despite the different sources for reform within the Soviet Union and Eastern Europe, the interests of the ruling Soviet elite and those of reformers in East Europe conspire to urge the 'demilitarization' of European and international politics. *Détente*, with the promise of *entente* and *cooperation* (as co-valuation) with the West and the United States, is a precondition for the success of internal Soviet and East European economic growth, technological progress, and the democratization of the Soviet Union and Eastern Europe. Relaxed and confident East–West relations are also a precondition for Soviet access to Western trade, credits, and know-how on a scale equal to the ambitious reforms now in train or contemplated. They are also a mechanism to lighten the burdens of Soviet imperial control over Eastern Europe, while transferring some of them to the West. Particularly heavy for the Soviet Union have been the political and economic costs of maintaining unpopular and incompetent communist rulers and managers in power. The competition of external markets and the application of market operations are needed to induce internal economic reform and to reduce the drag of governmental and party bureaucracies on economic development. Greater social and personal freedoms are also conceived as prerequisites for the stimulation of personal commitment on the part of an ever enlarging segment of the population to produce more – and more efficiently.

Converging incentives for superpower cooperation are also advised as a consequence of the relative decline in power of both powers *vis-à-vis* other states in the international system and of their receding ability – greater of course for the Soviet Union – to meet internal welfare demands. The immediate crisis, while immediately graver for the Soviet Union than for the United States, is no less a formidable concern for the United States if it is to sustain its relative position of economic development in light of emerging competition from Europe and Asia.

As this volume argues, incentives for superpower cooperation are also reinforced by the experience of both superpowers in their regional struggles in the postwar period. Other states and peoples, driven no less than the superpowers by national sentiment, have established an impressive record of successful resistance to the imposition of superpower solutions on local notions and norms of order, welfare, and legitimacy. These states have also progressively demonstrated, as the chapters below extensively explore, remarkable imagination, resourcefulness, and obstinacy in pressing their own interests and aims, thwarting superpower designs, and turning the latter, as often as not, to their own purposes at superpower expense.[24]

It is against this background of great effort and unrequited expectations that the rationale for this project can be best appreciated. Both superpowers have come to the realization, marked by differing rates of learning reflected in major shifts in policy aims and instruments and their slow – at times desultory, at times lurching and abrupt – disengagement from Cold War politics, that they have overextended their limited power often with dubious and untoward results abroad and not seldom with damaging consequences at home. Where one has been successful for a time at the perceived expense of the other – the Soviet Union in Vietnam or the United States in Iran – the long-term return on these investments has been meager or negative. They have also gradually, if not yet fully, internalized these 'lessons' within their domestic political processes. What were perceived as regional elements of a global struggle for hegemony in a zero-sum game – witness Vietnam[25] – were more often a struggle between local states and elites for ascendancy, with the superpowers as the objects rather than the subjects of manipulation for the advantage of clients and allies.

The opportunity costs of profligate intervention are now increasingly apparent. Not only have the superpowers checkmated each other's regional aspirations but regional forces have themselves supplied abundant countervailing power to superpower aspirations. Again, for different but convergent reasons, they now have less incentive – the Iraq crisis a partial exception – to try to project their will abroad. Greater confidence in each other as at least a sometimes reliable partner is as much rooted in commonly expressed values within their domestic political systems and in a slowly accumulating record of successful arms control and regional accords as it is a recognition of the exhaustion of both and the negative incentives at play to project their limited, and relative to other states, receding power abroad for questionable national gains. As Rome before them, both superpowers have slowly discovered, with Vietnam and Afghanistan as harsh lessons, that they 'had much less to hope than to fear from the chance of arms; and that, in the prosecution of remote wars, the undertaking became every day more difficult, the event more doubtful, and the possession more precarious, and less beneficial.'[26]

The superpowers have learned to accept and adjust to regional conflicts that neither wished and to rules of engagement that neither freely espoused or acknowledged. The division of Germany and Europe, as the chapters on West and East Europe suggest, is the most prominent example of second and third level choices or preferences prevailing since neither side had the power or the opportunity to compel the other to accept its views about how national power should be distributed in Europe and what socio-economic and political regimes should be instituted. Both powers have also gradually, if reluctantly, adjusted to the division of Korea and to their respective spheres of influence in the Middle East, Africa, and Asia although opportunities and instances of mutual challenge persist. Superpower regional adjustments on lesser outcomes and disagreeable rules – occasioned, to repeat, by mutual containment and local constraints and conditioned by the interdependent choices made by ruling superpower elites and, where relevant, home populations – can be considered forms of cooperation. The superpowers have had to accept lesser preferences than those that appeared to be animating their policies and the projection of their power abroad.

NOTES ON METHOD AND THE APPLIED AND THEORETICAL IMPLICATIONS OF A REGIONAL APPROACH

This approach differs from similar attempts to define the conditions under which rival nation-states, particularly the United States and the Soviet Union, can cooperate in managing or resolving their conflicts for limited, but mutual benefit. Policy studies, like those by Alexander George and Graham Allison and their respective collaborators, have largely focused on specific, functional issues, like crisis prevention, improvements in decision-making processes within both countries, or arms control and strategic problems.[27] More theoretical studies, like those of Robert Axelrod and the *World Politics* group, frame the problem of cooperation in general, abstract terms under conditions of anarchy. These analyses are designed to be widely applicable to all conflict and only incidentally to the superpower confrontation.[28] While drawing on these works and their insights, this volume departs from them in several key ways.

First, it examines superpower rivalry in terms of regional conflicts in which their power and purposes were actively engaged. For applied policy, a major concern of this volume, such an approach draws on the rich history of the superpower conflict at regional levels and the limited, but discernible, cooperation arising from their rivalry. Governmental pronouncements issuing from superpower capitals are largely cast in regional conflict terms rather than in specialized and rarified vocabulary of game theory, whether one is speaking of Berlin crises, the Palestinian problem, the Soviet invasion of Afghanistan, or US aid to the Nicaraguan rebels. Although the regional focus of this study cannot directly address superpower nuclear and conventional arms races, it does examine closely the local incentives that stimulate them.

Admittedly, from a strictly theoretical perspective, any specific regional conflict dividing the superpowers and the relative saliency of the conflict for them over time is not in itself crucial for understanding the general rules and dynamics driving the relationship, the incentives for cooperation and conflict, or the range of choices open to the players. For the theorist, these specific differences are less important than the underlying conditions and rules that frame and explain the structure of the conflict and the likely range of outcomes. For example, most analysts using Prisoner's Dilemma, a perennial in game theoretic analysis, do not attempt to specify the payoffs and values assigned by the subjects of analysis to any one play of the game, nor has it been widely believed to be necessary (or possible) to provide a satisfactory empirical basis for the analysis.[29] Nor are institutional processes, socio-economic and political structures or perceptual and valuational differences between the contestants, which may affect their decisions about the values, resources, and commitments that are to be assigned to an issue or particular regional conflict, systematically included in game analysis although, conceivably, these factors could be 'gamed'.

This volume, which owes much of its conceptual approach to the mixed motives of the player underlying much of game theory, is also very much interested in the specific aims and interests of the superpowers and ruling elites – what game theorists would call 'payoffs' for cooperation and defection and how they have specifically gone about coordinating their shared interests in their regional engagements. What the contributors seek to explicate are the considerations affecting superpower choices at the margin in their regional relations, where the two states and their ruling elites clash or collude, to understand more fully why conflict and cooperation arise and to examine the conditions under which one or the other is furthered and reinforced. A regional approach provides one way to look at these problems, an approach that remains to be fully exploited,[30]

Case studies of specific issue areas, while useful for some purposes, are ill-suited to the aims of this volume. Nor do statistical approaches that concentrate on a limited set of factors or variables over time provide sufficiently rich and textured discussion that will assist the analyst, the decision-maker, or the interested public to be aware of the required context and the complex incentives underlying the superpower struggle for cooperation across regions or at the global strategic level.

A regional approach obviously cannot do everything. It has to be supplemented in at least two ways that have implications for current thinking about international cooperation. First, as argued earlier, it has to be augmented by a systemic or global perspective that admits the force of three imperatives – order, welfare, and legitimacy – that are at work across international state-to-state and society-to-society relations and that frame the choices of ruling elites in their allocation of resources, particularly military, economic, and techno-scientific capabilities, and their access to power and influence over those capability domains. The superpower rivalry, however significant, is then but a species of a larger genus of behavior. We can learn a great deal about the systemic impact of these forces on state and societal change by examining the superpower relations closely as they evolve through a series of regional conflicts since World War II. In generalizing across the regional behavior of the superpowers over this half century, it is clear that they are engaged in a global struggle to define not only world and regional orders in ways favorable to their interests and values but also the socio-economic and political institutions of other nation-states to suit their preferences. Put another way, the superpowers and regional states are essentially responding to systemic incentives that act with force on all national states and societies. As the most powerful, at least militarily, the superpower conflict provides a window from which to examine this systemic process of globalizing principles of order, legitimacy, and welfare.

Within this global framework, a regional approach enriches our knowledge of the specific constraints and opportunities that appear to have shaped superpower choices and behavior. It also brings some sense of proportion to the range of power and the impact that the superpowers have had – and are likely to have – on their environment. That environment limits their ability to define the system in preferred ways. It highlights the limits of power of the United States and the Soviet Union as they have been compelled to adjust not only to the countervailing strategies that foiled the realization of their competing aims but also to the claims and leverage exercised by regional states in pursuing their manifold and divergent interests.

Secondly, the number of actors and the growing decentralization of military and economic power around the globe help explain superpower moderation in their regional conflicts. The evidence furnished in the following chapters indicates that the political pluralism and the growing multipolarity of decisional units within the international system, disposing often formidable economic and military capabilities, are key conditions for prompting (if not determining) superpower cooperation. This conclusion sharply contrasts with the intuitively attractive but empirically arguable assumption of the World Politics group that cooperation is fostered as the number of actors declines.[31] In the early stages of the Cold War that proposition may have more weight as the superpower struggle tended to be conceived as a zero-sum game and as contestants for regional and global influence had little choice but to follow superpower leads as a consequence of wartime destruction and dislocation, civil strife, or both. But even during this period, as the management of the Berlin crises and the joint superpower recognition of the state of Israel suggest, third parties still had some say over their fates and over superpower behavior if they cared enough to try.

As the Cold War developed and as the superpowers increasingly experienced opposition abroad and at home to the projection of national power and foreign entanglements, they have learned to differentiate between regions as to their relative importance and priority and to abandon commitment strategies and bargaining rules that linked and equated the importance of any specific regional conflict with the sum total and range of a superpower's values and interests everywhere.[32] The universal claims of the American Truman and Reagan Doctrines and the Soviet Brezhnev Doctrine are bankrupt, repudiated in deed if reluctantly in word by their most ardent partisans. It is now common for analysts to observe, as if it had always been the case, that the superpowers hold this or that region as one of low priority or salience. This generalization is reflected in the chapters below on Africa, North Africa, and Asia. But low saliency has not been as evident to the superpowers and to their ruling elites if one traces their conflicts since World War II. Places that now seem to be falling outside of the superpower struggle, like central Africa, were once areas of direct confrontation. Saliency has had to be learned by the harsh experience of wasted human and material resources for little or no purpose. In learning these lessons, the superpowers have gradually adjusted to the limits of their power and have assisted each other to disengage mutually from regions around the globe, a process that is by no means complete.

Disengagement will not be easy for many reasons – the resistance of internal groups and individuals to past policies or to the psychological traumas associated with withdrawal not the least unimportant among them. As the regional chapters indicate, confusion in both superpower capitals over each other's aims and intentions will remain for some time to come as both are likely to persist in efforts to retain their receding positions in certain regions – the US in West Europe and Central America, the Soviet Union in East Europe and Afghanistan – while remonstrating against the failure of the other superpower to assist in maintaining its ascendancy in what it perceives as its sphere of influence over which it insists on exercising a disputable *droit de regard*.

Contrary to some current thinking about the theory of cooperation, moreover, the experience of painful trial and error and the *shadow of the past* are quite relevant – indeed critical – in learning about the limits of national power in superpower attempts to impose unilateral solutions on intransigent allies and rivals.[33] As Victor Kremenyuk argues in the next chapter, the future cannot be confidently addressed, especially if one wishes to foster superpower cooperation, however defined, unless one has a record of the past on which to base expectations of the rival-partner's behavior if one cooperates and a theory, albeit incipient and provisional, of the systemic factors and shared values, internal to the states and societies themselves, that furnish both a structure and a source of enduring incentives for cooperation.

At the most theoretical level of analysis, the notion of history, as the accumulated and consciously shared interpretation of what we are as human beings and as human societies, how and why we got here, and where we might be going, cannot be underestimated as crucial for understanding the Cold War and for building on and beyond it to enlist both American and Soviet populations and their respective states and ruling elites in constructing a common global home. Without in any way denigrating the profound differences in aim and interest of the two countries nor minimizing the enormous efforts that each has made to prevail in their rivalry, whose inertial motion has by no means dissipated, the Cold War can still be viewed as cooperation. First and until now foremost, it may be viewed as a reluctant, even repugnant, set of accommodations by both parties to the limits of their power, defined by mutual and costly military stalemate and, increasingly, by a resistant international environment. It can also be viewed as a gradual recognition of mutual interdependence, partly conceived by the shared, if inevitably differential, experience of the limits of power and the disillusionment arising from only partially achieved (and only partially realistic) ideological ideals.[34] The incentives for security, economic, and political cooperation, as well as for increasing cultural exchange are generated from this common and unrequited condition.

Finally, there is an emerging basis, still ill-formed, fragile, and unreliable, for cooperation to be understood and extended in superpower relation as co-valuation. But that latter, Kantian ideal can hardly be the primary assumption to explain superpower behavior, even in a post-Cold War environment, or guide the policy decisions of either superpower. Progress in superpower cooperation depends instead on the proposition that more modest Grotian notions of cooperation are not only feasible in the future because they make sense but also because they are already present in the historical behavior of the superpowers since World War II. A record of ceaseless conflict has obscured the slow, non-linear evolution of cooperation. This volume highlights that evolutionary process as a precondition for its deliberate extension. So far, the superpowers, their ruling elites, and the perfecting social forces at work within their societies have not entirely acted on Hobbesian assumptions of war of all against all.

There has been much loose talk and not a little foolish effort expended on the disputable assumption that the Cold War was a zero-sum game. That notion no longer has much intellectual force nor experiential grounding. Eschewed, too, by the ruling elites of both superpowers has been the seemingly persuasive attraction of simple models of anarchy that supply analysts and modelers with a mythical pre-historic point in time that justify the erection of elaborate or simple schemes on which to base a new social contract.[35] If the history of the Cold War provides any insight into how effective and legitimate systems of order and welfare are constructed and sustained, it affirms the notion that social contracts can be better constructed by careful reinterpretation of the past than by leaping into the future on the assumption that there was once a point in time with no historical past that is the starting point for a new world order.

If the superpowers are able to reach accord on a social contract to regulate their affairs, it will in no small part be due to the social contract that is already partially inscribed in their own behavior, in the history of the Cold War, although the legacy may not be entirely clear to the legatees who have, paradoxically, bequeathed to themselves their own inheritance.

NOTES

1. Kenneth E. Boulding's analysis of political-military, economic, and social power provides a unifying framework to understand superpower relations as a species of a larger genus of human interaction based, interdependently, on threat, exchange, or affection. Kenneth E. Boulding, *Three Faces of Power* (Berkeley: Sage, 1989).

2. William McNeill, *America, Britain, and Russia: Their Cooperation and Conflict, 1941–1946* (London: Oxford University Press, 1954).

3. Thomas C. Schelling, *The Strategy of Conflict* (New York: Oxford University Press, 1960).

4. Schelling pursues his interest in defining winning rules in bargaining situations, where the rivals manipulate each other's expectations by threatening to 'kill, maim, damage and hurt' to get their way, in *Arms and Influence* (New Haven: Yale University Press, 1966). Schelling's approach, while logical and tightly reasoned, has elicited sharp and telling criticism when applied to nuclear deterrence and, doubly so, to regional conflicts. His game theoretic approach is a useful heuristic device to capture synoptically some of the essential elements of the superpower conflict, especially at the nuclear level, free from the specific issues and stakes at play. For a generic critique of game theory, which develops the limitations of this approach in greater measure than can be attempted here, see Robert Jervis, 'From Balance of Power to Concert: A Study of International Security Cooperation', *World Politics*, vol. XXXVIII, no. 1 (October 1985), pp. 58–79. See also the defense of game theory by Duncan Snidal, 'The Game Theory of International Relations', ibid., pp. 25–57. For empirically based critiques of the Schelling approach, see Alexander L. George and

Richard Smoke, *Deterrence in American Foreign Policy* (New York: Columbia University Press, 1974), especially pp. 1–103, 501–642, and Robert Jervis *et al* (eds) *Psychology and Deterrence* (Baltimore: Johns Hopkins University Press, 1985). This volume on superpower cooperation, while acknowledging its significant conceptual debt to Schelling, attempts to identify the critical reasons why the superpowers engaged in their global struggle – their definition of preferred payoffs and strategies – and why the Cold War is diminishing in force today. These primordial factors cannot be addressed by game theoretic analysis nor do proponents make so sweeping a claim. They are embedded in the imperatives of the international system as a whole (see the discussion below) and lie deep within the political and socio-economic processes and institutions of the competing states.

5. The editors have eschewed the application of formal regime theory, such as it exists, to superpower relations. Differences over power, values, and interests have been so sharp and conflicting that efforts to impose the complicated paraphernalia of regime analysis on superpower relations would have unduly constrained the contributors in analyzing the complex range of choices confronting states and regional players. These still need to be identified before one can realistically talk about regimes. On the other hand, the history of the Cold War, viewed within the larger context of the international system and the compelling force of the domestic political struggles of nation-states, evidences more than just power politics as the sole touchstone for explaining political behavior or outcomes. See the discussion below for an elaboration of these reservations. For a discussion of the rival schools of thought with respect to regime theory, see Stephen D. Krasner, *International Regimes* (Ithaca: Cornell University Press, 1983).

6. Raymond Aron portrays Schelling's more abstract conceptualization in the notion of 'brothers-enemies' who are bound by necessity to cooperate because each has the power to destroy the other. Raymond Aron, *Peace and War*, trans. Richard Howard and Annette Baker Fox (Garden City: Doubleday, 1966), pp. 536–74. Schelling's strategy of conflict is theoretically applicable to allies and adversaries since the focus is on payoffs as the margin – the next run of the game – and not on the value of the game rival as such.

7. Recognition of this political condition is certainly not new although it has been variously expressed by statesmen and observers since Thucydides through Machiavelli and Hume. Contemporary expositors and exponents of this partial characterization of the international system include *inter alia*, Hans Morgenthau, *Politics among Nations* (New York: Knopf, 1985, 6th edn) and, more recently, Kenneth Waltz, *A Theory of International Relations* (Reading: Addison-Wesley, 1979). For a useful general treatment of the security dilemma, see Robert Jervis, *Perception and Misperception in International Politics* (Princeton: Princeton University Press, 1976), especially pp. 3–57.

8. Hannah Arendt, *The Human Condition* (Chicago: University of Chicago Press, 1970).

9. Walter W. Rostow, *Politics and the Stages of Growth* (New York: Cambridge University Press, 1971).

10. The rival claims of these two approaches are systematically examined and evaluated in Robert Gilpin, *The Political Economy of International Relations* (Princeton: Princeton University Press, 1987).

11. The resistance to superpower rule on grounds of illegitimacy is at the heart of the Gaullist critique of the international system. See Edward A. Kolodziej, *French International Policy under De Gaulle and Pompidou: The Politics of Grandeur* (Ithaca: Cornell University Press, 1974).

12. Stalinist repression as well as Mao-Tse Tung's Cultural Revolution exemplify the problem. Alexander I. Solzhenitsyn, *Gulag Archipelago, 1918–1956: An Experiment in Literary Investigation*, trans. Thomas P. Whitney (New York: Harper and Row, 1974) and John King Fairbank's *The Great Chinese Revolution: 1800–1985* (New York: Harper and Row, 1986) make these points vividly clear.

13. This issue is first raised systematically by Alexis de Tocqueville in *De la Démocratie en Amérique* (Paris: Paguerre, 1950, 3rd edn). The American or Madisonian answer to the problems of preventing the rise of a destructive majority of the poor against the minority of the wealthy as well as of checking the disruptive force of factions is found in creating a mass democracy whose complex social and economic composition would furnish its own internal stability since no majority would be sufficiently controlling to deprive a minority of its rights and, presumably, its property. This argument is of course Madison's in Federalist 10, *The Federalist*, Edward Mead Earle edition (New York: Modern Library, n.d.).

14. The notion of international society is adapted from Hedley Bull's more restricted notion of a society of states: Hedley Bull, *The Anarchical Society* (London: Macmillan, 1977). According to Bull's persuasive analysis, the existence of this society is traced in the observance by states of elemental rules of behavior associated with their own survival, the keeping of contracts, and a respect for private property. On the strength of this line of analysis, Bull tentatively sides with the Grotians in affirming a basis for international society that cannot be satisfactorily reduced, either in logic or by observation, to the Hobbesian assumptions of a world at perpetual war and in an anarchical state that is ever 'solitary, poor, nasty, brutish and short'. The evolution of the superpower confrontation in regional rivalries as traced in this volume and their cautious approach to brandishing nuclear weapons suggest a much broader sharing of values and interests than has been previously supposed. The revolutionary changes which swept Eastern Europe in 1989 also suggest the expression of common political and economic values and interests across a previously unbridgeable ideological divide.

15. For overviews of US and Soviet strategic nuclear policies, see, *inter alia*, Lawrence Freedman, *Evolution of Nuclear Strategy* (New York:

St. Martin's Press, 1989, 2nd edn); Fred Kaplan, *The Wizard of Armaggedon* (New York: Simon and Schuster, 1983); and McGeorge Bundy, *Danger and Survival: Choices about the Bomb in the First Fifty Years* (New York: Random House, 1989).

16. This argument is developed by Kenneth Waltz in *The Man, The State, and War* (New York: Columbia University Press, 1959) and in his *Theory of International Relations*, n. 7.

17. The rise of US postwar economic hegemony is traced by Richard Cooper in *The Economics of Interdependence* (New York: McGraw-Hill, 1968); and by Harold van B. Cleveland in *The Atlantic Idea and its Rivals* (New York: McGraw-Hill, 1966). The fall is described, *passim*, in Gilpin, n. 10 and by Robert Keohane, *After Hegemony: Cooperation and Discord in the World Economy* (Princeton: Princeton University Press, 1984).

18. The hypertrophied military power of the Soviet Union at the expense of economic and technological development forms the thesis of Paul Dibb's *The Soviet Union: The Incomplete Superpower* (Urbana: University of Illinois Press, 1988).

19. The debate surrounding Paul Kennedy's *The Rise and Fall of Great Powers* (New York: Random House, 1987) is of course symptomatic of these concerns.

20. See, for example, Richard Rosecrance, *The United States as an Ordinary Power* (Ithaca: Cornell University Press, 1978).

21. Rejecting the simplicity of bipolarity does not readily produce a satisfying definition of what is properly *international* or a theory of international relations. For one not altogether satisfying attempt at developing an overarching theoretical framework, examine Robert Keohane and Joseph Nye, *Power and Interdependence* (Boston: Little, Brown, 1989, 2nd edn).

22. This paradox is not as strange as it may appear if one examines American politics. One speaks, for example, of the Jacksonian or Jeffersonian revolutions, signifying a fundamental change in how politics is played, who are permitted as players, what their roles are (mass, parties, and elites), and who gets what. Illustrative are Arthur Schlesinger's interpretations of the Jacksonian period and Leonard D. White's four-volume treatise tracing the evolution of American civil service practice. See, respectively, Arthur Schlesinger, Jr, *Age of Jackson* (Boston: Little, Brown, 1945) and Leonard D. White, *The Federalists* (New York: Macmillan, 1959) and *The Jeffersonians* (New York: Macmillan, 1959).

23. See the analysis of 'Z', 'To the Stalin Mausoleum', *Daedalus*, vol. CXIX, no. 1 (Winter 1990), pp. 295–344.

24. The Soviet experience is traced at length in Edward A. Kolodziej and Roger E. Kanet (eds), *The Limits of Soviet Power in the Developing World: Thermidor in the Revolutionary Struggle* (London: Macmillan; and Baltimore: Johns Hopkins University Press, 1989).

25. One is reminded, for example, of the much quoted rationalization for US intervention into Vietnam offered by Assistant Secretary of

Defense for International Security Affairs, John McNaughton, during the Kennedy Administration.

US aims:

70 per cent – To avoid a humiliating US defeat (to our reputation as guarantor).

20 per cent – To keep SVN ([South Vietnam] (and adjacent) territory from Chinese hands.

10 per cent – To permit the people of SVN a better, freer life.

Quoted in Neil Sheehan and E.W. Kenworth (eds), *Pentagon Papers* (New York: Times Books, 1971), p. 432.

26.   Quoted from Edward Gibbon, *The History of the Decline and Fall of the Roman Empire* (New York: J & J Harper, 1926), I, 18.

27.   These include Alexander George *et al.*, *Managing US–Soviet Rivalry: Problems of Crisis Prevention* (Boulder: Westview, 1983); idem, *US–Soviet Security Cooperation* (New York: Oxford University Press, 1988); Graham Allison *et al.*, *Windows of Opportunity: From Cold War to Peaceful Competition in US–Soviet Relations* (Cambridge; Ballinger, 1989); Nish Jamgotch (ed.), *US–Soviet Cooperation: A New Future* (New York: Praeger, 1989); and Roy Allison and Phil Williams (eds), *Superpower Competition and Crisis Prevention in the Third World* (Cambridge/New York; Cambridge University Press, 1990).

28.   Robert Axelrod, *The Evolution of Cooperation* (New York: Basic Books, 1984). Axelrod is explicit at the end of his treatise in summarizing guidelines for playing prisoner's dilemma games, which, for him, map most state-to-state rivalries including those of the superpowers: 'In the contemporary world this question [to control the blind forces of history] has become especially acute because of the development of nuclear weapons. . . . Perhaps if we understand the process better, we can use our foresight to speed up the evolution of cooperation' (pp. 190–1). The *World Politics* symposium on cooperation under conditions of anarchy, vol. XXXVIII, no. 1 (October 1985) widens the concern to include economic cooperation. Both share the assumption of inherent international anarchy that is challenged in this volume.

29.   Of interest is the recent and seminal work of Arthur Stein, *Forces of Circumstance: Structure and Choice in International Relations* (Ithaca: Cornell University Press, 1989), who makes extensive use of game theory analysis to conceptualize generic international relations choices. Superpower games are developed with precision in Steven Brams, *Applying Game Theory to Superpower Conflict* (New Haven: Yale University Press, 1985).

30.   An attempt to develop the notion of a regional approach to security analysis is found in Barry Buzan, 'A Framework for Regional Security Analysis', in *South Asian Security and the Great Powers*, Barry Buzan *et al.* (eds), New York: St. Martin's Press, 1986), pp. 3–33.

31.   See especially the lead article of the World Politics symposium by Kenneth A. Oye, 'Explaining Cooperation under Anarchy: Hypotheses and Strategies', *World Politics*, pp. 226–54.

32. The substitution of what appeared to be logical, almost mathematically determined, requirements of successful bargaining between rivals in mixed motive games of conflict and cooperation for what the subjects themselves believed to be their intrinsic interests is most extensively explored by Thomas Schelling's *Arms and Influence*, n. 4, and not always with what Patrick Morgan terms sensible (if logical) results. See Morgan's critique of first-wave deterrence theory in *Deterrence: A Conceptual Analysis* (Berkeley: Sage, 1983, 2nd edn), especially pp. 11–47.

33. See, again, the *World Politics* symposium and Axelrod's emphasis on the 'shadow of the future' as a determining factor encouraging cooperation. See n. 28.

34. Karl Mannheim's treatment of ideology as only a partial truth is still powerful and relevant. Karl Mannheim, *Ideology and Utopia: An Introduction to the Sociology of Knowledge* (New York: Harcourt Brace Jovanovich, 1955).

35. For complexity, see John Rawls, *Theory of Justice* (Cambridge: Harvard University Press, 1971); for simplicity, see Axelrod, n. 28. I would argue, with no claim to originality, that it falsifies our understanding of what human beings are and what the human condition is to posit a pre-historic state of isolated individuals who are perpetually at sixes and sevens in the search for a secure and, what is more difficult, a just order. Axelrod shows quite persuasively that beginning with the assumption of non-cooperation, one can relax but never satisfactorily solve the problem of non-cooperation or defection. But why assume the worst case? There is no necessary empirical basis for this assumption any more, admittedly, than the assumption on which this chapter rests, namely that men are social animals by definition – two or more – and that their perfection, as Aristotle's *Ethnics* and *Politics* argue, depends on their cooperation, rarely freely and unconditionally granted: *Introduction to Aristotle*, Richard KcKeon (ed.) (New York: Modern Library, n.d.), especially pp. 298–543, and Arendt, n. 8; and *The Politics of Aristotle*, trans. Ernest Barker (Oxford: Clarendon Press, 1961). From this perspective, superpower cooperation may be considered the normal state of affairs and their falling out as abnormal. This assumption underlies, for example, Quincy Wright's definition of war as 'the legal condition which equally permits two or more hostile groups to carry on a conflict by armed force. . . . This suggests that in spite of their hostility they are members of a higher group which originates this law.' Quincy Wright, *A Study of War* (Chicago: University of Chicago Press, 1965), pp. 8–9.

2 The Cold War as Cooperation: A Soviet Perspective

Victor A. Kremenyuk

INTRODUCTION

At first glance, to study superpower cooperation during the Cold War may seem strange, even absurd. There is a strong conviction among both scholars and practitioners that the Cold War is a classical example of a zero-sum game where the gain (perceived as real) of one is viewed as a loss by the other. Indeed, the Cold War, during which several crises arose that nearly led to war, appears to be the antithesis of cooperation. Although there are evident cases of cooperation – for example, the Geneva conferences of 1953 and 1954 and the Austrian State Treaty of 1955 – these were largely regarded as exceptions from the norms of the late 1940s and 1950s. In the historical analysis of that period, they were largely discounted as anomalies or disregarded or overlooked. The so-called traditional rationale of the Cold War makes the study of superpower cooperation essentially irrelevant.

The idea of Cold War 'cooperation' ceases to be strange if one simply reconsiders what 'cold war' means. Indeed, there is a clear distinction, both in theory and practice, between cold and 'hot' wars; the two are not the same. There were strong barriers that prevented the Cold War from becoming hot, and these barriers worked. The principal impediment was, of course, nuclear deterrence. Deterrence helped both superpowers to live through the dangerous times of the crisis peaks of the Cold War without a direct military confrontation. It is still arguable who deterred whom at that time, but, right as it may seem, this initial line of analysis does not fully explain the fact that both parties to the conflict managed to handle their relations in quite a cautious manner without either capitulating or colliding.

In brief, besides nuclear deterrence, there were other mechanisms that facilitated cooperation and made it conflict-proof, notwithstanding the inflammatory rhetoric, saber-rattling, propagandistic exchanges and the like. A second line of analysis comes to mind when one thinks of the Cold War as a specific type of 'cooperation' between the superpowers. They never existed in absolute isolation from each other; they were periodically in touch either directly, within the context of bilateral relations, or indirectly, through such mechanisms as the United Nations. There existed some implicit understanding, a certain code of relations, which helped them to continue their opposing foreign policies and to adhere to their proclaimed goals, while exercising prudence to exclude a direct military confrontation.

This consideration acquires special significance now, with the evident emerging possibility that the Cold War relationship can sink into the past. And, it would be naive to try to explain this evolution only as a result of some drastic changes in superpower thinking and behavior – what is sometimes portrayed as a bolt from the blue. In many respects these changes have come about as a result of accumulated practical experience, of disillusionments and fatigue from the permanent strain, of a concern over wasted human and material resources, time, and effort in regional conflicts of doubtful benefit or intrinsic worth, and of generational bitterness in both countries over fruitless and costly interventions abroad. All these are extremely important factors which to a large extent frame the thinking of the new generation of political leaders now and into the next century.

In this respect it is important to look back from a long-term historical perspective and to try to understand what conditions, mechanisms and patterns of thinking accompanied the Cold War relationship that helped to keep the whole world structure intact and to prevent it from falling apart in a crisis. If one is not to treat the notion of 'cooperation' only in a single, unidimensional sense or as a series of episodic and unrelated occurrences, then it would be appropriate to regard the whole period, especially from the vantage point of today, as a period of a special kind of cooperation, described by game-theorists as a conflict with mixed motives, or a 'conflict-cooperation' relationship.

IN WHICH SENSE 'COOPERATION'?

The Cold War of the 1940s and 1950s never resulted in a direct 'hot' war. More than that, it is possible now to talk about the end of the Cold War and to discuss its results.[1] This circumstance permits one to look back at the Cold War period as a type of 'conflict-cooperation' which in the long run evolved into coexistence. But if one accepts such a conclusion, then the whole relationship has to be studied anew tracing it back to preceding instances of cooperation while being still guided by a more or less strict definition of cooperation. What is of special concern are the particular types of relationships that the superpowers had in different areas of the world where their interests very often were incompatible. So, what permits us now to regard the Cold War period as a form of cooperation?

First, one should analyze the framework of superpower relations in the broad context of the existing international order. This structure was negotiated and agreed upon during World War II. In a series of summits and conferences, as well as through bilateral and multilateral negotiations during the war, the basic principles and mechanisms of the postwar order were discussed and accepted. Among them were the United Nations as a universal organization to secure peace, security, independence and justice for all the members of the world community; the UN Security Council as the major body of that organization responsible for security and based on the principles of unanimity of its permanent members; the other UN bodies with specialized interests in economic and social affairs, problems of colonies and dependent territories, world trade and finance, and international law.

Although this structure, reflecting the Cold War alignment, was polarized by the East–West division and embodied in the two main military blocks, it nevertheless appeared to be flexible and resistant enough to survive these and other tremors and to persist until now essentially intact. In assessing this fact it is important to note that to a large extent this structure survived because of, and due to, superpower cooperation. Only once, in 1950 after the Soviet walkout from the UN Security Council before the outbreak of the Korean War, was the idea of the UN put to a severe test. Afterwards, both the USSR and the USA were evidently interested in supporting the role of the UN and the Security Council at least as a meeting ground and as an instrument in curbing the dangerous consequences of the arms race. Their conclusion of the Non-Proliferation Treaty (1968) and their support of its regime are further evidence of their willingness to cooperate for mutual benefit.

The second important feature of the interaction of the superpowers during the Cold War is their specific attitude about the use of force in international relations. Each developed a huge and complex global military structure; each had its own version and interpretation of 'just' and 'unjust' wars; each used military force to pursue some foreign policy goals. But, having due respect for the military capabilities of each other, they were mutually sensitive to the high risks of using military force in a direct confrontation. After the condition of mutual assured destruction (MAD) emerged, they developed a joint interest in mutual survival which rather rigidly controlled their military efforts abroad, which interest was always strictly observed in their direct dealings. This restraint did not apply to the use of force against third parties, or to the use of force of their allies and clients (though with time there also appeared 'unwritten rules' in this area).[2]

The third very important dimension is the general attitude that both powers held toward national liberation movements. It is fashionable now among American experts (as well as among some Soviet counterparts), after the bitter polemics of the period of the Vietnam War and the experience of superpower conflict in the developing world of the 1970s, to overlook completely the fact that during World War II and immediately after both superpowers were very close in their positions about the future of the European colonies and dependent territories. To underwrite this conclusion mention must be made of the discussions of Stalin and Roosevelt at Tehran (1943) and Yalta (1945), the process of drafting the UN Charter, particularly those parts which regulated the problems of decolonization, superpower accord on the creation of the Israeli state (1948), and even the similar reaction of both powers to the Suez crisis (1956). It would be appropriate to state that in a very general form both powers shared the idea of decolonization and national independence for the colonies though each of them had its own views and approaches about how and when these goals could and should be achieved.[3]

But the main point should be emphasized here: with all the differences of an ideological and geopolitical nature, with all the harsh and bitter polemics, both superpowers indeed had some shared, or at least similar, general ideas of world order and of its survival. This fact, though overlooked, sometimes purposefully discounted, nevertheless played an important role in establishing norms of cooperation and coexistence with an atmosphere clouded by belligerent pronouncements punctuated by bellicose exchanges.

It would also be inappropriate to disregard completely the human dimension of the Cold War relationship. In the late 1940s and throughout the 1950s many of those who directly participated in Allied operations of World War II were still both alive and active in politics. These included President Dwight D. Eisenhower, the former

Supreme Allied Commander in Europe; Marshal G. Zhukov, the former commander of the Soviet troops which stormed Berlin, and Andrei Gromyko, the Soviet ambassador to Washington since 1943, as well as other important but less well known personalities. These people knew each other, sometimes personally (as did President Eisenhower and Marshal Zhukov), sometimes indirectly, but nevertheless they knew through their own experience the times of close cooperation and that knowledge could not go unnoticed in their thinking and decision-making.[4]

This brief mention of at least some of the facts that contributed to the possibilities of peaceful interaction during the Cold War years brings us closer to an answer to the question: in what sense can one speak of 'cooperation' at that time?

From the beginning one notion of cooperation should be absolutely excluded: namely in the direct, unidimensional sense of a close alliance relationship in managing international disputes. That, of course, never existed as a principle of superpower relations in the Cold War, and it would be misleading to use the term in this way. Since each side sought victory over the other, any possibility of direct cooperation at that time was simply unthinkable. But, as is evident, there were very serious constraints on both sides concerning the choice of means and methods in achieving those goals.

These constraints can be classified as follows:

(a) no direct use of force against each other, since it would be too dangerous, unpredictable, questionable and, hence, counter-productive;

(b) 'don't rock the boat', that is, maintain the postwar world structure, since the consequences of sudden change could bring results which would be dangerous to the self-interest of each side;

(c) conversely, while both sides could count on each other to observe these constraints, both felt free to use all other means to achieve victory.

In light of these mutually recognized constraints, one can speak about cooperation between the two superpowers in the years of Cold War. To substantiate such a conclusion, it would be appropriate to mention the so-called 'Zorin-McCloy Agreement' (1960) which thus far has not been studied in depth, perhaps because it never came to fruition. But if to assess properly the mere fact of the attempt on both sides to codify their relationship and to delimit what was 'acceptable' and 'unacceptable' for them (which, much later, in 1972 took shape as the Basic Principles Agreement), then it appears that the notion of 'cooperation' was not that alien to the thinking of the political leaders in the Soviet Union and United States though they proclaimed irreconcilable goals. This side of the relationship was reflected in Anatol Rapoport's book that appeared in 1960 and gave a push to the studies of cooperation.[5]

COLD WAR 'COOPERATION': REGIONAL ASPECTS

There were elements of direct cooperation between the United States and the Soviet Union in some regions after World War II as an offspring of the agreements and understandings achieved at the Tehran, Yalta, and Potsdam conferences. Though it is also well known that, right from the beginning, the Allies had sometimes absolutely divergent views of what those agreements meant and how they had to be implemented, it was understood at that time that the relationship between the Soviet Union and the United States included such regional matters and that regular discussions and consultations had to be held.

First of all, negotiations concerned Germany and other occupied territories in Europe as a result of the capitulation of the Nazi Reich. These discussions were extended to Japan and other occupied territories in Asia and the Pacific as a result of the collapse of the Japanese 'co-prosperity sphere'. In the restricted meaning of cooperation, outlined earlier, these negotiations were regarded as essential by both superpowers. In the long run, these consultations brought positive results in stabilizing these territories and countries. At the same time it is important to note that there was a difference between the situation in European and in the Asian-Pacific regions. As George Kennan notes, the American administration at that time was inclined to see what would happen in Asia when 'the dust is settled' whereas in Europe the situation was much more urgent and immediate.[6]

The elements of regional superpower cooperation largely survived until the early 1950s when they were abruptly ended with the signing of the US–Japanese Peace Treaty in San Francisco (1951) and with the Paris Agreements (1954) which brought West Germany into NATO. But even then elements of cooperation persisted, especially in the case of the treaty with Austria (1955), which ended the foreign occupation of that country and established its neutral status. In this aspect the signing of the Quadripartite Agreement on Berlin (1971) also reflected post-World War II allied cooperation although it was prompted by totally new developments.

Once the superpowers learned to manage their differences over Germany and Berlin, the most acute conflicts between them took place in the Third World which entered a highly volatile, dynamic and critical stage of national liberation and self-determination after World War II. To an extent both superpowers share responsibility for this phenomenon. The United States actively promoted self-determination in the Atlantic Charter (1941), notwithstanding the resistance of its British ally; the Soviet Union supported national liberation movements since the days of the Appeal to All the Muslim Working People of Russia and the Orient in December 1917. Both thought, as noted above, in similar terms during the wartime conferences, a convergence which did not go unnoticed in India, Indochina, Korea, Indonesia as well as in the North African colonies and elsewhere.

Perhaps this is not an appropriate place to speculate about who meant what in the declarations and pronouncements of these years. There are Soviet and American analysts who consider that the American position on colonialism during World War II was mainly motivated by the desire to get access to cheap resources and to break down the rigid economic barriers set by the British and French in their colonies.[7] There are American experts who consider that the Soviet position on national liberation was (and still is) motivated mainly by the dreams and ideals of world revolution.[8] Disputable as these arguments may be, they simply overlook the main issue: that both superpowers prompted national liberation revolutions in Third World countries, and when new regimes came into existence they became another area of confrontation and rivalry between the superpowers.

Two crucial events have to be singled out here: the Truman Doctrine (1947) and the Korean War (1950). The history of the Truman Doctrine is well known; there is no need to repeat it. What is less clear are its long-term consequences and its general impact on Soviet–American relations. Among American scholars, there are those who tend to disregard the importance of the Truman Doctrine, emphasizing that it was pronounced only for a specific situation; that it did not outlive its author; that it ceded in importance to John Foster Dulles's rigid policies, and so forth.

Partly, all this is true, but to a large extent this interpretation represents an attempt to downgrade the importance of a historical event simply because what happened later appeared much more important. To assess the original importance of the Truman Doctrine, one must recognize that it was apparently received in the Soviet Union as an unacceptable challenge and a decisive break with previous cooperation.

At that time the Truman Doctrine seemed motivated by a desire to keep the Soviets under permanent pressure, since it was evident to Moscow that revolutions in many countries were expected as a logical outcome of the disruptions caused by World War II. The pre-emptive US move, in attributing responsibility for any revolution in the world to the Soviet Union, was regarded as a declaration of war on the Soviet Union and an attack on its position, especially in Eastern Europe. It should also be noted that the Soviet Union's nuclear program was in progress by then. The events in Eastern Europe that followed demonstrated the ability of the Soviet Union to preserve its assets and to counter threats from the United States which extended to the dangerous Berlin crisis of 1948–9 which brought the superpowers to the brink of war. Thus, the hasty decision to issue the Truman Doctrine was taken largely due to two factors: an overestimation of American power and considerations of domestic politics (ousting Roosevelt's people from the government). Both factors played a crucial role in changing the entire context of Soviet–American relations at that time. Wartime cooperation ended and the Cold War started.

In this respect, the beginning of the war in Korea in June 1950 also played an important role. It is understandable that the war froze the positions on both sides; it also gave impetus to American initiatives in the Pacific (the peace treaty with Japan); to the formation of the defense treaty with Australia and New Zealand (ANZUS); to US involvement in Taiwan and Indochina; to the creation of SEATO in 1954; to the enlargement of NATO in 1952 to include Greece and Turkey; and to the expansion of US interests and influence in the 'Northern Tier' (Afghanistan, Pakistan and Iran). What was especially important was the progressive growth in US defense spending since 1950.[9]

Both events, the Truman Doctrine and the Korean War, left a significant imprint on the superpower relationship. In the case of Korea, it is still embodied in the strained situation on the peninsula, continuing unrest in the South, the presence of US nuclear arms and conventional forces, and the absence of genuine dialogue between the two Koreas. In other, more general, aspects, this imprint led to a formation of a certain system of beliefs which outlived the Cold War and which still persist. Among them the following may be cited:

(a) Third World regions were progressively regarded as 'safer' places for rivalry than Europe was. With the introduction of intercontinental ballistic missiles (ICBMs) in the USSR (1955) and growing stalemate in superpower strategic relations in some areas of the Third World, national liberation movements were looked upon by strategic thinkers as a possible battle-ground for 'local' wars, not excluding completely the use of nuclear weapons in these wars.[10]

(b) At the same time these areas were regarded as an integral part of the global superpower rivalry. Though both countries supported the notions of national sovereignty and independence, a 'spheres of influence' mentality appeared which was inclined to regard areas of the Third World as 'vital', 'important', or 'peripheral'. This meant that the freedom of action of the other rival in most regions was not welcomed or tolerated. Even the hint of intervention by one superpower in the 'sphere of influence' of the other superpower caused an overreaction, as with the United States in Guatemala (1954), or the Soviet Union in Hungary (1956).

(c) Rivalry in Third World areas had a dual meaning: geopolitical and ideological. Geopolitically, it provoked a strong Soviet reaction when the threat of the 'strategic encirclement', pursued by Dulles, became discernible by 1954. The Soviet government courted the non-aligned nations, assisted Gamal Nasser in Egypt, even prior to the Suez crisis, and established good relations with India and Indonesia, helping these states thus avoid becoming part of the US global system of alliances. Ideologically, the superpower rivalry prompted a strong American anti-Communist position spelled out in the resolution on 'Communist subversion in the Americas' (the 'Eisenhower Doctrine' for the Middle East (1957) and the 'Dulles Doctrine' for the Far East (1958)).

(d) The combination of geopolitical/ideological as well as 'spheres of influence' thinking in the general context of rivalry in the Third World produced a kind of symmetrical vision of the entire strategic and regional relationship between the US and

USSR on the Soviet side, a view vehemently rejected on the American side. The Soviet leadership was more inclined than its American counterpart was to approach this relationship from the point of view of achieving a global balance which later, toward the end of 1960s and early 1970s, was transformed into the idea of strategic balance. But in the late 1950s and early 1960s the Soviet notion of balance was assumed to be balance of influence in the Third World. For the United States the idea of 'balance' was generally unacceptable, since it contradicted the original idea of 'containment' which in practice meant the achievement of American superiority.

THE CUBAN MISSILE CRISIS: LEARNING COOPERATION

As is reported in recent Soviet publications on the Cuban missile crisis, Khrushchev's decision to deploy Soviet intermediate-range nuclear missiles in Cuba was prompted by two major considerations: (a) to deter a possible American attack on Cuba which was regarded as highly probable after the ill-fated Bay of Pigs intervention in 1961; and (b) to respond to the earlier American decision to deploy US Thor missiles in Turkey and Jupiters in Italy.[11] Both considerations seemed to him quite legitimate since his view of the Soviet–American relationship was evidently based on the idea of 'balance'. He did not consider this decision as a deviation from the 'rules of the game' and was sure that he was doing the right thing.

The story of the Cuban crisis of 1962 is well known.[12] But there is still a great need to learn from that crisis.[13] The need to turn back not only to the entire complex history of the Cold War and to the forms of cooperation that emerged but also to the study of separate episodes of that period, like the Cuban or Berlin crises, is self-evident. With the evolution of the superpower relationship, especially in the 1970s, it appears that the lack of study in this area permitted a great deal of misunderstanding. In the Soviet Union this misunderstanding turned mainly around the interpretation of the Basic Principles Agreement of 1972 that carried relations between the superpowers to the deadlock of Afghanistan. So, at least from this point of view, the lessons of the Cuban crisis deserve special attention.

There is also another dimension of the problem. The Cuban crisis played a central role in a series of regional events which happened at approximately the same time: the Congo (1960), Berlin (1961), and Laos (1962). It was evident that the superpower relationship, after the troubled but more or less stable stage of the 1950s, was entering less stable and hence more dangerous waters in the early 1960s. Readjustment in the patterns of behavior took place on both sides: the Kennedy administration launched a 'flexible response' doctrine, while the Soviet leadership evidently impressed by Sputnik regarded its prospects in the competition with the United States as quite bright. The Khrushchev–Kennedy meeting in Vienna in June 1961 evidenced these shifts.

In some US studies, stress is placed on the 'secrecy' of Khrushchev's decision to deploy nuclear weapons in Cuba as one of the major reasons for the powerful American reaction. It is hard to agree with this interpretation since the Cold War period was not one of openness and *glasnost*: Khrushchev's decision was consistent with a standard pattern of behaviour on both sides. Remember, for example, the U-2 downing over Soviet space in 1960 and the awkward attempts of the Eisenhower administration to explain that fact. No less awkward is the explanation of the Kennedy administration after the Bay of Pigs failure in 1961. One cannot regard 'Soviet secrecy' as one of the major reasons for American overreaction nor is it possible in terms of 'crisis management' to explain American behavior after the Cuban missile crisis was over.

In explaining the Cuban crisis, it is more reasonable to look at it from the point of view of the established norms of cooperation which were outlined earlier. In this respect, of course, the Soviet move caused great concern to the US administration and the general public. Military experts saw in the Soviet action an attempt to change drastically the military balance between the USA and USSR in the favor of the latter. In the tradition of 'worst case scenario' thinking, they were already counting American casualties if a military confrontation had happened. Political analysts thought in the terms of the 'Monroe Doctrine' and of more communist revolutions in the Caribbean and, perhaps, Central America. Decision-makers saw in Cuba an unexpected departure from what was perceived as standard Soviet behavior. As an aggregate result of these considerations, pressures mounted on President Kennedy to respond strongly, ushering in that ominous period of thirteen days in October 1962.

But something of this kind was bound to happen. Both the roles and assets of each superpower were gradually changing during the

1950s. The US lost its atomic monopoly as the Soviet Union became a nuclear power. The importance of this fact, however, was grossly exaggerated by the 'missile gap' campaign which partly misled both Soviet and American leaders. We now know from Robert McNamara's *Blundering into Disaster* that the real ratio was 18:1 in favor of the United States.[14] While during the 1950s the US turned increasingly away from national liberation movements, the Soviet Union developed close relations with political leaders in India, Indonesia, Ghana, Egypt, and even Yugoslavia. It also established close ties with Vietnam, Iraq and Cuba. All these were regarded as major assets in the superpower rivalry.

All these factors worked to readjust the rules and norms of Cold War cooperation, if not to revise them completely. Of course, this does not explain why Cuba happened to be such a pivotal crisis for superpower cooperation, and not Berlin. But the differences between the two situations are evident: Berlin was a 'front-city' where the military forces and political assets of both sides were almost equal; the construction of the Berlin Wall, although labeled by the West as 'unacceptable', did not much change the real correlation of forces; the city was never regarded as someone's monopoly since, on the contrary, it was an object of four-power control; and, finally, Berlin did not pose a direct threat to US territory. In the Cuban case the situation was entirely different on all these scores. It was clear to everyone that deployment of Soviet missiles meant a serious change in the superpower strategic balance and had, as the US administration thought, to be blocked even at the risk of nuclear war.

The Cuban crisis and especially its results have significantly changed thinking patterns on both sides. First, both superpowers approached a dangerous brink. It became evident to responsible observers that regional crises could very easily be turned into global crises despite the asymmetry of the interests at stake in a region. Second, both superpowers agreed that the existing means of communications between them were inadequate and that this seemingly technical matter posed a threat to crisis management. Third, it was understood that without some agreed upon rules of prudence, both sides risked Cubas all around the world. Even one mistake might lead to unthinkable consequences. Fourth, they also understood that even the kind of threat which appeared during the Cuban crisis would not divert them from rivalry and conflict. All in all, the task before both superpowers was enormous: to find ways to reduce the risk of war without significantly changing their conflicting foreign policy goals.

The conclusions reached by both sides partially converged and diverged. The American reaction can be characterized in the words of Robert McNamara after the crisis was over: there is no more military strategy, there is only crisis management (as quoted in Cora Bell's *Conventions of Crisis*).[15] As to the Soviet reaction, it was twofold: on the one hand, the Soviet Union accepted the idea of the 'hot line' which became a government-to-government agreement in 1963; on the other, it concluded that to speak to the US as an equal the Soviet Union had to achieve strategic parity with the United States.

Alongside these conclusions, the idea of more sophisticated and more elaborate patterns of superpower cooperation was also given serious examination by Washington and Moscow. There was some realistic possibility that this way of thinking could bring positive results. There is ample evidence of this notion at work throughout 1963. For example, there was the 'Hot Line' Agreement, the Partial Test Ban Treaty (PTBT), discussions of the non-proliferation of nuclear arms, and finally, President Kennedy's conciliatory speech at the American University in September 1963. The Soviet government tried to reciprocate in these moves. There was a Soviet proposal on disarmament which contributed to the general easing of tensions. The crisis played the role of a strong shock for both parties, contributing both an accelerated mutual learning process on both sides and a swing of the pendulum in their relations in the direction of a genuine cooperation as opposed to conflict. This movement had serious prospects for success since it was based on the recent experience of the worst crisis since 1945 which could very easily have erupted into a nuclear war and on the understanding that the US–Soviet relationship had to become an object of thorough scrutiny to introduce some basic principles and constraints on superpower behavior consistent with international legal practices. Unfortunately, this movement was abruptly checked by the assassination of President Kennedy on 22 November 1963.

But it would be wrong to disregard the general impact of the Cuban missile crisis on Soviet-American cooperation at that time and thereafter. It taught both sides some important lessons which were integrated into the patterns of their behavior toward each other. Among these lessons the most important was that the direct clash of Soviet and US armed forces had to be avoided at any price both in Europe and elsewhere. Even the slightest prospect of such an encounter was already regarded as an urgent political matter and merited attention at the highest levels of power in both countries. Contrary to the views of such theoreticians as Herman Kahn,[16] both governments strictly observed this principle.

Second, the matter of nuclear arms deployment in foreign countries acquired a heightened political dimension. This did not mean that the spread of nuclear weapons was arrested, but it turned that process into a highly sensitive issue. For many years, it became fashionable not to recognize officially the fact of such deployments. As an example, the statement of former US Secretary of Defense James Schlesinger in 1975, in which he acknowledged the existence of US nuclear weapons in Korea, produced an awkward situation for the Ford administration. The same experience characterized the Soviet position on SS-20s in the 1970s.

Third, the first attempts of joint crisis management were undertaken as a totally new aspect of the Cold War-type relationship. The establishment of the 'Hot Line' between Moscow and Washington was an attempt to establish close communications in case of an emergency for the purpose of having consultations whenever a conflict-prone situation emerged or when clarifications were needed. It became a part of the superpower understanding that in a crisis, it was absolutely necessary not only to keep communication lines open but also to discuss possible lines of action in advance. The system worked quite efficiently in the 1960s, according to President Lyndon Johnson.[17] Later, it was mutually decided to modernize this system (agreements of 1971 and 1985).

Fourth, the parties did not feel that this form of cooperation restricted their freedom of action elsewhere. The only exclusion by that time was the Soviet–American agreement on Cuba, which incorporated a US pledge to avoid direct intervention in Cuba. As to the rest the continuation of rivalry was regarded as self-evident and legitimate. Both sides regarded their obligations and perceived their resulting influence in the Third World as assets, accordingly, both were eager to keep them intact and to undertake new commitments.

Fifth, an interesting evolution resulted in their attitude toward the UN and the Security Council. After the 1960 Congo crisis, when the Soviet government grew skeptical about UN peacekeeping operations and their relevance (due partly to the fact that the UN force could not prevent the assassination of the Congo's Prime Minister Patrice Lumumba), there was a period when the prestige of the UN was rather low in the context of US–Soviet relations. But its usefulness in settling the Cuban crisis opened a new venue for both sides to cooperate in that body. Since then, it has often been used as a means for discussion and negotiations during crises.

One of the main results of the Cuban missile crisis was an evident acceleration of the process of cooperative learning between the US and USSR. Both sides came to an understanding that, alongside their rivalry, some measures of precaution had to be taken, especially in direct and indirect communication, in avoiding unacceptable interference with each other's allies and in deploying their nuclear weapons around the world. As another element of cooperation, the idea of consultations and notification has appeared as a possible part of the relationship though at that time it concerned primarily the conduct of both superpowers in international crises. But the thinking on both sides went much farther than that. Included also were cooperation in curbing the arms race (PTBP) and the spread of nuclear weapons (NPT).

VIETNAM: NEW ELEMENTS OF RIVALRY AND COOPERATION

The change in leadership in both countries at approximately the same time (US, 1963 and USSR, 1964) had an important effect on superpower relations. The elements of direct cooperation which appeared in 1963 were so fragile and based upon personal, non-institutionalized approaches that, with the new leaders in power, much had to be learned anew. The initial attitude on both sides was much less oriented toward observing the agreements already achieved than one of looking more for some fresh terrain to extend the rivalry where a possibility arose to gain ground and power. The anti-status quo power at that time was the USA. The proclamation of the 'Johnson Doctrine' in 1965, following the Dominican crisis, and growing US involvement in Vietnam channeled the American interests toward new zones of rivalry. The 'Johnson Doctrine' tied American involvement in Vietnam to the superpowers' global rivalry. It pointed to growing Soviet assistance to the Democratic Republic of Vietnam (DRV) and to closer relations with the Hanoi government. For Moscow, a US victory in Vietnam would be a major setback for the USSR at a regional level and would reinforce the SEATO alliance. A Vietnam victory could also be interpreted as a 'demonstration of force' useful for American prestige in other Third World areas. It seemed that one of the major elements of the American decision to intervene in Vietnam was a desire on Washington's part to control local wars. This shift is suggested by the ambitious American military strategy of preparing to conduct two and a half wars simultaneously.[18]

The Vietnam War became a focal point of Soviet–American relations in the late 1960s and early 1970s. Each side attributed a growing amount of attention to Vietnam, viewing it as a case of rivalry which could have a significant importance for their relationship in a long-term historical perspective. On the basis of the so-called 'Tonkin' resolution the Johnson administration acquired extensive authority to expand US involvement and to finance the war. The United States deployed approximately one-third of its standing military force in that war and spent almost $140 billion. The widely publicized Tet offensive (1968) of the National Liberation Front of South Vietnam demonstrated that the war was lost by the US. The special Advisory Group on Vietnam which gathered to advise President Johnson on the issue rejected the Pentagon request that the US armed force in Vietnam be increased by 200,000 men and recommended negotiation. President Johnson announced US readiness to negotiate the end of the war and to facilitate this decision he withdrew from the presidential campaign already underway.

But, accompanying the escalation of the American war in Vietnam, some new and additional elements of cooperation appeared in US–Soviet relations. The meeting between President Johnson and the Soviet Prime Minister Alexei Kosygin took place in Glassboro in 1967. The parties discussed the problems of bilateral relations, scientific cooperation, prospects for arms control and disarmament, and other matters of common concern. Unfortunately, the significance of this meeting was later overshadowed by the events in Czechoslovakia in 1968. There is no doubt that both sides welcomed the meeting since it permitted an exchange of views on the general situation in the world, opened the possibility of balancing the negative influence of the war in Vietnam on the state of US–Soviet relations with discussions on arms control, and initiated a process of defining common or parallel superpower interests in global politics: non-proliferation, denuclearization of the seabed and space, chemical weapons, and so forth. At least, both agreed that there was an urgent need to develop analytical tools that would permit both sides to use the same methods in evaluating common problems.

The significance of the Glassboro meeting is suggested by the fact that it placed on the agenda of both sides such issues as the discussions of anti-ballistic missiles (later developed into the ABM

Treaty 1972), strategic arms limitation (later also developed into the SALT 1 and SALT 2 treaties, 1972 and 1979), the discussions of an all-European conference which was later transformed into the so-called Helsinki process. Strange as it may seem, the war in Vietnam, although a focus of rivalry, was at the same time pushing both superpowers toward a search for new avenues of mutual understanding mainly in the area of bilateral relations on global issues and significantly less so in regional matters.

At the same time the quest for a 'balance' or for 'parity' was still one of the dominant forces in Soviet foreign policy. While the US was involved in a seemingly endless jungle war in Vietnam, Soviet strategic nuclear forces were enlarged by several orders of magnitude. They eventually approached in size those of the USA, creating a situation of strategic parity. The Western literature attached conflicting interpretations to this new strategic situation. George Kennan considered that the US involvement in Vietnam and the diversion of a significant part of its military expenditures to that war largely explained why the Soviet Union managed to achieve strategic parity by the end of 1960s.[19] The British analyst Alastair Buchan thought that the rate of growth of the Soviet strategic program after the Cuban crisis made it possible for the Soviet Union to build a strategic force equal to that of the USA even if there were no war in Vietnam and US involvement.[20]

These differences apart, the fact of strategic parity had become one of the major factors shaping superpowers interaction in the early 1970s. The war in Vietnam proved to be costly and purposeless; it brought no gain for the US and, conversely, it damaged its prestige and undermined the domestic foreign policy consensus. It was evident that the war had to be ended. The Atlantic Alliance was experiencing what Henry Kissinger labeled as a 'troubled partnership',[21] Armed clashes on the Soviet–Chinese border in 1969 also urged a rethinking of the US approach to China. Japan, partly due to significant US expense during the war in Vietnam, became a rising economic power. All these facts, together with the Soviet–US strategic parity, needed re-examination and a new conceptual framework devised for US foreign policy. This revision, known as the 'Nixon Doctrine', was embodied in a series of messages by President Richard Nixon to Congress between 1970 and 1973.

The three key elements of the doctrine – 'power', 'partnership', and 'negotiation' – had clear implications for US–Soviet rivalry and cooperation. The goal of enhancing American 'power' was evident.

After the Vietnam débâcle American presidents had to think of the US position in the world which at all times was closely tied to national 'power'. Preserving American power assumed top priority in the Nixon administration. In this case the notion of 'power' was not wholly concentrated on military might but also included the elements of technological and economic potential coupled with extensive US alliances in the developed world. As to developing countries, alliance relationships were regarded more as liabilities than as assets and were reassessed with an eye to abrogating unnecessary commitments wherever possible. The notion of 'realistic deterrence' (a code name for parity) became the governing standard.

'Partnership' was an offspring of 'power'. It was largely understood as sharing responsibility between the United States and its clients for controlling the events in different areas of the world. This was a substantial revision of the previous approach which emphasized direct US military involvement in local wars. But, once the conclusion was drawn, according to an unidentified US source, that 'a superpower cannot win a victory in a local war if the other superpower supports the other side',[22] it followed that there should be a policy of decentralizing the tasks of 'defending Western interests' to local allies and clients. Originally, this idea was spelled out by US Defense Secretary Robert McNamara in his speech in Montreal in May 1966; and, later, especially after the Arab–Israeli war in June 1967 it gradually assumed the status of a new policy for the United States, which was essentially adopted by the Nixon administration in its approach to the developing world.

Finally, the notion of 'negotiation' had direct relevance for US–Soviet relations. It was an important change in US foreign policy because prior to that time negotiations between the Soviet Union and the United States were always regarded as more the exception than the norm. This was the typical Cold War approach to cooperation oriented more towards unwritten, tacit rules which were generally defined during or after a crisis or which were negotiated in an indirect, Byzantine manner. President Nixon's (and Kissinger's) view was to try to make these rules explicit and to negotiate something like a *modus vivendi* with the Soviet Union. The effort took the shape of the Basic Principles Agreement (BPA) in 1972.

FROM THE BPA TO AFGHANISTAN: LOST OPPORTUNITIES FOR COOPERATION

It would be a mistake to regard the BPA signed in June 1972 in Moscow as a treaty designed to solve a specific dispute. The BPA was more a statement of principles, an attempt to specify the nature of the US–Soviet relationship and to codify the main rules of coexistence. By that time, it was already acknowledged that both superpowers could get along in spite of their controversies and opposing military arsenals. They could even try to start and conduct negotiations on such delicate issues as nuclear arms control, regional conflicts, and bilateral relations, concerned mainly with economic matters. Of course, there was still much to disagree about since mutual trust was negligible and deep suspicions governed thinking on both sides, yet the experience of the previous years was pushing the superpowers to recognize the need for some sort of negotiated accommodation.

Objectively, there were two approaches to a possible solution of this problem. One was to attempt to start the process of accommodation with some specific agreements on a concrete issue, such as modernization of the 'Hot Line', incidents at sea, an ABM treaty, or strategic arms limitations. This step-by-step approach could create, within a certain period of time, a necessary basis of confidence and in the long run lead to a more general agreement on the rules of coexistence. The other way was to try to formulate a joint approach, or a framework for coexistence, and to turn it into a formal agreement (or, as Alexander George termed it, a 'written norm')[23] which would be regarded as a legitimate basis for the construction of superpower relations. As we already know, both approaches were pursued during the early 1970s in what was regarded at that time as a major breakthrough in US–Soviet relations.

The Basic Principles Agreement established several major points of accord. It was agreed that peaceful coexistence should be the main principle on which to base US–Soviet relations. Differences in ideology and social systems were not to be obstacles to the bilateral development of normal relations based on the principles of sovereignty, equality, non-interference in internal affairs, and mutual advantage. Both sides attached major importance to preventing the development of situations capable of causing a dangerous exacerbation of their relations. They pledged to exercise restraint in their mutual relations and to negotiate and settle differences by peaceful means. They also recognized that efforts to obtain unilateral advantage at the expense of each other, directly or indirectly, was inconsistent with the objectives that both sides shared. As permanent members of the UN Security Council, they agreed to do everything in their power so that conflicts or situations that could increase international tensions would not arise.[24]

There were other mutual obligations agreed upon in the BPA. For the purposes of this study, the most important point was that both sides finally decided to codify some aspects of their conduct in order to avoid situations which could lead to the brink of war. This was one of the principal results of the previous period of Cold War-type cooperation, and it was finally put to paper as a written norm. At the same time, on the level of official thinking in both the USA and the USSR, there was little, sometimes no, understanding of the line between adherence to the spirit of this document and continuation of the rivalry which, of course, did not abruptly disappear after the BPA was signed.

The ambiguous approach of both sides toward the contents and significance of the BPA produced a volatile and unstable period from the mid-1970s on. Attempts to establish some cooperative relationship – for example in the Middle East following the 1973 Yom Kippur war or during the convening of the Geneva Conference under the Soviet–American co-chairmanship in 1977 – were paralleled by unilateral efforts which aggravated tensions. Soviet suspicions were raised by US subversive activity in Chile where the legitimately elected socialist president Salvador Allende was ousted as a result of the military coup in September 1973. Strong American reaction also followed the Soviet–Cuban support of the MPLA government in Angola to repel the South African invasion in the fall of 1975.[25]

The sole exception to the evolution of progressively enlarging superpower conflict in the developing world was the attempt of the early Carter administration (1977–8) to open a new chapter in the superpower relationship in the Third World. These included negotiations on the demilitarization of the Indian Ocean, conventional arms transfers (CAT), and a Middle East settlement. Initially, possibilities arose to extend these efforts to the entire list of Soviet–American tension points around the globe. But, as it turned out, the US administration at that time itself lacked consistency and necessary unity. This circumstance produced highly contradictory behavior (positive and negative signals alternated) and a serious controversy erupted within the administration between the president's national security adviser, Zbigniew Brzezinski, and his secretary of state

Cyrus Vance. It would be fair to acknowledge that the Soviet leadership also did not cooperate to the fullest extent since it was concerned about President Carter's 'human rights' crusade. All in all, the promising start of 1977–8 ended with no result. There were several objective conditions why Soviet–American cooperation could not progess in this period. First, the superpowers were ideologically in conflict, including the Soviet thesis that the ideological struggle could not contribute to the establishment of a normal working relationship. The same can be said about US foreign policy which added a 'human rights' dimension to the matter of economic ties (the Jackson-Vanik Amendment, 1974), giving birth to the idea of 'linkage' which flourished during the years of the Carter administration and persists until now, evidenced by the Bush administration's insistence on Soviet emigration liberalization as a precondition for conferring Most Favored Nation status on the Soviet Union. Second, the general policy lines of both superpowers were developing in opposite directions: while Soviet policy was expanding its obligations in the Third World (the treaties of friendship signed in the 1970s with Iraq, India, Somalia, South Yemen, Egypt, Vietnam, and several other countries), US policy was still looking toward limiting its links with Third World nations (e.g. US acceptance of the dissolution of SEATO, or the abortive decision of the Carter administration to withdraw American troops from South Korea).

Notwithstanding the impact of these contradictory factors, there were also extensive opportunities for a coming to terms on the 'rules of conduct' for both superpowers which might have ordered and systematized their relationship. At least, President Carter's thinking tended to treat seriously this possibility as a part of the general relations with the Soviet Union. This inclination was supported by policy papers circulating at the time as well as by the opinion of some political figures in the United States.[26] Nevertheless, the influence of countervailing factors appeared to be much stronger. Since 1978–9 relations between the superpowers regarding their contacts in the Third World became progressively strained. The 'linkage' politics practiced by Brzezinski only added to tensions without bringing any resolution.[27]

Until late December 1979, when Soviet troops entered Afghanistan, there were elements of cooperation in Soviet–American relations, extending to the Third World. Among the most important elements were, first, those associated with the pursuit of arms control negotiations. Although relations between them were getting worse since the days of the Somali–Ethiopian war and the beginning of the revolution in Iran, Soviet–American negotiations on limiting strategic arms steadily progressed. The March 1977 proposal by the Carter administration to modify the format of those negotiations (brought by Secretary of State Vance to Moscow) was rejected by the Soviet side. Nevertheless negotiations continued. Finally, they resulted in the summer 1979 Brezhnev–Carter meeting in Vienna where the SALT 2 treaty was signed.

Second, the idea of a 'code of conduct' was discussed as a possible part of Soviet–American relations. In the 1970s it was advanced principally by the US while the Soviet Union remained skeptical. Still, the idea was probed in different ways at the ministerial level and by experts at sundry meetings. These efforts corresponded to attempts to find solutions at least to the most divisive issues (Middle East, Indian Ocean, CAT). While both sides had reservations about the idea of a code of conduct (e.g. some US experts were rather skeptical about such 'general' agreements in line with their criticism of the BPA), they were inclined in practice to follow some 'code'. Finally, the Soviet side accepted this idea. On 27 April 1981, speaking to Libya's Muammar Qaddafi, Soviet Secretary General Leonid Brezhnev outlined the Soviet approach to a 'code of conduct'. The Soviet view contained five points mainly based upon the UN Charter.[28] But this initiative produced no result since the war in Afghanistan was already in full progress, and no US official could responsibly comment on it.

Third, it would also be unfair to overlook Soviet disillusionment with the record of the Carter administration. Soviet foreign policy at that time, following the state of stagnation in the country, was not ready to accept immediately any policy initiative whether it was productive or not. This attitude was illustrated by the Soviet reaction to the March 1977 US proposal on SALT 2 and to other overtures by the Carter administration. But, gradually, the Soviet government exhibited increasing interest in US proposals on Third World issues. However, the dynamics of the Carter administration manifested an ability, to cite an example, to sign a joint statement (on the Middle East on 1 October 1977) and then immediately to forget about it (the enthusiastic response of the United States to Egyptian President Anwar Sadat's decision to go to Israel announced on 7 October 1977), which was totally unacceptable to the USSR. Hence, the US administration was regarded as 'inconsistent', 'unstable', and 'untrustworthy'. No serious cooperation could be expected from it.

Fourth, the revolutions in Nicaragua and Iran in 1979, which destroyed regimes long friendly to the United States contributed to the further disruption of US–Soviet relations in the developing world. Following the disintegration of US friends and allies, the idea of the 'arc of crisis' was formulated by Brzezinski in order to mobilize US public opinion around the concept of a rapid deployment force to counter undesired events in Third World areas. On the Soviet side the American force was viewed as a sign of 'panic' and 'weakness' which bolstered the influence of those in the Soviet Union who were inclined to continue growing Soviet involvement in Third World areas as a means of improving the Soviet position in its rivalry with the United States. This inclination, as one can assume, prompted the ill-fated decision to send the Soviet forces to Afghanistan.

The Soviet intervention in Afghanistan almost reversed the entire pattern of Soviet–American tacit cooperation which had gradually emerged after the Cuban missile crisis. Taken, as one may suggest, as a result of the desire to counter the NATO December 1979 'dual track' decision (on the deployment of the US intermediate-range nuclear missiles in Europe), the decision to intervene in Afghanistan not only decreased Soviet leverage in its relations with the US but contributed to the sharpening of international tensions, to Soviet isolation both in the West and in the Third World, to heightened Chinese concern and resistance, and to anti-Soviet sentiment in the Islamic world. To speak directly of one important consequence for Soviet–American relations, the Soviet action in Afghanistan contributed greatly to the rise of conservatism in US foreign policy and even perhaps to domestic conservative opinion. In the first half of the 1980s, Afghanistan revived the worst days of the Cold War and prompted the expansion of new strategic nuclear programs by the Reagan administration. One may even conclude that the whole cycle of the reversal of the Cold War-type relationship between the US and USSR, starting with the easing of tensions after the Cuban missile crisis, was returning almost completely to its origins twenty years later.

CONCLUSIONS: LESSONS OF AFGHANISTAN AND US–SOVIET COOPERATION

The election of Mikhail Gorbachev as the Secretary General of the CPSU Central Committee in March 1985 and the advent of 'new political thinking' in Soviet foreign policy had a significant impact on US–Soviet relations. 'Gorbachev was beginning the huge task of *glasnost*. 'He was trying to get the country moving after almost a decade of stagnation. He needed a breathing spell in the competition with the United States in order to concentrate on problems at home. He wanted civil if not cordial relations with the other superpower, but not at the expense of any vital Soviet interest and not if this meant permitting the United States to have an important military system – like strategic defense, while the Soviet Union did not.'[29] This quotation provides in all its aspects a representative American comment on the essence of the 'Gorbachev factor' in the context of Soviet–American relations.

Indeed, the election of Mikhail Gorbachev as Secretary General occurred at the time that Soviet society was approaching a serious crisis. The decade of stagnation before 1985 resulted in significant and heavy consequences for the state of the national economy, for social welfare, including housing, education, health, and especially for the political and ideological climate of the Soviet Union. All spheres of life had to be critically analyzed, solutions found, and applied. Even without the 'new political thinking' in foreign policy, it was evident that the country needed a respite from the Cold War and a serious re-examination of its past, present and future. There existed no ready-made program of action, but the more the new Soviet leadership penetrated the depth of its problems, as well as those of the country, the more it understood that a significant, in some parts, a crucial restructuring, or *perestroika*, was needed.

The most critical area was, and still is, the economy. It operated at a declining rate of growth and actually was nearing stagnation. The country's huge and complex economic system was less and less effective. It could neither respond to the growing expectations of the Soviet people for greater welfare nor meet day-to-day needs (food, clothing, durable goods, services, etc.) at an appropriate level. This produced a widespread disillusionment with the system, growing apathy on the part of the majority of the population, and mounting criticism from the educated elite. The validity of the whole social system was questioned, a condition which could erupt into a serious political and ideological crisis.

But the efforts to look for some instant solutions in the economic area showed that without changing the political climate, without a substantial change in the government system, there could be no successful economic development. In order to promote political change, the policy of openness, or *glasnost*, and of democratization, was considered indispensable. Understanding the genuine value of the freedom of information and of choice came only later. With astonishing speed *glasnost* gained ground as a part of both governmental policy and the renaissance of the society. It made possible a major breakthrough in the governmental sphere of the USSR, leading to the first free election of the people's deputies and the creation of a working Supreme Soviet. It is evident that all these changes can be regarded as only the beginning of the creation of a new political system in the USSR since such important issues as the position of the Communist Party, its relation to the government, or the possibility of other political parties, are still to be reconsidered.

Meanwhile, as a reaction to years of neglect and mismanagement a whole new set of issues appeared on the Soviet President's agenda. Among them were growing unrest in some republics, especially in the Baltic area, wild-cat strikes in some critical areas, like the coal industry and parts of the railways system, and the growing emigration from the country. All these issues aggravated the situation and pushed the government to press reforms more energetically in the sphere of politics, economic management, and ideology. The general direction was to restructure completely the management of the economy by introducing new laws on property, status of enterprises, labor conflicts, rents, and local self-government. A sound basis for further restructuring is also expected from elections to the Supreme Soviets of the Republics and to the municipal Soviets.

This process which essentially led to the opening of the decision-making process in the Soviet system created a possibility for a critical re-examination of Soviet foreign and security policy. The primary source for such criticism was the Afghan war, which was unsuccessfully conducted for many years with little public knowledge about it. Several factors contributed to rising public demand to stop the war and to examine more seriously than before the foreign policy assumptions which led to it. These included the growing number of Soviet war victims, the gradual realization that the war was unwinnable, the excessive sacrifice in Soviet and Afghan lives, and the heavy expenditures needed in money, equipment, and national effort to carry on hostilities. Strongly supporting these factors was the determination of Mikhail Gorbachev to stop the arms race with the United States. For Gorbachev, this struggle proved increasingly dangerous as progressively more resources were consumed without adding to the security of the Soviet Union or of other states.

Since 1985 the Soviet leadership applied considerable effort to its foreign policy *perestroika*. Unilateral decisions, such as those to stop the underground nuclear tests (July 1985), proposals to create a non-nuclear world, and summits with President Reagan, French President François Mitterrand, British Prime Minister Margaret Thatcher, West German Chancellor Helmut Kohl – all helped to achieve a breakthrough in US–Soviet relations, leading to the INF Treaty in December 1987. In reassessing Soviet foreign and security policy, the general trend is directed toward reducing the Soviet Union's traditional obsession with the external threat. This focus led to overreliance on military power. The thrust of Soviet policy today is to rely more on political and diplomatic means to resolve differences and to find additional external resources for dealing with internal economic problems.

What was really important in this respect was the Soviet Union's desire to view its foreign policy and its results in the spirit of 'new political thinking'. This meant an emphasis on common human values, including a revision of ideology and its role and status in foreign policy decision-making; on avoiding nuclear war and annihilation of humankind involving, conceivably, complete nuclear disarmament; on resolving regional conflicts, encompassing both Soviet–American accommodation and mutual efforts to reconcile local antagonists; on recognizing the importance of human rights issues for confidence-building and for a normal working relationship with the United States; on pursuing *glasnost* or openness in foreign policy matters; and on initiating unilateral moves whenever they could help to break the existing deadlocks.[30] All in all, Gorbachev's approach to foreign policy matters created a qualitatively new situation in the Soviet–American relations with corresponding new opportunities for cooperation.

This cooperation started in several ways. The INF agreement, signed in Washington in December 1987, obliged the superpowers to destroy a whole class of intermediate-range nuclear weapons in Europe and Asia. Meanwhile, negotiations on START and space weapons continued in Geneva. Both superpowers actively pursued negotiations on possible solutions for the conflicts in Afghanistan and in southwestern Africa. They consulted actively on the Middle East and Persian Gulf and discussed other regional conflicts and possible solutions to them. The Soviet Union and United States developed a wide system of bilateral and multilateral contacts and consultations in political, military, and economic spheres. Cooperation in dealing with global issues has also become possible and desirable. For the purposes of this study, the issue of regional conflicts has acquired a special importance. First of all, both superpowers concentrated their efforts on settling the Afghan crisis. Taking into consideration its importance for the whole world situation and for bilateral relations, they had to find a solution which would not only be mutually satisfactory but that would also put an end to the endless and fruitless civil war. The negotiations which followed were coordinated with talks in Geneva between Afghanistan and Pakistan under the auspices of the UN Secretary General's special representative Diego Cordovez. The diplomatic activity which created a subsystem of bilateral negotiations (Afghanistan–Pakistan, US–USSR, US–Pakistan, USSR–Afghanistan, USSR–Pakistan and US–Afghanistan) finally led to the Afghan settlement, signed in Geneva in April 1988 with the Soviet Union and United States as guarantors of its implementation.[31] Within nine months after the signature of the agreement, the Soviet Union withdrew its forces from Afghanistan. On the other hand, the United States, after a period of deliberation by the Bush administration, decided to resume its arms supplies to the opposition thus fueling the continuation of the civil war in the country.

The lessons of Afghanistan, no less than the lessons of Vietnam, have a direct relevance for Soviet–American relations. They could and should be added to any attempt to construct a 'code of conduct' or other forms of cooperative relations between the superpowers because the cost of avoiding them, of pursuing policies to gain a unilateral advantage in different areas of the world, has become too high as well as politically and militarily counterproductive.

Four lessons might be taken into consideration. First, neither the Soviet Union nor the United States should directly employ its military forces in any region of the world. Currently there are no regional contingencies which would threaten the vital interests of either nation, and hence, there can be no justification for using their military forces, especially in large numbers, against local antagonists in other regions of the world. This convergence of interest coincides at least with two other trends: a proposed shift to a defensive posture in military doctrine with corresponding negotiated changes downward in military capabilities, and the growing ability of the legitimate sovereign governments of the Third World countries to contain any attempt by any illegal force to attack or to threaten the otherwise legitimate interests of the superpowers in those areas.[32]

Second, both sides should work for a negotiated solution of international conflicts and for national reconciliation in domestic conflicts. Afghanistan prompted a serious re-examination of the superpower attitude toward military violence in regional conflicts. Until recently, both superpowers had their caveats, or excuses, for their friends to use armed violence against their enemies. For the United States it was obsessed with 'legitimate self-defense'. This attitude encouraged such phenomena as the Israeli 'war machine', which is now playing a self-imposed role as an obstacle to any attempts for a peaceful resolution of conflict in the region. For the Soviet Union, it was the concept of the 'legitimate right of revolutionary self-defense' which also led to the growing amount of arms exports. On several occasions these arms exports have been used for purposes of aggression or for violence against the democratic movements of client-countries. This experience shows that there were no cases where these arms and the violence occasioned by them brought visible and stable political results. It seems that it is impossible under present conditions to count on a military solution of any conflict. It is preferable to work for a negotiated solution of international conflicts and for national reconciliation in domestic conflicts.

Third, very serious and sustained efforts should be undertaken in the area of establishing a permanent, standing mechanism for Soviet–American consultations on regional matters. The first attempts to create such a mechanism were discussed in the early 1980s at the Gromyko–Haig meetings although at that time they appeared to be abortive. But with the passing of time, the necessity to have open channels not only for crisis situations (for which the 'Hot Line' is perfectly suited) but also to discuss the interests of both sides in regional matters was becoming increasingly evident. The Soviet idea of a 'balance of interests' cannot be achieved in regional matters without a permanent and effective mechanism that permits a constant exchange of information, assessments and proposed actions on the basis of the acceptance of the legitimate interests of both sides. Such a mechanism would not only encourage the search for just solutions to existing conflicts, but it would also put on the superpower agenda issues for preventing them as well as measures for fighting terrorism and drug-trafficking.

Fourth, the United Nations should be allowed to play the roles for which it was originally created. The Afghan settlement led to the re-examination of the UN's police role. Since unilateral police actions of both superpowers, even taken with advanced notification, will always raise suspicions and create tensions, the need for policing conflict-prone areas could be satisfied by UN peacekeeping operations and other supportive activities where UN intervention could play a pacifying role. There is simply no other way than to revive those UN agencies and bodies which were designed for an international police role to deal with cases where the interests of both superpowers, their friends and allies, or neutral states might be threatened.

Some of these ideas have been already suggested for public discussion in both the Soviet Union and abroad.[33] They have to be studied and discussed because there is no way but to try to find approaches which could help overcome the heavy legacy of the Cold War relationship in the sphere of regional conflicts. This study, taken as a whole, can bring a very new, non-traditional approach to the examination of the whole period of the Cold War through the prism of the elements of cooperation which undoubtedly existed through this period of superpower tensions. Besides, it can stimulate a reassessment of information about how both superpowers avoided a direct confrontation in that dangerous period. Some US experts attempt to think about the Cold War in terms of its lessons for the future.[34] But to underline the importance of this study at present, it is evident that in the absence of a thorough study of all the elements and of the past areas of different forms of cooperation which existed between the Soviet Union and United States in different areas of the world, it would be naive and unrealistic to embark on such a task for the future.

NOTES

1. Michael Mandelbaum, 'Ending the Cold War', *Foreign Affairs*, vol. LXVIII, no. 4 (Spring 1989), pp. 16–36.
2. Graham T. Allison, W. L. Ury, and B. J. Allyn (eds) *Windows of Opportunity: From Cold War to Peaceful Competition in US–Soviet Relations* (Cambridge, MA: Ballinger, 1989), pp. 9–39.
3. V. A. Kremenyuk, 'SSR, SSHA i Razvivayushchiyesya Strany' (USSR, USA and Developing Countries), in *Sovetsko–Amerikanskiye Otnosheniya v Sovremennom Mire* (Soviet–American Relations in the Contemporary World) (Moscow: Nauka, 1987), pp. 235–9.
4. Cf. Anatolii Gromyko, *Pamyatnoye* (Memoirs), Moscow: Politizdat, 1988, vol. I. pp. 364–72.
5. Anatol Rapoport, *Fights, Games and Debates* (Ann-Arbor: University of Michigan Press, 1960).

60   Victor A. Kremenyuk

6.   George F. Kennan, *Memoirs: 1925–1950* (New York: Bantam Books, 1969), pp. 401–2.
7.   Gabriel Kolko, *The Politics of War: The World and US Foreign Policy, 1943–1945* (New York: Random House, 1968), p. 607.
8.   For example: Marshall D. Shulman (ed.), *East–West Tensions in the Third World* (New York: W. W. Norton, 1986); W. Raymond Duncan (ed.), *Soviet Policy in Developing Countries* (Huntington, NY: Robert E. Krieger, 1981); Jerry F. Hough, *The Struggle for the Third World. Soviet Debates and American Options* (Washington, DC: The Brookings Institution, 1986); Daniel S. Papp (ed.), *Soviet Policies Toward the Developing World During the 1980s: The Dilemmas of Power and Presence* (Maxwell Air Force Base, AL: Air University Press, 1986).
9.   One of the best accounts of the consequences of the Korean War for US foreign policy is in Dean Acheson, *Present at the Creation* (New York: W. W. Norton, 1969).
10. Thomas C. Schelling, *The Strategy of Conflict* (London: Oxford University Press, 1970), p. 253.
11. *Pravda*, 11 February 1989; *Izvestia*, 6 February 1989; 15 April 1989.
12. Graham T. Allison, *Essence of Decision: Explaining the Cuban Missile Crisis* (Boston: Little, Brown, 1971).
13. There is a special joint Soviet–American project studying the history of the crisis and the lessons that can be drawn from it, *Izvestia*, 6 February 1989.
14. Robert S. McNamara, *Blundering into Disaster: Surviving the First Century of the Nuclear Age* (New York: Pantheon Books, 1968), p. 154.
15. Cora Bell, *Conventions of Crisis: A Study in Diplomatic Management* (London: Oxford University Press, 1971), p. 2.
16. Herman Kahn, *On Escalation* (New York: Praeger, 1965).
17. Lyndon B. Johnson, *The Vantage Point: Perspectives of the Presidency; 1963–1969* (New York: Holt, Rinehart and Winston, 1971), p. 303.
18. Morton H. Halperin, *Limited War in the Nuclear Age* (New York: John Wiley, 1966).
19. George F. Kennan, *The Cloud of Danger: Current Realities of American Foreign Policy* (Boston: Little, Brown, 1977), pp. 156–162.
20. Anthony Lake (ed.), *The Vietnam Legacy: The War, American Society and the Future of American Foreign Policy* (New York: New York University Press, 1976), p. 1.
21. Henry A. Kissinger, *The Troubled Partnership* (New York: McGraw-Hill, 1965).
22. Cited in Yu. P. Davydov, V. V. Shurkin and V. S. Rudnev (eds), *Doktrina Niksona* (The Nixon Doctrine) (Moscow: Nauka, 1972).
23. Allison *et al.*, op. cit., pp. 45–66.
24. *USSR: Peace Program in Action* (Moscow: Novosti Press Agency, 1972), p. 15.
25. Henry A. Kissinger, *Implications of Angola for Future US Foreign Policy*, Statement of the Secretary of State (Washington, DC: Bureau of Public Affairs).
26. Later accounts on this issue see: Joan Gowa and N. H. Wessel,

Ground Rules: Soviet and American Involvement in Regional Conflicts (Philadelphia: Foreign Policy Research Institute, 1982).

27. V. A. Kremenyuk, 'Borba Vashingtona protiv revol'yustii v Irane' (Washington's Struggle Against Revolution in Iran), *Mezhdunarodnye otnosheniya*, no. 8 (1984), pp. 107–8. In one of my previous research efforts an attempt was made to outline this evolution in US–Soviet relations: the turn of the Carter administration from direct cooperation in its original days to confrontation and rivalry after the Somali–Ethiopian war (1977–8).

28. *Sovetskaya programma mira dlya 80 godov v deystvii. Dokumenty i materialy* (Soviet Peace Program for the 1980s In Action. Documents and Materials) (Moscow: Politizdat, 1982), pp. 36–7.

29. Michael Mandelbaum and Strobe Talbott, *Reagan and Gorbachev* (New York: Vintage Books – A Division of Random House, 1987), p. 4.

30. M. S. Gorbachev, *Perestroika and New Thinking For Our Country and For The Whole World* (Moscow: Novosti Press, 1987).

31. *The Geneva Accords: Agreements on the Settlement of the Situation Relating to Afghanistan* (New York: United Nations, 1988).

32. See, for example, Edward A. Kolodziej and Roger E. Kanet (eds), *The Limits of Soviet Power in the Developing World: Thermidor in the Revolutionary Struggle* (London: Macmillan, 1989).

33. The latest is Victor A. Kremenyuk 'Uroki Afganistana', (Lessons of Afghanistan), *SShA: Ekonomika, politika, ideologiya* No. 7 (July 1989).

34. See, for example, L. Wolfsy (ed.), *Before the Point of No Return: An Exchange of Views on the Cold War, the Reagan Doctrine, and What Is to Come* (New York: Monthly Review Press, 1986); J. L. Grabill, *Soviet–American Partnership: 1910s to 1980s* (Paper given at International Studies Association annual meeting, St Louis, April 1988).

Part II
Superpower Cooperation in Conflict Management: Regional Perspectives

3 Superpower Cooperation in Western Europe
Edward A. Kolodziej

INTRODUCTION

The Cold War in Western Europe began as cooperation. The superpower conflict in Europe was an extension of the flawed wartime alliance between the Western powers and the Soviet Union to defeat Germany and to destroy Hitler's Nazi regime. From the outset, as a matter of national survival, the Western democracies had to choose between one of two anti-democratic partners, both committed to their overthrow. The inevitable result was a peace compromised even before it was won.[1] As for the emerging superpowers, neither relished wartime alliance with the other. The German invasion of the Soviet Union in the spring of 1941 destroyed the Ribbentrop–Molotov agreement of 1939 designed to deflect German might from the Soviet Union to the Western democracies and to divide Polish and Balkan territories between these anti-democratic states as part of the agreed upon price for their temporary truce.

The Western–Soviet coalition, forged by necessity, was also split from the start by profound differences over strategy. The Soviet Union sought a second front as quickly as possible; Britain preferred an indirect strategy to disperse German forces against allied units by attacks on Germany's southern flanks through Italy, southern France, and the Balkans; the United States focused on raising a mighty invasion force to engage German armed forces directly to defeat them once and for all. If a compromise was eventually reached on strategy, based narrowly on the military objective of unconditional surrender, announced wartime aims remained fundamentally irreconcilable. The Atlantic Charter, signed by President Franklin Roosevelt and British Prime Minister Winston Churchill in September 1941, proclaimed Anglo–American commitment to the principle of national self-determination, to the right of peoples to define their internal political and economic institutions free from outside intervention, to peaceful change in revising national frontiers, and equal access of all states to trade and raw materials to foster their mutual prosperity. Even before the coalition formally took life, the Soviet Union (not to mention the British empire and its system of economic discriminatory practices) was in violation of the Charter.[2] The British–Soviet agreement on spheres of influence in the Balkans deepened the gap between Charter principles and balance of power politics. The Roosevelt administration widened the gap in repudiating traditional Big Power politics, preferring instead to place its confidence in a United Nations Organization based on the consensus of the victor powers.[3]

The wartime alliance held because differences over postwar Europe were suspended in the commitment of the Big Three to the unconditional surrender of Hitler's Germany. All could agree on that immediate aim. Left begging were three fundamental global or systemic issues at the core of the superpower struggle after World War II. Europe was not so much the cause of the Cold War but the effect of superpower differences over how the world should be organized and how that order should be guaranteed by military force; over how goods and services should be produced and distributed and access to needed raw materials assured – i.e. how global welfare would be achieved, whether through free or command markets; and over what principles of legitimacy should define the domestic political and economic institutions as well as human rights of peoples everywhere.

In Europe, the issue of order or, more pointedly, a balance of power favorable to one or the other of the superpowers centered principally on Germany. Central to each superpower was Germany's absorption into its sphere of influence. As for the issue of the postwar international economic system, the superpower struggle was defined by US insistence that Europe's economic recovery and development be incorporated into a global capitalist market system and by Soviet resistance to the dependency of its economy and those of its satellites on what was quite correctly perceived as an international economic system under US hegemony. Finally, the superpowers split over the question of defining the postwar frontiers of Germany and the East European states, over the legitimacy of the regimes instituted to rule these states and, as the Cold War evolved, over their opposing conceptions of human rights.

The first section of this chapter sketches the European components of the global regimes for order, welfare, and domestic political legitimacy that the superpowers had to accept or tolerate until the reform movement in Eastern Europe erupted in 1989. Neither superpower was able, alone or in alliance, to dictate its preferences to the other. Nor were they able to impose their views fully on their allies or neutrals. An analysis of these outcomes and the superpower rules of conduct sets the stage for the following section which defines the principal lines of current superpower conflicts in Europe and the cooperative measures pursued by them, not always by free consent, to resolve or manage those conflicts to their mutual satisfaction. A concluding section codifies regime rules of superpower cooperation in Western Europe and projects their likely evolution toward a Europe, from the Atlantic to the Urals, that promises to overcome the ideological Cold War division of Europe and the military bloc confrontation.

THE LURE OF LESSER PREFERENCES

Western Europe and global order and legitimacy

The struggle for Germany

The Potsdam conference essentially reaffirmed the recommendations of the European Advisory Commission (EAC) for the zonal government of Germany pending a peace treaty that would define the terms of Germany's restoration, frontiers, and internal governance.[4] The principal issue between the superpowers at this early postwar juncture was over reparations to be paid to the Soviet Union. The United States opposed reparations if they weakened Germany's ability to meet the needs of its own people or to resume as quickly as possible its central role in the European economy. For American planners this meant that Germany was to be treated as a single economic unit rather than as four zonal systems pursuing discrete economic policies and aims.

The United States pressed for the economic integration of the zones of occupation as the best way to ensure German and European recovery. The American plan included currency reform, a cap on reparations, free circulation of persons and material throughout Germany, and an export-import plan for the whole of the country.[5] Resisting these Western initiatives, the Soviet Union insisted on the unified administration of Germany through Four-Power consensus and on heavy German reparations, including access to the industrial Ruhr under Western control. The split grew deeper in February 1948 when the three Western zones were placed under unified German political administration and what was to become West Germany was included as an integral part of the European Recovery Program or Marshall Plan.

Superpower tensions then shifted to Berlin. The EAC placed the city, deep within the Soviet zone, under Four-Power rule. On 19 June 1948, one day after the implementation of currency reforms in the Western zones of Germany and Berlin, the Soviet rail and road blockade of Berlin commenced. Rather than use force to assert its occupation rights of access to Berlin, the West launched instead an airlift to supply the beleaguered city. On 12 May 1949, the blockade was lifted as abruptly as it had been instituted. Neither side could claim victory, but a military confrontation was avoided.

The Korean War catalyzed the process, prefigured in the blockade crisis, of dividing Germany and Berlin and of incorporating their western and eastern halves into NATO and the Warsaw Pact. In response to perceived Soviet support for North Korean armed aggression, the United States called for German rearmament, the creation of an integrated military command within NATO under American direction, the stationing of increased American forces in Europe, and expanded military assistance for West European nations. German rearmament was to proceed through the creation of a European Defense Community (EDC) that would have unified the military forces of France, West Germany, Italy and the Benelux countries in return for provisional West German sovereignty and independence, pending a final settlement of Germany's future.

France's defeat of the EDC in August 1954 led immediately to a British proposal to establish a Western European Union (WEU) by expanding the Brussels Pact to include West Germany. The treaty legitimated German rearmament but placed restrictions on German manufacture or possession of atomic, bacteriological, and chemical weapons without allied approval. The WEU bridged West Germany's entry into NATO in May 1955. Less than two weeks later, the Warsaw Pact was signed to counterbalance the Western military bloc. In another balancing move, the German Democratic Republic (GDR), which had been granted sovereignty by the Soviet Union in March 1954, was granted full membership in the Warsaw Pact. Unable to get the Germany it wanted, each superpower preferred a divided Germany and Berlin rather than lose its segment to its rival. Division was also preferable to a policy of mutual denial in which Germany would be reunited but neutralized. The resulting two-bloc security system for Europe, an outcome and aim neither superpower had articulated or anticipated in wartime Big Power negotiations, appeared preferable as a second choice to concessions by either opponent to the first choice of its rival – and decidedly more attractive than war. As Anton DePorte reminds us, 'the European system came to be what it is because . . . it divided least those with power to affect it.'[6]

With the militarization of the Cold War in Europe and its institutionalization in NATO and the Warsaw Pact, the remaining central issues to be addressed by the superpowers and their allies were a reliable regime for West Berlin, now *de facto* within the territorial limits of the GDR, the recognition of the GDR by the international community as a nation-state, and legitimation of the frontiers imposed by the Soviet Union on eastern Europe after World War II. The latter issue concerned tacit Western recognition of the Soviet Union's absorption of eastern Poland and, specifically, West German acceptance of the Oder–Neisse line separating East Germany and Poland and renunciation of prewar German claims in Czechoslovakia. Another twenty years of hard bargaining and periodic crises, most notably centered around Berlin between 1958 and 1962, were required to define an acceptable regime for their management.

Provoked by NATO's plan to deploy Thor and Jupiter intermediate-range ballistic missiles in Europe in response to Sputnik and to Western perceptions of increasing Soviet missile superiority, Soviet Premier Nikita Khrushchev threatened to transfer the Soviet Union's occupation rights to the GDR. The Western states would have been required to negotiate their transit and access rights with the GDR unless the Soviet compromise solution of a demilitarized free city were accepted in six months. Khrushchev's ultimatum appears to have been a calculated move to halt US IRBM deployment, at least in Germany, and to eliminate Western presence in Berlin. Khrushchev's ultimatum passed, as did several others over the next three years. The tensions over Berlin culminated in the summer of 1961 with the erection of the Berlin Wall to stem the swelling flow of refugees from East to West Germany.

Western acquiescence in the *de facto* division of the city had a profound change on German opinion. The Western allies and the West Germans could no longer view the Soviet hold over East Germany as temporary. However illegitimate the GDR may have appeared, the Communist government's control of its population, backed by Soviet arms, could no longer be gainsaid despite futile efforts by the United States and West Germany to isolate the East German government. West Germany's Hallstein Doctrine, which triggered a break in diplomatic relations with any nation recognizing the GDR, gradually lost credence in the 1960s as successive Third World states in the 1960s exchanged embassies with the GDR. Increasing superpower nuclear parity also undermined a strategy of negotiating from strength based on superior military capabilities to impose the West's views about Europe on the Soviet Union or its satellites. The Berlin Wall and the increasing assumption of authority by the GDR over East Berlin and the control of civilian access to the city ended any remaining pretense of exclusive Four-Power rule.

The Cuban missile crisis of 1962 overtook the Berlin issue. As in 1949, the Soviet Union desisted from further pressures on the city.[7] In lieu of crisis politics, the superpowers and their respective German allies, after a decade of hard negotiations,[8] peacefully regularized their discord over Berlin in a Four-Power accord signed in 1971. The complexity of the accord and its tortuous execution suggest the lengths to which all parties were prepared to go to make the agreements work while striving to bias its implementation in their favor. Berlin was not mentioned; only the 'area' in dispute was cited. The Soviet Union agreed to remove obstacles to civilian access between Berlin and West Germany. The German Federal Republic withdrew its claims to use West Berlin as the site for any of its governmental meetings and to consider the Western zones of the city as integral parts of the FRG. Implementation of the accord commenced with a meeting of GDR and FRG officials, representing separate governments and sovereignties, leading to the signature of a basic agreement between these 'two states in one German culture', as German Chancellor Willy Brandt characterized the formula to comprise East–West differences.

Each side got something. Neither got all it wanted. The West retained its occupation rights in the city and induced the Soviet Union to accept its Four-Power responsibilities. The GDR extended its hold over East Berlin and enhanced its international standing; Western efforts to forge a governmental link between the FRG and West Berlin were frustrated. At a non-governmental level, civilian exchanges between the FRG and Berlin multiplied and access to the city was finally resolved notwithstanding the Berlin Wall. Despite the complexity of the solution, involving a two-tier, six-state governing structure for the city (the Big Four and the two Germanies), it worked through the 1970s and most of the 1980s until its relevance was overtaken by the dramatic and unexpected dismantling of the Berlin Wall in November 1989.[9] Lesser preferences on both sides also proved compelling in the Helsinki understanding of 1975. The Brezhnev regime's notions of Soviet security interests resulted in formal US and European recognition of the status quo in Eastern Europe with respect to communist regimes and frontiers. On the other hand, in the West, the neutral states and reform elements in the Eastern bloc were furnished a process, the Conference on Security and Cooperation in Europe (CSCE), which has since proven to be a useful framework, as the discussion below suggests, within which to engage the Soviet Union in extracting human rights and arms controls concessions. Its long-term significance is as a framework within which to reconcile bloc preferences and within which to define a *novus ordo seclorum* in Europe. In exchange for assuring the Soviet Union's immediate needs for security – international recognition of East European frontiers and friendly regimes on its borders – the Helsinki process also expanded the definition of security to include freer exchange of peoples, ideas, and goods across European borders and human rights treatment by member governments.

As an added gain, the Helsinki understanding and process confirmed the United States as a European power. This was no small benefit in light of the frustrating history of US efforts since the Yalta understanding of the Big Three to foster democratic pluralism and liberal economic reform in Eastern Europe. Lacking the opportunity and will to intervene militarily in uprisings in 1953 (East Germany), Hungary (1956), and Czechoslovakia (1968) or to undo the Berlin Wall by force, the West and, specifically, the United States had little leverage beyond remonstrances and economic penalties to influence directly reform in the Soviet bloc. The CSCE essentially multilateralized US interest in fostering national self-determination in Eastern Europe as well as political and economic reform, including improved human rights treatment by all of the Warsaw Pact nations.[10] The United States was also able to rely on the CSCE process, substantially aided and abetted by the active support and initiative of the neutral states and its West European allies, notably to expand arms control and confidence-building measures between the East and West over Moscow's initial objections.

Militarization of a divided Europe
Hidden in the two-bloc confrontation was an implicit superpower

bargain to limit German rearmament and to control its security arrangements with other states.[11] Germany's division and the subsequent military integration of its two parts into multilateral alliances under the hegemonic leadership of a superpower testifies to the bargain. Of particular concern, too, was West German access to nuclear weapons. The WEU treaty prohibits manufacture of these weapons. While the WEU is an all-European group, its military effectiveness is an extension of NATO, which has since its inception been under the command of an American general. The permissive action links (PAL) controlling US assignment of nuclear weapons to German forces are additional US control mechanisms. Part of the explanation for the determined opposition of the Soviet Union to the multilateral nuclear force (MLF) for NATO, proposed during the 1960s, and the stationing of Pershing II missiles in Germany in the 1980s, can be traced to the fear that these controls might be relaxed. The MLF raised the possibility of direct German access to nuclear weapons. Pershing II, like Thor and Jupiter before it, threatened Soviet soil from bases in Germany, a prospect that violated Soviet expectations of permissible US and Western nuclear threats aimed at the Soviet Union.

A second set of superpower provisional understandings concerned SALT and START and their implications for European security. The United States historically preferred a technical definition of nuclear systems capable of delivering their payloads over a fixed distance (defined as 5,500 kilometers). The Soviet Union has argued for a definition of strategic weapons that includes any system capable of hitting Soviet territory. Based on Soviet assumptions, NATO's forward base systems were considered strategic systems. These included F-111 fighter-bombers stationed in Britain as well as Pershing II and land-based cruise missiles that were deployed in pursuit of NATO's two-track decision in the early 1980s. The US decision had the advantage of excluding these systems from considerations under SALT. By the same token the Soviet Union was able to keep the deployment of SS-20s and Backfire bombers outside the SALT treaty.

The superpowers pursued two different but not mutually exclusive strategies to get their way in Europe. The first, and the preferred method until the signature of the INF treaty in December 1987, was to rely on military threats to frustrate the designs of each other. The arms race within Europe and the institutionalization of two military blocs evidenced this preferred strategy; however, arms control accords gave witness to the limits of an armed clash as a solution to superpower differences. An alternative strategy, employed extensively by the Soviet Union, was to undermine the cohesion of the rival bloc by attempts to manipulate its political and psychological cohesion and to divide the alliance against itself. In so far as United States interests in Western Europe are concerned, the target of Soviety strategy inevitably centered on the necessarily provisional and, upon examination, implicitly contentious bargain made by the United States with its European allies. The central issue concerned Germany's political future and NATO's strategy to defend it.

Germany and nuclear weapons
The US–German bargain was delicate and extremely sensitive during the Cold War, as the Berlin crises revealed, to Soviet threats and blandishments. For, as Walter Lippmann recognized four decades ago, only the Soviet Union, and not the United States and the West, could ultimately satisfy Germany's political and security concerns. The Bonn government of Konrad Adenauer agreed to Germany's rearmament and entry into NATO in exchange for the political independence and sovereignty of West Germany whose security would be guaranteed by US troops and the American nuclear umbrella. Despite its strategic shortcomings, the United States also agreed to Bonn's insistence on a forward base posture to ensure the integrity of German territory. In permitting the stationing of American troops and nuclear weapons on its soil, the FRG implicitly coupled US strategic and German security interests. As long as both states saw eye-to-eye on those interests and on NATO's strategy to protect and promote them, the US–German bargain would hold.

This arrangement was initially predicated on US nuclear superiority. As that assumption eroded with the expansion of Soviet strategic and tactical nuclear forces in the late 1950s and early 1960s, the bargain of massive retaliation gave way to the strategy of flexible response. The Europeans and particularly the Germans assumed primary responsibility for the conventional defense of Europe while the United States underwrote NATO's nuclear deterrent posture. Implementation of this understanding was not fully satisfying either to Washington or to Bonn. If Bonn met Washington's expectations with respect to Germany's contribution to the conventional defense of Europe within an American-directed flexible response strategy, Bonn was never comfortable with US announced nuclear policy. Either it appeared threatening as in the latter stages of INF deployment or too weak and vacillating as during the Berlin crisis of the early 1960s.

In the 1960s, the MLF proposal channeled most European efforts to have a say within NATO over US nuclear policies. Many Western allies and the Soviet Union viewed the proposed multilateral nuclear force as a US–German rather than a NATO arrangement. Strong opposition from both quarters to enhanced German access to nuclear weapons scuttled the MLF that might have provided Bonn with a vehicle to participate in NATO nuclear operations through which it might also have been able to influence US nuclear policy.[12] Bonn had to be satisfied instead with membership in the Nuclear Planning Group, a NATO consultative committee, to advance its nuclear interests.

The SALT talks again raised German concerns about the credibility of the US deterrent and Washington's willingness to share equally the risks of nuclear confrontation with the Soviet Union over European and specifically German security interests. German Chancellor Helmut Schmidt first publicly raised this issue in an address before the International Institute of Strategic Studies in 1977. The SALT agreement excluded nuclear weapons in the European theater from consideration. This oversight again posed the decoupling issue: '[S]trategic arms limitation confined to the United States and the Soviet Union,' argued Schmidt, 'will inevitably impair the security of the West European members of the Alliance *vis-à-vis* Soviet military superiority in Europe if we do not succeed in removing the disparities of military power in Europe parallel to the SALT negotiations.'[13]

The American reply to Germany's nuclear concerns assumed the form of the two-track decision to deploy Pershing II and cruise missiles in Europe but to defer deployment of these systems if the Soviet Union dismantled its long-range nuclear theater forces, principally its SS-20 missiles targeted on NATO forces and bases. The two-track formula formally linked the European states and Germany to the superpower arms control process.[14] The two-track decision was incorporated into the START process in December 1985 after Soviet pressures on West European governments, particularly Bonn, failed to stop the initial deployment of Pershing II missiles in Germany and cruise missiles in Britain and Italy.

What had not been fully anticipated by the struggle over INF was the vulnerability of the Western security compact and German willingness to accept its terms of exchange. The Social Democratic party's alternative to German rearmament of the 1950s was Germany's neutralization and non-alignment with either bloc and its acceptance of restrictions on rearmament. In opting for security, sovereignty, and international rehabilitation by joining NATO, West Germany did not renounce in perpetuity better relations with Eastern Europe and the Soviet Union. Certainly, it did not wish to preclude improved intra-German ties.

There was also the unarticulated assumption that the United States would pursue nuclear and arms control policies that would not threaten to upset the global or the European nuclear balance and that these policies would not be an insurmountable impediment to better East–West relations. As the Brandt initiative to settle the Berlin crisis and West Germany's differences over frontiers with its eastern neighbors suggested, the ordered preferences of most Germans was for *détente*, deterrence, and defense. Those of the United States, given its global struggle with the Soviet Union and its geopolitical interests, were the reverse. The expansion of US nuclear strategic capabilities in the late 1980s, the failure to ratify the SALT treaty, and determined American deployment of intermediate-range nuclear forces in Europe – first in response to and, progressively, *despite* rising European public and governmental opposition – opened Washington to the charge that its nuclear policies were destabilizing the superpower nuclear balance and that NATO and the United States military presence was an obstacle to *détente*.

The Reagan administration's adoption of the zero-option stance in negotiating away long-range theater nuclear weapons and the Soviet withdrawal from the START talks in protest to Pershing II deployment temporarily blunted German and European criticisms of US nuclear policies. Ironically, the signature of the US–Soviet treaty to eliminate ground-based missiles between 500 and 5,500 km had the effect of weakening US–West German strategic cohesion. Where the Left in Germany was sympathetic to the total removal of nuclear weapons from Germany, the Right objected that the gap between US short-range and strategic weapons created a *de facto* strategic asymmetry between Germany and its allies. If nuclear war erupted in Europe, Germany would be the battleground for an East–West exchange, sparing the homelands of the superpowers. The assertion of US governmental officials, including President Reagan, about the possibility of fighting a limited nuclear war in Europe fueled German anxieties. The rapid movement toward German unification overtook these critical differences between Bonn and Washington. Only a resolution of the Cold War could relax the fundamentally contradictory strategic stances of Bonn and Washington on a nuclear weapons policy. This contradiction would of course re-emerge in different form in the wake of German unification, namely of the German state's possession of nuclear weapons, but on this point the Big Four shared essentially the same interest in precluding such a possibility.

Europe and the world economy

Superpower discord over how a stable and legitimate order could be achieved in Europe after World War II was also causally related, until the assumption of power by Mikhail Gorbachev, to their profound differences over Europe's postwar recovery and its subsequent integration into the world economy. Superpower differences over reparations reflected a more fundamental difference over welfare aims and strategies. American economic policy-makers reasoned that a major contributory cause to the rise of totalitarian regimes, including the Soviet Union, was the failure of the capitalist international market system to meet basic welfare needs in the interwar period. Following a Keynesian diagnosis, it was widely believed that chronic underinvestment, tight fiscal policies, and reduced governmental expenditures created unemployment, leading to widespread social strife and poverty. These crises were deepened by national protectionist measures, favoring high tariffs, competitive devaluations, and beggar-thy-neighbor policies, ranging from discrimination against foreign products and firms to subsidies for inefficient domestic enterprises.

At a global level, the United States and its Western partners addressed these problems through multilateral cooperation. The Bretton Woods agreement of 1944 created a stable monetary regime in which the currencies of all members of the International Monetary Fund (IMF) were pegged to the dollar set at $35 per ounce of gold. The IMF, in which the United States enjoyed a majority voting position, was charged to recommend revisions of national exchange rates in cases of chronic disequilibrium. In cooperation with the World Bank, the IMF was supposed to arrange loans to facilitate balance of payments adjustments among member states. The General Agreement on Tariffs and Trade (GATT), formed in 1948, rounded out the liberal economic regime promoted by the United States. It defined terms of non-discrimination and established Most Favored Nation principles for fair trade.

The integrated economic approach of US policy toward German reparations followed logically from American thinking about how to overcome the failings of the world market system of the 1920s and 1930s. A liberal international economic regime, based on the free movement of the factors of production as well as goods and services, was installed as a solution to the self-destructive protectionist measures of the interwar period. The Marshall Plan extended the logic of this regime in establishing as a condition of aid the creation of a plan for Europe's recovery and for its re-entry into the world economic system. The Organization for European Economic Cooperation (OEEC) was created to funnel US capital to the European states and to encourage recovery on the basis of their cooperative effort. In the absence of the Marshall Plan, neither GATT nor the IMF would have made much sense or long survived.[15]

In contrast, the Stalinist regime opted for a national-Marxist solution to economic recovery. Socialist ideology conspired with fears of dependence on the Western capitalist states to prompt Soviet rejection of the American invitation to join the Marshall Plan. Moscow also prevented the East European states which had signaled interest in participation from joining the Western grouping. The communist *coup d'état* in Czechoslovakia of February 1948 marked the eastern reach of the Marshall Plan and the principles of free markets and private property underlying it. The OEEC essentially covered those states, including the Western occupation zones in Germany, which were under the control of Western allied forces after World War II. These states formed the core of the NATO treaty signed in 1949 which formalized the US–European alliance.

In retrospect, it appears to be no accident that the Truman Doctrine and the Marshall Plan were initiated within approximately three months of each other. They comprise a remarkably coherent set of US foreign policy initiatives, all the more notable since they emerged from a political system riven by socio-economic divisions and by intense presidential–congressional competition, bureaucratic infighting, hotly contested special interest politics, and regional and civil strife. The Truman Doctrine and Marshall Plan rationalized and justified how American power would be used to shape the world environment to US liking. The solution to Europe's problems was conceived as an integral part of a task to construct an entirely new global system to replace the Eurocentric system. There is some justification for Dean Acheson's immodest remembrance of these times – *Present at the Creation*.[16]

As in the case of Western military strategy within NATO, the United States and its West European allies struck a bargain to support European economic and political integration. In its early incarnation, until the de Gaulle challenge of the 1960s, European and American policy-makers shared several objectives in their converging support for European unity. First, a strong West Europe was essential for its own economic and political stability. Until the Korean War, threats to democratic and liberal economic institutions in Europe were conceived to be essentially internal. European integration was expected to spur economic growth and to expand domestic welfare to preserve open Western societies. Second, a restored Europe was viewed as indispensable for the reform and regeneration of the world's capitalistic economy. World trade and investment would otherwise be impeded and economic growth frustrated; in the long run, there would also be fewer outlets for US products and capital.

Third, and more immediately important for the United States in the postwar period, was the strategic and political significance of European union. Four centuries of what might be viewed as an incessant civil war among European states might finally be resolved, particularly if Franco–German reconciliation could be achieved. A restored West Europe was also a precondition for a unified Western response to East–West and emerging North–South challenges.[17]

The United States tolerated European and Japanese discrimination against its products in world markets as the price of recovery. Discrimination assumed the form of currency controls on convertibility and, later, resistance to a downward adjustment in the value of the dollar as other Western economies and their currencies strengthened. It was institutionalized in the principle of community preference and in the European Community's Common Agricultural Policy (CAP). Meanwhile, America's allies accepted excess dollars through chronic balance of payments deficits to finance their trade and markets for their products. The adverse impact of Community preference as a contravening principle to a global free trade system based on GATT rules was expected to be softened by the anticipated entry of Britain into the Community. US interest in the European Community ideal gradually waned, partly due to sustained attacks by Gaullist France on US economic hegemony. France's blockage of British entry into the European Community during the 1960s directly challenged the American Grand Design and the US role and presence in Europe.

The crises of the late 1960s forced reformulation of the European–

American economic bargain and its relevance for the Cold War struggle. Repeated runs on the British pound and the American dollar led eventually to the Nixon administration's decision formally to end US support for the Bretton Woods regime: the fixed link between the dollar and gold was broken, the dollar was essentially devalued, and the stage was set for the adoption of a flexible rate exchange system. Unilateral US initiatives induced reluctant European and Japanese monetary support for the Vietnam War and for help with US balance of payments and inflationary problems. The oil boycott and the quadrupling of world oil prices also increased European dependency on the United States to guarantee access to Middle East oil even as a sense of heightened dependence led to a growing split between Europe and the United States over oil and Middle East policy, particularly toward the Arab–Israeli conflict.[18]

Gaullist opposition to British entry into the EEC was also overcome by the early 1970s as a consequence of French concern for their economic and political vulnerability. The May riots of 1968 underlined France's economic dependency on its European allies, especially Germany and the United States. German resistance to French claims for economic support within the European Community also made more attractive Britain's application to join Europe. Britain could be expected to counterbalance an increasingly more assertive and economically powerful West Germany. The Warsaw Pact's invasion of Czechoslovakia also reinforced France's security fears and appreciation for the balancing role of the Anglo-American powers. The German surge of interest in *détente* in the aftermath of the Warsaw Pact invasion of Czechoslovakia, dramatized by the Brandt government's *Ostpolitik*, also argued for a recalibration of French security and economic diplomacy in favor of a tilt toward the Anglo-Saxon powers.

Brezhnev's Soviet Union appeared insensitive to these differences within the Western alliance over economic and welfare policies or at least unsure about how it might exploit them. It continued to oppose West European economic and political integration. The European Community was still largely understood as a Cold War device to advance US economic and security interests and those of a resurgent Germany. Moscow's policies seemed oblivious to Washington's growing second thoughts about the Common Market.[19] The Gaullist challenge of the early 1960s, rising German economic and foreign policy independence in the 1970s, and growing protectionist sentiment in Europe belied the optimistic assumptions of the American

Grand Design. By the 1970s, the battle for Western Europe was therefore more a three-way contest than a straightforward clash between the superpowers. It was between the Europeans themselves, between the United States and the Europeans, and between the superpowers over a Europe which was both the subject and the object of their struggle.

SUPERPOWER COOPERATION IN WESTERN EUROPE TODAY: EMERGENCE OF A NEW SECURITY REGIME AND POLITICAL ORDER FROM THE ATLANTIC TO THE URALS

The Brezhnev years froze the Cold War regime for Europe into component parts comprised of two military blocs, whose armies confronted each other in Central Europe; into two political and ideological spheres, each led by a hegemonic power; two divergent sets of governmental regimes, the Western half based on open, pluralistic principles of democratic government, the Eastern half on one-party, Communist rule; and into contrasting socio-economic institutions and processes, one affirming the private ownership of property and the means of production as well as market practices, the other pursuing Socialist norms and dedicated to central planning and control of markets and prices.

This Cold War regime was consolidated in a series of accords between 1971 and 1975. These assumed the form of the 1971 Quadripartite Berlin Accords, the 1972 basic agreement between West and East Germany which acknowledged the existence of two German states, the 1972 superpower Basic Agreement, and, at the all-European level, the 1975 Helsinki understanding. These agreements marked the postwar highwater mark of the superpower *détente* process in Europe until the reform movements in the Soviet Union and in the Eastern Europe of the late 1980s led to the dismantling of Cold War barriers and to conventional and nuclear arms control and disarmament accords.

The last severe test of the Cold War in Europe in the decade before the Gorbachev era was the controversy over the deployment of Pershing II and cruise missiles in Europe. Fissiparous tendencies within each alliance and challenges to the hegemonic position of the superpowers were resisted across the range of issues touching on the Cold War regime. In the early 1980s the United States opposed closer

West European–Soviet economic and political exchanges, a policy exemplified in a campaign of legal action, political pressure, and veiled threats of retaliation to block a gas pipeline agreement between several West European states and the Soviet Union. Meanwhile, the Soviet Union pressured its satellites to crush internal dissension within the eastern bloc evidenced by the imposition of martial law in Poland and the suppression of the Solidarity union.

Amplifying these tensions in Europe during this period were the expanded superpower arms races at strategic nuclear and conventional levels. SALT limits were exceeded on both sides. The ABM treaty of 1972 (SALT 1) was also raised into question by President Reagan's Strategic Defense Initiative and by accusations of Soviet violations of the treaty, such as the construction of a phased-radar installation at Krasnoyarsk. The tensions arising from these efforts were aggravated further by the multiplication of superpower interventions in the Third World, pitting Moscow against Washington in the Middle East, southern Africa, South and East Asia, and Central America. Europe could hardly insulate itself from these struggles.[20] Further movement on European *détente*, aside from what had already been achieved between the superpowers, was stifled; conventional arms talks in Europe stagnated while those on INF and conventional arms transfers broke down. The CSCE process was paralyzed, serving more as a forum for ideological confrontation on human rights than as a mechanism to build confidence between governments and peoples on both sides of the ideological frontier.

This grim picture has radically changed since the middle 1980s. The supports for the Cold War regime in Europe and the incentives for continual testing of its limits are no longer present. On the other hand, how and in what way this international regime in Europe will be modified or redefined is by no means clear. While the specific form of the post-Cold War regime remains obscure and while its crystallization may yet be arrested, and even reversed by the reassertion of those forces that produced and sustained the Cold War regime in Europe, one can discern, however imperfectly, the general directions toward which Europe is moving if current trends persist. Most critically, if the socio-economic and political reform movement within the Soviet Union continues and thrives, it must eventually end the division of Europe between two opposed ideological blocs and transform the current military confrontation into a new, yet to be defined, security regime for a new all-European political order.

What French President Charles de Gaulle urged almost a generation ago – the end of bloc politics and a Europe built of *détente*, *entente*, and *cooperation* from the Atlantic to the Urals – is now in the process of forming.[21] The Europe inspired by Mikhail Gorbachev surpasses even de Gaulle's prescient projection of the future. De Gaulle (seconded by the Brezhnev and early Nixon administrations) worked for a superpower understanding based on the accord of both governments. That understanding was flawed on its face because of the unresolved differences that separated the superpowers and their bloc partners. If state-to-state differences could not be resolved, it appeared beyond the pale of the possible that superpower cooperation could emerge in the form of a convergence between the socio-economic and political systems of East and West Europe. No one anticipated that this possibility would be realized by a revolution led by Soviet leaders against the very system that brought them to power.

While it would be premature to minimize the formidable obstacles to reform in Eastern Europe, it is difficult to exaggerate the significance and ramifications of the unprecedented changes unleashed within the Soviet Union and Eastern Europe under Gorbachev's rule and their devastating blow to the European Cold War regime. Even Soviet reformers cannot be said to have fully anticipated the speed with which the Cold War regime in Europe unravelled. Moreover, one should not underestimate the fillip given to these forces for change arising from fundamental shifts of power and interests within the camp of the Western liberal democracies, including Japan. The European Community and Japan increasingly challenge US economic power and rival its political influence around the globe. This shift in power is quite independent of the East European reform movement. Together these forces from within the West and East form a synergistic field of reinforcing and converging pressures that are transforming the security, economic, and political landscape of Europe with powerful, arguably decisive, implications for international order and welfare.

Prospects for superpower security cooperation

The Cold War regime in Europe is fading fast in force and legitimacy. Challenging it are the same forces that have been driving world and European politics for several centuries: national self-determination, mass pressures for greater wealth – now – and demands of peoples everywhere for a greater say in their domestic political systems and for greater freedom of self-expression and association. The Cold War no longer serves these forces. On the other hand, as Europe's history makes plain, they are neither necessarily compatible nor moving in the same direction. Successive attempts to impose an imperial order on Europe from the Atlantic to the Urals have hardly resulted in greater harmony among the rival nations and divergent peoples comprising this slip of the Euro-Asian continent nor in promoting greater and more open economic and political exchanges within and between states. The Cold War provided a provisional solution to these conflicting imperatives based on limited superpower cooperation. When it no longer responded to these forces, particularly in fostering the socio-economic development and political freedom of the East European and Soviet populations, its demise was foreordained.

To ensure that a new European regime will succeed beyond the Cold War, cooperation must be extended to include all of the European nations and peoples. Whereas the European Cold War regime arose from the limits imposed by the superpower conflict, the new Europe will have to emerge principally from the initiative of the European nations and peoples themselves. Against their professed aims and in conflict with their preferred strategies, the superpower-driven Cold War, not altogether wittingly, has propelled Europe to its present state of evolution. The cooperation of all European states from the Atlantic to the Urals is a precondition for the reformulation of a new European regime. In a sense, the superpower struggle and the stalemated cooperation that it produced may still be the instrument of a level of European unity unprecedented since the height of Western Christendom.

Before greater European unity can supplant the Cold War regime, three crises – of order, welfare, and legitimacy – will have to be addressed. As Chapter 1 argues, these are but the European phases of larger global processes within which the Cold War has evolved since World War II and to which the superpower struggle was a transitory solution. As a consequence of the Cold War legacy, each of these domains of crisis in Europe is itself divided into three additional components, forming a kind of disassembled Rubik's cube. While no one can foresee how the European Rubik's cube will be solved, it is clear that it no longer admits to a Cold War solution.

At the level of order, the two-bloc confrontation no longer is a realistic basis for military planning by either side. As a consequence of the political reforms in Eastern Europe, conventional and nuclear arms accords between the superpowers, the Warsaw Pact and the Soviet Union no longer pose a clear and present danger to Western Europe or to the United States. Meanwhile, the Soviet Union has taken a series of steps since the publication of the Communist party's call for nuclear disarmament in January 1986 that have assured the Western states of Moscow's peaceful intentions. Illustrative are the Stockholm confidence-building measures reached within the framework of the CSCE in December 1986, the signature of the 1987 treaty to eliminate all missiles between 500 and 5,500 kilometers, the unilateral announcement of the Soviet withdrawal of 500,000 troops and the dismantling of 10,000 tanks in December 1988, and Moscow's agreement to negotiate limits on Soviet forces to 195,000 in Europe in February 1990.

The Western states would have been hard pressed to maintain defense spending at the Cold War levels of the early 1980s even if the Soviet threat had not significantly diminished. US budget and trade deficits drive political pressures to cut military budgetary authorizations. Service on the US debt at the end of the 1980s was approximately 15 per cent of governmental outlays, double the level of only a decade earlier. Savings and investment are hindered and, correspondingly, US competitiveness in world markets, arguably the key factor sustaining its power and influence, is weakened. European NATO states confront parallel financial and economic constraints. West Germany, the strongest economic power in the European Community, must assume the largest burden for integrating East Germany into a reunified Germany as well as for providing credits and grants to the emerging democracies and market economies of Eastern Europe. As these burdens multiply, demands for greater spending on domestic welfare across all NATO and EC countries will presumably continue unabated.

Finally, there is no ready and universally acceptable institutional substitute for the role played by the two blocs in overseeing and regulating European national conflicts. The division of Germany resolved only temporarily the potential threat posed by the creation of a single nation of 78 million energetic and talented people in Central Europe. If Germany no longer represents the threat it once did between 1870 and 1945, its economic and political power are a source of concern. The Cold War provisionally solved these issues. Its passing and Germany's unification raise these questions anew. With the demise of the Warsaw Pact, it would appear that only

NATO or an expanded CSCE – or some combination of the two – can assume in the long run some of the previous security functions of the two blocs. The Four-Power accord of fall 1990, which transferred sovereign control over German territory to a unified government of Germany, and Soviet approval of Germany's continued membership of NATO were steps in this direction. Moreover, the United States and the Soviet Union no longer appear either able or willing to bear the principal responsibility for resolving or dampening national and ethnic strife in Europe. Soviet military intervention in Azerbaijan to stop bloodshed may be tolerated, even encouraged by the West, but it is by no means clear that the use of Soviet military forces to prevent Baltic state separatism would be met with similar approval or acquiescence. In short, the Cold War developed rules for intervention which no longer apply, and new rules have yet to be defined and accepted by the superpowers and all of the states of Europe.

These three crises of order are joined by three others with respect to Europe's future welfare system. The first concerns the transition of the Soviet Union and the East European states from command to market economies. The obstacles to successful transformation are formidable, and surmounting them is by no means assured. Propriet- ary rights and ownership have to be defined and guaranteed to encourage foreign investment. At least temporary inflation and unemployment will have to be incurred, to bring the cost and true price of a product into line. The Soviet Union confronts special problems although it was the first to launch political and economic reforms. It lags behind its East European partners, especially Poland and Hungary, in accepting the discipline of the market. The resist- ance of Soviet workers as well as party and state functionaries to reform is notably stronger in the Soviet Union than among its former satellites. There is the double risk that the harsh, coercively based rigors of the Stalinist economy which worked at a low level of efficiency will be replaced by a system of incentives of little appeal to a skeptical work force and sullen *nomenklatura* socialized to a command economy. A reforming Soviet state may not have either enough sticks or carrots to ensure economic growth.[22]

The second welfare crisis concerns the size and working rules of the European Community. Aside from Ireland, the other members of the EC also belong to NATO. The Community decision to achieve a fully integrated European market by 1992 was implicitly based on Cold War assumptions. Neither East Germany nor the Slavic nations of Eastern Europe were included in Brussels' thinking. With German unification, membership in the EC must expand, to include at a minimum the inhabitants of East Germany. The East European states, particularly Hungary and Yugoslavia, have already indicated their desire to join the Community. Reaching the 1992 goal would have been difficult enough even if the revolutions in Eastern Europe had not occurred. Witness the slow progress toward monetary union. These impediments are magnified by the enlargement issue posed by an open Europe extending from the Atlantic to the Urals.

The third crisis of welfare turns on the question of whether the European Community will remain open and committed to the liberal economic regime established after World War II. Cold War needs justified US support for the European Community and for eventual political union. As the Cold War recedes in significance and salience, there is little incentive for the United States to tolerate the conferring of preferences to Community members at the expense of outsiders; conversely, as Europe's security depends increasingly less on the United States in a post-Cold War environment, European states have less need to make concessions to US economic demands in exchange for protection. It would be ironic that at the very time that Eastern Europe and the Soviet Union were seeking entry into a world capitalist system to spur their economic development, technological progress, and socio-political development – in effect conceding the failure of their socialist economies – the Western democracies might be moving away from a liberal international regime at the moment of its greatest triumph.

In tandem with the crises of order and welfare, two crises of political legitimacy have also emerged in Europe. The first is within the Soviet Union where the ruling faction under Gorbachev's leadership relies on the power of the Communist party and state to reform both from the top down. The success of reform, defined by President Gorbachev, as *perestroika*, *glasnost*, and democratization,[23] undermines the Communist party's monopoly of power, following the trends already well-developed in Eastern Europe and the Baltic Republics. Paradoxically, Gorbachev has enlisted his power as Communist party leader to end the party's monopoly of power without being assured that a pluralist party system will actually support his socio-economic reforms. Whereas the reformist leadership of the Eastern European states could count on the support of the populace from whence their revolutions sprang, this same legitimating force, as Chapter 4 sketches, has not been at work in proportional measure within the Soviet Union. Indeed, *glasnost*, which was supposed to propel *perestroika* and democratization, had the untoward effect of weakening the Soviet reform movement. The democratization in Eastern Europe raises an additional set of crises in legitimacy. None of these states has had much experience with pluralist systems based on rival parties within a constitutional system guaranteeing free expression and association. Opposing Communist rule cannot automatically be equated with a commitment to liberal democratic institutions and liberties patterned after Western models. Nor are demands for greater material welfare necessarily supportive of fundamental political reform as popular attacks on groups opposed to the Romanian ruling council suggest. Habits of democratic practice will have to be learned by populations long habituated to central direction, but whose patience is strained by the slow pace of economic development.

At this writing too many uncertainties have to be settled to speculate reasonably about how the European Rubik's cube will be solved. What can be argued with more certainty is that the Cold War and the largely implicit cooperation that it engendered between the superpowers kept the peace in Europe until a new generation could emerge within the East and within the West that would demand more in the way of national self-determination and security, economic welfare, and democratic practice than superpower bipolarity could provide.

NOTES

1. This is the argument of George F. Kennan's analysis of World War II in his *American Diplomacy, 1900–1950* (Chicago: University of Chicago Press, 1954), pp. 74–90.
2. For a discussion of the Grand Alliance and a review of selected original documents, consult Norman A. Graebner, *Ideas and Diplomacy* (New York: Oxford University Press, 1964), pp. 631–710.
3. The tension between announced US rejection of balance of power and spheres of influence politics and the gradual adjustment of the Roosevelt and Truman administration to these imperatives is traced in a vast and contentious literature over the origins of the Cold War. These historiographic controversies can in no way be recounted here. For a brief and balanced discussion of Roosevelt's thinking, see John Lewis Gaddis, *Strategies of Containment* (New York: Oxford University Press, 1982), especially pp. 3–24.
4. Anton DePorte's *Europe between the Superpowers* (New Haven: Yale

University Press, 1979) is the best Cold War analysis and explanation for Germany's and Europe's division. Neither he nor anyone else was able to envision the demand of the Soviet leadership under Mikhail Gorbachev and of the East European and East German peoples to end their isolation and to seek not only internal reform but to end the Cold War in Europe and Europe's division.

5. Jonathan Dean, 'Berlin in a Divided Germany: An Evolving International Regime', in Alexander George et al. (eds), US–Soviet Security Cooperation (New York: Oxford University Press, 1988), p. 86.
6. DePorte, op. cit. p. 165. See also David Schoenbaum, 'The World War II Allied Agreement on Occupation and Administration of Postwar Germany', in George et al., US–Soviet Security Cooperation, pp. 21–45. Domestic political considerations should not be slighted in explaining the decision of German Chancellor Konrad Adenauer in choosing West German sovereignty and membership in NATO over the hope of German unification. Aside from Adenauer's deep-seated suspicion of Protestant Prussia, his Christian Democratic party would have faced formidable electoral competition from the Social Democratic party which would have enjoyed considerable support in eastern Germany in sufficient number, quite conceivably, to have assured the SPD a ruling majority.
7. The Berlin crisis of the summer of 1961 is discussed at length in Robert M. Slusser, The Berlin Crisis of 1961 (Baltimore: Johns Hopkins University Press, 1973).
8. See, for example, Philip Windsor, Germany and the Management of Détente (New York: Praeger, 1971).
9. Dean, pp. 97–105, summarizes the history of the Berlin accords since 1971.
10. A useful summary of the Helsinki process is found in John J. Maresca, To Helsinki: The Conference on Security and Cooperation in Europe, 1973–1975 (Durham: Duke University Press, 1985). Useful documents and commentaries are found in Vojtech Mastny, Helsinki, Human Rights, and European Security: Analysis and Documentation (Durham: Duke University Press, 1986).
11. Josef Joffe accents this police and monitoring role as a major, if overlooked, benefit of the Western alliance in his The Limited Partnership (New York: Ballinger, 1987).
12. For a brief overview of alliance politics and the MLF controversy, see Richard Neustadt, Alliance Politics (New York: Columbia University Press, 1970).
13. Quoted in Strobe Talbott, Deadly Gambits (New York: Vintage, 1985), p. 28.
14. This is the argument of Christoph Bertram. See his 'Implications of Theater Nuclear Weapons in Europe', Foreign Affairs, vol. LX, no. 2 (Winter, 1981–2), pp. 305–26, 'Strategic defense and the Western Alliance', in Weapons in Space, Franklin Long, et al., (eds), (New York: W. W. Norton, 1986), pp. 279–96.
15. Postwar US thinking about international economic policy is covered in Richard Cooper's The Economics of Interdependence (New York:

McGraw-Hill, 1968) and in Harold van B. Cleveland, *The Atlantic Idea and Its Rivals* (New York: McGraw-Hill, 1966).

16. Dean Acheson, *Present at the Creation* (New York: New American Library, 1969).

17. For an overview of the Grand Design by a participant-observer, see Arthur Schlesinger, Jr, *A Thousand Days* (Boston: Houghton-Mifflin, 1965), *passim*.

18. These differences are detailed in Robert Lieber, *The Oil Decade: Conflict and Cooperation in the West* (New York: Praeger, 1983).

19. See, for example, Henry Kissinger's reservations about the economic dependability of the Europeans to adhere to an economically open Europe. Kissinger, *The White House Years* (Boston/Toronto: Little, Brown, 1977), pp. 425–9.

20. The superpower nuclear struggle to 1985 is detailed in Strobe Talbott, *Endgame* (New York: Harper, 1980) and in *Deadly Gambits*. Superpower regional conflict is reviewed in Edward A. Kolodziej and Roger E. Kanet, *The Limits of Soviet Power in the Developing World: Thermidor in the Revolutionary Struggle* (Baltimore: Johns Hopkins University Press, 1989).

21. De Gaulle's conception of Europe is sketched in Edward A. Kolodziej, *French International Policy under De Gaulle and Pompidou: The Politics of Grandeur* (Ithaca: Cornell University Press, 1974).

22. See the analysis of 'Z', 'To the Stalin Mausoleum', *Daedalus*, vol. CXIX, no. 1 (Winter 1990), pp. 295–344.

23. Speech of Mikhail Gorbachev to the Soviet Communist Central Committee in which he asked for the party renunciation of its monopoly of power, *New York Times*, 7 February 1990.

4 Superpower Cooperation in Eastern Europe

Roger E. Kanet

The present chapter focuses on the competitive-cooperative relationship between the superpowers in Eastern Europe and is divided into four major sections. The first examines the nature of the interests of both the Soviet Union and the United States in Eastern Europe. The second part traces the evolution of the East European security regime. Special attention is given to the evidence of superpower 'cooperative' arrangements as they evolved over the course of the past forty years. The third part of the chapter delineates the specific nature of the European community system and the rules of behavior (or 'operational code') that emerged during that period. The discussion responds to the question: to what extent has 'cooperation' become an operative element in Soviet–American relations as they relate to Eastern Europe? The final section of the chapter outlines the reasons for the recent revolutionary changes in Eastern Europe and the prospects for the expansion and strengthening of superpower cooperation concerning Eastern Europe.

SUPERPOWER INTERESTS IN EASTERN EUROPE

The years immediately after World War II witnessed a dramatic collapse of relations among the wartime allies, as the Soviet Union proceeded to establish political dependencies in the areas under its military control in East–Central Europe. Other authors have provided extensive documentation of the process which resulted by 1948 in Stalin's successfully sealing off the area from both the military power and the effective political influence of the West and creating the foundations for communist rule and Soviet dominance.[1] What is important here is an understanding of the key objectives of the Soviet leadership in the late 1940s and of the ways in which these objectives were at odds with US goals. In other words, what role did Eastern Europe play in the origins of the Cold War and superpower global conflict?

Soviet policy objectives in Eastern Europe emerged only gradually during the war. Even in the immediate postwar period Stalin's views concerning the nature of a future Eastern Europe had not coalesced completely.[2] As Stalin sensed the inability or unwillingness of the United States and Great Britain to oppose effectively his initiatives in the region, he pushed to incorporate Eastern Europe into the Soviet empire. The charges of revisionist historians notwithstanding, it is important to note that the evidence indicates only minimal US efforts, beyond diplomatic complaints, to intervene in Eastern Europe to influence political developments. As the Soviets and their East European communist clients imprisoned or executed non-communist political leaders, the United States stood by, seemingly paralyzed. In fact, diplomats stationed in the East European capitals were regularly instructed to avoid confrontation with Soviet officials. In Romania in 1944–5, for example, US representatives were precluded from meeting with local politicians, lest this might result in conflict with the Soviets.[3]

By 1948 Stalin's objectives in Eastern Europe had been clarified and implemented. They set the framework for Soviet policy in the region for the next four decades during which the Soviet leadership treated Eastern Europe largely as an extension of its domestic system – as a virtual fiefdom under Stalin or as a junior partner during the Brezhnev years.[4] Briefly, the Soviets viewed Eastern Europe from several, not necessarily mutually compatible, perspectives:

(a) *As a defensive bulwark.* In this sense Eastern Europe served as a buffer zone against possible attack from the West, as a zone of forward deployment of Soviet forces, and as a contributor to the overall defense effort of the region. In the ideological realm Eastern Europe was also seen as a bulwark against the incursion of Western liberalism into the USSR. In fact, changes in the nature of warfare since the 1940s have reduced the military security value of the region, and Eastern Europe has acted more as a conduit of Western ideas than as a barrier or filter, even prior to recent political developments.

(b) *As a basis for an offensive strategy.* This springboard conception, the reciprocal of the first factor, had three major aspects:

    (i) *Ideological.* Eastern Europe was viewed as the advance guard of the world communist movement and, along with the USSR itself, the spearhead of the global communist revolution.

(ii) *Political.* Eastern Europe has served as a base for policy
     initiatives, e.g. peace campaigns designed to influence
     Western Europe and split the continent from the United
     States. During the 1970s several East European states
     also became important partners of the USSR in the
     pursuit of global objectives, especially in the Third World.
(iii) *Military.* Eastern Europe served as a forward base for
     possible military initiatives taken against the West; this
     logistical contribution was especially important for both
     the GDR and Poland.
(c) *As the nucleus of an international bloc of support in world
    politics.* Though this East European role has been important
    ever since Stalin, it was especially emphasized during the
    1970s, when the Soviets spoke enthusiastically of the changing
    international correlation of forces and the important role of
    other socialist states in world affairs.
(d) *As a source of ideological and political legitimization.* Though
    there have been changes over time Soviet leaders seemingly
    were convinced that the existence of a bloc of states modeled
    after the USSR and publicly pursuing similar policies was
    essential to the political legitimacy of the Soviet system.
(e) *As an economic asset.* Initially, through reparations and other
    exploitative arrangements, Eastern Europe served as a source
    of capital and technology for the USSR. Throughout the 1950s
    and 1960s barter arrangements brought East European indust-
    rial and consumer goods to the USSR in return for raw
    materials. More recently, however, the economic benefit of
    Eastern Europe for the Soviets has become questionable;
    economic relations with most countries have resulted in a net
    transfer of Soviet resources.

The relative importance of these factors has changed over the
course of the past forty years. Ultimately what the Soviet leadership
has sought in Eastern Europe until very recently was a bloc of
prosperous, single-party states organically tied to the USSR in such a
way as to be fully supportive of all Soviet policy initiatives. The key
problem faced by those leaders in achieving this objective has
resulted from the basic tension or incompatibility between two
essential elements of that vision – the viability of East European
regimes and the cohesion of the Soviet-centered European communist system.

Virtually all of the political crises in Eastern Europe over the past forty years – including the developments of 1989 that led to the demise of communist systems – resulted precisely from this tension. In so far as East European leaders pursued policies consonant with Soviet interests, they generally did not respond to popular demands for national identity, expanded political participation and improved standards of living, as in the GDR and Hungary in the 1950s. On the other hand, when leaders responded to the popular will in the effort to generate greater domestic legitimacy and viability, they found themselves in conflict with the Soviet concern about bloc unity and adherence to the traditional Soviet conception of socialist internationalism – e.g. in Czechoslovakia in 1968 and Poland in 1956 and again in 1980–1. For the Soviet leadership from Stalin to Chernenko, the ultimate touchstone in evaluating its relations with Eastern Europe was Moscow's ability to dominate the area and to control key developments. It was precisely this aspect of Soviet policy, along with the role that the region played in the military balance, that brought it into conflict with the United States.

It is more difficult to outline the major interests of the United States in Eastern Europe in the postwar era, since they have never been as clearly developed as those of the USSR. For the most part these interests were initially defined primarily in terms of the emerging conflict with the Soviet Union in the region. Moreover, over the course of the past forty years the US response to Soviet domination of Eastern Europe has varied, depending upon the nature of US–Soviet relations at any given time. During the periods of *détente* in superpower relations the United States has tended to accept – at least not directly challenge – the Soviet sphere of influence in the region. At times of heightened tension, however, US policy has tended to treat the East Europeans as mere extensions of the USSR fit to suffer the penalties inherent in trade restrictions and coercive policies. Yet, throughout most of the past forty years, beginning with the Soviet–Yugoslav split, the general objective of US policy in Eastern Europe has been to stimulate and support diversity and political autonomy within the Soviet bloc, to implement a policy that might be termed reverse Finlandization. As Sarah Terry has put the issue: 'In the periods of "competitive coexistence" that have dominated the post-Stalin era, Washington has sought to encourage both domestic liberalization within the various East European countries and greater foreign policy "differentiation".'[5]

Already at the height of Cold War in 1949, the National Security

Council advised President Truman that the most realistic objective for the United States was to encourage the creation of regimes in the region that were free of Soviet domination, rather than pro-Western. Rhetoric during the 1952 presidential campaign concerning the immorality of containment and the need to 'roll back' the Iron Curtain in Eastern Europe notwithstanding, US policy during the Eisenhower administration pursued much more modest objectives: diversity within the Soviet bloc rather than liberation, and liberalization in domestic politics rather than full-scale democracy.[6] In effect, it was in the 1950s that the foundations for future US policy in Eastern Europe were firmly established. Objectives were limited to modest support for marginal change in the region, for they were based on the realization that the USSR viewed the region as a vital concern and that the United States was not in a position to provide active support for those who wanted major change – unless it was prepared to face a major military confrontation with the Soviet Union.

Although there was essential continuity in the pursuit of limited goals by Washington ever since the Truman administration, long-term objectives were often expressed in maximalist terms. This resulted in periodic incompatibility between stated principles and the reality of US policy. Never was that contradiction made clearer than at the time of the Hungarian Revolution in 1956. The rhetoric of the 1952 presidential campaign and the propaganda lines of Radio Free Europe led many in Hungary to expect US support; yet, the strategic and geopolitical realities of East-Central Europe meant that US support for the Hungarians was limited to public rhetoric and resettlement assistance.

Over the past four decades US interests in Eastern Europe, though real and significant, have been largely derivative and secondary. The primary objective in US policy, regardless of the region of the world, has been the limitation of the risk of nuclear confrontation with the Soviet Union. Another policy objective of great importance has been containment of Soviet control and influence, in Europe and else-where in the world. Within Europe the United States has been committed to maintaining the unity of the Western alliance system as a key element in containing Soviet expansionism. It is within the context of these policy objectives that US interests in Eastern Europe must be understood. In so far as Eastern Europe was perceived as a supporter of and adjunct to Soviet expansionist tendencies, US policy toward the region differed little from that toward the USSR itself.

However, Eastern Europe was also viewed as a weak link in the defense chain of the Soviet Union and, thus, a potential target of US initiatives. Given the level of Soviet concern about and commitment to the maintenance of its dominant position in the region, the US was forced to pursue a policy of 'peaceful engagement', to use the term coined by Zbigniew Brzezinski and William Griffith.[7] This policy meant that rivalry with the USSR in Eastern Europe would continue, but within circumscribed boundaries and by limited means. As will be discussed further below, the revolutionary changes that have affected Eastern Europe since 1989 have resulted in a new relationship between the superpowers, which diverges from past patterns.

EASTERN EUROPE AND THE EMERGENCE OF A NEW EUROPEAN SECURITY REGIME

After this brief examination of the interests of the two superpowers in Eastern Europe, we turn to a survey of major elements of superpower policy in relationship to Eastern Europe. Specifically, we shall examine those aspects of policy that can be termed 'cooperative' and that contributed to the emergence of the stable European security regime which characterized interstate relations after the late 1950s.

Nowhere was the conflict between the United States and the Soviet Union more pronounced in the years from 1945 until 1950 than in Central Europe. By 1949 the Truman administration concluded that little hope existed of cooperation with the Soviets to solve key issues such as 'the German question', the civil war in Greece, and concerns about democracy in the East European states. The Truman Doctrine of 1947 served as the foundation for a new US policy of containing Soviet expansion and influence, while the Marshall Plan promised the economic rehabilitation of European countries associated with the United States.

The Soviets viewed this new US policy as a direct and immediate challenge to their postwar position in East-Central Europe. At the founding meeting of the Cominform in September 1947 Andrei Zhdanov, the second-in-command to Stalin, proclaimed his 'two-camp' thesis and asserted that US policy was committed to the enslavement of Europe and the unleashing of a new war against the Soviet Union.[8] From the Soviet perspective, US policy posed a potential challenge to Soviet objectives. This required an adjustment of Soviet policies, especially in Eastern Europe, where Stalin accelerated the consolidation of communist regimes, as well as the extension of Soviet control over the East European communist parties. The result was a three-pronged Soviet offensive in the years 1948–50 aimed at consolidating Soviet power over its new empire. First, they attempted to impose uniformity on and control over the East European regimes. In Yugoslavia the attempt backfired, as Tito successfully resisted Soviet efforts and established a system which would continue to confound both the East and the West, as we shall note below. Elsewhere local party officials were purged for alleged political deviations and by 1950 leaders were in power who owed their very existence to Stalin.

The second element of Stalin's program was the establishment of centralized ideological dominance of the CPSU over other communist parties. This objective, which was closely related to the first, was accomplished through the creation of the Cominform and the imposition on all parties of the Soviet interpretation of 'socialist internationalism'. In effect, the interests of the CPSU and the USSR and the ideological interpretations of the CPSU were declared to be the interests and interpretations of the entire communist movement.

The third aspect of Stalin's initiative was his decision to test the West's commitment to the positions that it held in Central Europe. Specifically, beginning on 24 June 1948 the Soviets closed all access to Berlin, resulting in the first major potential military confrontation between the superpowers in the postwar era. During the ensuing eleven months, until the lifting of the blockade on 5 May 1949, the level of hostilities between the two superpowers was at probably the highest level during the entire postwar period (with the exception of the Cuban missile crisis of 1962). Yet, despite the Soviet attempt to coerce the West into withdrawing from Berlin and despite initial US consideration of using military power to force its way through to Berlin, the crisis was characterized by efforts on both sides to manage the level of confrontation.[9] Neither side was willing to push so far as to make a military confrontation inevitable. For example, the Western decision to supply West Berlin by an airlift and the Soviet response not to challenge directly that airlift reduced the likelihood of direct military confrontation. Moreover, throughout the crisis regular political consultations and negotiations among the four occupation powers occurred, though until spring 1949 they made virtually no headway.

Despite the high level of tension associated with the Berlin Blockade, once the West decided to stay but to challenge the blockade by an airlift rather than by direct military action, a stalemate ensued. Behavior on both sides was regularized. Key Western participants in the events, including Mayor Ernst Reuter and General Lucius Clay, were convinced that the Soviets did not want war and, thus, avoided measures which the Western allies would have resisted with force.[10] In other words, despite the high level of tension, both superpowers were careful to control their behavior, in order to reduce the prospects for direct military action. Moreover, once the Soviets recognized that they would not accomplish their primary objective of forcing the West out of Berlin, they were willing to cut their losses and drop the attempt.

Simultaneously with the Berlin Blockade another series of events occurred which would prove to be important for the development of the postwar security regime in Europe and for the nature of US–Soviet competition. Stalin's efforts to impose on Yugoslavia the type of dependency relationship that had been created elsewhere in Eastern Europe resulted in a major confrontation. Ultimately, Yugoslavia was expelled from the communist community, with the expectation that pro-Soviet elements in Yugoslavia would seize power and replace Tito and his supporters. After an initial period of foundering, Tito finally opted to turn to the West for economic and military support. The result was an independent communist state, hostile to the USSR and with close political, economic and security ties to the capitalist West. The decision of the Truman administration to provide support to Yugoslavia initiated a policy of differentiation in which the United States saw independent communist states as a positive alternative to those dominated by the Soviet Union.

However, over the past four decades Yugoslavia has represented something of a dual dilemma for the superpowers. While the United States supported Yugoslavia's successful attempt to pursue its foreign and security objectives independent of Soviet domination, it rejected the Yugoslav model of economic and political organization. At the same time, the Soviets did not fully accept Yugoslav foreign policy autonomy and found the Yugoslav claim to represent an alternative economic and political model of communism an irritant. Over the past forty years the specifics of Yugoslavia's place in Europe may have shifted, yet the essential element of its independence has remained stable. Though Yugoslav leaders' perception of world affairs has often been closer to that of the USSR than to that of the West, their ties with the West and with developing countries have been viewed as essential to maintaining their independence.

In the mid-1950s developments in both Eastern and Western Europe – e.g. West Germany's entry into NATO, the suppression of riots in Pilsen and Poznan, and the Soviet invasion and suppression of the revolution in Hungary – created conflicts that pitted the superpowers against one another. Almost simultaneously, however, other developments were occurring which reduced the overall level of tension, most notably the Soviet withdrawal from the naval base in Porkkala, Finland, and the signing of the Austrian State Treaty in 1955. Both actions contributed to the emergence of an increasingly stable European security regime. The second set of developments, along with the normalization of relations with Tito's Yugoslavia, was part of Nikita Khrushchev's efforts to gain Western acceptance for his policy of peaceful coexistence. After Stalin's death the new Soviet leadership was convinced of the counterproductive nature of Stalin's confrontational approach to the West. That policy had stimulated Western countermeasures including the establishment of NATO and Western rearmament and eventually West Germany's entry into the Atlantic Alliance. In other words, while consolidating Soviet control over its postwar East European empire, Stalin had also contributed to Western fears to the point that by 1953 the Soviets faced a militarily integrated and progressively more powerful Western alliance.

In justifying his position in the foreign policy struggle with Molotov, Khrushchev later stated that it was 'more important to give a widely visible clear signal of willingness to negotiate, than to cling to military positions of little significance'.[11] To reduce tensions and to gain general acceptance of his new approach to East–West relations Khrushchev made peace with Tito, returned naval facilities acquired from Finland in 1945, permitted Finland to join the Nordic Council, and invited German Chancellor Konrad Adenauer to Moscow to negotiate a normalization of relations with West Germany. It was within this context that the Soviets also agreed to withdraw from Austria as part of the postwar settlement in Europe. Though the agreement meant that Soviet troops would pull back in Central Europe, it also required the United States to give up its original goal of integrating Austria into the Western alliance system. Though there is some evidence that the Soviets had earlier hoped that the settlement in Austria might be viewed as a model for the solution of the Germany question, by the time of its signing West German entry into NATO was virtually assured.[12]

Another important element of the emerging European security

regime was the initial resolution of the German question through the long-term division of Germany, and of Europe, into roughly balanced regions each tied closely to one of the superpowers.[13] It has been this regime which, for the past thirty-five years or so, has provided Europe with a high degree of political and security stability – though the regime was not fully in place in 1955 and has also undergone some serious crises during the ensuing years.

Despite the partial normalization of US–Soviet relations associated with these developments, other events in East-Central Europe in the mid-1950s exacerbated tensions in relations between the two superpowers. The riots in Pilsen and in East Berlin in June 1953, and in Poznan in June 1956, were suppressed by the Soviets or their allies. In part because of the brief duration of these events, the Western response was limited to strong criticism of the communists for their brutal treatment of legitimate political dissent.

It was in the Polish and Hungarian crises of fall 1956 that the greatest possibility developed for a US–Soviet confrontation. Not only were these political crises of longer duration, but in Hungary full-scale revolution broke out, followed by the Soviet reoccupation of the country and the military suppression of all resistance to the reimposition of Soviet control. As we have already seen, despite the earlier calls for liberation and the implied commitments made in Radio Free Europe broadcasts that Western assistance would be forthcoming, the US response was limited to diplomatic maneuvering and political condemnation. Actual US behavior during the Hungarian Revolution was not based on the principles of self-determination of peoples or the rolling back of Soviet domination in Central Europe. Rather, it was based on the clear perception of US self-interest: specifically, on the realization that any move to support the Hungarians militarily would likely result in a direct military engagement with the USSR and the possible use of nuclear weapons. Even in the mid-1950s, when the Soviets lacked effective delivery systems to target nuclear weapons against US territory, the possibility of a nuclear exchange was viewed as a frightening prospect to be avoided at all costs.

During the Hungarian Crisis, as during all future East–West confrontations in Central Europe, US leaders effectively recognized Soviet hegemony over this region and avoided challenging that hegemony in ways that might have resulted in military confrontation. Thus, by 1956 several rules of the emerging European security regime (or of superpower behavior in East-Central Europe) had already been 'codified' through practice: do not challenge directly the core interests of the other superpower; avoid direct intervention in the other superpower's sphere of influence; and do not pursue actions likely to result in a direct military showdown. In the case of Hungary all of these imperatives were at work. First, Hungary was within the region viewed by the Soviets as their area of dominance. Moreover, US intervention in the region would have been perceived in Moscow as a challenge to Soviet security and, thus, might very likely have resulted in a military clash between the two countries.

To a very substantial degree the crises of the past thirty-plus years have largely followed the format laid out in Hungary in 1956. Only the Berlin Crisis of 1961 differed appreciably from this pattern. Beginning in 1958 the Soviets pursued a policy aimed at consolidation of the political system in the GDR and at strengthening the domestic and international legitimacy of its client. The key issue here was the inability of the GDR to consolidate effective control and to gain legitimacy among its populace or in world affairs, given the attraction of emigration to West Germany.[14] In this sense, then, the crisis that erupted in August 1961 was the result of one superpower's attempt to consolidate control which also challenged the position of the other in Central Europe. From November 1958 until summer 1961 the Soviets interspersed demands for the West to recognize the GDR's control over access routes to West Berlin with periods of willingness to negotiate a resolution of outstanding differences. The key issue, from the Soviet and GDR perspective, related to the problems that West Berlin posed for the viability of the East German state. As the GDR moved to finalize the process of collectivizing agriculture and of establishing a communist economy in the late 1950s, the number of refugees fleeing the country rose dramatically – to more than 70,000 during the first four months of 1961.

The problem for the Soviets was to find a policy which, while closing off access to the West, would not result in military confrontation. The decision to construct the Wall provided precisely such a policy. Despite the dramatic increase in the immediate level of tension – especially at the local level – it was clear that the West was not about to initiate actions that would challenge the USSR with force and, thus, run the risk of nuclear confrontation. According to Theodore Sorensen, a member of President Kennedy's 'inner circle', no responsible official in the United States, West Berlin, or West Germany recommended the use of force to tear down the Wall.[15] Thus, the outcome of the Berlin Crisis reinforces the points made above concerning the emergence of a European security regime and the rules of that regime. Though the Soviets did challenge the status quo in Berlin, that challenge never involved the threat of the use of force against the West. When the decision was finally made to solve the GDR's legitimacy and viability problems by sealing it off from the Western zone of Berlin, neither of the superpowers was willing to risk military confrontation. As events in Hungary five years earlier had demonstrated, the United States was unable to force the USSR to change its policies in areas considered of vital importance to the latter.

The next set of events in East Central Europe of direct relevance to the superpower security relations were those surrounding the 1968 reform movement in Czechoslovakia and the eventual military intervention in that country by the USSR and several of its allies.[16] Though the West was encouraged by the reforms and committed itself to supporting them politically and economically, it was unwilling to do more than that when the Soviet leadership decided that the evolution of events in Czechoslovakia represented a challenge to core Soviet interests. Throughout summer 1968, as the Soviets made increasingly clear their growing concerns, the Western response was limited almost exclusively to warnings of the negative implications of Soviet intervention for the emerging *détente* in East–West relations.

In many respects the negative effects of the invasion on relations within the communist movement were more lasting than those on East–West relations. Already by spring 1969 the momentum of *détente* had resumed. As we shall see below, the period 1969 to 1975 was one of great importance for stabilizing the postwar European security regime. During these six years most of the 'rules' of superpower behavior that had emerged on an *ad hoc* basis since the late 1940s were formally codified in a series of agreements that culminated in the Helsinki Accords. The early 1970s witnessed a whole series of bilateral and multilateral negotiations – between West Germany and, respectively, the USSR, Poland and the GDR concerning their mutual bilateral relations; among the four powers administering Berlin concerning the status of West Berlin; between the USSR and the United States concerning nuclear weapons; and among the thirty-five states which eventually signed the Helsinki Accords concerning a broad range of security, economic and human rights issues. Out of these formal negotiations emerged agreement on the postwar boundaries of East-Central Europe and the dominant position of the USSR in that region. However, agreement was also reached on issues relating to expanding East–West contacts and human rights guarantees in Eastern Europe.

A final series of problems faced by the Soviet Union that affected its relations with the United States concerned domestic political instability in Poland. In spring 1968 student demonstrations against the increasingly repressive policies of the regime of Wladyslaw Gomulka resulted in harsh repression. In December 1970 strikes and worker demonstrations in the major industrial cities along the Baltic Sea were initially crushed by the regime. However, this brought down the Gomulka leadership which was replaced by that of Eduard Gierek, who committed himself to reforms and economic modernization meant to solve Poland's endemic problems. Less than six years later, in June 1976, Gierek was faced with similar widespread labor disruption, as he attempted to raise prices of basic foodstuffs as part of a policy of economic retrenchment.

These domestic disturbances were short-lived and did not impact significantly on US–Soviet relations. Not until 1980–1, with the emergence of the major challenge to the Polish communist party mounted by Solidarity and the growing Soviet concern about a possible repeat of events in Czechoslovakia in 1968, did Polish developments become an important factor in US–Soviet relations.[17] Throughout the entire Solidarity period the United States warned the Soviet leadership of the negative implications for bilateral relations of direct Soviet intervention in Polish affairs. The imposition of martial law and the outlawing of Solidarity in December 1981 did not involve Soviet military forces. Convinced of direct Soviet involvement in the decisions of the government of General Wojciech Jaruzelski, the Reagan administration imposed political and economic sanctions against both the Soviet Union and Poland.

The growing hostility in US–Soviet relations associated with events in Poland, however, must be understood within the broader context of deteriorating superpower relations. Already in the mid-1970s there were those in the United States who questioned the wisdom of a policy of *détente*. In their view, *détente* had provided the Soviets with the cover to expand their influence within the Third World and to continue their unilateral military build-up in both the conventional and nuclear arenas. Even prior to the Soviet military invasion of Afghanistan in December 1979 and the imposition by President Carter of the grain embargo, the SALT 2 treaty was in danger of not being ratified by the US Senate. The election of Ronald Reagan in November 1980 brought to the White House a new political leadership convinced of the growing challenge to US interests emanating from 'the evil empire' and committed to re-establishing US military might and challenging the Soviet Union wherever possible. Thus, by December 1981 when General Jaruzelski imposed martial law in Poland, superpower relations had already deteriorated substantially toward what some analysts were calling 'Cold War II'.

Yet, despite the growing tension in US–Soviet relations, there was no question in 1981 of the possible use of US military force. In East-Central Europe this rule had long since been clarified. Despite its unhappiness with events in Poland and its conviction of the direct involvement of Moscow in those events, the Reagan administration never considered anything more than political and economic sanctions as an indication to the Soviets of the level of US indignation and as an 'inducement' to both the Soviet and Polish leaderships to modify their policies.

The final example of conflicting interests between the superpowers as they relate to Eastern Europe – though the issue was really one of broader European importance – concerned the Soviet introduction beginning by 1977 of SS-20 intermediate-range nuclear missiles targeted on Western Europe. In a very real way the deployment of these missiles threatened a possible shift in the overall military balance in Europe and, thus, a partial challenge to the security regime that had been in place for more than a decade. The introduction of Soviet missiles in the late 1970s and the NATO dual-track response contributed significantly to the deterioration of US–Soviet relations in the early 1980s. Only after a complete breakdown in superpower negotiations on arms control, much political posturing on the part of both countries, and the emergence of a new political leadership with a new foreign policy and arms control agenda, was the issue resolved in the breakthrough INF agreement of 1987 which called for the removal of all Soviet and US intermediate-range missiles. However, the initial Soviet decision to deploy this weapon system represented a challenge to the existing security regime in Europe. Despite Soviet claims that they were merely modernizing older weapons systems, both the qualitative improvements of the systems and the numbers of systems being deployed represented a major shift in theater nuclear capabilities.

Although the SS-20s have now been removed, the repercussions of this challenge remain, as the INF treaty and the ongoing unilateral withdrawal of some Soviet ground forces, including tanks, from Central Europe have encouraged widespread calls within NATO for fundamental reconsideration of the entire security strategy upon which NATO has been based for the past thirty-five years.

As should be evident at this point, despite US rhetoric and stated long-term objectives, American presidential administrations from Truman to Reagan recognized the reality of superpower interests and capabilities in East-Central Europe. Although the long-term objective of eliminating Soviet domination over Eastern Europe remained, it was tempered by the primary concern of not provoking a military confrontation with the Soviet Union. Thus, coexistence generally won out over the elements of competition in US policy in Eastern Europe. As noted above, US policy-makers pursued more limited objectives. As John Gaddis put it in speaking of the policy of the Eisenhower administration toward the Soviet Union: 'Since surrender was unthinkable, military victory impossible, and the cost of containment unacceptable, it seemed logical to explore possibilities for incorporating Soviet–American rivalry – which was certain to continue – within a mutually acceptable framework of coexistence.'[18]

By the 1960s and 1970s the United States expressed the competitive elements of the relationship by efforts to encourage the peaceful transformation of the Soviet bloc into a more diversified and pluralistic entity – i.e. by a policy of 'peaceful engagement'. In line with this objective, the United States granted Most Favoured Nation status to several countries deemed to be pursuing independent policies; during the early years of his administration President Carter visited Poland which he praised for its 'enlightened' policies; the United States returned the crown of St Stephen, the symbol of Hungarian statehood, to the government in Budapest, while also granting most-favored-nation status to Hungary; and at the Helsinki follow-up conference in Belgrade in 1978 Washington took a strong hand on the issue of human rights in Eastern Europe.

The revolutionary developments of 1989 and early 1990 have already restructured the domestic socio-political systems of the countries of the region and also the European security system that has been in place since World War II. Only four times during the past two centuries have events of such importance for the nature of domestic and international political relationships occurred in Europe: (a) during the French Revolution and the Napoleonic period when France attempted to destroy the old political order and replace it with a French-centered system of nominally independent and democratic states; (b) after the defeat of Napoleon in 1815, when the old order was in part re-established by the victors; (c) after World War I and the collapse of the traditional Central and East European empires and their replacement by a number of small states in Central Europe and a regime in Soviet Russia committed to revolutionary change; and (d) after World War II when the geographic and political map of Europe was modified once more by the collapse of the traditional European great powers and the emergence of the USSR and the United States as the dominant actors in Europe and the world.

The changes initiated in 1989 promise to have long-term consequences comparable to those associated with the four earlier periods of revolutionary 'restructuring'. Though the calls in Eastern Europe for the withdrawal of Soviet forces and the reunification of Germany challenge the foundations of the existing European security system, to this point at least, it appears that the leadership in Washington and Moscow are committed to ensuring that the changes do not lead to confrontation.

Thus, it was in Europe first – and particularly in East-Central Europe – that the two superpowers reached a form of accommodation which has permitted them to compete, while simultaneously limiting the extent of that competition lest it lead to military confrontation and, ultimately, to mutual destruction. It is also in East-Central Europe that the Cold War is coming to a close.

THE POSTWAR EUROPEAN SECURITY REGIME AND THE 'RULES' OF SUPERPOWER BEHAVIOR

After this examination of the nature of Soviet and US interests in Eastern Europe and of the evolution of postwar political and security developments there as they have concerned relations between the Soviet Union and the United States, we turn to a more systematic discussion of the nature of the security regime that emerged and of the general rules of behavior associated with that regime. We begin by emphasizing a point which, though central to the entire US–Soviet relationship in Europe and globally, has not yet been discussed directly in this chapter – namely the centrality of nuclear weapons and the nuclear stalemate in that relationship. The development of nuclear weapons and effective delivery systems by the superpowers created an environment in which both countries were concerned lest conflicts escalate to nuclear confrontation and, thus, the possibility of mutual annihilation. It has been precisely within the context of this nuclear stalemate that East–West and Soviet–US relationships have evolved in Europe.

Probably the most important security-related development for Europe that derived directly from this stalemate and the resulting commitment of both the United States and the Soviet Union to prevent confrontation was the evolution of a stable security regime in Europe in which warfare – or even the threat of warfare – had been eliminated. However, at the same time, the participants in this security regime – especially the two major military powers – committed large amounts of resources to their security systems and maintained large forces in being. In part as a result of the stabilization of the security regime in Europe, but also resulting from the increased importance of other regions of the world such as the Middle East and East Asia, Eastern Europe became relatively less important in the Soviet–American global competition and in international affairs generally. On the other hand, to an increasing degree until the growing economic problems of the 1980s, East European countries played a supporting role in the expansion of Soviet involvement throughout the Third World. Military, economic and political activities of individual East European countries – along with Cuba – often facilitated the expanded activities of the USSR and/or helped to distribute the Soviet costs of empire.[19]

Ever since the Second World War Eastern Europe has been an area viewed as essential to the vital interests of one of the two superpowers, while the other's interests were more marginal. In a very real sense until the revolutionary changes of 1989 Eastern Europe was viewed by the Soviets as a 'hard sphere of influence' in which they had important interests and over which they are able to exercise extensive control.[20] Although at one level the United States refused to accept the idea of permanent Soviet dominance over the area, in other ways it admitted that in times of crisis when the Soviet leadership saw a serious challenge to its interests in the area there was little that the United States could do to influence Soviet policy. Given the conventional military balance in the region and the implications of a global nuclear confrontation, American presidents since Truman have excluded the use of military power. Thus, the security regime that emerged in Europe was one based on the reality of the dominant role of the USSR in Eastern Europe.[21]

In fact, during the early 1970s the *détente* policy of Henry Kissinger was to a very great degree based on accepting the reality of Soviet dominance in Eastern Europe as a part of the cost involved in 'taming' Soviet behavior throughout the rest of the world. This viewpoint was expressed perhaps most boldly in the so-called Sonnenfeldt Doctrine of 1975 that referred to the 'organic' nature of the Soviet-East European relationship and seemingly accepted longstanding Soviet domination in Eastern Europe. However, this viewpoint incorrectly assumed that the imperial relationship between the USSR and Eastern Europe and the existence of political regimes viewed by the majority of the population as illegitimate could remain stable over time.[22] In fact, as we shall discuss in some detail below, at the very time when US policy accepted the stability of the status quo in the area, pressures were beginning to build up that a decade later would result in revolutionary change. Among these were the growing evidence of economic deterioration that would reduce the ability of the regimes to fulfill commitments for improved standards of living, the festering of popular resentment of continued Soviet domination, and the ongoing suppression of open political expression.

As we have already seen, throughout the past four decades there have been few actual confrontations between the USSR and the United States that had their origin in East European events. Only during the Berlin Blockade of 1948–9 – when the nature of the postwar European security system was still in flux – was there a significant possibility of direct military confrontation. But even in Berlin the two sides soon worked out tacit arrangements short of the use of military force according to which the remaining months of the struggle over the status of Berlin would be conducted. By the mid-1950s – and even more clearly after the Berlin Wall crisis of 1961 – the general outlines of the new European system had emerged in which the continent and Germany were divided into separate political-economic-military blocs. NATO and Warsaw Pact military forces have precluded each other's ability to make a military breakthrough. Moreover, the central role of the superpowers in this balance means that their global strategic nuclear capabilities are also integrally tied to the balance in Europe.

Out of this situation arose a pattern of expectations and controlled responses that contributed to the overall security stability of Europe, despite periodic challenges that have emerged, primarily from the challenges to the Soviets' control of their own bloc. This pattern of expectations and behaviors included several clear 'rules of prudence'. Seweryn Bialer and Alexander George provide listings of rules of prudence in conflict situations that have evolved over time to guide superpower relations.[23] But these rules depended on a Cold War regime that was of mutual interest. What no one foresaw was the eventual judgement of the Soviet leadership under Gorbachev that the Cold War regime no longer serves its interests.

In the crisis situations that we have discussed we find the type of behavior meant to limit conflict precisely because of the fear of escalation to the nuclear level. Though not all of the general 'rules' are directly relevant to US–Soviet competitive relations in Eastern Europe, those which are relevant have been observed virtually without fail. In all of the cases of actual or threatened Soviet intervention to reimpose control over recalcitrant allies – Hungary, Czechoslovakia, Poland – the US publicly stated its intention not to intervene. Recently, though there has been no evidence of Soviet intentions to intervene in the area to maintain or re-establish its dominant position, US officials have announced that the United States will not attempt to take unilateral advantage of the revolutionary changes that are redefining the nature of politics and security in Eastern Europe.[24]

In line with the 'rule' of caution in pursuing policies in areas where the vital interests of the other power are at stake, Western policymakers have been especially careful in developing relations with the East European countries. One important deviation from this caution was the first stage of West Germany's 'Ostpolitik' initiated in 1966 by the Kiesinger–Brandt Grand Coalition. The policy explicitly aimed at establishing direct relations between Bonn and the East European capitals and, in part at least, in weaning the latter away from their close dependency on the USSR, splitting the Warsaw Pact, and isolating the GDR. As a corollary of their military intervention in Czechoslovakia in 1968, the Soviets made clear the level of their opposition to this type of 'interference' in their sphere of influence. In the new version of 'Ostpolitik' initiated in 1969 the Brandt government, in effect, cleared matters with Moscow prior to initiating efforts to expand relations in Eastern Europe.

Another exception to this rule occurred in 1981 in Poland as US and Western labor unions, and other interest groups, actively supported the Solidarity movement. One of the major accusations brought by the Soviets against Solidarity was precisely the charge that it was functioning as an agent of Western interests. The imposition of martial law in December 1981 reduced these 'illicit' political contacts, though the Jaruzelski regime was never able to eliminate them entirely.

Throughout the entire postwar period negotiations and less formal political contacts have occurred during periods of heightened tension. For example, during the Berlin Blockade in 1948–9 regular consultations occurred between the Soviets and the three major Western governments.

The 'rules of prudence' in US–Soviet behavior concerning Eastern Europe resulted initially primarily from past behavior patterns and consisted of a kind of 'common law' in US–Soviet relations. During the *détente* period of 1970–5, however, a substantial number of these rules were 'codified' in a series of formal agreements. The treaties that emerged from bilateral and multilateral negotiations resulted in the formal recognition of existing postwar borders, commitments not to support change in the territorial status quo through coercive means, specific agreements concerning the status of West Berlin, and agreements on non-interference in the internal affairs of other states. Though it was never operationalized and was later the source of bitter criticism, the 'Basic Principles Agreement' on US–Soviet relations signed by President Nixon and General Secretary Brezhnev in 1972 also contributed to the environment of formalizing the rules of behavior in US–Soviet relations,[25]

As US–Soviet agreement and cooperation were formalized, they also became more complex. For example, in the negotiations over the status of West Berlin both sides came to the negotiating table with a specific list of objectives. For the West this was a list of rather limited goals of 'practical improvements' in the situation in and around Berlin. For the Soviet Union the key objective was Western recognition of the GDR. However, both sides had additional objectives the attainment of which the successful negotiations over Berlin might facilitate. For example, the Soviets recognized that they could not achieve the general objective of *détente*, nor the more specific objectives of Western recognition of the GDR and full Western participation in a Conference on Security and Cooperation in Europe, unless the Berlin situation were improved. Thus, the negotiations were based on bargaining strategies that cut across different issue areas. The final agreement on the status of Berlin did not meet the long-term objectives or ambitions of either side; rather it was a compromise in which both accepted what they were able to get at the time.[26]

Before turning to a concluding discussion of the importance of the dramatic recent changes in the USSR and Eastern Europe and their relevance for increased East–West and Soviet–US cooperation in relationship to Eastern Europe, it is well to summarize briefly the argument of this chapter to this point. By the mid-1950s – definitely by the early 1960s – a new security regime had emerged in Europe that included the division of the continent into conflicting military blocs. In addition, given the level of Soviet interest and involvement in Eastern Europe, the military balance in the area, and the implications of the superpower nuclear stalemate, rules of behavior emerged which resulted in careful and limited Western involvement in the region of a type that would not lead to superpower confrontation. By the 1970s this regime was largely formalized through a series of agreements that culminated in the Helsinki Accords of 1975. Though both superpowers have considered challenging the foundations of this security regime – the Soviets marginally by the deployment of SS-20s in the late 1970s and the United States more centrally through the effort embodied in President Reagan's campaign of military revitalization, including SDI, to shift the very nature of the global superpower military balance – it remained in place in 1985 when Mikhail Gorbachev took office. In the final section of this chapter we shall discuss the implications of Gorbachev's 'new thinking' and the revolutionary events of 1989–90 in Eastern Europe for expanding the cooperative aspects of the Soviet–US relations in the region.

THE EAST EUROPEAN REVOLUTION AND EXPANDED SUPERPOWER COOPERATION

Since 1985 when Mikhail Gorbachev assumed the leadership of the Communist Party in the Soviet Union – and even more since the spring of 1989 – revolutionary changes have occurred within Eastern Europe which are fundamentally transforming the European security system and the competitive-cooperative relationship between the two superpowers. At the beginning of 1989 Soviet leader Mikhail Gorbachev found only limited support among the communist political elites of Eastern Europe for his conception of political reform. Only the communist party leaderships in Poland and Hungary could be viewed as committed reformers. Elsewhere the concept of reform received mixed reactions: little more than lip service in Bulgaria, sharp criticism in Czechoslovakia and the GDR, or outright condemnation in Romania. Even in Poland and Hungary the pace of reform was slow and seemed on the verge of stalling. By the end of the year a Solidarity government ruled Poland, the Berlin

Wall had fallen and German reunification was but a matter of time, Ceaucescu's dictatorship had been overthrown in a bloody revolution in Romania, a world-renowned dissident playwright, Vaclav Havel, had been elected president in Czechoslovakia, and the Red Army was on the verge of moving out of much of the region at local request. Revolutionary change – in the full sense of the term 'revolutionary' – was in progress throughout the region, as the basic structures of domestic political power (including the formal institutions of governance) as well as the structures of the European interstate system were radically changing.

Though the economic and political tensions of forty years of Soviet domination, autocratic rule by local communist elites, and economic mismanagement and corruption had become increasingly apparent throughout Eastern Europe, little overt evidence was visible in early 1989 that events of such import were about to occur – though social pressures were building that would explode later in the year. Central to the dramatic changes throughout the region that resulted in the end of the Cold War and in the establishment of Eastern Europe's first non-communist governments since the 1940s was the new attitude of the Gorbachev leadership toward the area. In the past any movement toward reform met with strong Soviet resistance. By 1989 Soviet policy had shifted to the point where it encouraged reform and was even willing to accept the reality of expanded pluralism and the demise of communist dictatorships as the price for economic efficiency and political stability in the region and enhanced long-term stable political and economic relationships with the West.[27]

Yet the radical changes that occurred in Eastern Europe after spring 1989 must be viewed within the overall framework of state socialism as it had been institutionalized in the area and of the recent emergence of autonomous social groups demanding an end to communist party dominance and a recognition of the rights and interests of 'the people'. As developed in the Soviet Union in the 1930s under Stalin and in Eastern Europe after its imposition in the late 1940s state socialism consisted of a highly centralized economy that emphasized heavy industry, authoritarian political structures meant to ensure political control by miniscule and illegitimate communist party elites, and a strong dependency or patron–client relationship between the USSR and the smaller communist states of Eastern Europe. However, almost immediately after Stalin's death in 1953 and throughout the ensuing years evidence mounted that demonstrated both the political and the economic weaknesses of the system. Sporadically, though generally unsuccessfully until 1989, attempts were made in various of the countries concerned to reform portions of the state socialist system inherited from Stalin.

After the signing of the Helsinki Accords of 1975 organized movements committed to the protection of political and human rights were active (and under great pressure) in a number of European communist states – KOR in Poland, Charter 77 in Czechoslovakia, and Helsinki Watch groups throughout the region. Usually these groups based their demands for political reform on the commitments made by their governments in Helsinki and on the guarantees of the constitutions of their respective states.

Evidence also mounted throughout much of the region concerning the stagnation of economic growth and the fact that the socialist economies were falling even further behind their capitalist counterparts, including those of the East Asian NICs, in the development and adaptation of modern technology to the production process. In addition, the inability of the state to meet implied social commitments – i.e. the growing shortages of consumer goods and housing, the inability to halt the degradation of the environment, and related problems – contributed to increased dissatisfaction with the existing political system and to the demand for major political change that would extend effective participation beyond the narrow circle of the communist party elite. These attitudes were strengthened by the growing awareness of the success of 'capitalist' Europe in improving living standards.

Even before the emergence to political prominence of Mikhail Gorbachev and 'new thinking' in the USSR evidence existed of a growing awareness of the fundamental nature of the problems facing communist states, the imperatives (and perils) of initiating economic and political reform, and the necessity of expanding flexibility in relations between the USSR and its European allies. Thus, prior to spring 1985 when Gorbachev was elected the new head of the CPSU, the situation throughout much of the region was ripe for political change. However, only since 1985 have the efforts at reform expanded to the dismantling of key elements of the traditional state socialist system – from the dominance of central planning to the emergence of officially sanctioned pluralism and the decline of the dominant role of the communist *nomenklatura*.

Since the Gorbachev reform effort is central to the revolutionary changes that have occurred in Eastern Europe, it is important briefly to outline its most prominent contours. It is essential to recall that, when Gorbachev arrived on the scene in 1985, the Soviet Union was already in the throes of a major crisis. In the economic realm Soviet GNP had stagnated – according to key economic advisor Abel Aganbegyan real growth ceased by the mid-1970s; politically the population gave evidence of increasing levels of political ennui and withdrawal; alcoholism and incompetent medical care resulted in reduced life expectancy, especially among males, and in higher infant mortality rates.[28] Soviet allies in Eastern Europe were suffering from similar problems and had become a growing drain on the Soviet economy; clients in the Third World had proven incapable of establishing stable functioning political or economic systems and contributed to the growing 'costs of empire' for the Soviet state; the exponential growth of Soviet military capabilities had occurred at the expense of other portions of the economy; and many of the assumptions that had undergirded Soviet foreign policy during the Brezhnev years had proven to be false.

It was in this environment that Gorbachev proposed dramatic reforms as a means to rejuvenate the Soviet economic and political system. In effect, the initial Gorbachev message can be summarized as follows: The Soviet Union finds itself in an economic and political crisis situation that undermines its ability to provide basic goods and services to its population and threatens to erode its position as a global power. To deal with this problem revolutionary changes are required within the economy – including decentralization of decision-making, the establishment of competition within the system, the emergence of elements of a market economy, and related changes of a comparably revolutionary character within the context of the Soviet economy. Increased efficiency, enhanced quality, and the reduction of the technological gap with the West are among the central objectives of the economic reform.

Such reforms, however, will inevitably confront opposition within the party-state bureaucracy which benefits greatly from the perquisites associated with the present system. To overcome this opposition *glasnost* (or openness) and democratization will create an alliance between the reform-minded leadership and the masses of the population aimed at exposing the corruption, incompetence, and inefficiencies of the current system and, thus, contributing to the success of the reform effort. Initially, therefore, *glasnost* and democratization were viewed in rather narrow, instrumental terms as the means to facilitate the introduction of radical economic reforms.

There also existed the realization among many of the reformers that the centralization of political power and the absence of political participation and, thus, political responsibility had been key elements in explaining the failure of the Stalinist system. These attitudes contributed to the view that the entire reform movement also included an important political component that would open access to political decision-making to ever broader segments of the population. On the negative side, from their perspective, the reform leadership underestimated the degree to which *glasnost* and democratization would develop a life of their own, as the political agendas of the minority populations – Lithuanians, Armenians, Uzbeks, and others – emerged differently from the agenda of the reformers in Moscow. Yet, this development goes beyond the context of our current discussion, except as it relates to the growing pressures for political change that have impinged upon Gorbachev and his supporters.

Thus, *perestroika*, openness, and democratization have been intimately interrelated ever since the beginning of the Gorbachev reform program. Moreover, 'new thinking' and new behavior in foreign policy have also been an integral part of the Gorbachev reforms. First, the nature, scope, and cost of domestic reform would require an international environment in which the Soviet leadership was not concerned with a new cold war or arms race and would be able to devote more of its attention to the issues associated with reform. Moreover, the costs of Soviet foreign policy would have to be reduced dramatically, given the expanded investment demands of a successful revitalization of the economy. Since the past commitment of extensive resources to allies and clients in Eastern Europe and the Third World had not resulted in politically stable and economically productive states, those commitments would have to be reconsidered and in many cases reduced. Since the expansion of Soviet military capabilities and the building of bigger and better weapons systems had not resulted in expanded security, efforts to achieve security through accommodation and assurance strategies toward the West and, thus, to reduce the military burden would also be essential.

Soviet policy since 1985 has undergone more than mere rhetorical change. The dramatic shift in position on a number of key issues concerning nuclear weapons and arms control by the Gorbachev leadership was essential to the agreement to scrap all intermediate-range nuclear weapons in Europe and Asia. The announcement in December 1988 that the USSR would unilaterally reduce its military strength in Central Europe by 50,000 troops and upwards of 10,000 tanks – and the ongoing implementation of the first stage of that withdrawal – represented yet another shift in Soviet security policy. These moves were apparently meant to accomplish several important objectives. First, they indicated to the West that 'new thinking' in the foreign and security policy areas was more than rhetoric, that it presaged a dramatic shift in the way in which the USSR would deal with the outside world, in particular with the countries of Europe. Secondly, they were meant to encourage the West to enter into a mutual process of arms reduction. A third objective concerned the hope that arms reductions, especially in the conventional area, would eventually bring with them the economic savings required if the domestic program of economic restructuring and reform in the Soviet Union was to succeed.

An important component of Gorbachev's foreign policy initiatives has concerned bilateral relations with the countries of Eastern Europe. After at least 1987 Gorbachev's response to the growing economic and political problems of the region, as well as to the erosion of unity and cohesion within the socialist community, was to call upon the leaderships of the East European countries to reform their own political and economic systems. Unlike past Soviet leaders, Gorbachev argued that ultimately the decision on reform – as other major decisions – must be made by the East Europeans themselves. Moscow no longer viewed itself as the final arbiter of ideological orthodoxy for its East European allies, according to the new interpretation of socialist internationalism – an interpretation verified by Soviet reactions to the revolutionary events of 1989. High-level Soviet officials have stated that the USSR was wrong to intervene militarily in Czechoslovakia in 1968, non-communist governments in Poland and elsewhere have been accepted as partners within the Warsaw Treaty Organization, and Gorbachev himself virtually renounced past Soviet policies in statements made during his visits to Strasbourg and Helsinki in August and October of 1989. Even the integration of its key East European ally, the German Democratic Republic, into a reunited Germany has been acceptable in principle.[29]

Initially it appears that Gorbachev hoped that East European communists could reform their economies and their political systems in a manner to make them viable and productive. However, given the failure of East European communists to accomplish this task and the revolutionary changes that have brought non-communist or coalition governments to power throughout the region, he has accepted the idea of an Eastern Europe comprised of stable, economically efficient, though non-communist, systems as preferable to a continuation of the status quo of the 1980s. The effort to maintain politically illegitimate and economically inefficient regimes in Eastern Europe by force or threat of force has been abandoned in the hope that mutually beneficial relationships can emerge in the future between the Soviet Union and Europe's dominant economic power, Germany, and a revitalized set of 'Finland-like' systems in Eastern Europe.

In a way, by agreeing to dismantle its intermediate-range nuclear weapons, by announcing unilateral cuts in conventional weapons, by declaring its willingness to engage in wide-ranging negotiations for the reduction of strategic nuclear weapons, and by accepting the 'new order' emerging in Eastern Europe as a result of the revolutionary changes of 1989 the Soviets have challenged the very existence of the European security regime that has been in place for more than thirty years. The opportunity now exists of forging cross-alliance agreements that are already resulting in a dramatic lowering of the level of overt hostility in US–Soviet and East–West relations and in the development of a new European security regime in which the divisions of Europe might be appreciably reduced.

The dramatic changes that have occurred in the USSR, in Eastern Europe, and in East–West relations and have led to a changing European international security system are the result of both the domestic imperatives of the communist political systems and the Cold War environment in which they developed. The Cold War, defined in part as the emergence in Europe of a stable security regime that prevented war because of the dangers of escalation to nuclear confrontation, was a necessary condition for the recent revolutionary changes that have occurred in Europe. It created an international environment in which competition was diverted to areas of peripheral concern for both superpowers, though an environment in which ever greater amounts of military capabilities were being created and greater stress placed on domestic economies.

At the same time, however, within both alliance systems domestic political and economic developments ran their own course. In the West extensive political and economic cooperation contributed to an unprecedented expansion of both economic welfare and political participation. In the Soviet Union and Eastern Europe the experiment in applied Marxism-Leninism proved to be a failure. By the 1980s centralized economies could no longer provide adequately for the welfare of their populations (especially when compared with the almost unbridled economic success of Western states) and were faced with even greater demands for real political participation. In many respects George Kennan's prediction of the internal non-viability of the Stalinist political-economic model has proven to be accurate.[30]

As recent developments in both Eastern Europe and the Soviet Union itself imply, a reduction in centralized, authoritarian control within the Soviet bloc will not necessarily result in increased local stability. Traditional conflicts – as those between Magyars and Romanians, Bulgarians and Turks – may well increase, as the heavy hand of Soviet control has relaxed. However, assuming that the West does not attempt to intervene in such conflicts to the disadvantage of the USSR, they need not result in expanded superpower conflict.

The past forty-five years have witnessed a competition for power and influence between the Soviet Union and the United States which began in East-Central Europe and then expanded to cover most of the globe. In the process of pursuing that conflict the two countries have expended a tremendous amount of effort and capabilities. They have contributed to the exacerbation of regional conflicts and to the militarization of other societies. They have also come to the brink of nuclear disaster, as during the Cuban missile crisis. They are now faced with the possibility of resolving at least some of their outstanding differences and building upon the stability of the relationships that have existed in Europe. Serious common problems face both countries – from the threats of nuclear destruction and environmental degradation to the security dangers that might emerge from the unrequited demands of some of the less developed countries. Efforts to solve these and other problems may also contribute to an enhanced level of cooperation in the narrower, or co-valuational, sense of the term.

In sum, we currently live in a period when dramatic changes in US–Soviet relations are possible. Cooperation, in the sense of agreements based on shared values, seems more feasible now than it has been in the past. This does not mean that the two major global powers will not continue to compete and that their objectives will not come into conflict with one another. What it does mean is the possibility, especially in Europe, of expanding the arena in which their interests coincide and cooperation is possible.

NOTES

1. See the classic treatment of the process in Hugh Seton-Watson, *The East European Revolution* (New York: Frederick A. Praeger, 1956), 3rd edn. See, also, Zbigniew Brzezinski, *The Soviet Bloc: Unity and Conflict* (Cambridge: Harvard University Press, 1967), rev. edn.
2. See Vojtech Mastny, *Russia's Road to the Cold War* (New York: Columbia University Press, 1979).
3. Charles Gati, 'From Cold War Origins to Détente: Introduction to the International Politics of Eastern Europe', in Charles Gati (ed.), *The International Politics of Eastern Europe* (New York: Praeger, 1976), p. 6.
4. The following discussion of Soviet objectives draws on James F. Brown, 'Soviet Interests and Policies in Eastern Europe', in Richard D. Vine (ed.), *Soviet–East European Relations as a Problem for the West* (London/New York: Croom Helm, 1987), pp. 43–5; and Sarah Meiklejohn Terry, 'The Soviet Union and Eastern Europe: Implications of US Policy', in Dan Caldwell (ed.), *Soviet International Behavior and US Policy Options* (Lexington, MA/Toronto: Lexington Books, 1985), pp. 11–26.
5. Ibid., p. 31.
6. On the policy of differentiation see Charles Gati, *Hungary and the Soviet Bloc* (Durham: Duke University Press, 1986), pp. 219–20; Bennett Kovrig, *The Myths of Liberation: East-Central Europe in US Diplomacy and Politics since 1941* (Baltimore/London: The Johns Hopkins University Press, 1973), *passim*; and John Lewis Gaddis, *Strategies of Containment: A Critical Appraisal of Postwar American National Security Policy* (New York/Oxford: Oxford University Press, 1982), pp. 65–71.
7. Zbigniew Brzezinski and William E. Griffith, 'Peaceful Engagement in Eastern Europe', *Foreign Affairs*, vol. 39, no. 4 (1961), p. 642.
8. See Gati, op. cit., pp. 112–15.
9. An excellent analytic treatment of the crisis appears in Hannes Adomeit, *Soviet Risk-Taking and Crisis Behavior: A Theoretical and Empirical Analysis* (London/Boston: George Allen & Unwin, 1982), pp. 67–182.
10. Ibid, pp. 170–1.
11. Cited in Bruno Kreisky, *Die Herausforderung* (Dusseldorf: Econ, 1963), p. 103.
12. See Kurt Steiner, 'Negotiations for an Austrian State Treaty', in Alexander L. George, Philip J. Farley, and Alexander Dallin (eds), *US–Soviet Security Cooperation: Achievements, Failures, Lessons* (New York/Oxford: Oxford University Press, 1988), pp. 106–22.
13. A. W. DePorte, *Europe Between the Superpowers: The Enduring Balance* (New Haven/London: Yale University Press, 1979), pp. 165–6.
14. The following discussion benefits from Adomeit, *Soviet Risk-Taking and Crisis Behavior*.
15. Theodore C. Sorensen, *Kennedy* (New York: Harper & Row, 1965), pp. 593–4.

16. This discussion draws on Karen Dawisha, *The Kremlin and the Prague Spring* (Berkeley/London: University of California Press, 1984); Galia Golan, *Reform Rule in Czechoslovakia, 1968–1969* (Cambridge: Cambridge University Press, 1973); and H. Gordon Skilling, *Czechoslovakia's Interrupted Revolution* (Princeton: Princeton University Press, 1976).
17. This discussion draws from Roger E. Kanet 'The Polish Crisis and Poland's "Allies": The Soviet and East European Response to Events in Poland', in Jack Bielasiak and Maurice D. Simon (eds), *Polish Politics: Edge of the Abyss* (New York: Praeger, 1984), pp. 317–44, among other sources.
18. John L. Gaddis, 'The Evolution of US Policy Goals Toward the USSR in the Postwar Era', in Seweryn Bialer and Michael Mandelbaum (eds), *Gorbachev's Russia and American Foreign Policy* (Boulder, CO: Westview Press, 1988), p. 327.
19. On the role of Eastern Europe in the Third World, see Roger E. Kanet, 'Eastern Europe and the Third World: The Expanding Relationship', in Michael J. Sodaro and Sharon L. Wolchik (eds), *Foreign and Domestic Policy in Eastern Europe in the 1980s: Trends and Prospects* (London: Macmillan; New York: St. Martin's Press, 1983), pp. 234–59.
20. On the concept of 'spheres of influence' see Roger E. Kanet, 'Esferas de Influencia de la Política Exterior Soviética', *Foro Internacional*, vol. 14, no. 2 (1973), pp. 220–34; and Bennett Kovrig, 'Spheres of Influence: A Reassessment', *Survey*, no. 70/71 (1969), pp. 102–20. During the past two years official Soviet views of Eastern Europe have changed markedly. See note 28, below.
21. This coincides with Alexander George conclusions in 'Crisis Prevention Reexamined', in Alexander L. George (ed.), *Managing US–Soviet Rivalry: Problems of Crisis Prevention* (Boulder, CO: Westview Press, 1979), p. 384.
22. For an argument in favor of linkage in policy toward the USSR written several years later see Helmut Sonnenfeldt, 'Linkage: A Strategy for Tempering Soviet Antagonisms', *NATO Review*, vol. XXVII, no. 1 (1979), pp. 3–5, 21–2.
23. For the discussion of these rules see Seweryn Bialer, 'Lessons of History: Soviet–American Relations in the Postwar Era', in Arnold L. Horelick (ed.), *US–Soviet Relations: The Next Phase* (Ithaca/London: Cornell University Press, 1986), p. 91; and Alexander L. George, 'US–Soviet Efforts to Cooperate in Crisis Management and Crisis Avoidance', in George, Farley, and Dallin (eds), *US–Soviet Security Cooperation*, pp. 583–4.
24. Secretary of State James Baker, 'Points of Mutual Advantage: Perestroika and American Foreign Policy', *US Department of State, Current Policy*, no. 1213 (1989).
25. On the Basic Principles see Alexander L. George, 'The Basic Principles Agreement of 1972: Origins and Expectations', in George (ed.), *Managing US–Soviet Rivalry*, pp. 107–18.
26. On the Berlin negotiations see Jonathan Dean, 'Berlin in a Divided

Germany: An Evolving International Regime', in George, Farley, and Dallin (eds), *US–Soviet Security Cooperation*, pp. 83–105.

27.   During his address to the Council of Europe parliamentary assembly in Strasbourg on 6 July 1989 Gorbachev said: 'Social and political orders in one country or another have changed in the past and may change in the future. But this is exclusively the affair of the people of that country and is their choice. Any interference in the domestic affairs and any attempts to restrict the sovereignty of states – friends, allies, and others – are inadmissible.' *Pravda*, 7 July 1989. During a visit to Helsinki in October, he repeated his argument and set up Soviet–Finnish relations as a model for 'relations between a big country and a small country, a model of relations between states with different social systems, a model of relations between neighbors', *New York Times*, 26 October 1989, p. 7.

28.   This discussion draws from a number of sources. Especially important are Mikhail Gorbachev, *Perestroika: New Thinking for Our Country and the World* (New York: Harper & Row, 1987); Abel Aganbegyan, *The Economic Challenge of Perestroika* (Bloomington-Indianapolis: Indiana University Press, 1988); Tat'iana I. Zaslavskaia, *A Voice of Reform: Essays By Tat'iana I. Zaslavskaia* (Armonk, NY/London: M. E. Sharpe, 1989); Ed A. Hewett, *Reforming the Soviet Economy: Equality versus Efficiency* (Washington, DC: The Brookings Institution, 1988); and Jerry F. Hough, *Opening up the Soviet Economy* (Washington, DC: The Brookings Institution, 1988).

29.   For a perceptive analysis of recent Soviet–East European relations see Charles Gati, *The Bloc That Failed: Soviet–East European Relations in Transition* (Bloomington-Indianapolis: Indiana University Press, 1990).

30.   Kennan's 1947 'Mr X' article on containment is reprinted in Charles Gati (ed.), *Caging the Bear: Containment and the Cold War* (Indianapolis/New York: Bobbs-Merrill, 1974).

5 Superpower Cooperation in the Middle East
Galia Golan

BACKGROUND

The area of the Fertile Crescent, as well as the Middle East more generally, has been of importance to both superpowers. It has not, however, been of top priority for either. Mainly the conflicts in the region explain why it has been upon occasion catapulted to primary significance and urgency. Thus regional volatility shaped the interests of both superpowers, influencing their behavior as well as the nature of their commitments.

In so far as the United States had allies in the region, and its European allies had vital interests there, Washington had certain commitments to the area. These commitments were the product of a number of factors, not all of which were necessarily, nor always, connected to superpower competition. For many years the US commitment was the product of American loyalty and credibility with regard to its European allies and their requirements in the region. There was also an ideological, possibly moral, obligation to Israel as the only Western-style, Western-oriented democracy in the region. Certain domestic forces within the United States favored these commitments. In addition to the Jewish population and its lobby, there was a more general perception that the United States had an obligation to the cradle of the Judeo-Christian religions and Western values.

The American commitment was, however, linked to another set of factors or interests. There was a strategic interest connected with the protection of the southern flank of NATO, the deployment of the Navy's Sixth Fleet, and containment of Soviet forces. A political interest was generated by the competition with the Soviet Union, composed of both denial of access or expansion of the communist world and the extension of Western influence. An economic interest was linked to the supply of oil vital to Western Europe, Japan, and, though not vital, the United States.

The American perception of these interests and the degree of the commitment varied according to a number of factors. The first was the overall foreign policy line at any given time, for example, isolationism, Dulles's rollback policy (i.e. the creation of a network of alliances surrounding the Soviet bloc), the 'post-Vietnam syndrome' and so forth. A second factor was the interplay of bureaucratic or institutional forces, which included the State Department, the Defense department, the White House, and Congress. A third factor may have been the personalities of decision-makers from Truman to Reagan, or foreign policy advisors such as Secretaries of State Dulles or Kissinger. The priority of the region depended to a large degree upon all of these factors, that is, how each administration judged its various commitments, juggled bureaucratic differences, and viewed the superpower contest.

Soviet interests also fell into a number of categories, not all of which were directly connected with the superpower competition. Moscow had traditional interests in this area to the south of its borders. An area of security was sought in protection of the border; at the least the exclusion of hostile forces close to the southern border was sought. It was also the access route to and from the warm waters of the Mediterranean, vital not only for Soviet seafarers to exit the Black Sea but also for potential enemies to enter the Black Sea by way of the Dardanelles. There was also the ideological superpower interest in extending Soviet influence, possibly revolution, and to squeeze out first Britain then the United States, i.e. the West. Additionally, just as the United States had a commitment to Western-style democracy in Israel, in time the Soviets became committed to what they saw as progressive regimes in the area. One might interpret this in ideological or superpower terms; in either case it was basically a political interest.

Strategic interests eventually became a central factor in the Soviet commitment to the area. As Soviet military doctrine underwent changes, the region assumed importance for the forward deployment of the fleet, for anti-submarine warfare for power-projection as well as access denial. Gradually the Persian Gulf–Indian Ocean area assumed greater importance with regard to most of these strategic interests. The economic interest was generally secondary, although the heightened importance of this factor in Soviet foreign policy from the early 1970s onward affected Soviet interests in the region. While it generated an interest in hard-currency arms sales, the rise of the economic factor also contributed to a shift of primary interest from the Fertile Crescent to the wealthier states of the Persian Gulf area.

The Soviet perception of these interests and the degree of their commitment varied, as in the case of the United States, according to a number of basically domestic factors. The overall line in foreign policy was crucial, be it the idea of *détente*, the attitude toward the Third World, interest (or lack of interest) in promoting revolution, the priority of economics and what might be called a 'Soviet Union first' attitude. Bureaucratic politics or at least differing opinions, for example, between elements of the military such as the navy, or party ideologists, and/or pro-détentists had some effect. As in the case of the United States, personalities may have played a role, particularly with regard to Stalin and Khrushchev, and other officials involved such as Defense Minister Grechko or Commander of the Navy Gorshkov.

Each superpower had interests specifically defined in terms of the other superpower. For the Soviet Union this was the interest in removing the West from the region, limiting Western power, and gaining positions *vis-à-vis* the West for strategic, political, or ideological reasons. For the United States this was the interest in preventing the Soviet Union from taking over the region, halting the spread of communism, protecting the free world, and gaining positions *vis-à-vis* the Soviet Union. These too were for political, ideological, and strategic as well as economic reasons.

What provided priority for the region in the superpower relationship was the very fact that both superpowers were directly involved and committed in the region. This gave the area its high-risk quality for each superpower. Yet risk-taking on the part of each was often greater here than in a number of other Third World areas or conflicts. This was evidenced by such risk-related moves as the American landing in Lebanon in 1958, the use of the 'hot line' and US alerts in the 1967 Six-Day War, the initiation of Defcon-3 during the 1973 Yom Kippur War, and on the Soviet side, the missile threat of 1956, the assumption of Egyptian air defense and the introduction of SA-3s in 1970, the alerts and threats of the 1967 and particularly the 1973 wars. There were also the movements of the fleets of both countries in the Mediterranean at times of crisis and the actual presence of military personnel of both countries in Lebanon in the aftermath of the 1982 Israeli invasion. Precisely because the superpowers were both directly involved, the stakes were particularly high. And this in itself may have explained the readiness of both to engage in high-risk behavior, although the same circumstances dictated a large degree of risk avoidance.

This situation was the result of the fact that both superpowers, willingly or willfully, or not, became entangled in the Arab–Israeli conflict in pursuit of their own interests. This entanglement or attempt to manipulate and benefit from the conflict may have been more reluctant on the part of the United States than the Soviet Union. Given Britain's commitment to the Arab world, and American interests there as well, Washington only sporadically and relatively belatedly became Israel's primary champion. Surmounting hesitations regarding the creation of the state of Israel, the United States refused support of the Jews in the 1948–9 war and attempted to maintain an even-handed policy even after Israel abandoned its neutrality in favor of the United States in the Korean war. This was particularly apparent in the 1956 Suez-Sinai conflict and its immediate aftermath, when the United States applied strong pressures on Israel to desist from battle and return the territories taken during the conflict. Washington carefully avoided becoming Israel's sole or even main arms supplier, until France abandoned its unwritten alliance with Israel in 1967.

The Soviet Union too only belatedly grasped the potential of the Arab–Israeli conflict for promoting its superpower interests. Even after Soviet–Israeli relations cooled in the 1949–52 period, Moscow abstained from any support for the Arabs' positions in the context of the Arab–Israeli conflict. Stalin perceived the Arab world as basically belonging to the Western camp, ignoring what he dismissed as bourgeois, therefore pro-Western, forces such as the Free Officers who ultimately brought Nasser to power in Egypt after their revolution in 1952. It was only after the death of Stalin, and the change in Soviet policy toward the Third World altogether under Malenkov and Khrushchev, that Moscow had room for the bourgeois nationalist regimes emerging in the Arab world. Only then did the Arab–Israeli conflict appear an attractive vehicle for Soviet competition with the West, with Moscow backing the Arab states against the Western ally, Israel.

Yet as each superpower became involved, locked in competition on opposing sides, the risks as well as the stakes tied them into some mutual as well as competing interests. The principal such interest was stability, at least in the sense of avoiding escalation and direct military confrontation between the Soviet Union and the United States. The perception of what this meant, how far one was willing to go to achieve or preserve stability, just what each was willing to risk or the price each was willing to pay, were a matter of interpretation.

Nonetheless, this mutual interest did lead both superpowers to what George Breslauer has called *competitive collaboration* or the type of cooperation posited by this volume.[1] It was cooperation perhaps mainly of a tacit type, but it included instances of explicit cooperation as well.

INSTANCES OF COOPERATION

The following is a list of instances of cooperation, or attempts at cooperation, between the Soviet Union and the United States in the Arab–Israeli conflict up to the Gorbachev period. In addition to the occasions listed below, there were numerous points of tacit agreement on specific issues, the most important of which will be discussed below. Similarly, there were unilateral proposals presented by the United States, but they are excluded from the following list because they did not entail or propose cooperation with the Soviet Union.

Type of cooperation	Event
Tacit	End of British Mandate in Palestine – creation of the State of Israel
Tacit	Response to nationalization of Suez Canal
Explicit	Suez War and Sinai Campaign
Explicit unilateral attempt	1957 Soviet proposal for Four-Power Talks
Tacit	Pre-Six-Day War Crisis 1967
Explicit unilateral attempt	May 1967 Johnson proposal to Kosygin
Explicit	Six-Day War
Explicit	1967–70 negotiations: Glassboro talks; Resolution 242; two-power talks; four-power talks; Rogers Initiative.
Explicit/tacit	War of Attrition
Tacit	1971 prevention of war
Explicit	1972 Moscow Summit
Tacit	1973 prevention of war
Tacit	Outbreak of Yom Kippur War
Explicit	Yom Kippur War
Explicit	Geneva Conference
Explicit/tacit	Israeli–Egyptian, Israeli–Syrian Disengagement Agreements
Tacit	1974–5 preservation of cease-fires

Tacit	1973–7 moderation of PLO
Explicit	1977 efforts to resume Geneva joint
	Soviet–American Statement
Tacit	Israeli–Syrian missile crisis in
	Lebanon
Tacit/explicit	Lebanon War of 1982
Explicit unilateral attempt	Brezhnev Peace Plan of 1982
Tacit/explicit	American–Soviet presence in
	Lebanon
Explicit unilateral attempt	Soviet Peace Plan of 1984

Two examples from the earlier, less known period, reveal certain principles and even patterns of Soviet–American cooperation which became more distinct later, in the Brezhnev years.[2] The first instance of cooperation occurred at the very beginning of the Arab–Israeli conflict, when in 1947 the United Nations dealt with the future of the British Mandate in Palestine and the two peoples there. Despite the nascent Cold War, each of the two superpowers supported termination of the British Mandate and the plan to partition Palestine. They did so, however, for entirely different reasons. The Soviets had a Cold War objective in that they viewed the decision as an opportunity to reduce the British presence in the Middle East. Given the long-term as well as short-term nature of this objective, Moscow sought to limit the damage to future relations with the Arabs by initially favoring a solution short of partition, in the form of a bi-national state. The basically pro-British orientation of the Arab regimes at the time led Moscow, nevertheless, to support the Jews – temporarily – as the protagonist which clearly would not perpetuate British domination of the area.

Appreciating Moscow's intentions, the British sought to enlist American opposition to partition on Cold War grounds, arguing that support for the Jews would mean a zero-sum gain for the Soviets in the form of a new Marxist state in the region. The United States, however, chose the path of tacit cooperation with the Soviet Union, against its ally Britain, and in part against the advice of State and Defense Department officials concerned with US interests in the Arab world, in particular, the well-being of Western oil interests. Washington did so in the main for basically humanitarian reasons which were fortified by strong public sentiment in the United States in favor of the Jews. But it also saw the potential strategic and political advantage to what was already understood to be a Western-style democracy with strong links to American Jewry and, presumably, the United States itself. Unwilling to alienate the Arabs further, and harm Britain, the United States refrained from additional cooperation with regard to arms or other assistance to the Jews during the war. Acting more directly against Soviet interests, they sought a reduced role in the area for any UN body which included the Soviet Union, and on this basis resisted the dispatch of a UN force to impose peace. Thus Soviet–American cooperation was short-lived and purely tacit. It was fortuitous rather than intended, but nonetheless crucial to the decisions ending the British Mandate and permitting the creation of the State of Israel.

The nationalization of the Suez Canal by Nasser in 1956 once again placed the United States in a position of tacit cooperation with the Soviet Union at the expense of Britain, as well as Washington's other allies, France and Israel.[3] The two superpowers clearly differed in their attitude to the move itself. Washington obviously opposed Nasser's act designed to evict the British, while Moscow clearly welcomed the anti-colonial step. Yet they had one shared objective: to seek a negotiated solution to the crisis rather than a military move on the part of Britain and France. At the same time the Soviets had an additional objective, which was also operative during the earlier Mandate/Partition crisis, of achieving an active role as a co-participant with recognition of its legitimate interests in the region. These objectives led Moscow to join talks in London, even when its client, Egypt, refused to take part. And both Washington and Moscow sought to prolong negotiations in hopes that Britain's propensity for military action would be dissipated. At the same time both countries communicated directly with France and Britain in an effort to forestall such action.

Tacit cooperation became explicit following the outbreak of hostilities, although the Americans were initially unwilling to undertake explicit cooperation against their allies. Indeed the Soviets were not certain whether the United States would or would not stand by its allies. The Soviet proposals for cooperation for a cease-fire through the United Nations, and, later, the proposal for the dispatch of a joint Soviet–American force may actually have been intended only to embarrass or even test the United States. With regard to the cease-fire proposal, however, there were mutual Soviet–American interests in damage limitation, prevention of escalation, and the restoration of order. As a result, there was explicit cooperation, despite the involvement and opposition of America's allies.

On the matter of a joint force, US Ambassador to Moscow Bohlen expressed incredulity that the Soviets even thought that he would convey such a proposal to his superiors in Washington. Whatever the American response, the Soviets stood to gain. The expected US refusal would link Washington with the aggressive acts of its allies while the unlikely possibility of US agreement would create a serious rift in the Western alliance. In either case Moscow demonstrated its loyalty to the Third World victim and 'peace-loving' policy. However disingenuous the Soviet proposal was, it was accompanied by threatening messages to the British, French and Israelis, in what was a multi-sided effort to play a pivotal role in resolving the conflict. The threats as well as the proposal for a joint force were also gratuitous, however, for they came late, at a time when the crisis was nearing conclusion, to a large degree because of American pressure on its allies rather than any Soviet moves. Moreover, the threats elicited a confrontational response from Washington, which promised retaliation should Moscow try to implement its threats against Britain and France. This too was mainly gratuitous, for the Americans were most likely well aware of the Soviets' strategic and logistic weaknesses which rendered a Soviet military move, by missiles as threatened or by a military intervention in the field, close to impossible. It did demonstrate, however, the limits America placed on superpower cooperation when its own allies faced apparent danger. Even short of this, Washington most likely viewed its unilateral actions (pressures on Britain) as more important than the incidental, albeit explicit, cooperation with Moscow in the United Nations.

Something of a pattern in at least Soviet, if not American, behavior was set in the Suez crisis. Tacit cooperation would gradually become explicit as a new confrontation would simultaneously be accompanied by contradictory proposals for collaboration in a highly competitive context. This pattern repeated itself in the Six-Day and Yom Kippur wars, and to a much lesser degree in the 1982 Lebanon war.[4] If Soviet threats were often made, they usually arrived late, after the critical point in the fighting had passed. They usually did not prevent Soviet cooperation in seeking a cease-fire. In the interwar periods throughout the Brezhnev period, explicit attempts to promote a settlement of the Arab–Israeli conflict were superimposed upon nonetheless competitive relations, while both tacit and explicit cooperation were employed to maintain stability in the region.

For example, the period following the Six-Day War was one of acute Soviet–American competition, with each superpower fortifying literally with arms its relationship with its clients. Yet it was also one of the few periods of extended, explicit Soviet–American cooperation, as both superpowers sought a settlement of the Arab–Israeli conflict.[5] There is some question as to just how intensely or earnestly either superpower pursued this goal. It has been argued that the United States was preoccupied with Vietnam and could not, therefore, undertake a major, complicated diplomatic move in the Middle East. Under the increasing influence of Kissinger's policies, Washington eschewed cooperation, and postponed progress toward a settlement, in favor of an attempt to win Egypt away from the Soviet Union. The Soviet Union, for its part, may have considered continuation of the conflict situation beneficial to the pursuit of its interests in the region, at least in the early Brezhnev years.

THE CHOICE FOR COOPERATION

The major factor accounting for Soviet–US cooperation, be it explicit or tacit, was a mutual interest in preventing escalation of the conflict to the point of superpower confrontation. Under Khrushchev there had been the Soviet belief in the inevitability of escalation of local wars. Although Khrushchev's successors loosened this formula somewhat, they shared with the United States a concern that Israeli–Arab war might escalate. Both superpowers feared the necessity of intervening in the event of such a war. Both had to accommodate their own clients for the sake of credibility as patron and ally. The Soviets had the additional concern, however, that their client might shift to the other superpower. Both also sought to protect their weapons systems from capture and inspection by the ally of the other superpower.

A second factor dictating cooperation was the mutual interest, in the 1967–70 period, in stability and the achievement of a settlement in the area. Both superpowers had witnessed the ease and speed with which the Arab–Israeli conflict could and did break out into war. The lessons of the 1967 war pointed to both the lack of control in the hands of the superpowers and the risks of rapid escalation, from the outbreak of war to the possibility of superpower involvement. They also shared a concern over the arms race, Moscow because of the costs involved at the time, Washington because its supplies of advanced equipment to Israel conflicted with its other Middle East interests. The Soviets sought stability and quiet for the building of their naval and air bases in Egypt (in connection with their Mediterranean Squadron). They also were anxious to prevent another military débâcle on the part of their Arab allies, not only because of the costs of rearming but also because of the blow to the prestige and credibility of Soviet training and equipment. The Soviets apparently had little faith in the military abilities of the Arab armed forces. At the same time, the Soviet Union sought international recognition and legitimacy for its Middle East presence and interests. The United States, for its part, was additionally motivated by its concern over the ability of its ally, Israel, to sustain a long mobilization of its citizen army and to withstand a prolonged war and extensive loss of lives. Moreover, the polarization of the conflict hampered American interests in the region and relations with the Arab world.

After 1970 the superpowers had the additional mutual interest of preventing damage to their emerging *détente*. Polarization, such as that caused by instability and conflict in the area, threatened the atmosphere necessary for economic and other types of cooperation at the global level; it also encouraged opponents to *détente* within both countries. The superpowers may also have begun to share a concern over nuclearization of the Arab–Israeli conflict. Late in the 1970s the United States had a further interest in a settlement: Washington sought legitimacy for its clients, which by then included Egypt. It needed support for the Camp David accords and acknowledgement of the efficacy of its role as peace-maker. A settlement would allow Washington to regularize its relations with the Arab world.

On the Soviet side, there was concern over the growing independence of its Arab clients. Petro-dollar aid from the oil-producing countries contributed to this independence, as did increasing American inroads into the Arab world following the 1973 war. Diminishing Soviet influence was thus compounded by American gains in a zero-sum type competition. At the same time, Soviet interests were shifting. The focal point of military-strategic competition with the Americans was moving toward the Indian Ocea (due to a large degree to the Trident missile), while certain advances in Soviet military technology and logistics were reducing (somewhat) the need for sea and air facilities in the eastern Mediterranean. Furthermore, economic interests were beginning to dominate Soviet Third World policy in the early 1970s, generating a shift of Soviet interests to the Persian Gulf area, as distinct from the Fertile Crescent, in pursuit of the more favorable trade relationships obtainable from the wealthier oil-producing states. On the basis of a cost/benefit analysis, the Soviets had reason to share the American preference for a settlement of the Arab–Israeli conflict, provided they were a party to such a settlement.

What explains the choice of explicit over tacit cooperation or why did one or the other superpower decide to cooperate – or not – with the other? With regard to the United States, there was the claim made by Egyptian editor Heikal to Kissinger that to make war one needed the Soviets, to make peace one needed the Americans. If this were indeed true, one might conclude that in prewar periods of crisis the Americans would approach the Russians in an effort to prevent the outbreak of war, while in periods of peace negotiations they would not do so. In fact, this was only partially the case. There were occasions of overt moves by Washington to Moscow in order to prevent escalation once a war began. There was a value to explicit cooperation for the purpose of restraining the superpowers' clients once conflict broke out, but this did not occur in the prewar crisis period. In most if not all of the prewar crises there was only tacit cooperation. Moreover, there were also occasions, sometimes brief, upon which the United States pursued explicit cooperation with Moscow in peace negotiations, for example in 1967–70, postwar 1973, and 1977, rather than merely tolerating or preferring purely tacit cooperation.

The American choice of explicit or tacit cooperation would appear to depend upon four variables: (a) the overall policy of Washington toward the Soviet Union at the time, and, in particular, with regard to cooperation in Third World regional conflicts versus Cold War competition; (b) Washington's interest (or lack of interest) in linkage, that is, the extension of *détente* cooperation at the global level to regions where the United States itself was most active (such as the Middle East) as well as to areas where the Soviet Union was the more involved; (c) the estimate in Washington concerning the possibility of gaining US objectives without Soviet participation; and (d) the degree of urgency of the situation or seriousness of the American interest in achieving a settlement and, the counterpart of this, the US estimate as to the probability of a successful outcome to its efforts. In view of the domestic problems connected with pressing for a settlement, such as estimate was particularly important. American priorities were of the essence. Kissinger, for example, eschewed explicit cooperation except during war itself, believing that the United States could achieve a settlement without Moscow and could, thus, reduce

Soviet regional power in a zero-sum-game approach. Yet early in the Nixon administration, when Rogers had greater influence, there was willingness to engage in explicit cooperation, despite Kissinger's position. Under Carter and Johnson explicit cooperation was pursued, whereas the periods of Eisenhower, Ford and Reagan, Soviet overtures for explicit cooperation were rejected, with the exception, once again, of brief and limited cooperation in time of actual war.

The Soviet Union, as the United States, needed explicit cooperation in order to restrain both sides and prevent escalation in times of war. Explicit cooperation to prevent a war or to achieve a settlement was, however, subject to a number of considerations: (a) the overall attitude of Moscow toward cooperation with the United States, before and during *détente*. This may, in turn, have been affected by the balance of opinions within the Soviet leadership at any given time, that is, the relative strength of the pro-*détentists* versus the anti-*détentists*; (b) the Soviet estimate as to the urgency and probability of achieving a settlement. Whereas the United States had to weigh the domestic costs of dealing with this issue, the Soviets had to weigh the costs in Moscow's relations with its Arab allies. However, when Moscow accorded priority to a settlement and/or viewed it as probable, it sought explicit cooperation, for a settlement was unobtainable without Washington, at any time; (c) American mediation successes and inroads into the area. Moscow tended to raise its commitments and/or arms supplies at such times, presumably to compete with Washington, but this was also accompanied by efforts for explicit cooperation; (d) Soviet interest in linkage, not in terms of threatening tradeoffs at the expense of *détente* but rather invoking *détente* as a means of preventing American exclusivity. Thus, where linkage was invoked by the US for areas in which Moscow was active but not the Middle East where Washington was pressing forward, so too the Soviets denied linkage in their 'divisibility of *détente*' doctrine with regard to the Third World, but demanded it in the Middle East where they were unsuccessful in their competition with Washington; (e) Soviet search for legitimacy, including recognition of the importance of the area to the Soviet Union as well as of the Soviet Union to the area.

FACTORS DETERMINING SUCCESS OR FAILURE

Most, if not all, of the attempts at explicit superpower cooperation in the Middle East failed, or at best achieved only limited or temporary success. The reasons may be found in a number of factors. The first set are those connected with the willingness, or lack of willingness, of one of the superpowers to cooperate. This may have resulted from the existence of different objectives on the part of each. The Soviet objective was, generally, to achieve and ensure a role and presence in the area. To a large degree Moscow saw cooperation with Washington as a vehicle for remaining in, and even re-entering, the area instead of American exclusivity. The American objective, for the most part, was to remain in the area and remove the Soviet Union. Therefore, Washington more often than not saw cooperation with Moscow only as counterproductive.

The difference in objectives was compounded by the difference in the nature of their competition in the area. The US–Israel relationship made it imperative for the Soviet Union to deal with the United States; Washington was the key to Jerusalem and without this key there could not be stability or a settlement. It was clear that Moscow could not sever the US–Israeli ties, nor constitute an alternative to the United States in the eyes of Israel. Moscow's importance even to its Arab allies was in a way dependent on this US–Israeli alliance, for the Soviets proffered their weighty role *vis-à-vis* Washington as the crucial factor for obtaining US pressures for Israeli concessions. Ultimately and indefinitely the Soviets had to deal with a situation which included the United States in some, preferably limited role.

The United States, however, generally believed that it could deal with the area without the Soviet Union. Washington on many occasions, most notably but not only under Kissinger, did believe that Soviet–Arab relations could be severed. It was entirely possible for the United States to serve as an alternative to the Soviet Union and replace Moscow in the Arab world. The United States was not dependent upon the Soviet Union to reach or influence the other side, that is, the Arabs. Washington could go directly to the Arabs or though its allies in the Arab world – routes which were not open to Moscow. Thus there was a basic asymmetry in the objectives and capabilities of the two superpowers, which evoked opposite attitudes toward cooperation.

Another factor possibly affecting willingness to cooperate was the existence of divisions within the foreign policy decision-making elites. In the Nixon administration Secretary of State William Rogers was an advocate of the cooperative effort with the Soviets for the achievement of a settlement; he also demonstrated a sense of some urgency regarding the need for a solution. Kissinger, as the President's national security adviser, viewed the conflict more in terms of superpower conflict, seeking primarily a means of reducing Soviet influence in the region as elsewhere.[6] As Kissinger's influence in the White House increased over that of Rogers, the United States became far less responsive to Soviet proposals in the negotiations of the late 1960s, seeking rather to gain an advantage over Moscow *vis-à-vis* the parties involved, including Moscow's client, Egypt. The Kissinger–Rogers differences are the most notable, but the Carter administration faced similar problems. Carter's national security adviser Zbigniew Brzezinski had a much less positive view of cooperation with the Soviets than did his secretary of state, Cyrus Vance.[7] At the same time, the differences between Congress's priorities or concerns with regard to Israel and those of the Pentagon may have impeded superpower progress in achieving or sustaining cooperation.[8] The very existence of differences in approach within the American foreign policy elite may have provoked actions which impeded cooperation.

Similar problems existed, apparently, within the Soviet elite. Champions of *détente* had to answer their critics, possibly with more competitive behavior toward the Americans than they, the pro-*détentists*, generally favored.[9] Thus infighting in the Kremlin may have precipitated the type of hard-line position or increased assistance to the Arabs which mitigated against the possibility of cooperation with Washington. Pressures from the military – at least the navy, and, most likely, from Defense Minister and Politburo member Andrei Grechko – not only ignored the possible damage to *détente* but may even have sought to create such impediments to cooperation. Brezhnev had to deal with pressures also from the more ideologically motivated Soviet leaders such as Mikhail Suslov whose interest in promoting revolutionary forces and regimes coincided with – or dictated – opposition to cooperation with the United States. It is even possible that a unique, domestic form of linkage resulted, that is, 'divisibility of *détente*' in the sense of less Soviet cooperation in the Middle East in exchange for a freer hand to pursue *détente* at the superpower level. The fact that such a policy could not work – *détente* at the superpower level could not survive the lack of cooperation at the Third World, in this case, Middle East level – was obviously of little concern to the anti-*détentists* who encouraged the policy. In any case, the need to respond to the pressures of the anti-*détentists* may account in part for either unwillingness to cooperate in the Middle East or in the lack of success or attempts at cooperation.

Another limiting factor may have been the concern of each superpower about the effects or repercussions that cooperation could have had on their respective allies or friends. In 1948 and 1956 American consideration for Britain played a restraining role, limiting if not preventing altogether possibilities for successful or at least explicit cooperation. Later, this may not have been an important factor for Washington, but in the era of *détente* it became an important factor for the Soviet Union. Opponents to Moscow's *détente* policy existed not only within the Kremlin. For the benefit of Soviet interest in the Third World, and as leader of the world Communist movement, Moscow had to be careful not to appear to be selling out to the United States in the Middle East or elsewhere. The Chinese were ever waiting in the wings to exploit any such appearance of Soviet collusion or appeasement.

Yet for both superpowers, a connected but more crucial factor influencing the success or failure of cooperation was the position of each power's own client in the conflict. An important cause of the breakdown of the cases in which there was cooperation was the refusal of the relevant client to accommodate or abide by its patron's policies. Central to this was the degree of control or influence the Soviets had over the Arabs, namely Egypt and Syria, or the United States over Israel. There was a tendency of both superpowers to overestimate not only their own control but particularly that of the other superpower over its clients. Each most likely expected to be able to 'deliver' its own client when mutual Soviet–American agreement was reached, for example in the two-power negotiations of the late 1960s; each probably assumed that the other would be successful in bringing along its client. It was primarily the Soviet failure to bring Egypt along that led the Americans to abandon the cooperative approach at that time. It was American failure to bring the Israelis along, and in view of this the Egyptians, which led to the collapse of the Soviet–American peace effort of 1977.

There was a price to pressuring or trying to force a client into a particular policy; neither superpower could simply impose its will on its allies. An attempt to do so on the part of the United States, for example, would have to contend with domestic American opinion in support of Israel, including support within the US Congress. This support came not only from the 'Jewish lobby' but also from various circles (including the military) within the American public which viewed a strong Israel as an important American asset and accepted Israel's judgement as to just what consituted such strength. The Soviets, too, could not simply impose their will on the Arabs. Aside from the detrimental effect this might have on Soviet relations with other Third World states, such an effort stood a good chance of driving the Arabs into the hands of the United States. Moscow's value to the Arabs was mainly as their principle supporter; if such support were no longer forthcoming there was little to bind the Arabs to the Soviet Union. (Soviet arms supplies and sales were not a sufficient bond; Egypt pursued policies opposed by Moscow despite the latter's imposition of an arms embargo in 1972, and simply transferred to American suppliers when it so desired, despite the problems involved.)

It was also the case that cooperation, either explicit or tacit, broke down, even turning to confrontation, when a superpower sought to pressure the other to gain control of its client. In October 1973, it was the failure of the Americans to obtain genuine Israeli adherence to the Soviet–American cease-fire resolution which led to the panic-stricken Egyptian reaction, Soviet threatening behavior, and the transformation of superpower cooperation into the US Defcon-3 alert and near confrontation. In this and all of the Arab–Israeli wars, the United States was ultimately more willing to pressure its own client, Israel, than the Soviet Union was to pressure its. This may have been because the United States nurtured hopes of reaching the Arabs as well, and indeed did have allies within the Arab world which it had to consider. More likely, however, is the explanation that the Soviet Union, actually, felt more vulnerable inasmuch as its clients maintained the option of shifting to the other superpower – an option not open to Israel.

LESSONS AND RULES OF THE GAME

Years of dealing with each other in this region, competing but yet seeking to avoid confrontation, led each of the superpowers to develop elements of an individual code of behavior and rules of the game between them. These were unwritten, probably unspoken, and possibly merely circumstantial rather than consciously and deliber-ately worked out. Yet they appeared to be recognized and to some degree honored by both powers. The Soviet Union, for example, was generally willing to support its clients' initiation of low-level border warfare (on the Egyptian–Israeli and Syrian–Israeli fronts in the late 1960s, and on the Syrian–Israeli front after the Yom Kippur and Lebanon wars), but it drew the line (or attempted to draw the line) at full-scale war and signs of escalation to higher levels of warfare which might provoke more than sporadic Israeli reprisals. Similarly Soviet deployment of its weapons systems, such as the SAM systems, and the flight patterns of its pilots serving with the Egyptians during the War of Attrition appeared to be limited in a way designed to avoid provocation of the Israelis.

The superpowers appeared to have self-imposed limitations, or something of unwritten rules acceptable to both, regarding the types of weapons to be introduced into the region. Indeed American reaction to the placement of SA-3 missiles in Egypt in 1970 suggested that Washington believed the Soviets had violated these rules, leading, according to some accounts, to American agreement to provide Israel with additional F-4 (Phantom) aircraft and Shrike missiles.[10] American withholding of this and other equipment such as Skyhawk aircraft could be attributed to an interest in improving US relations with the Arabs (a competitive goal), though it may also have been designed to pry concessions from Israel. The decision to provide the F-4s and Shrike missiles, postponed several times, was finally taken in May, after the presence of Soviet pilots in Egypt was detected; it was conveyed to Israel only after the clash between Soviet and Israeli pilots at the end of July 1970.[11] Thus, although the offer was probably meant to persuade Jerusalem to agree to the American proposed cease-fire in the War of Attrition, it also appeared that Washington's reservations about further supplies were finally dispelled by the Soviet's violation of an additional unwritten rule: not to commit superpower personnel to combat in the region. Seeking to avoid an escalatory competition of this type of behavior, however, the Americans – and the Soviets – diplomatically refrained from any public mention of the presence of Soviet pilots or their participation in combat. Indeed the Soviets had partially honored this rule in so far as they had not committed their pilots to engagement with the Israeli air force. The dogfight occurred when Israeli aircraft entered previously avoided Egyptian airspace.

Soviet reluctance to provide Sadat with SCUDs and MiG-23s in the early 1970s may have been part of these self-imposed or tacitly agreed upon limitations, comparable to American hesitation to supply Israel with more than minimal quantities of advanced aircraft.[12] Yet Moscow rejected an American proposal for an arms limitation accord in the late 1960s, agreeing only that an arms embargo be part of an overall settlement. Later, the Soviets believed that Washington had overstepped its limitations when it was rumored to be considering the storing of Pershing missiles in Israel in the early 1980s. Both powers, however, scrupulously adhered to their mutual, albeit possibly tacit, agreement not to introduce or encourage the introduction of nuclear weapons into the region.

In keeping with their mutual restraint, the fleets of both powers limited themselves to intelligence-related activities, avoided provocative behavior *vis-à-vis* each other, and on the whole refrained from any direct involvement in hostilities. (The Soviet navy placed itself in Arab ports or off their shores at various times to deter Israeli attacks, but this did not involve direct intervention in battle.)[13] Rules of conduct in time of war maintained the avoidance of direct military involvement, not only at sea, but these rules may have undergone some change from war to war. The Americans appeared concerned over the Soviet resupply to the Arabs in the Yom Kippur War – Moscow had refused such an effort in the Six-Day War – and Washington responded with its own resupply airlift to Israel. More conciliatory behavior introduced in the 1967 war, however, became a pattern: immediate direct communication between the two super-powers, mutual notification in connection with (most) acts by one power which might be misinterpreted as intervention by the other, and joint action to bring about cease-fires through the restraint of respective clients.

Some of this behavior may have been the result of a learning process on the part of one or both of the superpowers. A lesson vital to cooperation in any form was the lack of control, even influence, each had on its own client. As each superpower learned this about its relationship with its own client, this undoubtedly had an effect on just what each superpower believed it could realistically propose to the other. For the Soviets, the lessons of its inability to control its clients and the demonstrated depth of the American commitment to Israel's survival, together summed up as the perhaps only gradually compre-hended danger of superpower confrontation resulting from this conflict, led to more moderate or realistic negotiating positions designed to reach a settlement. For the Americans, at least under Kissinger and Reagan, the understanding that the Soviet Union had little influence over its clients led to the conviction that Moscow could be excluded from the peace process.

Whether simply a continuation of competition or the result of learning, both superpowers sought to expand their options somewhat by seeking to deal with nations traditionally linked to the other superpower. In the case of the Soviet Union, there was a realization that the kind of Arab unity encouraged at earlier stages tended to augment Arab independence and, therefore, did not always work to the Soviet's advantage. Toward the end of the Brezhnev period there were signs that Moscow had decided to abandon its more militant effort to create a bloc of radical states and, instead, seek a broadening of its options in the area through relations with conservative states such as Jordan and some of the Gulf states.

There are a number of lessons that should have been learned, but it is not certain that they were, in fact, grasped by either side, at least in the pre-Gorbachev period. For example, both the United States and the Soviet Union should have and probably did realize the risks of the arms race in the area, but neither power did more than attempt to slow the race somewhat. With the exception of the withholding of nuclear weapons, each continued to contribute, however reluctantly, to the spiraling arms race. Nor did either act on the conclusion which must have become obvious to them: that control over the supply of arms did not accord them control over client decision-making. Rather, the provision of arms merely encouraged and facilitated the clients' decisions to go to war, while suspension of arms failed to deter at least the Arabs (the effect on Israel was more successful because of Jerusalem's limited alternative sources).

A negative lesson which appears to have been learned by both concerned the absence of linkage. Even hostile superpower competition in the Arab–Israeli context did not significantly interfere with the superpower relationship at the global level; conversely, cooperation at the one level did not necessarily produce cooperation at the other (regional) level.[14] Nonetheless, both the Soviet Union and the United States learned quite early that direct involvement or even the appearance of direct involvement in an Arab–Israeli crisis could lead to superpower confrontation and that, therefore, speedy, direct communication as well as cooperation in damage control and crisis management were essential. They did not, however, take all the measures necessary to create mechanisms for ensuring this; nor did they undertake effective measures for crisis-prevention.

GORBACHEV AND THE FUTURE OF COOPERATION

It is only under Gorbachev that some of the lessons have been fully grasped, revised, or expanded upon. Indeed, emerging changes in Soviet policy toward the Arab–Israeli conflict may be the result of a learning process; certainly factors directly connected with the region have played a role.[15] Yet it would appear that the very interpretation and application of lessons derived from factors specific to the Arab–Israeli conflict are today a function, first of all, of the overall changes in Soviet foreign policy and Moscow's approach to the world under Gorbachev. Virtually every aspect of Gorbachev's 'new thinking' on the world has some application in the Middle East: the theory of interdependence of states and the need for a mutual balance of interests, the priority of domestic considerations (a Soviet Union first attitude), the political resolution of conflict and need for settlement of regional conflicts, the end of the zero-sum game approach to superpower relations, and the 'de-ideolization' of foreign policy.

If 'new thinking' does in fact determine Soviet behavior, then one may expect more explicit cooperation, as distinct from implicit, on the part of the Soviets, based on a new motivating factor. Rather than cooperation superimposed upon competition, apparent throughout the years of 'peaceful coexistence' of the two competing systems, cooperation may in fact become the objective. In terms of the Arab–Israeli conflict, one could pose the following hypothesis: whereas in the past a settlement of the conflict through cooperation was sought by the Soviets as a means of competing with the United States and preserving if not augmenting Soviet assets in the area in a zero-sum relationship with Washington (and was therefore rejected by the Americans), in the conditions of 'new thinking' a settlement is a desirable objective in and of itself, and cooperation is the only way to achieve it. Past concerns that the resolution of the conflict might eliminate a situation which could be exploited to the advantage of Moscow no longer appear relevant in a non-zero-sum situation. The abandonment of competition and ideologically dictated behavior not only permits but even demands the resolution of this regional conflict, for cooperation at the bilateral level of superpower relations, and other related objectives, cannot be achieved in conditions of continued regional strife.

This would appear to be the major lesson Gorbachev has been willing to learn from past Soviet behavior, in this region as well as elsewhere. If cooperation at the superpower level is genuinely sought, competition in regional conflicts is neither tolerable nor, for that matter, necessary. Aside from the perhaps limited concern that this ongoing conflict drains reserves and efforts from the important domestic tasks of *perestroika*, a more profound realization has been that competition with the United States in this region could endanger the economic and other benefits sought and needed from the West, while, as in the past, exploitation of the conflict runs the risk of escalation and superpower confrontation. The past effort to juggle global cooperation with regional competition, relying upon only sporadic, often purely tacit, cooperation to prevent direct confrontation, has been perceived under 'new thinking' as ultimately impossible. Linkage is now clearly recognized, even in the very specific terms of the potential harm to Soviet–US arms agreements such as INF under the circumstances of a continued arms race in the Arab–Israeli context.

Stripped of its global competition component, the Arab–Israeli conflict may become solvable, on the basis of balanced interests. If there is no longer a zero-sum game approach, Moscow need not fear the reactions of its allies in the area, Syria and the PLO, to pressures for greater moderation *vis-à-vis* Israel's interests. The threat of a client shifting to the other superpower becomes inoperative. For this reason, direct American contact with Soviet allies in the conflict becomes tolerable, just as direct Soviet contact with America's ally, Israel, becomes less risky from Moscow's point of view in its relations with the Arabs. Indeed, if settlement of the conflict, rather than competition, is the purpose, an important lesson learned from the past is the necessity of dealing directly with Israel. Presumably the extensive and significant improvement of Soviet–Israeli relations, albeit still short of the resumption of full diplomatic relations, is a sign of such a conclusion.

All of this opens up new prospects for Soviet–American cooperation in the Arab–Israeli context. If the United States becomes convinced that Moscow has abandoned competition in the area, that is, that the Soviet quest for cooperation is no longer directed at blocking American interests, Washington may be more willing to enter into such cooperation. Indeed, a lesson the Americans themselves might now be willing to learn from past experience is that exclusion of the Soviet Union hampers the pursuit of a settlement. Although the United States has in the past been successful in wooing at least one state, Egypt, away from Moscow, there are a number of Arab parties to the conflict, including Washington's own ally, Jordan, which are not willing to reach an agreement without the Soviet Union. Rather than submit to paralysis, out of reluctance to permit any Soviet headway at America's expense, the United States might under the new circumstances be willing to enlist Soviet assistance. A new American attitude toward the Soviets might alter Washington's objections to the convening of an international conference. Yet, by the same token, the change in Moscow's thinking might render such a conference less critical to Soviet policy. If the objective is no longer Soviet participation so as to prevent a *Pax Americana* but rather to achieve a settlement, almost any channel for negotiations should become acceptable. Thus the Afghan and Angolan negotiation models become feasible, and bilateral and multidimensional talks such as US–PLO, USSR–Israel as well as Soviet–US and, possibly, Israeli–Palestinian are added to the usual superpower-client contacts. Both the United States and the Soviet Union would be in a better position to pressure their respective clients, including Syria, once the zero-sum-game pressures were removed. Even the Lebanese conflict might benefit from the superpowers' willingness to cooperate in the Arab–Israeli context. And the role of Egypt as a mediator in the Arab–Israeli context is enhanced by the reduction of Soviet–American hostility.

There are, of course, limitations to the ability of each superpower to bring its clients to accept a solution, but a cooperative venture by the Soviet Union and the United States would be much more difficult to resist than the unilateral proposals or pressure of each separately. Moreover, such cooperation would change both the international and local climate, creating new pressures on the parties involved as well as weakening the forces of rejection in each local camp. The latter could no longer benefit from manipulating the Cold War propensities of the competing superpowers; nor could they hope to gain the support or aid necessary to maintain their intransigence. There have already been some signs of this in reported Soviet cooperation with the West in connection with counter-terrorist measures, including even terrorism employed by Palestinian groups.[16] And Soviet pressures were clearly brought to bear upon the PLO to meet America's specific requirements regarding recognition of Israel's right to exist and renunciation of the use of terror, opening the way for US–PLO talks and American pressures on the Shamir government to alter its positions.

Another area of potential cooperation is that of the arms race in the area. Past tacit cooperation with regard to types and even quantities of weapons supplied to each side might be transformed into formal agreements reached by the superpowers, as often proposed by the United States in the past. Growing Soviet concern not only over the possible nuclearization of the region but also over the appearance of chemical warfare (in the Iraq–Iran and Iraq–Kurd contexts), as well as Iraqi alteration of Soviet equipment (the SCUDs) to extend their range, appear to be of greater concern to the Gorbachev regime than to its predecessors. Israel's development of the Jericho missile, which can target the Soviet Union itself, has prompted some concern, and Foreign Minister Shevardnadze has enunciated Moscow's linkage of the presence of intermediate range missiles (presumably including those provided to Syria by the Russians themselves) in the Middle East with the INF agreement conducted by the two superpowers in 1987. This was, indeed, part of a call for an arms control agreement in the Middle East.[17]

At the same time, however, the 'Soviet Union-first approach' of the Soviet leadership under Gorbachev, that is, the priority given domestic well-being and economic *perestroika* argue for continued arms sales which constitute a serious portion of needed Soviet hard-currency earnings. At the very least, those remaining opponents of 'new thinking' with regard to the Third World (be they elements in the military or ideologists) or even those Russian nationalists who oppose any change in Soviet Middle East policies (preferring strong support for the Arabs over any *rapprochement* with Israel), could use the foreign currency argument against the idea of a Soviet–American arms agreement in the region. *Glasnost* has thus far produced only very limited discussion of Soviet arms sales, even as linkage has been officially advocated.[18] Arms control in the region, therefore, would have to be made somehow economically attractive. One possible direction this might take is suggested by the nascent economic arrangements initiated with Israel, particularly in the areas of Israeli technology and agricultural know-how. Introduction of the United States or Europe into this equation might go a long way toward compensating for whatever economic advantages Moscow might lose from reduced arms sales to the region.

Finally, crisis prevention could be approached cooperatively. Shevardnadze, while in the Middle East in January 1989, proposed the creation of a regional military risk-reduction center, as well as the idea of on-site monitoring and other security arrangements.[19] While these suggestions related primarily to Israel's demands for security in the event of a settlement of the conflict, they might be taken as the nucleus of crisis-prevention measures even prior to a settlement. Whether a purely Soviet–American device, or within some UN or regional framework, an on-the-spot crisis prevention mechanism would provide for immediate, direct communication and cooperation presumably at an early enough stage to prevent a budding crisis from escalating or developing into hostilities. If the basic superpower relationship is one of cooperation rather than zero-sum-game competition, this kind of communication and joint effort might provide guarantees to the local parties that pre-emption would be unnecessary. Provided there is superpower trust that mutual cooperation will outweight loyalty to one or the other local adversary, the presence of both powers might well forestall precipitous action. Israel is wary of placing its security in the hands of any other body or nation; it presumably would remain suspicious of Moscow's loyalties. Nonetheless, determined and clearly joint actions, directed not only at restraining the parties involved in an equal and impartial manner, but also at allaying the fears of each, might provide the type of security necessary for a permanent settlement of the conflict.

NOTES

1. George Breslauer, 'Soviet Policy in the Middle East, 1967–1972: Unalterable Antagonism or Collaborative Competition?', in A. George, *Managing US–Soviet Rivalry* (Boulder, CO: Westview, 1983), pp. 65–103
2. For the earliest period, see Christopher Sykes, *Crossroads to Israel* (London: Collins, 1965); Yaacov Ro'i, *Soviet Decision-Making in Practice* (New Brunswick: Transaction Books, 1980); Jacob Hurewitz, *Middle East Dilemmas: The Background of United States Policy* (New York: Harper, 1953).
3. Superpower behavior in this crisis is discussed in Peter Calvocoressi, *Suez Ten Years After* (London: BBC, 1967); Carol Ann Fisher and Fred Krinsky, *Middle East in Crisis: A Historical and Documentary Review* (Syracuse: University of Syracuse Press, 1959); Ilan Troen and Moshe Shemesh, *The Suez–Sinai Crisis: A Retrospective* (London: Frank Cass, forthcoming); Mohamed Heikal, *Sphinx and Commissar: The Rise and Fall of Soviet Influence in the Middle East* (London: Collins, 1978); Yaacov Ro'i, *From Encroachment to Involvement: A Documentary Study of Soviet Policy in the Middle East, 1945–1973* (New York: John Wiley, 1974); Oles Smolansky, 'Moscow and the Suez Crisis 1956: A Reappraisal', *Political Science Quarterly*, vol. 80, no. 4 (December 1965), pp. 581–605; Hugh Thomas, *Suez* (New York: Harper and Row, 1967).

4. For the Six-Day War see Michael Brecher, *Decisions in Israel's Foreign Policy* (New Haven: Yale University Press, 1975); Arnold Horelick, 'Soviet Policy in the Middle East', in Paul Hammond and Sidney Alexander (eds), *Political Dynamics in the Middle East* (New York: American Elsevier, 1972); pp. 581–91; Lyndon Baines Johnson, *The Vantage Point* (New York: Holt, Rinehart and Winston, 1971); Walter Laquer, *The Struggle for the Middle East: The Soviet Union in the Middle East, 1958–1968* (London: Routledge and Kegan Paul, 1969); William Quandt, *Decade of Decisions: American Policy Toward the Arab–Israeli Conflict, 1967–1976* Berkeley: University of California Press, 1977). For the Yom Kippur War, see Galia Golan, *Yom Kippur and After: The Soviet Union and the Middle East Crisis* (Cambridge: Cambridge University Press, 1977); Mohamed Heikal, *The Road to Ramadan* (New York: Quadrangle Books, 1975); Marvin Kalb and Bernard Kalb, *Kissinger* (Boston: Little, Brown, 1974); Quandt, *Decade of Decisions*, Henry Kissinger, *The White House Years* (Boston: Little, Brown, 1979). For the Lebanon War see, Galia Golan, 'The Soviet Union and the Israel Action in Lebanon', *International Affairs*, vol. 59 (Winter 1982), pp. 7–16; Dina Spechler, 'The Politics of Intervention: The Soviet Union and the Crisis in Lebanon', *Studies in Comparative Communism*, vol. XX, no. 22 (Summer 1987), pp. 115–43.

5. For these negotiations see, Breslauer, 'Soviet Policy in the Middle East'; Quandt, *Decade of Decisions*; Lawrence Whetten, *The Canal War: Four Power Conflict in the Middle East* (Boston: MIT University Press, 1974).

6. For a discussion of this, see Breslauer, 'Soviet Policy in the Middle East', and Quandt, *Decade of Decisions*. See also Henry Kissinger, *The White House Years*, pp. 569–73.

7. See William Quandt, *Camp David: Peacemaking and Politics* (Washington, DC: Brookings Institution, 1986), pp. 39–40.

8. George Kent, 'Congress and American Middle East Policy', in W. A. Belirᵉ (ed.), *The Middle East: Quest for an American Policy* (New York: State University of New York Press, 1973); Robert Hunter, 'American Policy in the Middle East', *Royal Central Asian Journal*, vol. 55 (October 1968), pp. 265–75; William Quandt, 'The Middle East Conflict in US Strategy, 1970–1971', *Journal of Palestine Studies*, vol. 1 (1971), pp. 39–52.

9. Galia Golan, 'Soviet Decision-Making in the Yom Kippur War', in Jiri Valenta and William Potter (eds), *Soviet Decisionmaking for National Security* (London: George Allen and Unwin, 1983), pp. 185–217; Galia Golan, *The Soviet Union and National Liberation Movements in the Third World* (London: Unwin and Hyman, 1988); Dina Spechler, *Domestic Influences on Soviet Foreign Policy* (New York: University Press of America, 1978); Spechler, 'The Politics of Intervention'. pp. 115–43.

10. Quandt, *Decade of Decisions*, pp. 81, 88.

11. Ibid., pp. 81–103.

12. Golan, *Yom Kippur and After*, Chapter 2; John Glassman, *Arms for*

the Arabs (Baltimore, MD: Johns Hopkins University Press, 1975); Anwar Sadat, *In Search of Identity: An Autobiography* (New York: Harper and Row, 1977); Mohamed Heikal, *Road to Ramadan* (New York: Ballantine Books, 1975).

13. For analysis of naval 'rules of the game', see Bradford Dismukes and James McConnell (eds), *Soviet Naval Diplomacy* (New York: Pergamon Press, 1979), pp. 240–80.

14. For a detailed examination of the question of linkage in the 1970s, see Galia Golan, 'The Arab–Israeli Conflict in Soviet–US Relations', in Yaacov Ro'i, *The Limits to Power* (London: Croom-Helm, 1979), pp. 7–31.

15. For a somewhat different analysis of these, see George Breslauer, 'Learning in Soviet Policy Toward the Arab–Israeli Conflict', in George Breslauer and Philip Tetlock, *Learning in US and Soviet Foreign Policy* (forthcoming).

16. Cited in Galia Golan, *Gorbachev's 'New Thinking' on Terrorism* (New York: Praeger and the Center for Strategic and International Studies, 1990), pp. 54–64.

17. TASS, 23 February 1989 (Shevardnadze speech in Cairo).

18. Hinted at by Foreign Ministry official Andrei Kozyrev, 'Confidence and the Balance of Interests', *Mezhdunarodnaia zhizn'*, no. 10 (October 1988), pp. 3–12, and by Evgenii Primakov, 'Sovetskaia politika v regionalnikh konfliktakh', *Mezhdunarodnaia zhizn'*, no. 5 (May 1988), pp. 3–9, when he was still head of the Institute for World Economy and International Relations. The subject was somewhat more directly addressed by Africa Institute Director Anatoli Gromyko in a published dialogue with visiting American scholars. He called for the Soviet Union and the United States to discuss an end to the 'flow of arms' into the Third World, 'where most of the regional conflicts were occurring'. A Foreign Ministry-*Mezhdunarodnaia zhizn'* symposium later in 1988 went much further, devoting a good deal of attention to the Soviet Union's contribution to the arms race in the Third World. Deputy head of the Africa Institute, Alexei Vasilyev, along with Oleg Peresypkin, rector of the Foreign Ministry's Diplomacy Institute, and Victor Kremenyuk, shortly to become Deputy Director of the Institute for the Study of the United States and Canada, all called for a cutback in Soviet arms deliveries to conflict areas, arguing that little political influence could be gained by such deliveries. Peresypkin called upon the Soviet Union to 'discard double moral standards' whereby it spoke of resolving conflicts but went on supplying arms.

19. TASS, 29 January 1989.

6 Superpower Cooperation in North Africa and the Horn
I. William Zartman

There is no better example of the contrasts of competition in Soviet–American relations than the evolving situations in the two northern corners of Africa. Northwest Africa, or the Maghrib, is a region of enough importance to both the United States and the USSR for the states of the region to balance their relations successfully with both superpowers so as to keep them interested suitors but never fully engaged. There is little prospect for change in this pattern as the world moves toward greater cooperation, and yet it can serve as a good example for other regions which have not yet arrived at this state of cooperation. Northeast Africa, or the Horn, is a region of greater importance to the superpowers, who have divided it into clients, if not satellites. However, despite their deep engagement, the superpowers actually changed partners with relative ease in the 1970s, as the region was engrossed in its own turmoil. Yet the superpowers were only scrambling to hang on; it was the regional states that made their own shifts, for reasons of domestic and intra-regional politics. Because of these characteristics, there are more lessons for change and cooperation in the Horn than in the Maghrib, although of course no assurance that they will be learned or applied.

This chapter contrasts these two regions in their handling of Soviet and American interests and relations, and then turns to the degree of competition, cooperation and conflict that has been found there, with an explanation of the particular levels found in the two regions. It examines the Maghrib first, and then the Horn, before turning to a combined conclusion that analyzes and evaluates possibilities for the future.

SUPERPOWER INTEREST IN NORTH AFRICA

North Africa has been of only secondary importance to both the

United States and the Soviet Union, its value depending above all on its relation to somewhere else. As a self-identifying and interactive – and even integrating – region, the Maghrib compounds the importance of its member states by making relations with any of them impinge on relations with all of them and with the other broader Arab and African regions with which the countries identify. The Maghribi states are of interest to the United States and the USSR as part of the Mideast and Africa, but even more so as the southern flank of the Mediterranean.

The Maghrib has long been America's entry point to the Mideast and Africa. From the Barbary pirates and the shores of Tripoli to the Vichy forces of 'Casablanca' and the North African landings, the US has met North Africa on the way to other areas, such as Europe or the eastern Mediterranean. In the postwar period, North Africa is important as a source of support or resistance to American policies toward the Arab–Israeli dispute, toward African security issues, and toward Third World (G-77) questions, as well as toward a wider range of general foreign policy matters.[1] Morocco has a special position in this array of concerns, since it has long institutionalized its World War II beachhead role by serving as an American military foothold on the African continent. For two decades after the war, it hosted US naval and air bases, and then revived this role again in the 1980s.[2] But this position merely reinforces the secondary nature of US interests, for the bases are now staging facilities for the Mideast Rapid Deployment Force, a stepping stone to somewhere else. The two-decade interim between the two periods when Morocco had US bases or facilities was a time when Spain filled the need, showing that Morocco's strategic importance to the US is not absolute but conditioned by the availability of alternatives.

Other aspects of US interest in the region are also variable and of relatively low priority. The United States has been Algeria's primary trading partner during some of the high oil price years, but none of the Maghrib countries ranks very high in US economic interests. Nor are social ties or domestic clientele interests high in importance to the US; other Arab countries are closed to the US and France is still the closest country of the West to North Africa.

It is the sea that gives the Maghrib its greatest value to the US.[3] Much of this value is pre-emptive, since the United States has no naval bases or facilities in the region. It is of great importance that the Soviets not have such bases either. But it is also important that the states of the south shore not try to establish their own regime for the sea, limiting its free naval use to littoral members, for example, or decreeing it a nuclear-free zone. Free access to the Mediterranean for merchant and naval vessels is a vital interest for the US. It allows direct contact with equally vital land areas at the other end of the sea, and direct communication and cooperation with NATO allies and other associates on all four shores, from Spain clockwise around the sea to Egypt. Through the Suez Canal, US commercial and naval power reaches into the Arabian Sea. Thus, the southern shore may be passively neutral but not actively so for that would deny the strategic use of the lake to external powers such as the United States; similarly, friendliness to the Soviet Union beyond normal port visits would also put North African states in conflict with US interests.

Soviet interests in the region are much the reverse.[4] Direct economic, social and political affinities with North African states are few. The USSR has benefitted from hard-currency arms purchases by Algeria and above all Libya, but these countries are not major Soviet trading partners. No Maghribi state, not even Libya, has had any deep ideological resemblance to the heartland of communism. In the strict sense of the word, Libya may be a Soviet client and Algeria a Soviet military client, but neither is a satellite. Although there has been much military cooperation with Libya, the Soviet Union has never been able to obtain bases there, nor *a fortiori* in Algeria. Libyan foreign policy has often been on a parallel course with that of the Soviets, but Libya does not do the Soviets' bidding. Similarly, the USSR has often held positions close to Algeria's, but that is a case of coincidence not alliance. At most, Algeria and Libya, because of this coincidence and the understanding of Soviet positions that it provides, give the USSR an entrée into Third World fora.

Although closer ties and military cooperation with Maghribi countries could provide the Soviet Union with stepping stones to the Atlantic, much as cooperation with the US provides a path to the Middle East, that close cooperation does not exist. As a result, Soviet relations with the region are carried out at a minimal level for their own sake and for the general access to the Third World circle that they may provide, rather than as a stepping stone to a geographic area. More than its land value, however, it is the relation to the seas that makes the Maghrib attractive to the USSR. One of the seas is the Atlantic, not for its naval value but for its content of fish that the Soviets consume; the other sea is the Mediterranean, which represents one of the avenues of exit from the Soviet heartland. It is of vital interest to the USSR to keep the Mediterranean from being a

NATO lake from which it would be excluded, and therefore of vital interest to preserve neutralism and non-alignment on the southern shore, even if bases and facilities are not made available. The Soviet position is more precarious than the American, since it has no naval base west of Latakia, whereas the US and its NATO allies hold almost the entire northern shore. On the other hand, neutralist surges in the past, involving Algeria and Libya, have tried to exclude from naval use of the sea all countries not on its shores or its tributaries – that is, exclude the US but not the USSR. There seems to be little support for such measures at the beginning of the 1990s, however.

The Mediterranean, therefore, is a lifeline for the Soviet Union as it is for the United States, although of somewhat different dimensions. For the US it represents a direct access route to the Levant and Israel and also to the very (Black Sea) shores of the Soviet Union; it is also a short cut to the Arabian Gulf and the Indian Ocean, vital for rapid access even if not the only path. For the USSR, the Mediterranean is the only way out of rimland encirclement between the frozen north of the Baltic and the Arctic, and the frozen east of the seas of Japan and Okhtosk. Without Mediterranean access, the USSR is bottled in; without Mediterranean access, the US is bottled out. Thus, each has a separate interest in keeping the other out. But both have a joint interest in keeping the sea open. As the world moves from Cold War to *glasnost*, this Prisoner's Dilemma becomes easier to move to at least tacit cooperation.

THE SUPERPOWERS AND NORTH AFRICAN AUTONOMY

East–West relations with the Maghrib have been a mixture of competition and tolerance, unmarred by any shadow of cooperation. North Africa was a French and British preserve at the end of World War II, and only the Algerian nationalists' warm relations with the East during their revolutionary war (1954–62) changed that picture at the time of independence. The Soviet Union was distinctly unwelcome in monarchical Libya during the 1950s and 1960s. It was admitted for its threat value as an alternative source of arms and political relations by Morocco and Tunisia, but between France and the United States the West was generally attentive enough to the two states' basic needs and the Soviet Union unforthcoming enough to keep the threat within bounds. Morocco bought some Soviet arms, Tunisia did not, and both countries developed a small amount of trade.

Algeria – especially through the Trotskyite heyday of Ben Bella (1962–5) – admitted Soviet advisors and set the pattern for arms dependence on the USSR that continues to this day, but the advisors were kept at arm's length, and trade in non-military items remained secondary in importance. It soon became clear that Algeria's primary foreign policy goals were leadership of the Third World along paths blazed by its own experience and restoration of a privileged relation with France to resolve its primary outstanding issues.[5] That left little place for the Soviet Union (or the United States).

In all cases, Soviet relations have been falling off rather than intensifying, while relations with the US have been greatly intensifying (often to the discomfiture of the French). Only in the case of republican Libya have ties with the Soviet Union gradually been reinforced, changing from one of the East–West poles that the Third Way sought to avoid to the major superpower support for a policy aimed above all at countering perceived American imperialism (and all its other minions). Yet, again except for Libya, these varied relations with the USSR were observed and tolerated by the West from its dominant position (just as in Libya, the USSR tolerated remaining Western contacts – primarily economic – with its client).

There has never been any cooperation or coordination between the Soviet Union and the West (US and France) on any element of relations with North Africa. At most, there may have been some tacit unilateral coordination of aid projects, as the US Aid Mission or the Soviet bilateral commissions take each other's activities into account to avoid duplication. Some aid projects may involve conscious competition – for example, technical education in Algeria. But even competition is lacking in general. Although the two camps (or even different members within the pluralist West) are certain to bring different development formulas, for example, or different foreign policy platforms, these broad policy orientations are domestic choices in North Africa, where broad political positions are rather well developed. Embassies will weigh in competitively on specific issues but have little influence over broad orientations. The USSR may not have approved of structural adjustment for more efficient development, with its corollary of privatization and state divestment, but Maghribi membership in the Western (global) economic system and the dependence on Western aid gives the USSR little leverage behind its views (even if they were to have proven successful somewhere). The limits of even the most tacit coordination appeared during the American bombing raid on Libya in April 1986. The Soviet ship offshore in the Gulf of Sirte made no effort to come to Libya's defense, but instead was lit up like a Christmas tree so that American planes could be sure to avoid it. Generally, other aspects of Soviet activities in North Africa have followed the same patterns of avoiding contact with the West. Except for rhetoric on foreign policy issues, the Soviets and the West have avoided cooperation, coordination, or even competition within North Africa.

Not only has there been general coexistence throughout North Africa, but it has also been peaceful. Although the region is not without its share of conflicts, they have not become battlefields of the Cold War, even in the Brezhnevian era of the early 1980s. Despite some rich potentialities, neither the Western Saharan nor the Chadian conflicts, nor any of the lesser inter-Maghribi disputes, has been polarized into an East–West confrontation. In both of the two major conflicts, opposing sides fought with Soviet and Western armaments, and they were supported in the UN and other foreign policy fora by opposing Cold War camps. Yet the Soviet arms came only indirectly to the combatants, passing through Libya and on to the Transitional National Unity Government (GUNT) in Chad and the Popular Front for the Liberation of Saqiet el-Hamra and Rio de Oro (Polisario) in the Western Sahara, although Libya itself was also directly involved in Chad. Furthermore, the USSR never recognized the Sahrawi Arab Democratic Republic (SADR) of the Polisario nor even the Polisario as a national liberation movement, nor did it recognize the Libyan claim over the Aouzou Strip of Chad nor the continuing claim of the GUNT to be the government of Chad. Despite a woolly leftism on the part of the GUNT and Polisario leaders, neither of them became a Marxist-Leninist movement or even a Third World socialist organization. The same is true of Libya and Algeria in the course of the 1980s, as they pulled away from earlier orientations. Algeria has gradually dropped socialism from its national Charter and Leninist party notions from its constitution, in 1985 and 1988 respectively, and Libya, while sidling closer to the USSR from a formerly independent Third Way, has nonetheless remained unrecognizable to any Communist criteria and is never referred to by the Soviets as a socialist system. In a word, Soviet identification with its own 'side' in the conflict is weak.

Western identification with its 'side' is more direct but still not deep. Neither the United States nor anyone else has recognized Moroccan sovereignty over the Western Sahara, only its administrative control, until the long-planned referendum of self-determination is held. US and French *matériel* backs the Moroccan claim, but US military attachés do not travel to the Western Sahara. The US and France are much more direct in their support of the internationally recognized government of Hissene Habre in Chad, although they differ slightly in tactics. But since the Soviet identification with the opponents is distant, the Western support for the government in both cases does not make for an East–West conflict. Furthermore, in the Saharan case at least, the US has made no effort to portray the Polisario as a player in a Cold War dispute. The same is not true of Libya, of course, but it is of the GUNT in Chad, which is seen as an agent of Libya but not of the USSR.

The only East–West conflict in North Africa concerns Libya. Here the conflict is neither direct nor of US–Soviet origin, but rather derives from conflicting policies with regard to the Libyan regime. Where the Soviet Union gives support to shared Third World and East–West policy positions and to a revolutionary regime under fire from the West, the US – particularly under the Reagan administration – has used Qaddafi's regime as its whipping boy for the Middle East, a scapegoat for the greater evils of other less vulnerable actors such as Syria and Iran. The demonstration effect was deemed useful to American foreign policy, although it reinforced the Libyan–Soviet ties up to a certain point.[6] Yet the Soviet Union was wary of too close association, and after the American raid in 1986 it publicly counselled Libya against foreign policy adventurism rather than coming across with more tangible support. Since 1986, all parties pulled back from the confrontation until the very end of the Reagan administration, when the issue of the Libyan chemical warfare plant arose. President Reagan announced that another raid was one of the conceivable – and momentarily rejected – options, and the Soviet Union expressed doubts that the plant was capable of making chemical weapons at all. The incident blew away, unresolved, in the change of administrations. In sum, Qaddafi's Libya was useful to Reagan's policy, for it was symbolic of a hardline opponent in the Middle East and gave the US the opportunity to show how far it could go in response (even if the response was inapplicable to other countries).

To the Soviet Union, Libya was less useful. As long as it refused to concede a naval base, it could not replace the lost facilities of Alexandria, which was the hope that turned the USSR to Libya in the first place in the mid-1970s. Short of that close cooperation, Qaddafi was a loose cannon, a potential embarrassment to the Soviet Union and more and more so as the pragmatism and conciliation of *glasnost* took over. Libya's usefulness to each of the great powers was not dependent on its usefulness to the other, and too great attachment to the Soviet Union of Gorbachev might actually impede his other policies. Libya was not a major East–West conflict issue, despite the rhetoric.

The one aspect of the region that is characterized by a strong amount of both coordination and conflict is the Mediterranean Sea. In many ways, the maritime picture is the same as the terrestrial situation: predominant Western presence, shared strategic importance, competitive coexistence, danger of collision, impossibility of unilateral exclusion, and mutual interest in avoiding direct confrontation, among others. The difference between East–West relations on land and sea is that the Mediterranean is covered by a tacit set of rules of the road that regulate coexistence and prevent collision. They begin with standard maritime rules, which have traditionally been established to regulate responsibilities and expectations, but they extend to less formal and less explicit rules of coexistence on a busy thoroughfare for Soviet and NATO warships. While these rules have not prevented frequent incidents and more frequent close calls, they have been effective both in avoiding worse conflicts and in minimizing those which nonetheless occur, to the point where one can accurately speak of a Mediterranean naval regime.

Such a regime has not prevented either party from carrying out its policies as it deems necessary, nor even from testing the limits of the regimes and needling the other party within its restrictions at times when it was useful to wave the threat of greater conflict. Indeed, the regime itself has served the useful purpose; it not only limits accidental conflict and regulates coexistence, but also, by establishing such regulations, it allows a clearer distinction between accidental and purposeful conflict, making signals in either direction clearer and less ambiguous. The success of a regime on the sea can have possible implications for similar regulation of activities and expectations on the land.

In fact, some very rudimentary rules of the road may already exist in North Africa.[7] They are scarcely comprehensive enough to be called a regime, and they are probably not specific or limited to the Maghrib. They begin with an avoidance of direct confrontation, based on an understanding that the region is not important enough or secure enough to warrant direct challenges between the US and the USSR. This rule in turn implies deference before the party that gets there first, with 'there' identified according to both activity and level of intensity; this prevents ratcheting escalation. A third proto-rule is that intentions should be announced so that there are no surprises; parties use 'brakelights' and 'turn-signals' to avoid collisions. Finally, as seen, neither of the superpowers identifies fully with any Maghribi state and its policies, so that Maghribi conflicts with superpowers do not engage other superpowers, nor do Maghribi conflicts with other Maghribi states. Yet these rules are minimal, implicit, and inchoate. They do not explain the level of East–West coexistence in North Africa.

Part of the explanation comes from the strong position of the states of North Africa themselves. Although new in modern terms, these states have a historic and established identity; although developing, they still have the means to carry out an autonomous policy. Neither ideologically nor practically are they dependent on the USA or the USSR for their existence, orientation, approval or policies. More so than many states of the Third World, they have a sense of their national interests and an established policy tradition. Second, for all the conflicts that trouble the region, there is nonetheless a sense of limitation, operating within a sense of regional brotherhood.[8] Brotherhood and unity should not be taken too euphorically. One should also remember the Maghribi segmentarian saying, 'My cousins and I against the outside, my brothers and I against my cousins, myself against my brothers.' North African conflicts have not involved the direct intra-regional confrontation of a Kampuchea, Ogaden or Angola; the longest one, in the Sahara, is a proxy war in which direct combat between Moroccans and Algerians is explicitly excluded by regularly renewed rules of the game; and one member state, Tunisia, periodically rises in Maghribi circles to plead unity when the centrifugal forces of conflict threaten to tear the region apart. Third, the Maghribi states have been extremely skillful in crosslinking the superpowers so that none is free of ties with its ally's enemy.[9] These ties tend to be commercial, contrary to the politico-ideological ties with the ally, and they make it too expensive for any superpower to side unequivocally with any one North African state and polarize the region. Behind the commercial ties between Morocco and the USSR, Algeria and the USA, and even Libya and Europe, however, is also a desire not to alienate an important political actor on the southern shore of the Mediterranean.

In sum, North African states themselves have generally worked to keep the Cold War out of the region, and in their various conflicts have not sought to borrow power competitively from the US and the USSR to the point where they polarize their relations. They have their own interests and issues, and at the same time seek to manipulate the context to favor them; superpowers, like others, do their best to maintain good relations with North African states and are forced by them to take North African interests into account. Algeria, with its feisty independence, and Morocco, with its pursuit of its 'national integrity' (Saharan) issue to the point even of a pact with the Libyan devil, are cases where North African states followed the dictates of their own interests, as they saw them, even against the wishes of the superpower friends. Even Libya, usually the odd man out, fits this characterization. Despite the American pressure, Qaddafi has not always fostered Soviets' interests and has thereby kept the relationship more distant than it otherwise might have been. At the other extreme, even when Morocco granted the US standby facilities for the Rapid Deployment Force, with the admitted risks that this posed for King Hassan, it did so under its own terms and in the process gave itself more leverage over the US than the reverse. North African interests determine the strength and direction of East–West relationships, and none of the parties sees its interests in polarization.

SUPERPOWER INTERESTS IN THE HORN

The Horn's value to East and West, like the Maghrib's, depends on its relation to somewhere else, but it is much closer by. The Horn is practically part of the Middle East, the Soviet Union's border region and the home of United States' economic and political allies, and the countries of the Horn are key members of Zhigniew Brzezinski's 'arc of crisis'. Curiously, the importance it derives from its position in Africa is only secondary, since Africa is only of secondary importance to the superpowers. Like the Maghrib, the Horn also draws much of its interest to the US and the USSR from its maritime relations, as the western shore of the Red Sea and the Indian Ocean.

American interests in the Horn are by no means historic, but they began with some intensity in the early postwar period,[10] with the disposal of the Italian colonies, and then in the 1950s with the distinguished Ethiopian role in the Korean operation, the friendship treaty of 1951, and the arms and base agreement of 1953. Thereafter, the Ethiopian Empire became a strong American client, with many advisors pressing to move it into the twentieth century. When Sudan became independent in 1956, it maintained good ties with the US, although not of nearly the same intensity, until the leftist interlude that came with Colonel Jaafar Numeiri's coup in 1969. Similarly, American relations with Somalia were friendly upon its accession to independence in 1960, but cooled as early as 1963 when Somalia found the Western arms package inadequate for its irredentist designs. They took another turn for the worse in 1969 as well, when General Mohammed Siad Barre came to power with his own brand of Somali Scientific Socialism, but less active irredentism. Surrounded by hostile countries who were also hostile to the US, Ethiopia was a bastion of anti-communism and stability, strategically located on the Red Sea and its strategic straits of Bab al-Mandeb. Its 25,000-man US-armed army was the biggest and the best in the region, and the Emperor was the Elder Statesman of Elder Statesmen (as well as King of Kings) in the African continent, father of the Charter of the Organization of African Unity (OAU). Only in trade were relations not of the same intensity between the US and Ethiopia, whose historic markets were with Europe instead.

In the 1970s, the kaleidoscope turned and the whole picture changed.[11] On the American side, where the change began, communications satellites made the Kagnew communications station obsolete, and its 25-year agreement was to be allowed to lapse when it expired and gradually to fade out up till then. The Emperor's request in 1973 for an expensive military modernization was therefore turned down. Furthermore, efforts at modernizing were bogging down in the feudal system of the country, and prospects for a smooth and enlightened succession to the aging emperor were dim. Haile Selassie had mediated a settlement of the southern Sudanese war in 1972, and the Sudanese expelled both the Communist party from government in 1971 and the Soviet advisors from the country in 1977, so American relations returned to normal on Ethiopia's western flank. American advisors, however, were dismayed at the emperor's handling of his own catastrophic drought at the same time, and when the issue turned his people and his army against him, the US felt helpless to save him and helpless to set up good relations with his unstable military successors. In December 1976, General Mengistu Haile Mariam contracted an arms agreement with the USSR and in February 1977 massacred his remaining rivals to control the new

People's Democracy of Ethiopia. The US, with its small group of professional Ethiopians, was out, without having put up much struggle.

Instead, the US interest shifted to Somalia, where the Soviet Union had been evicted with similar unceremoniousness. With extraordinary scrupulousness, the US waited for nearly three years until Somalia met American insistence on the removal of Somali troops from Ethiopian soil – part of *Somalia irredenta* – before supplying arms and establishing close relations, including the inheritance of the major Soviet base at Berbera. Having lost its Red Sea position, the US now had an Indian Ocean facility, along with a poor, drought-ridden, unstable, irredentist ally. If some of these characteristics were also to be found in Ethiopia, Somalia had none of the foreign policy clout in its region, where its irredentism made it a pariah. Gradually, the US has been trying to work its way back into Ethiopian graces without offending Somalia, something the USSR had been unable to do (under admittedly different circumstances) in reverse.

Soviet interests in the region are historic. Ethiopia, with its Coptic church and its Christian empire besieged by Muslims, had both traditional relations and affinities with tsarist Russia. Propinquity to the critical region of the Middle East and profession of a local socialism made the chance to develop special relations with the new military regimes of Sudan and Somalia attractive. The USSR had no compunctions about arming irredentist Somalia in 1963, a relation that was eventually to prove its undoing, and it received in turn a base with wharf, runway and storage installations at Berbera on the Gulf of Aden. When a new military regime in Ethiopia overthrew the imperial American client and feudal monarch, proclaimed a socialist workers' state (not just an African socialist government), and then cried for help against a serious invasion in defiance of international law, the Soviet Union saw clear situations that it recognized in its own terms. Soviet specialists on Ethiopia and on Marxism saw the Ethiopian revolution as a replay of the Soviet revolution, *mutatis mutandis*, and they brought heavy pressure on the military committee to set up an Ethiopian Workers' party as their next step to a communist state. For a brief half-year, in mid-1977, they tried to maintain good relations both with Somalia and with Ethiopia, and Soviet President Nikolai Podgorny and Cuban Premier Fidel Castro proposed a socialist confederation of the Horn to overcome the nationalities question. Forgetting that socialist confederations have only been set up by Soviet armies, they failed in this proposal. However, in exchange for Somalia and Berbera, the Soviets received the larger and more influential African leader, Ethiopia, and a new well-equipped Red Sea base on the Dahlak islands. For the enormous arms deliveries for the new Ethiopian army, costing $1.5 billion in 1977–8 and twice that amount again in 1979–86, the USSR received the Ethiopian coffee crop, mortgaged for a long future.[12]

Despite their basic and continuing competition, superpower positions on major regional issues have been very similar. The leading issues are all ones of territory and sovereignty, on which both the US and the USSR subscribe to UN and OAU declaration of *uti possedetis*, colonial state succession, self-determination, and international law. Somalia receives no support from either superpower for its irredentist policy, and superpower positions have not changed with their change in clients. Soviet policy in the late 1960s and 1970s was naive and contradictory on Somali claims, to be sure, since it armed and trained the unnecessarily large Somali army and even the Western Somali Liberation Front (WSLF), but did not support their irredentism. When the Ogaden war broke out, the USSR reaffirmed its lack of support for the Somali claims and urged Siad not to use Soviet arms for the purpose. The USSR paid for its contradiction by being expelled from Somalia. The US position has been equally supportive of established boundaries, in defense of which it provided arms to Ethiopia and Kenya. US policy did not change after the Ethiopian revolution, and the US delayed military aid to Somalia until Somalia had verifiably removed its last troops from Ethiopian territory, the result of some very painful bargaining with Somalia. When the formerly Ethiopian-supported Somalia National Movement (SNM) raised a rebellion in northern Somalia after the conflict management agreement, Ethiopia disassociated itself from the action and the USSR did not support the particularist rebellion either. Both the US and the USSR supported the end of French colonial rule over the Territory of the Afars and Issas and its transformation into independent Djibouti in 1977, and thus again rejected Somali irredentists claims over the territory. In all cases, the recognition of an important principle of conflict reduction in Africa and support of an issue of concern to more African states than Somalia's cause were two important elements in both the US and the Soviet position.

In the southern Sudan, where US–Soviet conflict was less sharp, both superpowers again supported the territorial integrity of the country, although the US may have been somewhat more concerned about the conditions of the southern Sudanese. John Garang, leader of the Sudanese People's Liberation Movement and Army (SPLM/A) claims a certain Marxism but has not benefitted from direct Soviet support; unlike his Anyanya predecessors, his movement claims not to be separatist but revolutionary for all Sudan. There have always been the basic ideological differences between the superpowers in support of various Sudanese positions and issues, but this has not translated into different positions on the basic issues of the south.

The Red Sea is of equal interest to the US and the USSR, for it offers rapid access to the Indian Ocean.[13] But no state in the Horn guarantees access to the Red Sea; they only provide support facilities to back up Soviet bases at Aden and Socotra and US facilities in Mombasa and Ras-al-Banat. Rather, Ethiopia and Somalia, and to a lesser extent Sudan, offer close ties with second-string players on the edge of the Middle East, along the Arc of Crisis. As the history of the region shows, either superpower would be in Ethiopia even if the other were not in the region, but the presence of the other escalates the need in times of Cold War. Yet all of these three states are albatrosses, with tremendous problems of their own that inevitably weigh down their great power patrons. The three are among the world's poorest, with their poverty exacerbated by endemic drought. Each has its own internal rebellion, and each exacerbates its neighbor's rebellion with support, sanctuary, and eventually use as blackmail against the neighbor's similar use. Each has serious problems of instability in its governmental system. Each has a restive military, offended by the inadequacies of the government but bereft of any solution to the basic problems if it were to throw the rascals out. The US and the USSR are caught in a very different situation than in the Maghrib.

US–Soviet relations in the Horn have been those of competition and, indirectly, conflict, with some, but very little, cooperation or coordination. Individual countries were almost the exclusive preserve of the superpower with which they maintained close relations. For long periods during the 1970s and 1980s, the US had no ambassador in Ethiopia, and the embassy staff was rather constrained in its compound. Before the volte-face of 1977, Somalia had had a friendship treaty with the Soviet Union, signed in 1974. Thereafter, it was Ethiopia that had a friendship treaty. During the period of the Soviet treaty with Somalia, the US embassy asked Washington for a more competitive policy challenging the Soviets on their client's turf but were told that Somali support of the USSR and terrorism did not make it worthy of better relations.[14] Even before the Soviets moved in on Ethiopia, the Carter administration implemented a decision of its predecessor and cut off military aid to Ethiopia for human rights abuses, leaving the country to the USSR by default. Once the revolution had fully come to power, the tables were turned: it is the US that has slowly come around to a policy of seeking better relations with Ethiopia, only to find itself blocked by a total absence of Ethiopian receptiveness, other than in words, and particularly by an absence of Ethiopian moves to meet any of the legal requirements for compensation for nationalized property that stand in the way of renewed economic relations. The one area of exception in US–Ethiopian relations concerns drought aid, which the Ethiopians receive in large quantities but often refuse to facilitate or even acknowledge, while the Soviet patron stands by giving little such aid. The broader exception to the absence of East–West cohabitation is Sudan, where warmer relations with the East or the West over the past three decades have not prevented the maintenance of active relations with the other side.

The Horn was the region on which the great debate on linkage was focused, ending in the resignation of Secretary of State Cyrus Vance (ultimately over a different issue, the Iran rescue operation) and in the end of East–West *détente*, 'buried' – as Brzezinski put it – 'in the sands of the Ogaden'. At a time when new Soviet capabilities for intervention were available, along with a legitimate cause for assistance to friendly governments under aggression by invasion by a neighbour, the Soviet Union was willing, after a long debate, to avail itself of a window of opportunity and achieve foreign policy benefits which seemed quicker and surer than the vagaries of *détente*.[15] The rapid intervention of 1,000 Soviet advisors and 11,000 Cuban troops into Ethiopia followed the introduction of larger numbers into Angola beginning in 1975, and was accompanied by a perception (probably quite erroneous) of support for successive invasions of Zaire by rebels from the south in 1977 and 1978. In fact, the military commitment was expensive to the Soviets and unreliable for the African states, and the economic support was kept from being expensive only by being small. Yet indirect confrontation, challenge and replacement were the nature of East–West relations in the Horn.

Despite these pervasive characteristics, there have nonetheless been some rather unusual examples of coordination between the US and the USSR in the region. One was overt and explicit, others less so. In February 1978, as the Ethiopian armies pressed the Somali

invaders back toward their border, the US intervened diplomatically
to keep the pursuers from crossing the frontier and reversing the
aggression.[16] The assurance of respect for the border came from the
Soviet foreign minister. The effort was successful in the short run, for
it was not until four years later, in a somewhat changed context, that
Ethiopian troops with 'their' Somalis crossed the border at two small
salients and camped on Somali soil, reminding Somalia of the
possibility of going further. The 1978 *démarche* was conducted jointly
with the Soviets, even though they were in a very different position
from the Americans in regard to the combat and were indeed seen by
the US as using the conflict to spike the canons of East–West
cooperation. The USSR was, after all, the best advocate for the US
position in the courts of the Derg. Even in the time of the greatest
conflict, there was some cooperation, even explicit. It was the type of
coordination practiced by laywers on behalf of their adversarial
clients, making signals plain and avoiding conflict.

A second case is broader and implicit. On reflection, it is remarkable that the *renversement des alliances* in the Horn in 1977–8 took
place so smoothly. In a remarkably short space of time, the superpowers changed horses in the middle of the stream without a hitch, to
the point where Soviet-supported Ethiopian pilots flying American
planes cleared the sky of American-supported (albeit more lightly)
Somali pilots flying Soviet planes. There were no Soviet–American
incidents, no direct contacts in the changing of the guard, no
obstacles placed by the outgoing patron in the path of the incoming
patron, and yet no real interlude between the tutelage of one patron
and its successor. Horses were changed in mid-stream as if by
established rules of the game, yet nowhere else in Cold War history
has such a double exchange occurred. If the two superpowers were
operating according to some coordinated rules, there is at least no
evidence that they were established for or in the Horn of Africa.
Rather, they were established as a result of a sense of 'rules as you go'
and *ad hoc* rule-respecting so as to avoid direct confrontations,
incidents and accidents. This is the loosest possible meaning of
coordination, according to which parties mutually circumscribe and
reorient behavior so as to avoid conflict. It is the self-coordination of
the pedestrians on the sidewalk.

The third case of coordination is a case of volunteers pushing
stalled cars, as a result of the new, Gorbachev policies. In the first
half of the 1980s, a number of Western countries, notably Britain but
also the US, were instrumental in pressing Siad Barre toward

reconciliation with Kenya. Once this had been accomplished, press-ure was renewed to bring about a softening of Somali policy on the Ogaden, in order to entice a more conciliatory position from Mengistu. Italy was most active in this direction, but the US was also involved. After Siad made his conflict management offer at the IGADD summit in Djibouti in 1986, the ball began an aimless roll in Mengistu's court for two years without a response. At this point, the USSR was the main source of pressure, since many other Western countries – and especially the US – were in no position to claim leverage or even access. These efforts, in turn, came to fruition in 1988, when Mengistu accepted the Somali plan and conflict manage-ment measures were formalized between the two countries, including an agreement to study directly the basic border problem.[17]

Why is the pattern of East–West relations so different in Northeast from Northwest Africa? What can be learned about what to do and what to avoid in creating better patterns of relations? The questions are particularly important since both sides have invested large amounts of resources in aid and arms in the region, passing through a *renversement des alliances* which left them no better off but more deeply engaged. As in the other corner of the continent, much of the explanation comes from the internal position of the states them-selves, in this case very weak. Because of their extreme poverty and underdevelopment, juxtaposed with their high goals and demands on the regional and international system, the states of northeastern Africa had a heavy need for the superpowers and were willing to sell themselves – several times over – to the highest bidder. Sudan has long been the second highest recipient of American aid in Africa (after Egypt); Somalia has also been high on the list from time to time, and Ethiopia's drought-driven needs have returned it to the aid list even after all other forms of relations with the USA were reduced to zero. Somalia was a heavy target of Soviet aid up to the point when it bit the hand that had fed it, after which Ethiopia began to consume unusually larger amounts of Soviet aid, the largest regular annual sums in Africa, and mortgaged its coffee crop in payment of the rest.

Second, other restraining features of the Maghribi system were absent in the Horn. Because of ethnic diversity and centuries-old enmities, there is no sense of regional systemic unity in the Horn. Instead, there is a sense of Muslim encirclement of the Christian highlands, doubled on the north by a sense of Arab colonization of the Black jungles.[18] Similarly, there is no skillful crosslinking of the superpowers so that each has an interest in the neighbor's camp as well. Instead, polarized regional relations polarized global alliances. States of the Horn remained constant enemies; they merely flung their external allies around in function of their enmities. Had the states not been so strategically placed, neither external party would have played the game.

PROSPECTS FOR THE FUTURE

The Cold War has been relatively benevolent in North Africa, and dangerous in the Horn. Is a change for the better conceivable? A change for the worse? And under what conditions can the status quo in the Maghrib serve as an example for other, more polarized regions such as the Horn? The Maghrib of the 1990s has launched itself on another of its efforts to pull together.[19] Faced with the closing of its traditional European market behind the common tariff walls of the European Common Market of 1992, the five Maghrib states formed a Union on 15 February 1989 to develop economic cooperation and to provide a frame for overcoming political conflict. Economic self-support was to offer a new focus that would contain the adventuresome proclivities of Libya's Qaddafi and would encourage progress toward a political solution for the Saharan dispute. Thus, a *détente* in intra-Maghribi tensions parallels the current *détente* in East–West relations. Either *détente* can fall apart, and the effects on each other can be analyzed beforehand. In the Horn, there is a damper on Somali tensions with its neighbors and an amplifier on Sudanese–Ethiopian tension, in contrast to the East–West *détente*.

If both *détentes* continue, they work for the continuation of current conditions in the Maghrib. There is not a large array of new or intensified opportunities for East–West cooperation or even coordination. Whereas some regions of the world might benefit from a coordinated aid effort, or relief measures, or development cooperation, no such possibilities stand out in North Africa. Similarly, whereas some regions could be helped by a coordinated effort of conflict management to overcome a major dispute currently dominating interstate relations, no such challenge appears in the Maghrib. In general, it should be expected that superpower–Maghribi relations would at best continue along the same path as in the past, there being nowhere better to go.

In specific, however, there are a few instances where it may appear that there are opportunities for improvement. One might be the

Saharan conflict.[20] The ups and downs of conflict and conciliation in Western Sahara have shown that third party pressure and mediation were sorely needed at some crucial moments. Yet the superpowers are ill-suited for the mediating role that was finally played effectively by King Fahd of Saudi Arabia, with a little help from Tunisia, and with some crucial technical assistance from the UN Secretary General, Javier Perez de Cuellar, and his office. The superpowers are both too involved and too distant to play either role. At best, but discreetly, they could pressure Algeria and Morocco to accelerate preparations for a referendum. Neither party would want to put teeth on that pressure, for example by holding up arms deliveries or establishing linkage to other elements of their relations, so that the pressure would be only diplomatic.

A second area of activity with slightly greater potentialities, concerns Libya's adventures. It would be useful to have Libya's external patron exert some pressure on its client to calm its encouragement of wayward causes and join a more conventional practice of foreign relations. This is indeed a role that the Soviet Union can play, reinforcing Qaddafi's new policy mood at the end of the 1980s. The USSR has already urged restraint on Libya, particularly after 1986, but it has few means of pressure to make its advice stick. Considering its delicate relations with its client, in which each party is somewhat dissatisfied with the performance of the other, the USSR has little leverage over Libya. Too strong pressure on Libya would do little but convince Libya of the further unreliability of the USSR, with no corresponding gain for either. Only if the USSR were able to cover Libya in exchange for the latter's promise to behave after a specific incident might the calming role be played, and then only lamely, after the fact.

In the Horn there is a real opportunity for East–West cooperation in conflict resolution, in regard to all the conflicts. Coordinated pressure on Sudan and Ethiopia (behind the SPLM/A) by the USA and USSR, respectively, and on Ethiopia and Somalia by the USSR and the USA, respectively, and one superpower's support for the other's mediation efforts between the EPLF and Ethiopia could be effective in moving these conflicts toward management and solution. Such mediations are difficult, and the need for coordinated participation compounds their delicacy. Yet a US role – official or unofficial, as in the mediation attempts of former President Carter in the Eritrean conflict in 1989 – is viewed as legitimate, and someday the Soviet Union may develop a better sense of how to go about doing

the same thing; for the moment it supports the Carter *démarche*.
Improved East–West relations made the concerted efforts leading to
the Mogadishe agreement of 1988 possible, and continued *détente*
should be accompanied by continued pressure to move the conflict
management agreement to conflict resolution. Otherwise, one side or
the other will notice the unfulfilled promise, as it did in the
mid-1970s, and a new crisis will arise. Neither party is very easy to
pressure in the Sudanese dispute, but both superpowers have developed enough distance from their clients to permit them more
freedom of action in pressing for internal changes that would
facilitate an agreement – an end to Ethiopian support for the
SPLM/A and an end to the Sudanese measures of cultural dominance
in the South.[21]

A broader area of US–Soviet cooperation could concern armaments and related items, a matter of concern in regard to the
neighboring regions of the Middle East and even Africa as well.
Currently there is shared concern about missiles and chemical
weapons in the area, particularly in the hands of the Libyans. A
superpower embargo on either item would be useless; since the
tripartite arms embargo on the Middle East of 1950, there are always
alternative suppliers, and particularly small powers now in the arms
business. On the other hand, joint statements, combined monitoring
and generally coordinated diplomacy might have some possibilities.
Had the US and USSR agreed on a common position on the Libyan
chemical plant, the matter might have been handled in a manner both
more conclusive and less hair-raising. There is probably little interest
by any of the parties in a nuclear-free land or sea zone. Nuclear-free
land area must be seen in the Middle East context, for northern
African states – and particularly Libya – will not subscribe unless
Israel does too. The US would also be uninterested in a nuclear-free
area as long as it values the Moroccan air and Somali air and naval
facilities for potential rapid deployment use, and the Soviet Union
might not be interested either as long as its nuclear vessels use Libyan
ports. Similarly, while North African states have subscribed to a
nuclear-free Mediterranean on occasion, there is no support from the
superpowers.

The Mediterranean offers potentialities for cooperation and any
measures about the Western Mediterranean would necessarily involve the Maghrib states. It is in the interest of all to keep the sea
open to all naval and maritime traffic, and also to develop programs
to keep such commerce and also the riparian states from polluting its

waters. Military concerns are more and more a past issue for the western basin, and security is increasingly becoming associated with the issue of resources and pollution. It is the superpowers who would have to make the case for their presence in conferences and cooperative projects dealing with these issues, yet it would be important for them to do so, to learn, to help, and to assure their continuing presence in the sea. They would definitely be the invited, not the invitors, if they were to be present at all, underscoring the independent position of the south- and north-shore states. The Red Sea, on the other hand, would seem to carry fewer chances for cooperation, other than in the basic rules of the road.

However limited, those positive possibilities could be reversed only by a collapse in *détente* on both power levels at the same time, leading to a Horn-like situation. If Maghrib cooperation breaks down, it would not be likely to polarize the region on global dimensions unless East–West cooperation broke down at the same time. Even so, North African states would be expected to revert to their policies of counterbalancing their ties and hobbling the one-sided sympathies of the superpowers. Similarly, if global *détente* collapsed, North African states could be expected to resist superpower attempts to polarize the region or to win over exclusive clients, particularly but not exclusively if Maghrib cooperation remained. If both levels of *détente* collapsed, however, and the world returned to the 1970s, one might see the testy sparring over and among the states of North Africa that would be a far cry from today. The necessary conditions for such an eventuality are distant indeed.

How useful then is the Maghrib as a model for better East–West relations in odd corners of the globe? It does tell us that under certain desirable conditions it is possible for the superpowers to operate within a region, side by side, unequally, but staying out of each other's way. It also suggests that those conditions include strong states with a sense of their own interests joined together within an identifiable region that exerts restraint on the centrifugal temptations of conflict. The region must not be unimportant to superpowers for such conditions to operate smoothly, but it must not be an area of their vital interests that would impel them to seek exclusive advantage. Yet such conditions also mean that superpower roles, both in limiting regional conflict and in promoting cooperation, will be limited, since an absence of clients means an absence of leverage. For other regions that look like that, the Maghrib is an encouraging example.

The Horn, on the other hand, represents a model of what to avoid. Unfortunately, avoidance is not primarily in the hands of the superpowers, except to the extent that they can provide such assistance as to overcome the chronic poverty of the area. Yet such assistance would only augment its dependence, and therefore accentuate its polarization at the same time. The most that can be said of dependence is that it facilitates entry and influence if the patrons were to decide on policies of conflict reduction. The reduction of tensions between the superpowers permits them to run more easily the risks of a loss of clients that such pressures might well entail. If offended clients have nowhere else to go, and if patrons are not strongly competing for clients, superpower mediation becomes easier, even if not easy. An end to regional conflicts, in turn, would permit cooperation and more efficient programs to meet more fundamental needs of the impoverished region. If more strategic conflicts nearby, such as those of the Middle East which give the Horn some of its importance, are reduced or are at least the subject of East–West cooperation, military bases in the Horn may become less necessary. But more importantly, they may become less threatening to the other superpower even if they remain, and that is a more immediate benefit. In other words, reduced East–West tensions may not allow much fruitful East–West cooperation beyond mediation measures, but the greatest benefit may be to allow a more relaxed attitude toward clientship and competition in the region.

NOTES

1. On the USA and North Africa, see Charles Gallagher, *The United States and North Africa* (Cambridge: Harvard University Press, 1963); Richard Parker, *North Africa* (Boulder, CO: Westview Press, 1984); John Damis, 'US–North African Relations', in I. William Zartman and Mark Habeeb (eds), *State and Society in Modern North Africa* (Boulder, CO: Westview Press, 1991, for the Middle East Institute).
2. On the Moroccan bases, see I. William Zartman, *Problems of New Power* (New York: Atherton, 1964), Ch. 2, 'Agreement between the United States and Morocco, . . . 27 May 1982', *US Treaty Series 10399* (Washington: GPO, 1982); *New York Times*, 20 May 1982.
3. See I. William Zartman, 'The Mediterranean: Bridge or Barrier?', *US Naval Institute Proceedings*, vol. XCIII, no. 2 (1967), pp. 63–71; Adachiara Zevi (ed.), *Europa Mediterranea: Quale cooperazione?* (Rome: Istituto Affair Internazionali, 1975); Giacomo Luciani (ed.), *The Mediterranean Region* (New York: St. Martin's Press, 1984).

4. See Carol Saivetz, 'Soviet–Maghribi Relations', in Zartman and Habeeb (eds), op. cit.; I. William Zartman, 'Soviet–Maghribi Relations', in Edward Kolodziej and Roger Kanet (eds), *The Limits of Soviet Power in the Developing World* (Baltimore: The Johns Hopkins University Press, 1989).

5. See John Entelis, *Algeria: The Revolution Institutionalized* (Boulder, CO: Westview Press, 1986); Nicole Grimaud, *La politique étrangère de l'Algérie* (Paris: Karthala, 1984); Bahgat Korany, 'The Foreign Policy of Algeria', in Bahgat Korany and Ali Dessouki (eds), *The Foreign Policy of Arab States* (Boulder, CO: Westview Press, 1990, 2nd edn).

6. See, as a sample, Jay Peterzell, 'The Secret War Against Qaddafy', *The Nation*, 21 January 1984; Alex Rondos and I. William Zartman, 'The US Role in Chad', *The Baltimore Sun*, 3 September 1983; Alex Rondos, 'Why Chad?' *CSIS Africa Notes*, vol. 18 (31 August 1983).

7. On security regimes and other rules of the game see, Cora Bell, *Convention of Crisis: A Study in Diplomatic Management* (New York: Oxford, 1971); Miriam Camps, *Management of Interdependence* (New York: Council of Foreign Relations, 1974); Alexander George (ed.), *Managing US–Soviet Rivalry* (Boulder, CO: Westview Press, 1985); Robert Jervis, 'Security Regimes', *International Organization* vol. XXXVI, no. 2 (1982), pp. 362–8; Robert Jervis, 'From Balance of Concert', *World Politics*, vol. XXXVIII (1985), pp. 58–79.

8. See I. William Zartman, 'The Foreign Relations of North Africa', *The Annals of the American Academy of Political and Social Science*, vol. 489 (1987), pp. 13–27; Mary Jane Deeb, 'The Maghribi Community', in Zartman and Habeeb (eds), op. cit.

9. See I. William Zartman, *Ripe for Resolution: Conflict and Intervention in Africa* (New York: Oxford University Press, 1989, 2nd edn), Ch. 2.

10. See Tom Farer, *War Clouds on the Horn of Africa* (Washington, DC: Carnegie, 1979); J. Bowyer Bell, *The Horn of Africa* (New York: Crane and Russak, 1973); Zartman, *Ripe for Resolution*, Ch. 3.

11. Barakat Habte Selassie, *Conflict and Intervention in the Horn of Africa* (New York: Monthly Review, 1980); David and Marina Ottoway, *Ethiopia* (New York: African, 1978); Volker Matthies, *Der Grenzekonflikt Somalias mit Aethiopien und Kenya* (Hamburg: Institue für Afrika-Kunde, 1977).

12. Soviet arms and aid figures from *World Military Expenses and Arms Transfers* (Washington: ACDA, annual) and *Warsaw Pact Economic Aid to Non-Communist LDCs* (Washington: Department of State, annual).

13. See Ali Dessouki *et al.*, *The Red Sea* (Cairo: Al-Ahram Center for Strategic Studies, 1983).

14. See Raymond Thurston, 'The United States, Somalia and the Crisis in the Horn', *Horn of Africa*, vol. I, no. 2 (1978), pp. 11–20.

15. See Larry C. Napper, 'The Ogaden War', in George (ed.) op. cit.; Marina Ottoway, 'Superpower Competition and Regional Conflicts in the Horn of Africa', in Mark Kauppi and Craig Nation (eds), *The Soviet Impact in Africa* (Lexington: Heath, 1984).

16. See Napper, op. cit.: Zartman, op. cit.

17. See David Laitin, 'Security, Ideology and Development on Africa's Horn', in Robert Rotberg (ed.), *Africa in the 1990s and Beyond* (Lexington: Heath, 1989); Zartman, Ch. 2; *The New York Times*, 5 April 1988.
18. Terry Lyons, 'The Regional System of the Horn of Africa', in Howard Wriggins (ed.), *Regional Systems around the Indian Ocean* (pending).
19. See Deeb, op. cit.
20. See John Damis, *Conflict in Northwest Africa* (Stanford: Hoover, 1984).
21. See Paul B. Henze, *Eritrean Options and Ethiopia's Future* (Santa Monica: Rand, 1989, N-3021-USDP).

7 Superpower Cooperation in Central Africa
Crawford Young

INTRODUCTION

Africa entered the field of foreign policy vision of the United States and the Soviet Union at a time when the Cold War was at peak intensity. Initially, both superpowers plunged into the African arena with vigor and enthusiasm, mirroring the mood of optimism concerning future prospects for the continent. Quickly, however, both parties encountered disappointments that drove African affairs downwards on the priority listing. Long before the desperate decade of African crisis in the 1980s, both powers had come to rank Africa at the bottom of their scale of strategic concerns.

Northern and southern Africa will be considered in other chapters; the focus here is upon the great stretch of Africa below the Sahara and the Horn, and above the southern Africa conflict zone. Central Africa has experienced its share of trauma: the 'Congo crisis' of 1960, the 1963–5 rebellions and the Shaba I and II episodes in 1977 and 1978 in Zaire; the Nigerian civil war of 1967–70; the endless confusion in Chad since 1965; the Burundi massacres of 1972 and 1988; the capricious tyrannies of Idi Amin (Uganda), Jean-Bedel Bokassa (Central African Republic), and Francisco Macias Nguema (Equatorial Guinea). On the whole, however, American–Soviet competition has been subdued in most times and places in Central Africa. Indeed, a retrospective glance informed by the contemporary perspective of diminishing intensity of US–USSR rivalry in the Third World suggests a higher degree of implicit cooperation than was generally recognized at the time.

DETERMINANTS OF SUPERPOWER REGIONAL CONFLICT

Only the sudden and unexpected acceleration of the decolonization process in the late 1950s placed Africa on the policy agenda for both powers. In the American case, this was symbolically marked by the creation within the Department of State of a Bureau of African Affairs in 1958. On the Soviet side, abandonment under Khrushchev of rigid Stalinist dogma on the bourgeois nature of African nationalism and of funneled relationships through the metropolitan communist parties opened new possibilities for flexible action. Both powers perceived major opportunities to become key players. The highly visible entry of each onto the African stage triggered pre-emptive concerns for the other. As the parameters of post-colonial politics became clearer, hopes and fears of superpower gains or losses in the region subsided.

Since that brief moment of intensely competitive entry, both superpowers have exhibited substantial policy stability. The fundamental premises, interests, and major policy directions have an underlying continuity on both sides. Within the overarching parameters of persistence, there have been important fluctuations, to which we will return. But let us begin by identifying the vectors of policy reproduction over time.

UNITED STATES' AFRICAN POLICY

Running through American policy toward Africa are several basic premises. The Central African region in particular enjoys little policy priority save at moments of crisis; American economic, strategic, and political interests in the area are relatively slender. African states are perceived as weak and fragile, and unusually dependent on external patrons. This view originates in the uncertainties attending an independence so swiftly achieved within exceptionally artificial boundaries and insecure territorial identities. It has been reinforced by the devastating economic crisis of the 1980s. However, whatever its seeming irrationalities, the existing state system required preservation. The liberal economy and polity were preferred, but the low policy priority and perceived weakness set a context for these values. The pervasive statism across the African ideological spectrum engendered a combative response only in the 'structural adjustment' decade of the 1980s. Similarly, the predominance of autocratic forms of rule triggered only subdued responses, a tacit acceptance of African regime arguments that consolidation of state and nation required single parties, military tutelage, or both. African crises were presumed to bear a fatal tendency to acquire an East–West dimension, even if originally locally rooted.[1] Deeply embedded in the operational code shaping American policy thought is the postulate that Soviet influence is harmful, and should be minimized; Henry Kissinger spoke for all seasons in articulating this axiom: 'To foreclose Soviet opportunities is . . . the essence of the West's responsibilities.'[2] Corollary to it is a zero-sum conviction; a Soviet gain is necessarily an American loss, and vice versa.

The modest policy priority of Central Africa reflects in turn the relatively slender interests which might drive towards engagement. Economically, only 2 per cent of American foreign direct investment was located in Africa between the Sahara and the Limpopo; the USA took a quarter of Africa's exports, but provided only 10 per cent of its imports over the past decade.[3] Although there are significant imports of oil from Nigeria, Gabon and Cameroon, tantalum from Nigeria and Zaire, and cobalt from Zaire and Zambia, the strategic mineral issue relates above all to southern Africa.

Central African strategic importance is minimal for the USA. There are minor military facilities in Liberia, transit access to Dakar, and since 1987 utilization of Kamina air base in Zaire for Central Intelligence Agency (CIA) supply of *União Nacional para a Independência Total de Angola* (UNITA) insurgents. None of this makes Central Africa a consequential strategic theater.

To the extent that American Central African policy has been interest-driven, the predominant determinant has been political. Minimally correct and maximally quasi-tutelary relations are sought with a handful of exceptions of states deemed conjuncturally hostile (for example, Congo-Brazzaville from 1967–77). The political interest lies above all in African state behavior as it relates to broader global interactions. Non-alignment – a principle of diplomacy invoked by almost all African states, however differently interpreted – has always been acceptable; the Dulles era of sinful neutrality and frenetic alliance-building was over before African policy was formulated. At issue was the direction of the tilt.

A minor but not entirely negligible factor in the configuration of interests, important when catalyzed in the public mind by traumatic events, is the humanitarian dimension. The disposition of state discourse to cloak policy in moral clothing means that formal rhetoric cannot be accorded face value, but a residual humanitarian impulse does lurk in the official mind. Moreover, there is a significant humanitarian constituency in civil society which becomes activated on certain issues, composed above all of African American activist groups (Transafrica) and church-related organizations. Southern African questions occupy most of the energies of the humanitarian constituency, but on occasion Central African issues evoke this interest – human rights in Zaire or Liberia, disaster relief in the Sahel.

Major policy themes shaped by these premises and interests begin with a counter-Soviet disposition. The landscape is carefully scrutinized for Soviet initiatives, which are certain to engender responses. Similar concern attends involvement by members of the 'camp of socialism' viewed as Soviet 'proxies' (especially Cuba and East Germany), or states deemed so fundamentally hostile to Western interests as to provide – in zero-sum logic – support for Soviet positions (Egypt under Nasser, Libya since the 1970s). A comparable counter-Chinese dimension existed during the 1960s, when for a time Maoism seemed an even more dangerous doctrine than Soviet Marxism-Leninism; this began to fade when Chinese African policy fell into eclipse during the Great Proletarian Cultural Revolution, then lost its anti-imperial intensity during the 1970s. Indeed, for a time in the late 1970s the anti-Soviet determinant of Chinese policy was so powerfully asserted that China became virtually an unacknowledged ally.

Several considerations drove policy toward coordination with European allies, particularly the former colonizers. The higher priority commanded by the European theater, and the North Atlantic Treaty Organization (NATO) solidarity imperatives, made frictions undesirable in a secondary zone. Once initial enthusiasms about American developmental skills as applied to Africa subsided, a sobering recognition of the value of accumulated policy knowledge and human resources available in the former metropoles set in. As well, European aid levels were higher in most African states. Thus American policy has generally been deferential to European concerns.

The political cultivation of African states in some instances has engendered degrees of intimacy which approach client state relationships. Liberia and Zaire are the most sustained examples, although Senegal and Kenya also have had a special status. The reciprocities in such relationships are evident: on the African side, provision of security-related services and sensitivity to American policy concerns in their own diplomacy; for the US priority to such states in its aid program and informal but often decisive protection for incumbents. American patronage does not assure compliance with US wishes; the spectacular failure of repeated American-backed economic and political reform schemes in Liberia and Zaire are dramatic examples. Yet in such instances the widespread public belief that rulers enjoy an American security guarantee is crucial to their survival. Development assistance plays a significant part in the policy ensemble, even though the absolute levels for Central Africa – well short of a billion dollars – are not large, and during recent years have been shrinking, after a striking increase of 250 per cent in the 1975 to 1984 period.[4] For all but the oil-wealthy states (Gabon, for example), at least a modest aid program is a necessary lever for diplomatic voice. For African states providing security or diplomatic services to American policy a more generous aid level is an indispensable reward. The political significance of aid is only loosely related to its developmental effectiveness, generally evaluated as mediocre at best.[5] The weaker Central African states were exceptionally dependent on aid; for countries such as Niger or the Central African Republic, aid accounted for the bulk of foreign exchange and public investment. American aid levels available for Africa are now tightly constrained by the federal budget impasse, the political hammerlock Israel and Egypt have on 40 per cent of total aid, and the escalating demands by countries providing major military bases (Philippines, Greece, Turkey, Spain), and the new clamor to reward East European reform regimes.[6]

In summarizing the overall thrust of American African policy, we need also note – alongside the overall continuities – some vectors of fluctuation, arising from two primary sources: contending doctrinal orientations within the policy community, and the exceptional fragmentation of the American state. Two ongoing lines of cleavage may be detected: globalism versus regionalism, and activism versus restraint.

None of these tendencies is found in pure form; within the policy apparatus, they represent nuances rather than categorical perspectives. A disposition toward globalism – to view African developments as tributary to broader East–West rivalry realities – was pronounced in the Kennedy years, during the period of Kissinger stewardship, then again from late Carter through Reagan. The affinity to regionalism – perception of African conflict as locally rooted – was strongest under Johnson, the first part of the Carter administration, and now appears re-emergent in the Bush era. Activism characterized the Kennedy and Reagan years, although it was little manifest in actual policy determination in the Central African zone.[7]

The carefully constructed fragmentation of the state designed by the framers of the Constitution likewise serves as a counterpoint to policy continuity. The unending conflict between the executive and congressional branches over foreign policy is inherent to the separation of powers and a state apparatus founded upon checks and balances. Since the 1970s, in Africa the struggle has pitted the Congressional Black Caucus (created in 1977), and the Subcommittee on Africa of the House of Representatives under its last three chairs (Charles Diggs, Stephen Solarz, and Howard Wolpe) against the executive branch. Southern Africa has been the primary topic of discord, but Central African issues have figured as well (policy toward Zaire and Liberia, aid levels and rationale).

Within the executive branch, somewhat different policy perspectives characterize individual agency players: the bureaucratic politics and organizational process identified by Allison.[8] When issues are processed through routine diplomacy, the working personnel of the Department of State Bureau of African Affairs are in command, with regionalism and restraint likely to predominate. When conflict escalates, policy determination moves up the ladder to involve participants from the White House, the National Security Council, and the top State Department personnel, who will inevitably view the issue in more globalist perspective. The security agencies – the CIA and Department of Defense – contemplate policy choice within a different bureaucratic culture. Zaire is a case in point; sustaining Mobutu in power is a higher priority for the CIA than it is for the State Department, because of the nature of the cooperation he is prepared to offer in return for a security guarantee.

In sum, continuity predominates. But significant policy fluctuations are observable, reflecting changing political balances over time, the uncertainties of the fragmented state, and reactions to perceptions of Soviet intentions and African circumstances. Perhaps the best measure of the enduring force of continuity is to recall that over the last three decades three Presidents have assumed office with a commitment to policy change in Africa: Kennedy, Carter, and Reagan. In all three cases, the policy shift was most visible at the beginning of the administration. Over time, bureaucratic routines pulled it back towards the center.

SOVIET ACTION IN CENTRAL AFRICA: PREMISES, INTERESTS AND POLICIES

Soviet Africa Institute director Anatoli Gromyko told a visiting group of American Africanists in 1979 that, 'Soviet policy in Africa has never changed. Only opportunities have changed.' Notwithstanding important fluctuations over the years, this lapidary formulation in many respects holds for Central Africa, *perestroika* notwithstanding. To seek out the stable elements in the Soviet operational code for African policy, we turn first to summarize its premises and interests, then recapitulate the main dimensions of policy.

Soviet policy premises in good part mirror those of the United States. As point of departure, Central Africa ranks near the bottom of regional priorities. It is far removed from Soviet borders, and had no historic relationships with Moscow. Soviet policy instruments within most Central African societies are few and feeble.

Central Africa is seen as hampered in its developmental prospects not only by the imperial impact, but also by its intrinsic 'backwardness'. As one Soviet analyst put it, 'It is impossible to build a socialist society in countries with age-old backwardness in the shortest period of time.'[9] The backwardness exists at both base and superstructure. African social formations are particularly refractory; as Kiva writes:

A developed working class is practically lacking there, and as for the communal-patriarchal peasantry, its level of organisation and political consciousness is extremely low . . . the bulk of the population . . . is still shackled by the archaic social and spiritual ties of a tribal society and abides by the laws of past epochs.[10]

Not only was social structure unfavorable, but also the state itself was exceptionally weak. State socialism – the Soviet vision of the socialist commonwealth – required above all an effective state. African polities were states without history, and singularly ill-adapted to serve as weapons for progress.[11]

Nonetheless, the Soviet Union, as a global power, insists upon a presence and a voice in Central African affairs. Although perceived as entitlement, this role, in Albright's words, 'must be self-asserted, self-achieved, and self-sustained'.[12] An active Soviet presence, and in the long term the strength of the camp of socialism, can facilitate African evolution toward a socialist future. Meanwhile, Soviet diplomacy, like American, holds a zero-sum assumption about East–West struggles for influence in the region.

Soviet interests in Central Africa are minimal, although not non-existent. Trade relations with Central Africa are slender and unlikely to increase. However, the Soviets do value access to some Central African resources, in particular bauxite and fish;[13] in the latter case, the importance of fish meal for livestock feed has led to negotiation of a string of fishing rights accords with littoral states at some policy costs in other spheres because of widespread African belief that the terms proved unfavorable, and that the Soviets regularly exceed the stipulated harvest limits.[14] In strategic terms, the forward Soviet naval strategy and global power projection ambitions of the 1970s, and commitment to an improving 'correlation of forces', placed some premium on port facilities, airfield access and overflight rights. As with the United States, the most fundamental interests were political: nudging African non-alignment in an anti-Western direction, although not to the point of rupture.

Translated into policies, the Soviet Union has sought to maintain a presence everywhere, and to provide privileged support for states articulating congenial policy or ideological positions.[15] Pragmatism has always had its place, and correct relations even with westward-leaning (Kenya, Zaire) or resolutely capitalist states (Nigeria) are sought. But radical anti-imperialism and socialist orientation have been clearly preferred.

Soviet policy has consistently maintained a preference for the creation of conditions ultimately favorable to the construction of socialism in Africa, with fluctuating perceptions of what policies most surely advanced this goal. In the early phase, Soviet economic assistance was significant in several instances. It focused upon state industrial projects, or state farms (although not introduction of collective agriculture); the subtext was encouragement of state domination of the economy, fostering a social structure (a working class) eventually supportive of socialism, and pre-empting the emergence of an indigenous capitalist class. Exemplary of this policy orientation (and its shortcomings) was the large Soviet commitment to the costly and ineffective Ajaokuta steel complex in Nigeria, and the spectacular fiasco of state farms in Nkrumah's Ghana. As time went by, attention shifted from economic to military assistance, and to devising means to consolidate the power of regimes perceived as well-disposed, particularly those of socialist orientation. Thus we find a greater stress placed upon the construction of a 'Leninist core' to the would-be African socialist state: a politically controlled security and communications apparatus, often with East German assistance, and a Leninist party. After the wave of coups eliminating leaders such as Kwame Nkrumah and Ben Bella in whom hopes for 'revolutionary democracy' had been vested in the early 1960s, the ephemeral nature of power and reversibility of orientations became evident. As one recent Soviet commentator wrote, 'There has been, regrettably, quite a few instances in Africa's political history when the forces coming out for social progress failed to retain their positions. The irreversibility of the choice of socialism, proclaimed by many revolutionary democrats and sometimes recorded in the constitution, reflects a desire rather than a reality.'[16]

Support assistance pointed toward regime reproduction naturally strikes a responsive chord among incumbent rulers. It corresponded to the emergence in Soviet ideological debate of the thesis that military regimes had progressive potential; this argument had particular application to Central Africa, in that all its Afro-Marxist regimes were of military origin. Former Africa Institute Director Solodnikov wrote in 1973:

It would be mistaken to regard the army in the Asian and African countries as standing aloof from the class struggle, as being neutral in that struggle. The experience of . . . [several] countries demonstrate that the army can become an important progressive factor in the political struggle for further development of the national-democratic revolution.[17]

The officer corps were of petty bourgeois origins, with other ranks drawn from the peasantry. Its budget came from the state, and thus the military was unconstrained by ties to capitalism.[18]

There have been significant policy fluctuations over time, roughly corresponding to poles of activism and restraint. Moments of peak activism occurred in the early 1960s – age of the 'hare-brained scheme' – and the late 1970s – era of 'the stagnation'. The activism/restraint policy balance in turn reflected changing ideological interpretations of Central African evolution, and dominant notions of Soviet resource constraints.

Although the Soviets always scorned the 'African socialism' discourse which dominated the first years of independence, they did have initial hopes that Central African ventures in 'national democracy' such as those in Ghana, Guinea, and Mali could create from above the preconditions for a non-capitalist route to socialism. The shock of the demise of these regimes, and the (short-lived) popular joy which celebrated their disappearance, forced a reappraisal of the prospects of such governments, leading to a recognition of their fragility, lack of a supportive social structure, shallow ideological commitments, and poor economic performance. A period of retrenchment ensued, marked by a de-emphasis upon ideologically flavored preferences in African state relationships; the most important Central African initiative of this era of restraint was the shrewdly calculated and politically profitable support for the Nigerian government faced with the Biafran secession.

The emergence of a second wave of African socialist regimes, now explicitly invoking Marxism-Leninism as ideological reference, and the new strategic opportunities opened by the collapse of the Portuguese regime and the Ethiopian monarchy in 1974, kindled new interest in what was now termed 'socialist orientation'.[19] From the debris of the Portuguese empire, and through ideological declaration by military regimes, at one point eight African polities claimed Marxist-Leninist commitment, by far the largest Third World concentration of such states. Kosukhin expressed a dominant view in 1980 in saluting these trends:

> Today the policy of socialist orientation has ceased to be merely a slogan there, a political abstraction. The revolutionary democrats are an organised influential force, implementing their programme aimed at creating the socio-economic, ideological and political foundation of new social relations, the development of the state sector in the economy and co-operative ownership in agriculture . . .
> . . . *the change-over to the positions of scientific socialism and the creation of vanguard parties acting in accordance with the ideology and organizational principles of Marxism-Leninism. The emergence of such parties reflects a new stage in the ideological and political evolution of revolutionary democracy.*[20]

In Central Africa, this brought a Treaty of Friendship and Cooperation with Congo-Brazzaville in 1981. Soviet nurture and support also came for a Leninist core to these states. Economic aid, however, was minimal in this activist phase.

By the early 1980s, especially after the death of Brezhnev, a movement toward restraint gathered force, doubtless motivated in part by increasingly severe resource constraints, but also accompanied by ideological doubts.[21] Deputy Foreign Minister Leonid Ilyichev, summarizing foreign policy debates at the 19th All-Union CPSU Conference in 1988, noted consensus that Third World developments generally 'had entered a difficult, even contradictory stage.' No one disputed the assertion that 'our science and diplomacy had failed to fully predict many of the current processes in the Third World.' Pragmatism in inter-state relations was back in fashion; 'we should develop relations with these countries on realistic lines, with due regard to the peculiarities of each particular country, and, first and foremost, to our actual possibilities.'[22] Kiva reported queries from Soviet audiences as to the efficacy of socialist orientation in Africa, 'in the light of the fact that many socialist-oriented countries are developing more slowly than other newly free states and that people there live in dire poverty and are even starving in some cases . . .'[23] While he reflects that Africans might have found unpalatable Soviet advice that no other road to socialism was open save through the construction of capitalism, yet today, 'we cannot understand why we judged the law-governed development of capitalism and socialism so simplistically or why we expected in good earnest to spare hundreds of millions the ordeal of capitalism by offering the concept of national democracy and non-capitalist development and yet had no clear idea of the components of the problem.'[24] Senior Africa Institute member and former diplomat Tarabrin added, 'we are not going to go on spending money on armed forces for nothing. Angola has cost us billions . . . We need the money for other purposes.'[25]

Symbolic of the new Soviet mood towards African commitments was the 1981 decision of the Council for Mutual Economic Assistance (CMEA) to reject Mozambique's application for membership; subsequent overtures from Ethiopia were similarly rebuffed. In 1982, a high-ranking Ghanaian delegation implored the Soviets to provide economic rescue permitting retention of a radical populist orientation; Ghana was told to turn to the International Monetary Fund.

The present era of restraint appears likely to persist for some time. At the same time, the elements of continuity in Soviet policy thought should counsel caution in assuming that recent trends are necessarily permanent. The nature and depth of the African economic crisis of the 1980s, however, is an improbable source of opportunities for renewed activism, always triggered in the past by sudden openings for advantageous Soviet action. Previous gains have invariably proved short term.

THE AFRICAN MAGNETIC FIELD AND GREAT POWER POLICY

Crucial to grasping great power involvement in Central Africa is the central role played by African events in conditioning their intervention. The low policy priority the region commands in both Washington and Moscow is pertinently recalled; the default option is inaction. At most times and places in this zone, low-intensity rivalry prevails between the powers. When crisis occurs, great power involvement comes in good measure in response to earnest African solicitation rather than by pure external initiative.

The 'Congo crisis' of 1960 may be taken as illustrative of the interactive dynamic of African participants in a conflict setting seeking external support, in turn triggering a competitive great power response largely shaped by the respective images of the other's actions and intentions.[26] Within a week, Zairian leaders issued separate appeals for US, Ui l Nations, and Soviet military intervention. Americans and Soviets each believed the other to be committed to a lunge for domination, and responded accordingly; as a counter-Soviet operation, American policy was a clear success, as the sharp limits of Soviet power projection capabilities in 1960 were clearly revealed. How salutary this Cold War triumph was in the longer run is far less clear; its policy legacy was a permanent entanglement in Zairian affairs and close identification as sponsor with a regime under whose stewardship state and economy have experienced prolonged decline.

Thus, the nature of what we might term the African magnetic field weighs heavily in the policy equation. The relative weakness of the African state, and the nature of its political processes, tend to reinforce a disposition to turn outwards for support. The blockage of succession mechanisms, and the prevalence of the coup as primary instrument of regime change, create conditions favorable to external involvement. Regimes value assistance from external security and intelligence agencies in monitoring opposition activity and providing advance warning of conspiracy; in addition to the US and USSR, the French and Israelis have special skills in this domain. Opposition groups as well plead with possible external patrons for their support – although in recent years usually without effect.[27] African militaries that acquire sophisticated weapons systems also purchase a logistical dependency necessitating continuing supply and skilled personnel involvement; in turn, the emergence by the 1970s of several sustained crisis zones produced regional arms races. Above all the deepening economic crisis could not be overcome with internal means; governance was an unending search for resources to meet immediate liquidity needs.

Thus in important respects great power African policy is best understood as less the product of conscious global design than the cumulation of responses to particular stimuli and solicitations arising from within the regional environment. Nothing compels a great power to respond to such invitations; distance and disengagement is always a possible choice. In periods of mutual restraint such an option is frequently exercised. But the underlying affinity of each to policies pre-empting the other, and apprehensions that the adversary may exploit inaction, within a framework of shared zero-sum assumptions, invariably cast their shadow upon the decision-making process.

Operating in conjunction with the African magnetic field is the interactive impact of policy. The initial activism of Kennedy and Khrushchev had a pwerful racheting pull. The first surge of activism spent itself, and the mood of lowered expectations and commitments which set in on both sides by 1966 was mutually reinforcing. Both sides found themselves confronted by new choices by the convulsive reconfigurations of the entire African political landscape in the wake of the 1974 Portuguese and Ethiopian coups. Brzezinski concluded that *détente* was buried in the sands of the Ogaden; Casey assumed control of the CIA convinced that 'the Soviets were on the move' throughout the Third World, and fashioned activist strategies to combat them. The first covert operation authorized on his watch was in Chad, to facilitate Habre's march to power.[28]

OTHER REGIONAL ACTORS: THE FRENCH CONNECTION

Central African states entered the international arena as sovereign actors as a product of decolonization, beginning only in 1957 (except for Liberia) with Ghanaian independence. At the moment of power transfer, the tutelage of the withdrawing power in most cases remained extensive, with expatriate presence strong in the senior ranks of the public service and especially security forces. Economies, which had developed as metropolitan appendages, were intimately linked into the orbit of the former colonizers. There was reason to believe that, for a prolonged period, the external linkages of the newly independent states would remain largely mediated through the erstwhile imperial occupants.

In the event, only the French connection remained critical. British pre-eminence in tropical Africa eroded with surprising speed, and by the end of the 1960s London was only a secondary regional player. For different reasons, mismanaged or aborted decolonizations in the Belgian, Portuguese, and Spanish instances swiftly reduced their role. But the French, in contrast, became in some respects even more salient actors. The French sphere of action enlarged from the 14 successor states to the 'African bloc' of the former French empire to incorporate former Belgian and Spanish colonies.

The unusual form of terminal French colonial policy produced a generation of African political leaders who had participated in French parliamentary politics, and had in many instances intimate contacts within the French political class. Successive French Presidents, from Charles de Gaulle on, had close personal ties with many African heads of state in the francophone orbit. The maintenance of a convertible franc zone has provided a crucial economic cement to the political ties. Equally important is the security guarantee represented by French detachments stationed in Senegal, the Ivory Coast, Gabon, and the Central African Republic, and deployed in Chad. Emblematic of their importance is the arresting fact that usually the francophonic summits attract more African heads of state than those of the Organization of African Unity (OAU).

The French presence in tropical Africa actually increased after independence, reaching a peak of 180,000 around 1970. Since that time, these numbers have begun to decline, dwindling to 133,000 in the late 1980s.[29] There are some indications that this shrinkage may portend a broader diminution in the French role in the 1990s. The prospective 1992 changes in the European Community, as well as the new situation in Europe, may require a redeployment of energies and resources away from Africa. Indications grow that the increasing costs of sustaining a convertible African franc are increasing to a point where a re-evaluation of its benefits to France may lie ahead.

Nonetheless, the densely woven, multi-stranded French connection has insulated most of the countries concerned from the direct impact of the superpower rivalry. There have been instances of rupture for a time (Guinea and Mali in the early post-colonial period), which drew in the US and Soviet Union. More striking is the durability and solidity of *francophilie*; even Benin and Congo-Brazzaville, in espousing Afro-Marxism, remained within the franc

zone and preserved relatively amicable ties with Paris.
Soviet or American linkages with particular francophonic states may be important (for example, Soviet Friendship Treaty links with Congo-
Brazzaville, or the United States' close ties with Zaire and Senegal),
but the saliency of France as regional actor is a fundamental factor in
the Central African equation.

LESSONS OF EXPERIENCE: TOWARD MUTUAL RESTRAINT AND COOPERATION?

Only in retrospect would one characterize superpower relations in
the Central African region as including a cooperative dimension. A
mere decade ago, the competitive dimension appeared to be of
exceptional virulence. In the intervening years a new era of *détente*
has emerged. amd the mutual hostility evoked in formal state
discourse has greatly diminished: 'evil empire' rhetoric has faded into
the background on both sides. One may detect significant areas of
tacit cooperation; in interpreting these spheres of mutual restraint,
we must keep in view the underlying conflictual dispositions of the
two powers.

The deeply embedded counter-Soviet and counter-Western impulses are far too fundamental to vanish from policy premises.
Diplomacy as human agency contains internalized routines and
mentalities rooted in the presumption of conflict as the normal
condition. Careful surveillance of the adversary and suspicion of his
motives is instinctual. Notwithstanding the burden of these caveats,
the growing importance of an emergent operational code of mutual
restraint merits close attention.

This nascent code departs from the radically different *Weltan-
schauungen* of the two societies, but converges upon some shared
postulates which incorporate the three decades of policy learning. A
recent meeting of Soviet and American Africa specialists developed a
list of common assumptions which may serve as a point of departure.

(a) factors internal to the region are relatively more important for
understanding and coming to grips with conflicts than global
strategies that affect specific regions;
(b) nevertheless, interventions by outside powers, including arms
sales, have intertwined with and exacerbated local conflicts;

   (c) internal social divisions and the residues of historical differ-
       ences are as important as the intentions of present govern-
       ments in Central Africa;
   (d) both the US and USSR are limited in their abilities to set the
       terms for conflict management.[30]

The implications of these areas of accord are considerable, if one
may interpret them as representative of perspectives extending
beyond the purely academic community.

If internal dynamics dominate external factors in explaining political outcomes within Central African states, the stakes in the denoue-
ment are lowered for both sides in two senses. First, the frequent
suspicion, especially in the early years, that outcomes are orchestrated by the adversary loses its force. And second, the incapacity of
either side to master the vectors of domestic politics diminishes the
temptation to try. If superpower interventions have limited rationality in terms of their ability to control outcomes, their potential costs,
often hidden and unanticipated in terms of the risks of sharpening
internal cleavages or comporting inconvenient obligations, assume
greater importance.

In other terms, the pedagogy of post-colonial Central African
history instructs both sides that fostering coups is unproductive.
Although this mode of diplomacy has been more frequently employed in the region by the United States (Zaire in 1960 and 1965,
Ghana in 1966, Chad in 1982), its attractiveness as strategy clearly
has diminished for both superpowers. American advocates of activism admittedly can point to a Zairian role as strategic junior partner
on a number of occasions (especially in Angola, but also in Chad),
and Chadian collaboration in anti-Libyan operations (such as the
creation of a Libyan 'contra' group from Libyan prisoners captured
during the spectacular Chadian military triumphs in 1987 with
American and Israeli intelligence backing).[31] On the Soviet side,
although the gamut of Marxist-Leninist fragments in such states as
Senegal and Burkina Faso invariably includes those labelled 'pro-
Moscow', the actual support received is minimal; such identification
serves above all as a point of external reference for obscure factional
struggles involving a narrow intellectual/professional stratum.[32]

The saliency of ideology as a litmus test of regime orientations has
clearly declined for both Washington and Moscow. For both sides,
this issue arose above all with rulers articulating Marxist-Leninist or
populist socialist perspectives, which in the mid-1970s had the

appearance of a powerful trend; those of capitalist orientation have eschewed ideological declaration, characterizing themselves as 'pragmatic'. Even in those instances where 'scientific socialism' as discourse of state was most intense (Ethiopia, Congo-Brazzaville, Benin), there was always a degree of skepticism as to the depth and significance of doctrinal permeation of state and society. In this region, the Soviet pole of reference had its greatest impact in Ethiopia; in Brazzaville, the remarkable suffusion of public rhetoric with Marxist-Leninist semiotics made of the doctrine a '*discours d'acces*', a vocabulary necessary in instrumental transactions with the state.[33] Soviet and American diplomats maintained private skepticism about the underlying significance of formal rhetoric; for both sides, deconstruction rather than content analysis was the appropriate methodology for grasping its real meaning. Only in Ethiopia, where by the 1980s regime ideology became intricately interpenetrated with the personal autocracy of Mengistu Haile Mariam and high-voltage Soviet military backing, did it appear to have real weight. Everywhere, the dramatic deterioration of African economies in the 1980s, and the narrowing set of policy choices that the crisis permitted, devalued sundry forms of socialist discourse, even as symbolic dogma.

The sheer intractability of the economic crisis was also instructive. Every passing year made clearer the depth and probable duration of the economic crisis. In such circumstances, encouragement of a non-capitalist pathway became impossible. A bankrupt country with a hemorrhaging public sector could not avoid disengagement of the state. Experiments in communal forms of agricultural production, or state farms, had such uniformly disastrous results that continued prescription of socialist form in the rural sphere was impossible. As the 1980s wore on, it became abundantly clear that Soviet policy had reached two crucial conclusions about the African economic crisis: first, that in these circumstances the policy package commonly associated with 'socialist orientation' could not be effective; and secondly, that the Soviet Union could not possibly afford the economic commitment that might improve its prospects. These judgements concerning the parlous condition of the African state spilled over into the sphere of military aid as well; between 1983 and 1988, the number of countries receiving Soviet arms help shrank from 22 to seven.[34] The painful lessons of investment in the non-capitalist pathway powerfully urged restraint. The Soviet Union could well counsel Ghana or others to turn to the IMF and the West for economic rescue, and might conclude that a capitalist stage was unavoidable. It was not, however, the responsibility of the Soviet Union to design or finance structural adjustment of Western prescription.

Initially the emergent African economic crisis stimulated more activist impulses on the American side, coinciding as it did with the articulation of an assertive liberal economy doctrine in the early years of the Reagan administration. Into the interstices of the policy apparatus flowed some ideologically motivated operatives with a missionary faith in the therapy of the market-place. Over time the political and economic limits of privatization and structural adjustment remedies became more apparent; so also did the severely circumscribed American capacity and disposition to support African recovery. The politics of the federal budget deficit capped African public aid at slowly declining levels, while the private sector – international banks and multinationals – offered nothing but praise for structural adjustment.

Even during the periods of mutual activism, and application of globalist policy reason, one may note important elements of policy restraint. Both sides have on occasion sought some military facilities, but neither has tried to enlist Central African states in formal military alliances. In the Zairian crises of the early 1960s, after the initial Soviet effort to match and counter Western intervention was foiled by September 1960, real military support for dissidents and insurgents was always inconsequential. The Soviets provided only verbal backing to the 1963–5 wave of rebellions, though some arms of Soviet origin did filter in after the key insurrection had been defeated in late 1964. The ineffectual Che Guevara venture in eastern Zaire was a purely Cuban fiasco in 1965. In Nigeria, although the Soviet Union provided arms assistance to the Federal government, it remained at arm's length from the conflict, as did the United States. In the convoluted history of the Chad imbroglio since the post-colonial order began to unravel in 1965, Soviet policy has always been circumspect. Libyan immersion in Chad affairs, often audacious and at times brazen in the 1973–88 period, was wholly independent from Soviet inducement, despite the high level of Soviet arms sales to Qaddafi.

Evolving circumstances in Central Africa have altered the African magnetic field; the didactics of history are at work here too. Economic survival has increasingly come to dominate the policy agenda. As only a handful of states can contemplate this question without urgent reference to external supporters, to stave off creditors and sustain minimal levels of state operation, negotiating access to debt rescheduling and economic assistance has a policy precedence which it lacked in the first two decades of independence. Disappointments with American policy in this respect may be legion. The set of perspectives which brought demands for a 'New International Economic Order' in the mid-1970s and undergirded the initial African response to deteriorating economic conditions, the 1980 Lagos Plan of Action with its 'dependency theory' overtones, continues to suffuse the policy thought even of such moderate leaders as Felix Houphouet-Boigny. But the sharpening constraints of immediate survival have fundamentally narrowed the options; 'structural adjustment' by the mid-1980s was the only game in town.

Socialist orientation, and the Soviet point of reference, had diminishing policy value, for those states which had found instruction in its postulates, for several reasons. Afro-Marxism and populist socialism were never doctrines extending beyond ruling groups and elite strata; by the 1980s the inability of policies grounded in such doctrines to deliver a stream of benefits to the broader population, and thus serve as instrument of legitimation, was everywhere manifest. The Soviet Union had made abundantly clear that irrespective of ideological companionship no significant economic aid was available. The West, for the most part tolerant of African socialist experiments until the 1970s, as evidenced by relatively high aid levels for such states as Tanzania and Guinea-Bissau, now came to insist on liberalization as the ransom for assistance.

To these factors must be added a dramatic deterioration in the credibility of the Soviet – and also Chinese – 'models of development'. Three decades ago both these pathways commanded enormous prestige. In Laidi's terms, in validating 'the universality of its historical experience, the rapidity of its economic development or the effectiveness of its diplomatic action, the USSR sought to position itself in the three privileged sites of its image in the Third World: that of political legitimation, state construction, and national affirmation.'[35] The necessity for both the Soviet Union and China to justify sweeping reforms by stigmatizing the failures of the past left the model stripped naked; *perestroika* had no blueprint, and 'the stagnation' appeared as an all-too-familiar description of Africa's plight rather than as an uplifting prescription.

Thus, the African magnetic field seemed destined in the immediate future to exercise a reduced and uneven attraction. The Soviet Union largely escaped from its field. This very fact lessened its pull upon the West. But there was no other direction to focus its diminishing force.

COOPERATION: A NEW PATTERN OF SUPERPOWER INTERACTION IN CENTRAL AFRICA?

At the beginning of the 1990s, a new political conjucture in Central Africa seems at hand. Indeed, one influential publication characterized it as an epoch of 'the most far-reaching great-power agreement on Africa since the Berlin conference of 1885', with the US and USSR 'now cooperating to such an extent that it is hard to resist the conclusion that they have reached an informal agreement to redefine their spheres of interest in the world, including Africa'.[36] *Détente* in Africa occurred before, but this version appears to have a more comprehensive policy impact.

The parameters of the conjuncture are marked by policy evolution by both powers. The shift toward thorough-going restraint, indeed virtual disengagement, is most striking on the Soviet side. Important changes in overall ideological doctrine concerning the character and destiny of the world, and in authoritative reading of Central African realities, command greater restraint in a zone of peripheral concern. So also – with even greater insistence – do Soviet resource constraints, unlikely to ease in the coming decade.

For the United States, policy evolution can be best characterized as a 'recentering', a return to its more basic moorings after the departure toward globalist activism in the early Reagan years. A prolongation of the period of Soviet restraint and relative quiescence would foster a consolidation of this orientation, by eroding the validity of the 'counter-Soviet' element in policy determination. Within the fragmented arena of American state action, this would reduce the weight of conservative militant groups, and the security agencies, both forces – in different ways – pushing toward globalist activism. The operation code of the professional foreign policy establishment would tend to prevail, with its affinity – in a low priority area – for restraint and regionalism.

From a sustained period of mutual restraint in the Central African zone might emerge a code of conduct, tacitly accepted, which curbed interventionist tendencies. A fundamental plank in such a platform would be elimination of zones of armed conflict, and inhibiting their future emergence. No conclusion stands out more starkly for both sides than the difficulty, in African circumstances, of extinguishing such conflicts once they become institutionalized. Three decades of such strife in the Horn has brought violent death to tens of thousands, starvation to millions, and pauperization to most. Strategic and political advantages to either side have been marginal, and always subject to reversal. The ultimately ephemeral gains could not possibly justify the investments required to maintain them.

If the incidence of regional conflict is reduced, along with the zonal arms races such struggle tends to beget, an era of restraint in the pursuit of politico-strategic advantage in this region may evolve. Zero-sum psychosis is deeply implanted on both sides, as is mutual suspicion. A long period of tacit cooperation would be required to reduce its weight. An unacknowledged moratorium on seeking military facilities or fostering security clientage would contribute to this end. So also would the declining supply of military equipment, although in this sphere mercantile motivations often drive policy.

If the major regional conflicts were removed from the agenda, the issue whose imperatives would govern African external ties would be the economic crisis. Here one may anticipate that restraint, on the Soviet side, will manifest itself above all through relative silence. The USSR could hardly be expected to fund the era of capitalist development which its doctrine now recognizes as inevitable and necessary. Moscow will surely continue to absolve itself from any blame for the debt crisis, declining terms of trade for the region's main commodities, and other external determinants of the African crisis. But it may well refrain from the fervid denunciations of Western economic linkages and African acquiescence in the structural adjustment game which have been staples of its discourse in the past.

A policy challenge which pushes the Soviet Union to the sidelines does not necessarily make the United States the key player. The weakening economic position of the United States will circumscribe the American role. The fragmented state apparatus appears incapable of the decisions that will alter the constraints imposed by endemic federal budget and international trade deficits. In an era of great power mutual restraint, and concomitant decline in the saliency of the strategic currency of power, the mercantile states of the world assume greater importance. Federal budgetary politics in the deficit context will deny to American policy operatives the economic leverage required to fill the space opened by Soviet disengagement. American international banks and multinational corporations find Central Africa unattractive. The European Community and Japan seem destined for leading roles.

Soviet commentators have for some time suggested that sub-Saharan Africa may prove a valuable laboratory for great power collaboration. Their gaze is particularly fixed upon southern Africa in such visions, but Central Africa may as well lend itself to such a scenario. The low policy priority the region commands, the improbability of significant and enduring superpower advantage in the outcome of regional or local conflicts, and the disastrous condition of African economies all point toward a prolongation of the political restraint exhibited by both sides in the recent past. Institutionalization of restraint, and a pattern of communication and consultation which enhance it, could over time alter the pathologies of great-power rivalry and competition in the region.

In any event, a more cooperative mode of superpower interaction in Central Africa needs to persist for some period of time before a trend is declared. Analytical caution is a prime lesson from review of three decades of superpower encounter in this region. The axiom of adversarial conduct is deeply engraved in the official mind on both sides; we are far from effacing its effects. Such a perceptual prism could again yield inflamed suspicions if the prolonged and enduring economic crisis should trigger political breakdown in a major state (Nigeria and Zaire are doubtless the two most potentially volatile, and too important to ignore).

Perestroika itself remains reversible, and with it some of the new doctrinal premises that condition Soviet African policy. One may speculate that any reshuffle of the ruling oligarchy in the Soviet Union which drew back from some of the new policy directions which *perestroika* has come to symbolize would not initially affect policy in Central Africa. Difficulties on the domestic front – nationalities issue or economic stalemate – or in the most sensitive foreign policy sector – Eastern Europe – are the most likely triggers for a neo-conservative restoration. The disposition to active cooperation on eliminating zones of regional conflict might diminish, but the reluctance to commit scarce resources to zones of peripheral interest would surely endure.

Whether the analyst in the next century will look back upon the Namibia settlement and allied alteration in the mood of great-power relations with Africa as a moment of fundamental mutation, a landmark event ranking with the Berlin congress in redefining the parameters of external involvement in African affairs, remains to be seen. In the short run, indisputably there has been a dramatic transformation in at least the 'atmospherics'. A fair measure of the magnitude of the change is that the question of possible paradigm change even arises.

NOTES

1. This presumption is common across the spectrum of American policy operatives. Assistant Secretary of State for African Affairs Chester Crocker forcefully advanced this argument in a debate on American policy at the 1983 African-American Institute meetings in Zimbabwe; his predecessor, Richard Moose, asserted the dangers to American policy of any power vacuum in Zaire at a hearing of the House of Representatives Subcommittee on Africa in March 1978 on the grounds that the Soviets 'tend to get their act together more quickly' than do local forces enjoying Western support.
2. Henry Kissinger, *The White House Years* (Boston: Little, Brown, 1979), p. 119.
3. Donald Rothchild and John Ravenhill, 'Subordinating African Issues to Global Logic: Reagan Confronts Political Complexity', in Kenneth A. Oye, Robert J. Lieber, and Rothchild (eds), *Eagle Resurgent: The Reagan Era in American Foreign Policy* (Boston: Little, Brown 1987), p. 394.
4. Carol Lancaster, *US Aid to Sub-Saharan Africa: Challenges, Constraints, and Choices* (Washington: Center for Strategic and International Studies, 1988), p. 1.
5. Despite the indisputably good intentions and often dedicated labors of the aid apparatus and their counterparts in African states, only a few really bright spots can be found. Certainly the disaster relief efforts are one; countless lives have been saved by these efforts in Ethiopia, Sudan, and the Sahel region during the drought years. Hampering the aid effort are high administrative overheads, constant churning of policy doctrines, political priorities in its distribution, the innumerable compromises made in the gauntlet a project runs from field request to congressional approval, its bureaucratic bias toward larger-scale projects, administrative weaknesses in the recipient states, and the many difficulties in the developmental environment. See Jennifer S. Whitaker, *How Can Africa Survive?* (New York: Harper & Row, 1988), pp. 57–86; Donald R. Mickelwaite, Charles F. Sweet, and Elliott R. Morss, *New Directions in Development: A Study of US Aid* (Boulder, CO: Westview Press, 1979); Virginia A. McMurtry, 'Foreign Aid and Political Development: The American Experience in West Africa', PhD dissertation, University of Wisconsin–Madison, 1974).
6. David R. Obey and Carol Lancaster, 'Funding Foreign Aid', *Foreign Policy*, vol. 71 (1988), pp. 141–55; Carol Lancaster, 'US Aid to Africa: Who Gets What, When, and How', *CSIS Africa Notes*, vol. 25 (31 March 1984).
7. Bob Woodward in his lengthy exposé of the CIA under William Casey devotes only a handful of passages to Central Africa: assistance to

Hissene Habre in Chad, minor assistance to an Ethiopian opposition movement; *Veil: The Secret Wars of the CIA 1981–1987* (New York: Simon and Schuster, 1987).

8. First advanced in Graham T. Allison, 'Conceptual Models of the Cuban Missile Crisis', *American Political Science Review*, vol. 69, no. 3 (1969), pp. 689–718.

9. L. Ratham and H. Schilling, 'The Non-Capitalist Development in Asia and Africa – Balance, Problems, Prospects', in Research Center for Africa and Asia, Bulgarian Academy of Sciences, *Developing Countries and the Non-Capitalist Road* (Sofia, 1974), cited in Marina Ottaway, 'Soviet Marxism and Socialism', *Journal of Modern African Studies*, vol. 16, no. 3 (1978), p. 480.

10. Aleksei Kiva, 'Socialist Orientation: Reality and Illusions', *International Affairs* (Moscow) (July 1988), p. 85.

11. This point emerged repeatedly in informal conversations with Soviet African specialists at the conferences bringing together Soviet and American African specialists in Berkeley in 1982, in Moscow in 1984, and again at Berkeley in 1986.

12. David E. Albright, *The USSR and Subsaharan Africa in the 1980s* (New York: Praeger, 1983), p. 35.

13. An estimated 20 per cent of Soviet bauxite needs were supplied by Guinea by the late 1970s; Elizabeth K. Valkenier, *The Soviet Union and the Third World: An Economic Bind* (New York: Frederick A. Praeger, 1983), p. 17.

14. East European COMECON partners probably have a stronger interest in a number of African commodities, as the Soviet Union itself becomes less able to meet their raw material needs; for evidence, see Christopher Coker, *NATO, the Warsaw Pact and Africa* (New York: St. Martin's Press, 1985). Soviet imports of other African commodities (Ethiopian coffee, for example) are largely in payment for military supplies. An intriguing debate broke out at the 1984 Soviet–American conference on African affairs on the concept of 'interest'. On the one hand, Soviet participants claimed that, as a socialist state, the USSR had no 'interests' in Africa. On the other, they took umbrage at a statement earlier that year by a ranking State Department official that the Soviet Union should refrain from intrusion in African affairs, because it had no 'legitimate interests' in the region.

15. Valuable recent reviews of Soviet African policy include the chapters by David E. Albright, Elizabeth Kridl Valkenier, and Francis Fukuyama in Marshall D. Shulman, *East–West Tensions in the Third World* (New York: W. W. Norton, 1986); Michael Clough (ed.), *Reassessing the Soviet Challenge in Africa* (Berkeley: Institute of International Studies, University of California-Berkeley, 1986); Zaki Laidi, *L'URSS vue du Tiers Monde* (Paris: Editions Karthala, 1984).

16. Lev Entin, 'African Countries: National Statehood in the Making', *International Affairs* (January 1988), p. 46.

17. Carol R. Saivetz, 'The Soviet Perception of Military Intervention in Third World Countries', in W. Raymond Duncan (ed.), *Soviet Policy in the Third World* (New York: Pergamon Press, 1980), p. 144.

18. This thesis is by no means unchallenged. Kiva asks rhetorically in a 1988 article, 'Why should patriotic, nationalist-minded army officers strive to build socialism as we conceive it? For what objective reasons? ... It is we who attributed to them the intention to follow a non-capitalist path in its Marxist sense.' Kiva, 'Socialist Orientation', p. 84. On this subject, see also Mark N. Katz, *The Third World in Soviet Military Thought* (Baltimore: Johns Hopkins University Press, 1982).
19. See, for example, Nikolai Kosukhin, *Revolutionary Democracy in Africa* (Moscow: Progress Publishers, 1980); *The Ideology of African Revolutionary Democracy* (Moscow: Social Sciences Today, 1984).
20. Kosukhin (1980), op. cit., pp. 164–6. Emphasis in original.
21. Elizabeth Kridl Valkenier, *The Soviet Union and the Third World: The Economic Bind* (New York: Praeger, 1983); Francis Fukuyama, *Moscow's Post-Brezhnev Reassessment of the Third World* (Santa Monica: Rand, 1986).
22. *International Affairs* (Moscow) (October 1988), p. 49.
23. Kiva, 'Socialist Orientation', p. 78.
24. Ibid., p. 81.
25. *Washington Post*, 9 October 1988.
26. Particularly valuable sources for this thoroughly documented episode are Madeleine G. Kalb, *The Congo Cables* (New York: Macmillan, 1982); Richard D. Mahoney, *JFK: Ordeal in Africa* (New York: Oxford University Press, 1983); Stephen R. Weisman, *American Foreign Policy in the Congo 1960–1964* (Ithaca: Cornell University Press, 1974).
27. To capture this dimension of the external factor in African politics, see Pierre Pean, *Affaires africaines* (Paris: Fayard, 1983).
28. Woodward, op. cit., pp. 92–7.
29. *World Development Forum*, vol. VII, no. 14 (15 August 1989).
30. Harvey Glickman, 'Perspectives on Africa from the Fourth American–Soviet Symposium on Contemporary Sub-Saharan Africa', *Issue*, vol. 17, no. 1 (1988), p. 5.
31. *Africa Confidential*, vol. 30, no. 1 (6 January 1989).
34. *New York Times*, 11 January 1989.
35. Laidi, op. cit., p. 25.
36. *Africa Confidential*, vol. 30, no. 5 (3 March 1989).

8 Superpower Cooperation in Southern Africa
Daniel R. Kempton

THE EVOLUTION OF SUPERPOWER INTERESTS AND OBJECTIVES

The possibilities for superpower cooperation in any region are highly dependent on the importance of the region to each of the superpowers. However, determining a region's significance to the superpowers is itself a serious and challenging task. The typical answer to this question points to the idiosyncrasies of the region being analyzed that give the region special or unique importance. In the case of southern Africa, this results in a now well-known litany. Southern Africa's unique importance for the superpowers is attributable to three major features of the region. First and foremost, we must look to its mineral wealth. While southern Africa is a major source of numerous commercially significant minerals, the greatest attention is usually given to platinum, chromium, vanadium, and manganese, none of which is readily available elsewhere in the non-communist world. Additionally, neither the sheer financial lure of the deposits of gold and diamonds which account for much of South Africa's financial success, nor the strategic importance of the uranium deposits which dot the region, can be easily ignored. Second, the coastal states of southern Africa border one of the world's great sea transit routes, along which pass numerous military vessels and much of the Gulf states' oil trade. Finally, the region contains South Africa, by far the wealthiest state in Africa, as well as the most troubled.

However impressive the above litany may appear, for both superpowers the importance of any region can accurately be understood only from a comparative perspective; and for both the Soviet Union and the United States, southern Africa's importance is rather low relative to the other regions of the world. Given its great distance from the superpowers, southern Africa does not hold the strategic importance that Central America holds for the United States or that Eastern Europe holds for the Soviet Union. Economically, its importance clearly pales in comparison with that of Western Europe, the Middle East or Japan. Thus, southern Africa is a region which holds great importance for both superpowers but, relatively speaking, is not critical to the economic or military security of either. US interests in the region clearly predate those of the Soviet Union. In its policy toward southern Africa the United States has pursued two sometimes contradictory objectives. First, and probably of highest priority, the United States has sought to contain communism in the region. Secondly, the United States has sought independence for the region's colonial territories and the gradual transition to black rule in the white-ruled states.[1] In the initial Cold War atmosphere which characterized superpower relations following World War II, the search for allies to implement its geostrategic notion of containment was clearly the guiding force in US policy. The practical result of this was close cooperation between the United States and both the region's white minority regimes and the Portuguese colonial empire, all of which boasted impeccable anti-communist credentials. This cooperation ensured continued US access to the region's resources and limited the Soviet threat to the sea lanes.

Over time, the United States felt increasingly impelled to come to terms with the growing wave of independence in the Third World. Although the United States remained firm in its anti-communist objectives, it had to take into account the newly independent regimes and those forces fighting for independence in the remaining colonial territories. If the eventual independence of these territories was inevitable, as the Kennedy administration perceived it to be, US interests were best served not by blocking the process, but by promoting a gradual transition thereby ensuring that the resulting regimes would at least not be pro-Soviet, even if they were not necessarily pro-American.[2] This policy entailed the development of US ties with some of the region's less radical revolutionary movements and a growth in US pressure on the white minority regimes. However, as Vietnam grew to preoccupy US foreign policy not only was a higher premium again placed on loyal anti-communist allies, but southern Africa as a whole was given less prominence in US policy.

In 1969 a major review of US policy toward southern Africa was conducted by the newly inaugurated Nixon administration.[3] The resulting study concluded that there was little chance of the region's black revolutionary movements coming to power by virtue of their own armed struggles. Thus US interests were best served by the continuation of friendly relations with the Portuguese and white-ruled regimes in southern Africa. Yet US officials were not oblivious to the long-term dangers of their policy. First, if US ties to these regimes were viewed as too close by other African and Third World regimes, US relations elsewhere could suffer. Second, while these regimes were deemed to be stable in the near term, future decades would see a steady erosion of their stability if progress was not made toward majority rule. The United States would, therefore, continue to push for gradual movement toward black rule in Rhodesia and South Africa and for independence for Portugal's colonies, but much of the sense of urgency and idealism previously attached to this task dissipated.[4]

Prior to Portuguese decolonization Soviet objectives, as those of the United States, were viewed in largely zero-sum terms. Moscow sought to weaken the US grip on the region through its military and economic assistance to revolutionary movements in Angola, Mozambique, Rhodesia, South Africa, and South West Africa. Soviet assistance to these movements was a relatively low risk and inexpensive, yet reasonably effective policy.[5] In time, a minimal amount of Soviet assistance could seriously weaken US interests by helping to destabilize, if not overthrow, US allies in the region. Moreover, the Soviet willingness to provide support for the liberation effort was a major asset in its attempt to improve its ties with the existing black regimes in the region. With Zambia, in particular, Soviet assistance to the region's revolutionary movements became a cornerstone in what remained a relatively friendly relationship throughout the 1960s and 1970s.

THE EVOLUTION OF SOVIET INTERESTS AND OBJECTIVES

For both superpowers the process of Portuguese decolonization and its impact on southern Africa led to a significant restructuring of interests and objectives. With the ascent to power of Soviet-backed revolutionary movements in Angola and Mozambique, for the first time the Soviet Union developed a direct and major interest in the region. In both cases the revolutionary movements brought with them well-established ideological commitments to Soviet-style Marxism-Leninism and a close working relationship with the Soviet bloc. As a result, from the outset both regimes looked to the Soviet Union as their closest non-African ally. The resulting alliance relationship entailed a large and rapidly growing flow of arms, the provision of modest levels of economic assistance and close cooperation on a number of regional and international interests. A not inconsequential by-product of Soviet ties to Angola and Mozambique, and later Zimbabwe, was a steady improvement in Soviet political, economic and in some cases even military ties to some of the region's non-Marxist governments. As the Soviet presence in the region increased, the Soviet Union emerged as an acceptable and safe counterweight to dependence on South Africa and the West.

In recent years, however, there is growing evidence that many Soviet analysts and decision-makers are not satisfied with their new socialist allies in the Third World and the accompanying pattern of relations. One major complaint is that, despite the official commitment to scientific socialism on the part of both Angola and Mozambique, neither has progressed very far toward that goal. As then General Secretary Andropov argued, 'it is one thing to declare socialism as one's goal and another to build it.'[6] Aleksei Kiva argues that while Angola and Mozambique may have the commitment to socialism they simply do not have the economic and technical basis to build it. As a result, in both countries the social foundation of the revolution is now much weaker than it was at the beginning of the revolution.[7]

The poor performance of the existing regimes of socialist orientation has stimulated a rather heated debate among Soviet analysts. One group of analysts argues that when Third World regimes attempt to implement socialist policies immediately after independence they can cause immeasurable harm to their economies.[8] This may lead to a heavily bureaucratized socialism (such as that which existed under Brezhnev), which may actually inhibit the eventual development of true socialism.[9] Instead they need to develop policies which are more in keeping with their level of development. In practice this may include promoting capitalist development. As Kiva interprets Marx, no social system goes out of existence until it has exhausted its possibilities for development, and capitalism – at least in the Third World – has not.[10] Other analysts, however, are still relatively supportive of attempts to implement socialist transformations in Third World societies.[11]

Second, the costs of the new alliances are undoubtedly much greater than anyone in the Kremlin had expected. While aiding revolutionaries may be a relatively inexpensive endeavor, keeping them in power typically is not. Because of the combined effect of continuing civil wars and a variety of economic blunders both the Angolan and Mozambican economies have performed miserably. In general, their economies have not even kept pace with the modest economic results of their capitalist neighbors. This has been an embarrassment to the Soviet Union, and has resulted in a seemingly insatiable demand for foreign economic assistance that the Soviet Union is either unable or unwilling to meet. Some Soviet diplomats now privately consider Angola 'a bottomless pit into which the Kremlin has already poured too much money.'[12] Overall, the Soviet Union has poured about $8.2 billion into Angola over the past thirteen years.[13] While the total cost of Soviet assistance to Mozambique, both military and economic, is undoubtedly less, there is less chance that Mozambique will ever be in a position to repay the assistance it has been receiving. The rejection of Mozambique's 1981 application for full membership in the Council for Mutual Economic Assistance was a clear sign that the Soviet Union, and/or its allies, were unwilling to bear the financial burden of salvaging Mozambique's economy. As one Soviet diplomat explained, foreign economic ties should be designed to enrich the nation but 'at times we lose our own national income through such ties.'[14]

The Soviets may have underestimated the ultimate costs of their new alliances, and probably overestimated the potential benefits. Admittedly, on most major international issues, particularly those which do not concern southern Africa, Angola and Mozambique have steadfastly supported the Soviet position. However, Angola and Mozambique have yielded few strategic benefits. Soviet reconnaissance planes now use Angolan airfields to stage routine surveillance flights over the South Atlantic and Soviet ships use the facilities of Luanda Harbor.[15] However, neither Angola nor Mozambique has provided the Soviet Union with routine access to basing facilities. In Mozambique, for example, Soviet vessels are given access to specific facilities only on a case-by-case basis. To reinforce their position, both Angola and Mozambique have adopted constitutional clauses which strictly forbid the granting of foreign bases on their territory. In 1988, Mozambique went a step further by allowing a US warship to make a port of call for the first time since 1975.[16]

The growing Soviet disillusionment with the regimes resulting from past liberation struggles also led to a growing Soviet ambivalence toward the remaining liberation struggles, such as those in Namibia and South Africa. Not only have the past results of Soviet support been disappointing, but Soviet analysts have become increasingly concerned that superpower involvement in national liberation struggles might escalate into an unwanted superpower confrontation. How has the Soviet reassessment affected its interests and objectives in southern Africa? Although it may be too soon to draw definitive conclusions, there is considerable evidence that, while Soviet objectives may be relatively unchanged, the level of commitment to those goals has declined. The maintenance of its established allies in Angola and Mozambique is still the Soviet Union's primary objective in the region. However, the Soviet Union is not willing to provide the economic and military assistance necessary to ensure the survival of the existing Angolan and Mozambican regimes. Despite the growing Mozambican need for military assistance, the dollar value of Soviet arms transfers to Mozambique was actually less in 1982 and 1983 than it was in 1978 and Moscow is reported considering even further reductions in its assistance.[17] Although the level of Soviet military assistance has actually increased, both in terms of the quantity and quality of aid, the Soviet Union has attempted to cut its costs in Angola through a negotiated settlement of Angola's conflicts with South Africa and UNITA.[18]

THE EVOLUTION OF US INTERESTS AND OBJECTIVES

How were US interests and objectives in the region affected by Portuguese decolonization? As with the Soviet Union, US interests were most affected by the emergence of three new self-proclaimed socialist regimes. And, as their Soviet counterparts, US decision-makers differed considerably in their assessments of the meaning and importance of these changes. Ironically it is the conservatives within Congress, such as Jesse Helms in the Senate, and not those in the White House who have judged the existence of these regimes to be most injurious to US interests in the region. After an initial period of icy relations with Mozambique, the Reagan administration haltingly committed itself to providing economic assistance to Mozambique and resuming relatively normal and cooperative relations. And, if not for Congressional resistance, the administration might have provided Mozambique with military assistance as well. In Zimbabwe, after a steady deterioration in US–Zimbabwean relations throughout the early 1980s culminating in the Carter fiasco of 1984,[19] the Reagan administration pursued the normalization and gradual renewal of relations. Currently the United States is Zimbabwe's second leading trade partner (surpassed only marginally by Great Britain). The case of US policy toward Angola is unique. Although the United States remains Angola's leading trade partner, the Reagan administration refused to recognize the People's Republic of Angola and since 1986 actively sought its overthrow through US support for the *Uniao Nacional para a Independencia Total de Angola* (UNITA).[20] The explanation for this discrepancy in US policy is apparently not that the United States is any more concerned about Angola's willingness to assist revolutions elsewhere or that it found Angola's brand of Marxism-Leninism any more repugnant than Mozambique's. There are, however, two differences which help explain the US position. First, the United States found the use of Cuban troops in Angola an unacceptable precedent in the East–West rivalry in the Third World. This would account for the extraordinary emphasis the United States placed on the withdrawal of Cuban troops from Angola. Second, unlike the situation in Mozambique or Zimbabwe, the United States believes it has a viable alternative in Angola to the existing pro-Soviet regime, this being Jonas Savimbi and UNITA. Although US support for UNITA remains controversial, the Bush administration still sees the reversal of what it perceives as a major Soviet gain in the region as important enough to justify continued aid.

The primary US objective in the region, however, remains guaranteeing continued Western access to the resources of southern Africa. The above discussion suggests that, at least for the Reagan and Bush administrations, the spread of Soviet-backed regimes is no longer seen as the major threat to that objective. US support for the current Mozambican government and its discussions with the ANC would otherwise be inexplicable. Instead the US government appears to be increasingly taking the broader view that US interests, primarily access to minerals, are most likely to be threatened by the proliferation of conflicts in the region, somewhat irrespective of the role of the Soviet Union or its allies in these conflicts. This accounts for the growing US emphasis on negotiations and its increased willingness to normalize relations with the region's Marxist-Leninist governments and liberation movements.

CHANGING PATTERNS OF SUPERPOWER COOPERATION

Until recently southern Africa has been notable for the relative lack of superpower cooperation. Precisely because neither superpower regarded the region as critical to its economic or military security, both the United States and the Soviet Union tended to act in the region with relatively little fear of overly aggressive reactions by the other superpower. In other words, while the region offered fewer temptations for intervention than other regions, it also provides fewer inherent constraints on superpower conduct.

Not surprisingly, the pattern of superpower relations in southern Africa prior to Portuguese decolonization was overwhelmingly discordant. The two major tracks of Soviet policy were support for national liberation movements and growing cooperation with those existing black regimes which actively encouraged national liberation elsewhere in the region. This Soviet strategy left little room for cooperation with the United States. Although the United States found both white minority rule and colonial rule repugnant, it clearly viewed US interests as being tied to the continuation of those regimes until a transition to majority rule could be negotiated. From the US perspective the optimal solution would be an eventual transition to majority rule which eliminated, or at least minimized, the role of the Soviet-backed liberation movements. Conversely, from the Soviet perspective any transition to majority rule which did not result in a major, if not dominant, role for its allies was viewed as illegitimate. Thus, there was a direct clash in both the interests and the strategies of the superpowers, with little room for compromise.

At the same time, the steps taken by the superpowers in this period to avoid the escalation of local conflicts into superpower conflicts can be viewed as an important form of informal cooperation. The attempt to avoid escalation can be seen in the unwritten code of conduct to which both superpowers have generally adhered. For example, even during the height of the Cold War neither superpower introduced troops into the region's numerous conflicts.[21] In southern Africa the superpowers have demonstrated greater restraint in their commitment of military advisors to conflicts than elsewhere. When the United States committed military advisors, they were relatively few in number, and the government attempted to keep the operation covert.[22] While the Soviet Union has generally been more willing to commit military advisors, in every case it has refused to send military advisors until an official government has been declared and recognized.

In fact, superpower conduct in southern African conflicts has generally been significantly more restrained than that of their allies. In Angola, not only did Cuban advisors appear before independence, but the number of Cuban combat troops in Angola surpassed 50,000 in 1988. On this point it is also worth remembering Castro's claim, and the supporting evidence, which suggests that the Soviet Union was not even consulted prior to the introduction of these forces.[23] Similarly, during the second Shaba crisis, it was France, not the United States, which took the lead in opposing the incursion. The US role in the conflict was largely limited to supplying the carrier aircraft needed to ferry French and Belgian contingents to Zaire.[24]

Until the spring of 1975 it could be argued that the superpowers were relatively restrained in their arms deliveries to southern Africa, both in term of the quality of the weapons systems being provided and the sheer quantity of arms reaching the region. However, in 1975 it became clear that the future of Angola was to be decided on the battlefield. As a result, in the spring of 1975 there was a dramatic increase in the provision of arms by both the United States and the Soviet Union provided to their respective allies among the revolutionary forces in Angola. In the view of many American observers it was the Soviet bloc which, through a massive infusion of arms and the provision of Cuban troops, broke the unwritten code of superpower conduct in the era of *détente* that had theretofore prevented an escalation of superpower conflict in the region. The fact that American involvement in Angola was also increasing dramatically prior to the congressional intervention greatly undermines the validity of this argument. Regardless of the accuracy of the American accusations, Brezhnev must have judged the charges as serious enough to merit a prompt and unequivocal response. At the 25th Party Congress, he argued that,

> Some bourgeois leaders affect surprise and raise a howl over the solidarity of Soviet communists, and the Soviet people, with the struggle of other peoples for freedom and progess. This is either outright *naïveté* or more likely a deliberate befuddling of minds. It could not be clearer, after all, that *détente* and peaceful coexistence have to do with interstate relations ... *Détente* does not at all abolish, nor can it abolish or alter, the laws of class struggle.[25]

For neither superpower can it be argued that the only reason for restraint was the avoidance of superpower confrontation. However, this was an objective shared by the superpowers, albeit with different priorities. Furthermore, the principal result of this restraint was undeniably an informal cap on the discordant behavior of both superpowers. Thus, throughout the 1970s both superpowers tended to view superpower relations in the region in zero-sum terms. The effect was largely to limit superpower cooperation to various forms of conflict limitation. The importance of this, however, should not be undervalued. Between 1975 and 1980 southern Africa experienced a number of conflicts in which the superpowers had an interest: the Angolan civil war, Shaba I, Shaba II and the Rhodesian revolutionary war. Each of these had a potential for escalation which was averted.

The transition to black rule in Zimbabwe during the late 1970s marks a transition point in superpower relations in southern Africa because it presented a situation in which the interests of the rival superpowers were not directly opposed. By then the United States was convinced of the dangers of letting revolutionary struggles run their course. To avoid a repetition of the events in Angola, in 1976 then Secretary of State Henry Kissinger sought to bring about a negotiated settlement in Rhodesia between Ian Smith's white regime and the black opposition. Kissinger believed that this would shorten the revolutionary process and thus would prevent the further radicalization of the black opposition.[26] It would also end the black opposition's need for Soviet weapons and open the way for an improvement of their relations with the United States. The US hope was that negotiations and subsequent elections would lead to the emergence of a black regime led by the internal opposition rather than by either of the two revolutionary movements.

The Carter administration, however, realized that the likelihood of excluding the revolutionary groups from a successful negotiated settlement was extremely slim and was prepared to deal with whatever regime resulted. In fact, of the two revolutionary movements, the United States was clearly more comfortable with Joshua Nkomo's Zimbabwe African People's Union (ZAPU) than with Robert Mugabe's more radical Zimbabwe African National Union (ZANU). The main reason was that Nkomo's ties with the West, especially with the Western business community, were quite strong. The Soviet Union, ZAPU's major arms supplier, was repulsed by ZANU's Maoist ideology and tactics and rudely rejected ZANU's desperate pleas for arms and other assistance. Thus, if faced with a choice between the two revolutionary movements, both superpowers would have preferred to see ZAPU, rather than ZANU, emerge as the dominant black political force in Rhodesia.

Although the superpowers preferred ZAPU for very different reasons, their interests were nonetheless complementary. But, for cooperation to occur, both sides must be aware of the opportunities for cooperation and willing to accept the tradeoffs involved. In Zimbabwe, this was clearly not the case. In 1979 when the Lancaster House Agreement was signed, the Soviet Union was deeply suspicious of any agreement with the white regime, particularly one which was negotiated under British and US sponsorship. The Soviet trepidation may have stemmed from their realization that because of ZANU's larger base of ethnic support it was likely that ZAPU would fare poorly in the elections mandated by the Lancaster House Agreement. This, however, does not appear to have been the main reason for the Soviet hesitancy to endorse the agreement. The available historical evidence suggests that the Soviets, as most outside observers, were quite surprised by ZAPU's resounding defeat in Zimbabwe's first elections. Instead, the Soviets believed that because of ZAPU's superior military potential it would benefit most from a military resolution of the conflict. Thus, even after the Lancaster House Agreement was signed, the Soviet Union sought to undermine it by increasing the flow of arms to ZAPU.[27] On the US side, the Western decision to exclude the Soviet Union from the negotiation process did little to allay Soviet fears that their interests would be ill-served by the resulting agreement.

One major impact of the Soviet reassessment of its policy in southern Africa was to make its interests more complementary with those of the United States. But for the level of cooperation to increase it was necessary that the United States recognize and respond to the growing compatibility of superpower interests. In the early 1980s the primary US objectives in the region were to prevent the creation of new Soviet-backed regimes in South Africa and Namibia and to undermine the Soviet position by supporting efforts to destabilize the existing Soviet-backed regimes. The pursuit of these objectives entailed the resumption of US aid to UNITA in 1986 and turning a partially blind eye to South Africa's efforts to destabilize black-ruled states throughout the region. However, by the end of 1987 the United States was also beginning to rethink its objectives and policies in southern Africa, albeit to a lesser extent than the Soviet Union.

The American reassessment, to the extent that the label is appropriate, takes into account a number of recent changes in the region. First, as the Soviet Union has distanced itself from some of its allies in the Third World, Western governments, including the United States, are being actively courted by these regimes. Despite the tentative US reaction to this opening, a number of other Western nations have significantly strengthened their economic ties to these regimes. Second, neither Mozambique nor Angola has presented the kind of threat to US interests in the region which was predicted by many Western analysts in the 1970s. This has allowed for a significant improvement in US relations with Mozambique, as well as with some of the non-Marxist frontline states. Third, it is becoming increasingly apparent that, as the Soviet commitment to the remaining liberation movements is wavering, the United States has less to fear from Soviet-backed revolutions. Although the revolutionary forces remain strong, and are in many ways growing, there is less reason to view them as mere appendages of the Soviet Union. This accounts for the growing US interest in the opposition forces in South Africa, which culminated in the 1986 meeting between then Secretary of State George Shultz and ANC President Oliver Tambo.

At the same time, changes in US and Soviet thinking have not resulted in a significant calming of the region's conflicts. An explanation for this is that as the growth of Soviet involvement in southern Africa's conflicts subsided, South Africa's involvement dramatically increased. In the view of some, by the middle of the 1980s South Africa had supplanted the Soviet Union as the primary military actor in the region.[28] In fact, largely because of South Africa's efforts to destabilize its neighbors, the region is potentially as unstable now as on the eve of the Portuguese decolonization. In the view of Joseph Hanlon, South Africa has been conducting an undeclared war against its neighbors in order to defend apartheid in South Africa itself.[29] This leads to the conclusion that South Africa's policy of destabilization is itself a threat to US interests in the region because it is ultimately the escalation of the current conflicts, rather than the long-feared transitions to majority rule, that is disrupting Western access to goods and markets in the region. While signs of a 'new thinking' in US policy toward southern Africa were just emerging in the waning years of the Reagan administration, it is too early to determine decisively the orientation of the Bush administration. But the modest nature of Bush's policies elsewhere would suggest that the United States will become even more open to future opportunities for superpower cooperation in southern Africa.

Thus far I have argued that beginning in the early 1980s a number of changes occurred in Soviet objectives and policies in the region, and to a lesser extent the objectives and policies of the United States, which made superpower cooperation increasingly possible. But in order to understand the forms of cooperation which are beginning to characterize superpower behavior in the region, it is necessary to discuss actual instances of such cooperation.

Even in the early 1980s there was evidence of new forms of informal superpower cooperation in the region. When the needed Soviet assistance failed to materialize, both Angola and Mozambique realized that critical to the recovery, or merely to stabilizing the downward spiral, of their respective economies was the acquisition of Western economic assistance and an end to South Africa's destabilization efforts. Thus, both governments eventually began pursuing a *rapprochement* with the West, including the United States. Initially, the Soviet Union was somewhat resistant to the policy shifts. Soviet officials and analysts frequently warned their allies of the 'dangers of conducting business with the West'.[30] Eventually, however, Moscow warmed to the advantages of having the Western nations and Western-based international financial organizations remove some of the financial burdens Angola and Mozambique represent.

The Soviet Union initially maintained similar qualms over the growth of US diplomatic contacts with its allies. This can be seen most clearly in the initial Soviet disdain for the US-facilitated Lusaka accords between Angola and South Africa, and the US-encouraged Nkomati accords between Mozambique and South Africa. These agreements essentially provided for an end to South African support for the counterrevolutionary forces in Angola and Mozambique in exchange for which Angola and Mozambique were required to end their assistance to the Soviet-backed revolutionary movements in South Africa and Namibia. These agreements frustrated the Soviet Union in a number of ways.[31] To begin with, most in Moscow at that time were quite optimistic about the prospects for revolution in South Africa; yet the loss of the ANC's facilities in Angola and Mozambique could seriously weaken its ability to maintain its links with the growing internal resistance. Second, Moscow viewed the agreements as an admission of the failures of its earlier policies. Third, the agreements, if successful, could reaffirm the United States' role as the primary external mediator in the region. Finally, 'Angola's decision to not only "deal with the enemy" but to do so without consulting' them must have been especially grating to the Soviets.[32] It is therefore noteworthy that both agreements were eventually accepted, although certainly not welcomed, by the Soviet Union.

Although neither the Nkomati accords nor the Lusaka accords were successful, they marked an important shift in superpower cooperation. For different reasons both superpowers sought to reduce the growing civil conflicts inside Angola and Mozambique. Moreover, both professed a clear desire to halt South Africa's policy of destabilization.

In Mozambique, the coincidence of US and Soviet interests has continued. Currently, both superpowers support the Mozambican government in its civil war against the Mozambican National Resistance (RENAMO). Although the Soviet Union has not kept up with Mozambique's ever growing requests for additional arms, it remains Mozambique's leading arms supplier. Despite pressure from some conservatives in Congress, the Reagan and Bush administrations also refused to open even informal contacts with the RENAMO. In 1985 the Reagan administration proposed an aid package for Mozambique which for the first time included limited non-lethal military supplies, but the House of Representatives imposed a number of restrictions on the package which effectively prohibited all but food aid. Since 1985 the amount of American food aid has increased gradually, but there has been no change in US policy on military aid, despite the fact that Mozambique receives military assistance from a number of the US's Western European allies.

For the United States, providing an alternative to Mozambique's excessive economic dependence on the Soviet bloc is certainly a prime motive for its recent aid. More precisely, the United States acknowledges the Soviet desire to reduce its military commitments in Mozambique and seeks to promote that process. To the extent that Mozambique's growing economic ties to the United States and other Western states have lessened the pain of the Soviet disengagement, for Mozambique this informal superpower cooperation has been successful. Nonetheless, this represents a dramatic reversal from the Reagan administration's early antipathy for the Mozambican regime. More importantly, for the first time in recent history, the Soviet Union and the United States are both providing assistance to the same side in a major southern African conflict.[33]

The December 1988 Angola–Namibia Accords provide tangible evidence that superpower cooperation in southern Africa is now moving to a new stage of formal cooperation. In brief, the Accords entailed four major provisions. First, South Africa was required to withdraw its military forces gradually from Namibia (thus ending its direct support for UNITA). The last South African troops had to leave Namibia before 1 November 1989. Second, the estimated 50,000 Cuban troops were to withdraw gradually from Angola, with the last troops leaving on or before 1 July 1991. Third, as the South Africans left Angola, elections supervised by the United Nations were held to determine Namibia's first independent government. Fourth, the withdrawal process and the subsequent elections were monitored by the United Nations. A joint appeals commission, including representatives of both the United States and the Soviet Union, was formed to arbitrate any ensuing disputes over the implementation of the Accords.

It is ironic to recall that superpower relations in Angola, up until last year, were even more directly discordant than superpower relations elsewhere in the region. In 1985 the Reagan administration finally succeeded in repealing the decade-old Clark Amendment banning aid to UNITA. During 1986 and 1987 the United States provided UNITA with approximately $15 million in annual military assistance, including Stinger surface-to-air missiles. The increase in US aid, combined with a growth in aid from South Africa and other US allies, had a profound effect on UNITA's fortunes on the battlefield, and by 1987 UNITA forces were able to strike throughout the country and were thought to be dominant in almost one third of the territory.

By 1987 it appeared as if the superpowers were again facing a growing regional conflict in which they provided military assistance to opposing sides. This was precisely the type of conflict that risked further escalation and could spill over and significantly sour superpower relations. Possibly to avoid this precise scenario a direct dialogue between the superpowers developed. In 1986 US and Soviet officials met twice to discuss regional conflicts in accordance with the agreement reached at the November 1985 Reagan–Gorbachev summit. During these talks the Soviet Union was reportedly quite eager to discuss southern Africa, and Angola in particular.[34] At the 1987 Washington summit the issue of Angola was again raised as President Reagan unsuccessfully sought Soviet backing for a US regional peace plan. However, in subsequent bilateral meetings between US Assistant Secretary of State Chester Crocker and Soviet Deputy Foreign Minister Anatoly Adamishin significant progress was made.[35] At the heart of the matter the Soviet Union and the United States were ultimately able to agree in principle to the idea of a mutual withdrawal of Cuban forces from Angola and South African forces from Namibia. It was this understanding which formed the basis of the subsequent Angola–Namibia Accords.

Crocker, who is not generally known for his glowing accounts of Soviet behavior, described the Accords as 'a rather remarkable case study of US-Soviet cooperation to recognize actual historical realities and work together to solve a regional problem.'[36] During the negotiations there were numerous signs of Soviet-American cooperation, at times even to the consternation of their respective regional allies.

The Soviet Union reportedly pressured Angola and Cuba during the negotiations by warning that further Soviet assistance might not be forthcoming if they were intransigent.[37] At one point Adamishin himself explained, 'We did not give our friends advice on how to conduct the negotiations. They did this very well on their own – but we assisted in ensuring that a settlement was achieved.' He believed that, were it not for the role played by the Soviet Union, 'there would have been no accord.'[38] The effectiveness of Soviet pressure is illustrated by this story. In November of 1988, during a critical juncture in the negotiations, Crocker remarked to his Soviet diplomatic counterpart that Pretoria had responded to a proposal on troop withdrawal, but, as of yet, he had not received an answer from Angola. 'The Soviet official told Mr Crocker the reply would be coming shortly. It did; the next day.'[39] Similarly, it can be assumed that South Africa was acutely aware of the United States' desire to reach an agreement and the possible ramifications for itself if South Africa was seen by the United States as the major barrier to an agreement. A South African observer has even suggested that 'the US State Department may have acted by omission in order to enhance the utility of the Cuban military thrust, in pushing South Africa to the table.'[40] Additionally, a US columnist sympathetic to South Africa reports that the United States threatened to refuse to roll over South Africa's loans or advance new credits if South Africa did not yield on Angola.[41]

Despite the fact that the United States acted as the principle mediator in the negotiations, the Soviet Union consistently supported the process. From the perspective of at least one Soviet observer, the Americans 'assumed the role of an honest broker at the talks. They conveyed the proposals of the two sides technically without expressing their own attitude toward them.'[42] Because the Soviet Union did not have formal ties to one of the major participants, South Africa, the Soviets were satisfied with their lesser observer status. At the same time, the US willingness to have the Soviet Union participate in the talks, even as an observer, must have been seen as a major cooperative step, and one that is uncharacteristic of past US practice in the resolution of regional conflicts. Certainly, Soviet observers were not welcome at the Lancaster House negotiations. Despite initial denials, Adamishin eventually admitted that unofficial observers attended all eleven rounds of talks.[43]

There was also strong evidence of superpower cooperation in the controversy which surrounded the cost of the UN peacekeeping forces. As permanent members of the UN Security Council, the Soviet Union and the United States were obligated to pay a major share of the estimated $650 million cost for the 7,500 person peacekeeping force requested by Black Africa and the non-aligned nations. When the Soviet Union and the United States, along with the other permanent members of the Security Council, raised the possibility of reducing the costs of the peacekeeping force some allies of both superpowers reacted negatively. South Africa was concerned that a reduction in the peacekeeping force would make it more difficult to monitor Cuba's withdrawal, but checking for Cubans who might have acquired Angolan citizenship was not one of the tasks of the UN forces. Moscow's allies in the Third World, as well as the majority of the non-aligned states, opposed the reduction on the grounds that a smaller peace keeping force might not be able to prevent South African manipulation of the independence process in Namibia. On these grounds Robert Mugabe, the prime minister of Zimbabwe and former president of the non-aligned movement, repeatedly appealed to Moscow to oppose the proposed reduction.[44] SWAPO's foreign secretary, Theo Ben Gurirab, complained that for 'the first time the Big Five have ganged up on an issue' and consequently the non-aligned movement could no longer take for granted the support of either the Soviet Union or the People's Republic of China.[45]

While the United States is relatively accustomed to criticism from these quarters, the Soviet Union was not. The initial Soviet response was understandably cautious. The Soviet ambassador to Zimbabwe told his host that although the Soviet Union was not 'indifferent to the costs of peacekeeping', it was opposed to any reduction in forces.[46] The next day, however, an official Soviet spokesman said that the Soviet Union was 'ready to search for ways to economize' if it could be done without lowering the effectiveness of the UN forces.[47]

However, US and Soviet pressure ultimately prompted United Nations Secretary General Perez de Cuellar to recommend slashing the UN forces for Namibia to 4,650 troops. The cost of deploying these troops, and the other needed personnel would still be a hefty $416 million.[48] However, if this number proved inadequate the UN commander would still have the option of calling in additional troops up to, but not in excess of, 7,500.

During the negotiations both superpowers also agreed to act as guarantors of the agreement. As a result, the United States and the Soviet Union both sit on the joint commission to resolve the problems which arise from the withdrawal process and the transition to independence for Namibia. By the spring of 1989 the joint commission had already been called on to deal with a number of alleged violations of the Accords,[49] but by far the most serious was the infiltration of armed SWAPO forces into Namibia in early April. With the future of the Accords in the balance, the superpowers again placed peace above the wishes of their allies. The UN Security Council, including the Soviet Union, basically sanctioned the South African effort militarily to root out the SWAPO incursion. Interestingly, while Soviet journalists tended to deny SWAPO's culpability for the incursion, claiming that the clashes were 'accidental' or the result of a South African attack,[50] Soviet diplomats were quite willing to blame SWAPO.[51] Meanwhile both superpowers pushed hard for a cease-fire. It is too early to surmise how successful the Angola–Namibia Accords will ultimately be.[52] It should not be forgotten that both the previous agreements between South Africa and its Black neighbours have been openly violated when convenient.

What conclusions do the Angola–Namibia Accords provide concerning superpower motivations? In one way, superpower cooperation in Angola can be seen as a continuation of the processes observed in Mozambique, because the same basic motivations and objectives were involved. For the Soviet Union, the key to the Accords is reducing its own commitment and expenses in the region without the immediate fall of a major ally, Angola, and without a significant loss of face. For the Soviet Union, independence for Namibia, which brings black-rule one step closer to South Africa, is probably only a secondary, but nonetheless meaningful, benefit of the agreement. For the United States, as in Mozambique, the key is in promoting the further disengagement of the Soviet bloc from the region. In this case this entails not only an anticipated reduction of Soviet influence in Angola, but sending home an estimated 50,000

Cuban forces. Additionally for the United States, if the Accords are successful, it will mean an end to the embarrassment and political condemnation it has received from Black Africa and the non-aligned movement for the South African occupation of Namibia.

What conclusions can then be drawn about superpower cooperation in southern Africa? The obvious conclusion is that for most of the Cold War there has been very little superpower cooperation. Until the early 1980s the way the superpowers defined their interests and objectives typically left the superpowers supporting competing outcomes. Even in cases where superpower interests were complementary, the rigid zero-sum lens through which both superpowers tended to view the region resulted in missed opportunities, as was the case in Zimbabwe in the late 1970s.

The dominant form of cooperation in southern Africa has been informal, designed to avoid an escalation toward direct superpower conflict. To this end, both superpowers appear to have adopted a minimum code of conduct. In practice this meant that while both superpowers were prone to becoming involved in regional conflicts, they tended to avoid military intervention and restrained their military involvement in a variety of ways. Apparently, the operative assumption for both superpowers was that there was little in the region for which it was worth risking confrontation. While this axiom certainly does not hold true for other Third World regions, for the Middle East or Latin America for example, it has remained consistently true for southern Africa. On a more cautionary note, short of overt military involvement, the low salience of the region also leaves both superpowers free to meddle in the region with little fear of overreaction by the other superpower.

Aside from crisis management, informal cooperation can at times also be seen in superpower policy toward the region's minority regimes and the Portuguese colonies. The US and Soviet sanction programs against Rhodesia and South Africa can be seen in this light. While the superpowers envisioned different outcomes, their policies were mutually reinforcing to the extent that both were designed to promote a transition to black rule. A similar argument can be made for the US and Soviet efforts to encourage Portuguese decolonization. Because the Soviet Union was more consistently committed to decolonization, the extent to which superpower policy was reinforcing was largely a function of the twists in US policy. Parallel superpower action was greatest, therefore, during the Kennedy and Carter years.

Since the early 1980s, however, a new trend in superpower cooperation in southern Africa has emerged. In this period there have been new incidents of informal cooperation. Not only have both superpowers continued to push for a regime change in South Africa but they have undertaken actions which more directly reinforce the interest of the other superpower. Examples of this practice would be shared support for the Mozambican government in its ongoing civil war and the financial support which both superpowers have provided for the South African Development and Coordination Conference (SADCC) and a number of frontline states.

A more dramatic change is the introduction of formal cooperation into superpower relations exemplified by the Angola–Namibia Accords. The agreement was continuous with past practice in that both superpowers continued to view their interests in a competitive framework and generally preferred to see a reduction of the other's involvement in the region. But for the first time the Soviet Union and United States formally worked together for an extended period of time to bring about a mutually agreed upon result, the simultaneous withdrawal of Cuban forces from Angola and South African forces from Namibia. It is important to note again that while the final arrangement was acceptable to all of the local actors, they were at times pushed toward this end by their superpower allies. One cannot, therefore, assume that greater superpower cooperation will necessarily serve the interests or desires of the local actors.

THE FUTURE OF SUPERPOWER COOPERATION

What then is the future of superpower cooperation in southern Africa? If one's judgement is guided strictly by the historical evolution presented above, the clear conclusion is that southern Africa is likely to witness a continued growth in both informal and formal superpower cooperation in the 1990s. Unfortunately, straight-line projections from historical trends have frequently proved to be an unreliable basis for prediction in the social sciences. To understand better the future prospects for superpower cooperation, therefore, one must focus on two queries. First, to what extent is the current superpower willingness to cooperate likely to continue? And, second, are there opportunities in southern Africa where superpower cooperation is likely to prove beneficial to both superpowers?

To begin with, one can assume that for both superpowers, or at least for the current leaders, some 'political learning' has occurred. The Soviet Union has clearly come to the conclusion that supporting the creation of Marxist-Leninist regimes is in all likelihood a costlier and riskier strategy than was once believed. Furthermore, the political and military rewards of this strategy, even when successfully implemented, are fewer than previously anticipated. Thus, even when Soviet involvement in the region successfully undermined US influence, the Soviet position was not necessarily improved. The United States has also learned to be more skeptical of formal proclamations of Marxism-Leninism. To the extent that such commitments are serious, the United States can no longer discount the possible evolution of the system. Moreover, the existence of these regimes has not been as detrimental to Western economic and military interests as was once feared. Presumably, the successful negotiation of the Angola–Namibia Accords has demonstrated to both superpowers the advantages of working together. On a more cautionary note, however, if either side fails to live up to the Accords, or allows its allies to violate the Accords, the lessons of the Accords are likely to be rapidly reinterpreted.

To put the recent trend toward superpower cooperation in southern Africa in perspective, however, one must seriously consider the possibility that the present superpower interest in cooperation will evaporate. This could happen for a variety of reasons. One widely mentioned possibility is that Gorbachev will be overthrown by some of his more conservative colleagues. An even more likely scenario is that Gorbachev, in an attempt to consolidate the centre in Soviet politics, will himself move to a more conservative position. However, one should not discount the numerous sources of change in US policy. In recent US history shifts in US policy have accompanied not only executive changes, but also bureaucratic shifts within a given administration. For example, the growing conservatism of the final Carter years is often attributed to Brzezinski's rise to prominence and the weakening of Vance's role and his eventual removal. Similarly, during the two Reagan administrations the growing interest in superpower cooperation documented in this volume coincided with the gradual replacement of neo-conservatives (e.g. Haig, MacFarlane and Weinberger) with less ideological figures (e.g. Shultz, Powell, and Carlucci). One should also recall the volatility of US public opinion and how it reacted not only to the Soviet invasion of Afghanistan, but also to unplanned incidents such as the downing of KAL-007. Finally, with regard to southern Africa, it is sometimes more difficult to obtain cooperation between the US Congress and the president than between the superpowers. Thus, on both sides, the present commitment to formal superpower cooperation must be seen as very tenuous.

The question remains, however, does the regional environment present opportunities for fruitful superpower cooperation? Southern Africa certainly does not lack for problems in which cooperation could be fruitful. Bringing Namibia to independence is certainly a process which will require continued superpower cooperation. While they may differ on whom they would like to see rule, both seem fully committed to the independence process. The problem of national reconciliation in Angola and Mozambique, however, is a much more intractable one. Recent developments would provide some basis for optimism. Not only are both superpowers now calling for national reconciliation, but both the Mozambican and Angolan governments now appear committed to the process. In Angola progress can be seen in terms of the willingness of both sides to commit themselves to a cease-fire in preparation for negotiations. In Mozambique progress can be found in the government's nascent talks with South Africa as well as the superpowers, a step preliminary to talks with RENAMO. President Chissano even suggested that the Angolan cease-fire is an example which can be followed in Mozambique.[53]

Unfortunately, in neither case has significant progress been made on the political problems which are necessary to end these conflicts permanently. In both cases, national reconciliation probably requires a willingness of both parties to accept, at least in the short term, some form of shared governance. Given the long history of antagonism and the alleged atrocities in both conflicts, this will prove a difficult hurdle. Moreover, the path is certainly not clear for superpower cooperation. In Angola, the main problem is that Congressional support for Savimbi will make it difficult for the United States to place too much pressure on UNITA. This, of course, will make it difficult for the superpowers to reach a consensus on what role UNITA will play in a future Angolan regime. Conversely, Soviet prestige will be harmed if the Soviet Union places too much pressure to compromise on the Angolan government. In Mozambique the problem is somewhat different. Here the question is what pressure either superpower can place on RENAMO in the absence of formal diplomatic ties. Thus, while superpower cooperation would be easier to obtain in Mozambique, it is less critical to a resolution of the conflict.

Ultimately, the most intractable problem in southern Africa concerns South Africa itself. When discussing the South African problem there are two related, yet logically distinct, areas with which one must deal. The first and more challenging problem is that of apartheid and the accompanying political conflict. Second, there is the South African policy of destabilizing its neighbors.

With regard to South Africa's internal problems, there again is some initial room for optimism. In recent years there have been policy changes on the part of both superpowers which would make cooperation more possible. On the Soviet side there is growing evidence that the Soviet Union would be willing to accept a negotiated settlement in South Africa, and possibly one in which the ANC–SACP alliance did not emerge as the dominant actor in post-apartheid South Africa.[54] Recently numerous Soviet leaders, including Gorbachev himself, actively called for the negotiated settlement of all regional conflicts in the Third World, including those in southern Africa. A pair of the Soviet Union's leading Africanists, both of whom are deputy directors of the prestigious Moscow–based Institute of Africa, have gone further by suggesting a negotiated settlement in South Africa that entailed constitutional guarantees for whites, such as those granted in Zimbabwe, and the creation of a federal system along ethnic lines with a great amount of local autonomy. They also suggest that the Soviet Union should act as one of the international guarantors of such a settlement. Finally, there is some evidence that the Soviet Union is seeking to improve its ties with progressive whites and black opposition groups other than the ANC with the realization that these groups could play a significant role in a post-apartheid South African government.

The change in United States policy, albeit a lesser one, is also significant. In 1987 for the first time representatives of the US government officially met with representatives of the ANC. The US position, like that of South Africa, is that the ANC must first renounce terrorism before these relations can be normalized in any meaningful way. The United States has also actively encouraged the ANC to break with the SACP. While these may still represent a significant barrier to a US–ANC dialogue, a change has occurred to the extent that the US now appears ready to accept a major ANC role in any settlement of the South African problem and has even tacitly encouraged a government dialogue with the ANC.

Since the start of negotiations between the ANC and the South African government in the spring of 1990, the chances of a negotiated settlement in South Africa are far better than at any time in the past. It must be understood, however, that the negotiation process in

South Africa is only beginning and the potential pitfalls are numerous. Moreover, the ability of the superpowers, even with close formal cooperation, to promote a resolution of South Africa's domestic problems is extremely limited. Neither the Soviet Union nor the United States has demonstrated much ability to effect changes in the behavior of any of the disputants in South Africa. Unlike the case in Angola and Namibia, in South Africa the major disputants have expressed strong reservations about superpower involvement and have clearly indicated a preference for direct negotiations, free from external mediators or guarantors. Given that a failed superpower attempt to resolve the South African problem may actually undermine the existing trend toward cooperation in the region, and given that the chances for success are slight, the growth of superpower cooperation on this particular problem may be prudently slow.

The issue of South Africa's destabilization campaign offers greater possibilities for superpower cooperation. Here not only are superpower objectives complementary, but the chances of superpower cooperation succeeding are relatively good. For the Soviet Union, ending South Africa's destabilization campaign would strengthen its allies in Angola and Mozambique as well as the other friendly frontline states. Ultimately this would reduce the demand for Soviet military assistance. For the United States the end of South Africa's destabilization campaign would reduce the dependence of the frontline states on Soviet military assistance and, ultimately, could lead to a decrease in the Soviet presence in the region. Additionally, a general reduction of regional tension would reduce Western concerns about a possible disruption of the resource flow and would lessen the threat to Western economic investments.

Together, the superpowers could also apply considerable pressure on South Africa. The real threat that the US could pose is not the strengthening of its overall sanctions program, which is aimed largely at promoting domestic change, but a strengthening of US ties to South Africa's competitors – the frontline states, SWAPO and the ANC. In particular, if the United States were to provide military assistance to the frontline states to defend themselves against South Africa's destabilization campaign, this would significantly undermine South Africa's self-image as the major defender of Western interests in the region. While a modicum of US military assistance may have a great psychological effect on South Africa, it is the significant growth in Soviet military assistance which has increased the economic and human costs to South Africa of its destabilization campaign.

Daniel R. Kempton

In conclusion, the present trend in southern Africa is toward greater superpower cooperation. This has entailed a wide scope of informal cooperation. However, the most significant change is the recent willingness of the superpowers to cooperate formally in the resolution of regional conflicts to their mutual advantage. In the Angola–Namibia Accords the superpowers doggedly pursued a settlement, even when they were faced with significant resistance from their southern African allies. It now appears likely that informal superpower cooperation will continue, albeit on a sporadic basis. The superpowers have a shared interest not only in avoiding the escalation of regional conflicts into superpower confrontations but also in a variety of regional issues. In South Africa, for example, while the superpowers ultimately prefer different successor regimes, both at present seek to promote a transition to black rule. In Mozambique and elsewhere the interests of both superpowers would be served by a stabilization of the existing regime. However, whether the 1990s will witness more incidents of formal cooperation as exemplified by the Angola–Namibia Accords is still an open question.

NOTES

1. For an excellent summary of US policy in southern Africa prior to 1975 consult Thomas J. Noer, *Cold War and Black Liberation: The United States and White Rule in Africa, 1943–1968* (Columbia, MO: University of Missouri Press, 1985).
2. Ibid., p. 253.
3. On the Kissinger study see Anthony Lake, *The Tar Baby Option: American Policy Toward Southern Rhodesia* (New York: Columbia University Press, 1976) and Mohammed El-Khawas and Baring Cohen (eds), *The Kissinger Study of Southern Africa* (Westport, CT: Lawrence Hill, 1976).
4. During the Carter years there was of course a de-emphasis of East–West factors in US foreign policy and a return to the emphasis on promoting change which was characteristic of the early Kennedy years.
5. For an in depth discussion of Soviet strategy during the 1970s see Daniel R. Kempton, *Soviet Strategy Toward Southern Africa: the National Liberation Connection* (New York: Praeger, 1989), pp. 1–33.
6. *Pravda*, 16 June 1983.
7. Alexei Kiva, 'Socialist Orientation: Reality and Illusions', *International Affairs*, no. 7 (1988) 86.
8. Advocates of this argument include Boris Asoyan, *Literaturnaya gazeta*, no. 46 (1988); Alexei Kiva, op. cit. (1988), pp. 78–86;

'Developing Countries, Socialism, Capitalism', *International Affairs*, no. 3 (1989), pp. 54–63; Nikalai Kosukhin, Radio Moscow in Portuguese, 19 January 1989, translated in *FBIS-SOV-89-031* (16 February 1989), pp. 32–4; and Igor Zevelev and Alexei Kara-Murza, 'The Destiny of Socialism and the Afro-Asian World', *Asia and Africa Today*, no. 3 (1989), pp. 2–6.

9. Zevelev and Kara-Murza claim that building socialism in underdeveloped societies contrary to the lines of capitalism may lead to *étatism* (op. cit., 1989, p. 4), while Kiva fears the development of 'a nonproletarian socialism behind a Marxist-Leninist facade' (op. cit., 1989, p. 59).

10. Kiva, op. cit., 1989, p. 61.

11. For a clear juxtaposition of the two position see the arguments presented in Vladimir Lee and George Mirsky, 'Socialist Orientation and New Political Thinking', *Asia and Africa Today*, no. 4 (1988), pp. 64–70 and Ivanov's critique of Mirsky in Yuri Ivanov, 'Some Problems of Non-Capitalist Development', *Asia and Africa Today*, no. 6 (1988), pp. 66–9.

12. E. A. Wayne, 'US negotiators walk a minefield in bid for peace in Angola', *Christian Science Monitor*, 18 February 1988, p. 5.

13. E. A. Wayne, 'African leaders want US mediation in Angola, but no rebel aid', *Christian Sicence Monitor*, 18 April 1988, p. 7.

14. Ivan Ivanov, 'Problems of Foreign Economic Ties', *International Affairs*, no. 11 (1988), p. 41.

15. John Marcum, 'Bipolar Dependency: The People's Republic of Angola', in Michael Clough (ed.), *Reassessing the Soviet Challenge in Africa* (Berkeley, CA: University of California, Institute of International Studies, 1986), pp. 12–30.

16. To add salt to the wound of this insult to the Soviet Union, President Chissano made a point of visiting the US ship, Peter Younghusband, 'Chissano emerges as Calm Broker', *Washington Times*, 18 October 1988.

17. The Soviet Union is reportedly considering withdrawing all of its advisors from Mozambique in 1990 and reducing its military assistance by about 40 per cent, E. A. Wayne, 'US Seeks End to Mozambique War', *Christian Science Monitor*, 12 July 1989, p. 8.

18. It should be noted that most Soviet arms transfers are not gifts; they are to be paid for by the recipients. By 1987 the total Angolan debt to the Soviet Union was approaching a staggering $2.6 billion.

19. During an international conference on apartheid hosted by Zimbabwe, the Zimbabwean Minister of Youth, Sport and Culture, David Karimanzira, delivered a scathing attack on US policy in southern Africa. The US delegation, led by former President Jimmy Carter, walked out in protest. The irony was that few Americans had done more to oppose apartheid than Jimmy Carter.

20. In the early years of the Carter administration the United States seriously considered recognizing the Angolan regime. But with the presence of Zbigniew Brzezinski and Hamilton Jordan in Carter's inner circle it was apparently difficult to reach the consensus of opinion

Carter generally required to act. After the Shaba incursion, for which Carter vehemently condemned Cuba, Angola and the Soviet Union, the feasibility of recognizing Angola probably dissipated rapidly.

21. Since 1986 the South African government has repeatedly claimed that Soviet personnel have been flying actual combat missions, but this has never been completely verified. Moreover, even if these allegations are true they would be unlikely to stimulate the same US reaction as would the involvement of Soviet ground forces.

22. Stockwell and other CIA operatives covertly monitored the anti-MPLA forces as part of the US support effort; John Stockwell, *In Search of the Enemy* (New York: W. W. Norton, 1978).

23. Kempton, op. cit., pp. 44–5.

24. 'Zaire', *Africa Contemporary Record* (1978/79), p. B576.

25. *Pravda*, 25 February 1976.

26. David Martin and Phyllis Johnson, *The Struggle for Zimbabwe* (New York: Monthly Review Press, 1981), pp. 235–6.

27. For an in depth discussion of the Soviet Union and the Lancaster House Agreement see Kempton, op. cit., pp. 115–18, 130–6.

28. Robert I. Rotberg, 'South Africa and the Soviet Union: A Struggle for Primacy', in Robert I. Rotberg *et al.* (eds), *South Africa and its Neighbors: Regional Security and Self Interest* (Lexington, MA: Lexington Press, 1985), pp. 55–67.

29. For a thorough examination of South Africa's policy of destabilization see Joseph Hanlon, *Beggar Your Neighbors* (Bloomington, IN: Indiana University Press, 1986).

30. See, for example, Premier Tikhonov's warning to Lucio Lara in *Pravda*, 21–24 January 1982.

31. For a discussion of the Soviet reaction to the Nkomati and Lusaka agreements see Peter Clement, 'Moscow and Southern Africa', *Problems of Communism*, vol. 34, no. 2 (1985), pp. 29–50.

32. Ibid., p. 36.

33. This situation differs from the Zimbabwean civil war in that the USA, despite its preference for ZAPU relative to ZANU, did not provide assistance to either combatant.

34. Colin Legum, 'The Southern African Crisis', *Africa Contemporary Record* (1985/1986), pp. A73–A74.

35. The critical breakthrough apparently came during the Moscow summit, which Crocker attended as part of the US delegation.

36. E. A. Wayne, 'Big prize for southwestern Africa', *Christian Science Monitor*, 22 December 1988, pp. 1, 28.

37. Ibid., p. 28; on this point also see *The Sun* (Baltimore), 5 April 1985; *Washington Post*, 15 December 1988.

38. Anatoly Adamishin, Moscow Television Service, 1 April 1989, translated in *FBIS-Sov-89-0621*, 3 April 1989, pp. 16–19.

39. Robert S. Greenberger, 'Indefatigable Crocker's Southern Africa Accord Shows Value of Persistence, Timing and Luck', *Wall Street Journal*, 22 December 1988.

40. Sean Clear, 'The Impact of the Independence of Namibia on South Africa', *South Africa International*, no. 3 (1989), pp. 117–29.

41. Pat Buchanan, 'Conservative Criticism of Accords', *Washington Times*, 21 December 1988.
42. Mikhail Khrobostov, 'A Step towards Each Other: An Interview with Vladillen Vasey', *New Times*, no. 31 (1988), pp. 9–10.
43. Adamishin, op. cit., p. 16.
44. Radio PANA in English, 25 January 1989, printed in *FBIS-Sov-89-016*, 26 January 1989, p. 30.
45. Ethan Schwartz, 'UN Council Votes Peace for Namibia', *Washington Post*, 17 February 1989.
46. Radio PANA, op. cit.
47. TASS in English, 26 January 1989, printed in *FBIS-Sov-89-021*, 2 February 1989, p. 40.
48. 'Costs May Force UN to cut Namibia Force', *Chicago Tribune*, 25 January 1989, p. 2.
49. For discussions of allegations of South African violations of the Accords see James Brooke, 'Pretoria Accused of Creating Namibia Rebels', *New York Times*, 8 January 1989; A. Kamorin, 'Cuban Troops Return Home', *Izvestiya*, 12 January 1989; 'A Frail New Infant in Africa', *The Economist*, 4 February 1989.
50. Interestingly, while Soviet journalists tended to deny culpability for the incursion, claiming that the clashes were 'accidental' or the result of a South African attack (Valintin Korotov, 'Namibia Lesson', *Pravda*, 12 April 1989; Nikolai Reshetnyak, 'Southern Africa: A Troubled April', *New Times*, no. 18 (1989), pp. 14–15), Soviet diplomats were willing to blame SWAPO.
51. Boris Asoyan, 'UN Plan Under Threat', *Izvestiya*, 6 April 1989; Anatoly Adamishin, 'Namibia Situation Remains Tense', *Izvestiya*, 16 April 1989; TASS in English, printed in *FBIS-Sov-89-70*, 13 April 1989, p. 25.
52. For a discussion of some of the weakness of the accords see 'The Brazzaville Protocol', *Washington Times*, 19 December 1988.
53. E. A. Wayne, 'US Seeks End to Mozambique War', *Christian Science Monitor*, 12 July 1989, albeit to a lesser extent than the Soviet Union.
54. For an extensive discussion of the recent changes in Soviet policy toward South Africa see Kempton, op. cit., pp. 185–212.

9 Superpower Cooperation in the Caribbean and Central America

W. Raymond Duncan

Central America – the scene of civil war upheavals, Soviet expansionism, Cuban intervention and United States anxiety – merits attention as a unique arena in which to assess superpower cooperation in conflict management. This is so for at least three reasons. First, Central America's geographic location makes it a high priority in US security policy. Like other great powers, the US has resisted political developments in neighboring states that pose unacceptable threats to its national security.[1] US concern about Central America has been exacerbated by the region's political turbulence since World War II, dramatized by radical leftist movements and the emergence in 1979 of Sandinista Nicaragua as a major US security issue. Until the Sandinista's stunning election loss in February 1990, the US viewed Nicaragua, like Cuba, as an opportunity for Soviet expansionism.

Second, Cuba plays a unique role in Central America, owing to shared geographic and cultural ties. In backing leftist regimes and movements in Central America, associating with Moscow, and pursuing anti-US policies, Cuba has impeded superpower cooperation in conflict management. Havana's links to Managua, forged in the Sandinista struggle against Anastasio Somoza in the late 1970s, Fidel Castro's insistence on exporting revolution into Central America, and continued Soviet weapons transfers to Cuba, has especially hindered Soviet–US cooperation.

Third, despite hostile rhetoric on both sides, material support for opposing groups, and US intervention in Grenada in October 1983 that put Soviet and Cuban personnel under US fire, superpower conflict has not led to direct confrontation. Indeed, a close look at Soviet–US relations in Central America reveals various forms of *informal* (or tacit) cooperation. While *formal* (or explicit) Soviet–US security cooperation has been limited, the record of tacit cooperation under competitive conditions makes this a useful region to explore. Indeed, both forms of cooperation have been increasing with the evolving policies of Mikhail Gorbachev's 'new political thinking' as applied to the Caribbean and Central America.

SUPERPOWER INTERESTS IN CENTRAL AMERICA

Superpower cooperation in conflict management in Central America has been impeded during much of the decade of the 1980s because of the adversarial character of Soviet–United States relations in this region.[2] Soviet–US adversity stems from numerous factors – including Moscow's opportunity-seeking in a volatile Central America, Washington's traditional security sensitivities in the Caribbean Basin, Soviet ties with Cuba and President Ronald Reagan's 'Doctrine' of 'rolling back' communism in leftist Third World states like Nicaragua during the 1980s.[3] Rather than developing the conditions for incentives to cooperate, each side has tended to act in ways that have produced mutual suspicions, reinforced conflict of ideological perceptions, and uncertainty as to the other's intentions.[4] Each side's support of antagonistic third parties in the region fits this portrait of undermined superpower cooperation – as in Moscow's backing of Castro's Cuba and Sandinista Nicaragua, and Washington's links with the anti-Sandinista Contras.

Nicaragua and El Salvador illustrate how the superpowers have bolstered preferred clients with economic support to stay afloat and military assistance to resist opponents. Moscow extended about $1 billion annually to Sandinista Managua, divided roughly equally between economic and military assistance, without which the Sandinistas could not have survived economically nor defended successfully against US-backed Contras.[5] The US, meanwhile, has pumped approximately $4 billion into El Salvador since 1980 to resist Cuban-backed guerrillas operating in the Farabundo Martí National Liberation Movement (FMLN).[6] Missing in this structure of Soviet–US relations – at least until recently – has been strong encouragement of Soviet and US-backed clients to enter into negotiations to craft power sharing arrangements and a process of national reconciliation. Gorbachev's pressure on the Sandinistas to hold elections in Nicaragua is a key exception to this pattern.

Washington's security apprehensions regarding the 'spread of communism' in Central America is not unlike a number of civil wars in the modern period that have alerted the security concerns of great powers concerning areas immediately adjacent to their borders.[7] The most recent Central American version of this phenomenon unfolded with the July 1979 Sandinista victory in Nicaragua, subsequent civil war in El Salvador and guerrilla activities in Guatemala.

These events raised US security fears by convincing top decision-makers during the Reagan administration that events in Nicaragua and El Salvador were part of a 'well-orchestrated international communist campaign' to disrupt the region from Panama to Mexico.[8] Perceiving events through Reagan Doctrine lenses, Washington launched an all-out effort to sweep Soviet influence from the region – utilizing massive economic and military aid to friendly governments like El Salvador and Honduras, making Honduras a secure base for US military training and war-game demonstrations, backing the Contras, developing concepts of 'low intensity warfare' to deal with the problem, mining Nicaraguan harbors in 1984, working around congressional impediments, and utilizing other means, including extra-legal measures revealed in the Iran-Contragate affair.

Still, Soviet–US competition has by no means been devoid of cooperation. Both sides have accepted situations and conditions not high on their preference list, and each party has avoided actions that might have led to direct confrontation. Soviet–US relations in Central America since the early 1960s reflect several events of reluctant compromise where neither side could fully get its way nor impose solutions on the other side at an acceptable cost or risk. Moscow assumed a low profile during the US invasion of Grenada in 1983, and of Panama in 1989, and Washington eschewed direct intervention in Nicaragua, notwithstanding its deep dislike of the Sandinistas. Each side has followed policies avoiding direct con-frontation with the other – as in Moscow's refusal to introduce MiG fighter planes into Nicaragua, despite Sandinista insistence on receiv-ing them, because the United States had made clear such action would cross a line of acceptable Soviet behavior.[9]

The superpowers appear to be entering the 1990s with greater prospects for cooperation, although of a limited nature. The new era has been shaped especially by Mikhail Gorbachev's 'new political thinking', with its emphasis on East–West *détente*, deideologized foreign policy and negotiated political settlements to resolve Third World regional conflicts.

IMPACT OF LOCAL, REGIONAL AND INTERNATIONAL FORCES

Superpower competition in Central America has stemmed largely from local, regional and international forces. Each superpower has intervened in Central America's turbulent power setting in pursuit of vital interests, the US defending traditional security concerns in a geographically contiguous and sensitive area, the USSR seizing opportunities to project its presence in competition with the US. Superpower policies in turn have reinforced Central American conflict as well as older pre-existing tensions between the superpowers based on mutual suspicions and adversarial motivations. While this cause and effect setting has complicated superpower cooperation, it has not completely inhibited cooperative lines of action.

Local conditions

Local conditions in Central America have spawned state settings high in domestic conflict. Because the region generally lacks historical experiences conducive to pluralist democracy as practiced in the US, Central American states have found it difficult to adjust to modern pressures for change – frequently in the form of demands for power and economic sharing by new middle and lower sector groups. The result has been breakdown in political order, as in Nicaragua's 1979 revolution against Somoza, El Salvador's civil war pitting leftist insurgents against entrenched oligarchical and right-wing military elites; leftist insurgencies and guerrilla movements in Guatemala; and other forms of civil unrest and repressive rule in Honduras and Panama. Only Costa Rica has been spared the political and social turbulence at work elsewhere in the region. Yet even here terrorism is not an unknown event.

Local conditions producing these settings include:
(a) Entrenched political elites unwilling to adjust to pressures for change, responding instead with heavy-handed violent repression, typically citing 'communism' in an effort to enlist middle sector, predominantly conservative, and right-wing military groups to deal with 'subversion'.
(b) Intense domestic political competition between have and have-not groups, with leftist insurgents representing the have-nots

struggling against wealthy elites, and both sides using violence
to pursue political ends.

(c) Political cultures noted for emotionalism as fulfillment of self
    and demonstrating power, where legitimate political authority
    frequently is perceived as residing not in institutionalized rules
    and procedures associated with pluralist democracy, but in
    charismatic individuals whose policies often result in violence.

(d) Social and economic conditions contributing to political insta-
    bility – population explosion, rapid urbanization, income
    maldistribution, unemployment, and overall grinding poverty.

How have these local conditions affected the superpower struggle
in Central America? The key point is that Central America's conflict
societies – reflected in El Salvador's and Nicaragua's civil wars – have
shaped the norms of conduct in superpower competition. Moscow
and Washington have pursued their national interests less through
tacit or explicit bilateral cooperation than by intervening on behalf of
antagonistic clients, typically by supply of arms, military advice,
security training and support of exiles or ruling governments, and
sometimes, as in the US occupation of Grenada in October 1983,
through full-scale intervention by US forces. This form of Soviet–US
competition during the 1970s and 1980s – mirroring local problem-
solving through militant competition and coercive forms of influence-
seeking rather than cooperation – in turn has magnified the scale of
conflict and transformed the region into a major Cold War zone.

Regional conditions

Regional conditions have played a major role in accentuating Central
America's domestic conflict settings and patterns of superpower
behavior. Intraregional tensions stem from a legacy of failed Central
American union, provincial rivalries, and resentment against past
Guatemalan domination. Even before today's intraregional frictions,
El Salvador and Honduras erupted in the famous soccer war of 1969,
with El Salvador invading Honduras to seize a major part of
Honduran territory. Although US and Organization of American
States (OAS) pressure led El Salvador to withdraw from invaded
territory, formal diplomatic relations between the two countries
remained suspended until 1981.
    More recent regional tensions have resulted from cross-border

policies pursued by those groups locked in the struggle over how to change and govern during a period of rapid transition. Examples abound – from Sandinista Nicaragua's providing safe-haven for El Salvador's leftist guerrillas, to Honduras serving as the base for Contra attacks into Nicaragua, Cuban training of Central American leftists and Costa Rica hosting conferences expressive of anti-Sandinista positions. The political spectrum of contending groups in Central America is wide indeed, from the far left to the far right, and their struggle admittedly has been made possible by external assistance from Soviet, Cuban, East European, US and other sources backing favored clients. Yet Central America's intraregional tensions are home grown; superpower policies did not create intraregional conflict, but have used it to advance their own agendas.

On the cooperative side of the ledger, Central and South American presidents have taken the lead in attempting to forge a process of negotiated settlements to Central America's crises. The foreign ministers of Colombia, Mexico, Panama, and Venezuela met on Panama's Contadora island in January 1983 to try to negotiate peace in Central America – the first to exclude the US. Argentina, Brazil, Peru, and Uruguay later supported Contadora initiatives; the whole group soon became known as the Group of Eight. Central America's presidents subsequently met in a location in Guatemala – Esquipulas – in August 1987 to adopt a plan first proposed by Costa Rican President Oscar Arias Sanchez to initiate a process of national reconciliation and democracy in Central America – a meeting also excluding the US. Following the failure of this plan to meet its objectives, the presidents of Central America met again in Costa Rica in February 1989, where they agreed to draft a plan to disarm Nicaragua's rebels, dismantle their bases in Honduras and repatriate them voluntarily to Nicaragua.[10]

The superpowers have endorsed these peace-keeping initiatives, using the Central American presidents' call for Nicaraguan democracy and an end to regional subversion as a hook to find common ground for Soviet–US cooperation. With the George Bush administration in place in Washington, superpower interest in a Nicaraguan settlement began to percolate on the front burner. In a series of remarkable political moves, Gorbachev publicized a Soviet cut-off of arms shipments to Sandinista Nicaragua after 1988, pressured the Sandinistas to support Central American peace proposals and insisted that they go through with the February 1990 elections.[11] The US – among other actions – scaled back manuevers in Honduras (which threatened the Sandinistas), closed the Contras' political office in Miami, and joined with the Soviets in pledging that both countries would respect the results of free and fair elections in Nicaragua.[12] Such efforts have set the scene for further cooperation to end the war in El Salvador and to help solve the toughest problem of all: untangling the Soviet–US Cuban knot.[13]

International forces

International forces at work in Central America include the Organization of American States (OAS), the United Nations (UN) and international law. While these factors traditionally have not acted persuasively in diffusing regional tensions and moderating intraregional conflict, they recently have become more viable forces in managing Soviet–US cooperation in the Caribbean and Central America. Since President Violeta Barrios de Chamorro's February 1990 victory in Nicaragua, the OAS and UN have actively participated in the Contras demobilization, and the UN previously played a distinct role in monitoring the Nicaraguan electoral process – activities strongly backed by Moscow and Washington. Given Gorbachev's strong endorsement of the UN as a major actor in his 'new political thinking' – with its stress on national reconciliation and politically settling Third World regional conflict – UN and OAS would appear to hold promise as even greater factors in Soviet–US cooperation.

International law has not been totally inactive in the Central America conflict. The International Court of Justice (IJC) accepted in 1984 a case filed by Nicaragua against the United States in which Nicaragua charged the US with arming and training rebels seeking to overthrow Nicaragua's Sandinista government. The Court found in Nicaragua's favor in June 1986 and ordered the US to halt its arming and training of the Contras. In response, the US dismissed the Court's ruling, stating that the Court was not equipped to handle complex international issues. While the USSR has also stonewalled the World Court's jurisdiction, Gorbachev's recent statements – as in address to the General Assembly in December 1988 – suggest a growing willingness to acknowledge the broadened role of UN and World Court jurisdiction in regional conflicts. This development suggests the possibility of strengthened international organizational and legal practices that could move superpower relations onto a more cooperative track in the future.

UNITED STATES, SOVIET AND CUBAN STAKES IN
CENTRAL AMERICA

United States stakes

Observers familiar with US policy in Latin America since the early
nineteenth century will quickly reach several key conclusions. To
begin with, Central America historically has been vastly more
important to Washington than to Moscow or Cuba, a fact shaped by
history, power politics, and geography. Since the early nineteenth
century when US leaders first pronounced the Monroe Doctrine
principles for Latin America – with its notions of no future colonization by any European power, a distinct western hemisphere 'sphere'
into which European political systems should not enter, and where
common 'republican' traditions would flourish – US policy in Latin
America focused on the Caribbean Basin and Central America as
vital zones for North America's national security. Indeed, US
preoccupation with preventing or excluding foreign influence south of
the Rio Grande produced what some observers describe as an
attitude of 'domination' – expressed in turn-of-the century interventions like the 1898 Spanish–American War, Theodore Roosevelt's
'Corollary' to the Monroe Doctrine, and his 'taking' of the Panama
Canal.[14] America's growing preoccupation with its 'strategic rear' as
a special security zone occurred well before Russia's 1917 Revolution.

Again and again the US has demonstrated sensitivity to external
threats in this part of the world – from saddling Cuba with the Platt
Amendment, building and protecting the Panama Canal, and intervening repeatedly before and after World War II.[15] Indeed, the
US used military force in Central America and the Caribbean Basin
135 times between 1823 and 1983 to quiet political turmoil and assert
its power.[16] The first key episode in the region of Cold War conflict
and US intervention occurred in Guatemala in 1954. When Guatemalan president Jacobo Arbenz Guzman came to power in 1951, he
initiated a series of radical economic and social reforms and allowed
communists substantial influence in Guatemalan politics.[17] In reacting to this perceived security threat, the US sponsored a Guatemalan
exile force, led by Colonel Carlos Castillo Armas, which invaded
Guatemala from Honduras in June 1954.[18] Although the Arbenz
government appealed to the UN Security Council, the UN deferred
the matter to the US-dominated OAS over Soviet opposition.

Colonel Castillo took over the government before the OAS fact-finding team arrived and Arbenz was sent into exile.[19]

United States intervention in the Dominican Republic in April 1965 again illustrates efforts to defend against politically unacceptable events in geographically neighboring areas. The most violent of US actions during this period, it occurred following the dictatorship of General Rafael Trujillo in 1951 when the US sent in approximately 23,000 troops out of fear that communists had joined in a rebellion and threatened to take control. President Lyndon Johnson stated that US action stemmed from the goal to 'help prevent another Communist state in this hemisphere.'[20] Unlike the Cuban Bay of Pigs episode, the US was able to legitimize this action by working to receive OAS endorsement of its intervention, demonstrated by a token Latin American military contribution that transformed the occupation into an international peacekeeping force.[21]

Soviet-backed Cuba has been the focal point of Soviet–US Cold War competition. The Cold War dramatically entered the Caribbean Basin as US–Cuban relations deteriorated during 1959–61 and Castro turned toward the USSR for economic and military assistance and adopted Marxism-Leninism as Cuba's guiding ideology. Well-known events are the US-backed Bay of Pigs invasion of Cuba in April 1961 and the October 1962 missile crisis as Soviet–Cuban relations developed and Castro's revolution turned anti-US and pro-socialist. The 1961 invasion failed miserably and fueled Castro's determination to draw more closely into the Soviet orbit, and the missile crisis triggered a major confrontation that narrowly avoided nuclear war. On the positive side, the missile crisis provided a shared Soviet–US shock that led the two governments to examine seriously ways to reduce the threat of nuclear war.[22]

Cuba, however, has remained a perceived threat to US interests and the focal point of Soviet–US Cold War competition in the Caribbean Basin – underlined by the Soviet-operated Lourdes intelligence-gathering facility manned by about 2,100 technicians, 7,000 Soviet civilian advisers, a 2,800-man combat brigade, and another 2,800 military advisers.[23] The Lourdes intelligence installation is the most sophisticated Soviet collection facility outside the USSR.[24] Cuba's strategic location provides Soviet monitoring of US Caribbean and Gulf of Mexico maritime routes, US East Coast and Caribbean military forces and installations, and for deployment of Soviet naval combatants in Caribbean waters.[25]

US concern over Soviet naval activities in the Caribbean, including deployments of Soviet surface ships and submarines, naval exercises and port calls in Cuba, and the building of a Soviet nuclear submarine facility in Cienfuegos, is not without reason. It comes as no surprise that the 1980s, following the leftist Grenadian and Nicaraguan Revolutions, produced a Republican Party platform condemning the 'Marxist Sandinista takeover of Nicaragua and the Marxist attempts to destabilize El Salvador, Guatemala and Honduras.'[26] In the perceptions of the then incoming UN Ambassador, Jeane Kirkpatrick, Central America was '. . . the most important place in the world for the United States today.'[27]

Soviet stakes

For the Soviet Union, in contrast, Central America's attraction is less vital in nature and more recent in history. Moscow's attention to Latin America sharpened after Fidel Castro's 1959 Revolution, with its turn to the USSR and Marxism-Leninism, Castro's stirring of cloned revolutionary forces in Central America and the Caribbean Basin and his success in challenging the 'colossus of the North'. Central America's allure for Moscow lay not in its role as a zone of pressing Soviet Interests – physical security, economic survival or defending political values against proximate alien adversaries – akin to Moscow's position in Central Europe or Afghanistan. Rather, the region offered a playing field to pursue secondary and tertiary Soviet interests, less pressing in priority, yet highly valued in the never-ending game of superpower politics. Soviet competition with the US could be played out through state-to-state activities, party-to-party ties, 'active measures', such as disinformation, propaganda, and front organizations – and indirectly by backing Cuba's own adventures in Central America.[28]

Nicaragua's 1979 revolution, while not fomented by the USSR, raised Soviet interest in the region and, for a short period of time, gave Moscow cause to believe that armed struggle might produce additional revolutionary victories in this arena.[29] Although Soviet enthusiasm for armed struggle subsequently waned, Moscow's high military aid and substantial economic assistance to the Sandinistas suggests that Soviet leaders perceived Managua as a valued asset. The Sandinistas provided a safe haven to El Salvadoran leftist guerrillas seeking power next door, pursued a socialist version of development, and diverted US attention and resources from more sensitive Soviet arenas. These activities gave the Soviets a foothold in Central America – a presence on territory contiguous with their superpower competitor and a client whose foreign policy has aided leftist insurgents in the region. The Sandinista defeat in early 1990, however, left Cuba as the major Soviet-backed player in the region.

That both superpowers had substantial commitments in Central America during much of the 1980s is illustrated by resources each side has invested in this part of the world. Table 9.1 compares Soviet aid to Cuba and Nicaragua with US assistance to Central America.

Of special note in Table 9.1 is the comprehensive nature of US aid, which goes to several countries – Panama, Guatemala, Costa Rica, Honduras and El Salvador – and serves a wide range of assets, compared to the overwhelming proportion of Soviet aid going to

Table 9.1   US Aid to Central America compared to Soviet–East European Aid to Cuba and Nicaragua (in millions of US dollars)

	1982	1983	1984	1985	1986
US economic and military assistance to Central America	418	704	1,017	1,135	1,133
Soviet–East European economic and military assistance to Cuba and Nicaragua	6,585	5,935	6,570	7,340	8,030
US economic assistance to Central America (a)	337	566	616	755	736
Soviet–East European economic assistance to Cuba and Nicaragua	4,775	4.465	4,880	4,940	5,930
US military assistance to Central America (b)	8	138	401	380	397
Soviet–East European military assistance to Cuba and Nicaragua	1,810	1,470	1,690	2,400	2,100

(a) Data are 'total official gross' disbursements as reported on a calendar-year basis by the Development Assistance Committee of the Organization for Economic Cooperation and Development in Geographic Distribution of Financial Flows to Developing Countries. 'Total official gross' disbursements is the Western measure most comparable to estimated Soviet economic aid deliveries.
(b) Data are for fiscal years and include deliveries under the following programs. Military Assistance Program, Foreign Military Sales, Military Assistance Excess Stocks, Military Construction Sales, Military Assistance Merger Funds, and IMET (training).
Source: US Department of State, *Soviet Bloc Assistance to Cuba and Nicaragua*, October 1987.

Moscow's chief client, Cuba. Soviet aid to Cuba, reaching approximately $5.4 billion in 1986 – after running about $4.5 million since 1981 – supports Cuban foreign policies which in turn advanced Soviet interests in Third World settings like Sandinista Nicaragua and elsewhere in Central America. Soviet interests in Central America and the Caribbean Basin have varied significantly before and after the emergence of Gorbachev on the scene. Before Gorbachev, Soviet interest centered on distinct goals in superpower competition:

(a) undermining US power in order to augment Soviet strength in the world political system;
(b) enhancing Soviet prestige and legitimizing the USSR as a responsible superpower actor capable of playing an important role in regional politics – such as backing Central American peace initiatives and supporting nationalist sentiments;
(c) seeking political equality with the US in terms of superpower status;
(d) bolstering Moscow's key regional client, Cuba, whose own foreign policy advances Soviet interests;
(e) advancing Moscow's interests in trade, commercial relations, and access to natural resources.

Since Gorbachev, Moscow has been seeking ways to reduce tension with the US – essentially through demilitarized and deideologized competition and cooperating with the US to politically negotiate regional conflicts and work toward national reconciliation. Within this framework the above list of interests probably stands firm, with the exception of item number one – undermining US power by militarily backing Soviet clients.

The Cuban factor

Cuba's Revolution has greatly affected Soviet interests, policies and diplomacy in the US 'strategic rear'. Before the fall of Fulgencio Batista in 1959, Soviet policy-makers perceived Latin America – especially the Caribbean Basin and Central America – as a place commanding little or no attention. Lagging Soviet interest stemmed from the area's geographic distance from the USSR, lack of knowledge about Latin American history, culture and politics, relative weaknesses of Latin America's communist party organizations, and a recognition of US power and influence.[30] These perceptions changed dramatically with Cuba's Revolution. Havana more or less fell into Moscow's lap, when Castro, in need of external economic and military support to defend against US pressure, turned to Marxism-Leninism, invited himself into the Soviet camp, and began to pursue a range of policies advancing both the interests of Havana and Moscow. Because Castro's own anti-imperialist and 'international proletarian' foreign policy agenda provided the USSR with power projection capabilities it might not otherwise have enjoyed to bolster leftist causes in Central America, Cuba became a principal actor affecting superpower cooperation in conflict management.

Cuba traditionally has advanced Soviet interests in three ways. First, Havana played a major role in helping the Sandinistas monopolize power, advance their revolutionary agenda, and deflect US-backed threats to their regime. By 1985 about 7,500 Cubans were in Nicaragua, of whom an estimated 3,000 were military or security personnel attached to the armed forces, internal security and intelligence organizations.[31] The rest of the Cubans were engaged in construction, teaching, medical and other programs, although many of these individuals were younger men who had received some military training.[32] Second, Cuba backed other leftist insurgent groups in the region, allowing the Soviets to assume a lower profile which lessens the risk of direct confrontation with the US. As Castro stated in an interview with NBC reporter, Maria Shriver, in February 1988, Cuba gives El Salvador's leftist insurgents 'all the support we can give them', which includes training, and political and moral backing.[33] Third, Havana has crafted a foreign policy designed to parallel Moscow's approach to the region.[34] These efforts include improving ties with established governments throughout Latin America, thus enhancing Cuba's status as a legitimate regional actor without departing from its consistent anti-American and Third World identity, and generally supporting Central America's regional peace efforts.

PRINCIPAL FORMS OF SOVIET–US COOPERATION IN CENTRAL AMERICA

In approaching the issue of Soviet–US cooperation in managing conflict in Central America, we adopt here the notion of cooperation as something different from the traditional definition of shared values. We identify cooperative behavior as those actions falling under two modes: (a) *informal (tacit) cooperation*, such as parallel actions that avoid the risk of direct confrontation between the two superpowers, and (b) *formal (explicit) cooperation*, as when formal agreements are reached in which both parties are openly involved.

Illustrating *informal* types of cooperation in Central America are Moscow's moderating the scale of conflict by restricting resources to favored clients in Nicaragua, El Salvador, and Guatemala and Soviet resistance to Cuba's pressure to take a stronger stance against US assertive actions, as during the 1962 Cuba missile crisis (discussed below) and when the US intervened in Grenada in October 1983. Both Soviet reactions occurred out of anticipated reactions in the US.

Formal coordination of policies includes formal efforts to establish rules of conduct, cooperation in a process of discussion and initiatives that may lead to new codes of behavior in regional settings, or working together with international organizational support – as through UN auspices. While the superpowers have not established formal accords for rules of conduct in Central America since Gorbachev assumed political leadership, they have formally cooperated on the Nicaraguan issues and held other discussions on Cuba and Central America. Moscow's reduced military aid to Nicaragua is a case in point.[35]

Assessing the principal forms of superpower cooperation in Central America is best approached in terms of the periods before and after Gorbachev's emergence as General Secretary of the CPSU in March 1985. Superpower cooperation before Gorbachev was essentially informal; after Gorbachev, efforts to establish formal coordination emerged as a distinct trend – a consequence of Moscow's efforts to revive a sagging economy through *perestroika*, *glasnost*, and 'new political thinking' – with its emphasis on reduced East–West tensions, arms control initiatives, and negotiated political settlements to Third World regional conflicts.[36] Moscow's 1988 pull-out from Afghanistan, pressure on Cuba and cooperation with the US in the Angola and Namibia Pact, and new initiatives with UN peacekeeping efforts illustrate new Soviet inclinations to untie regional knots. As outgoing Secretary of State George Shultz said in December 1988, 'The Soviets have been very cooperative and good in working with us on the southern African situation . . . and even in Central America, we've had at least some exchange.'[37]

Informal cooperation before Gorbachev

Informal superpower cooperation before Gorbachev is mirrored in several aspects of Soviet and US policies. The October 1962 missile crisis highlights this type of behavior. In the missile crisis both superpowers accepted non-preferred optimal outcomes and sought to avoid direct confrontation as the crisis unfolded. Khrushchev bowed to intense US pressure to dismantle Soviet missiles in place in Cuba in return for an American pledge not to invade the island. This outcome aborted any Khrushchev designs on using Cuban territory to address the US nuclear advantage. At the same time it put to rest a US plan to 'use . . . open US force to aid the Cuban people in winning their liberty', setting October 1962 as the target date for Castro's overthrow following a US-supported insurrection on the island.[38] The subversion plan, code-named Operation Mongoose, was discarded once the superpowers stepped back from nuclear confrontation in October 1962.[39]

Informal cooperation occurred elsewhere in Soviet–US behavior after the missile crisis – most probably the result of both parties being deeply attuned to the imperatives of prudence in crisis management in order to avoid nuclear war. The missile crisis, according to one observer, reinforced a key rule in managing Soviet–US rivalry – that 'neither superpower should exploit its advantage in a crisis to impose on the other a policy dilemma between backing down in defeat or desperately initiating the use of force.'[40] After the missile episode, both sides acted in ways to accept non-preferred outcomes or situations in order to avoid direct confrontation. This point is underscored by stalemated civil wars in Nicaragua and El Salvador since the late 1970s, where Moscow and Washington continued to support opposing clients in 'no win' situations. Neither side was willing to take higher risks to assure a 'win' over opposing forces. Moscow kept its military manpower numbers low in Nicaragua, supplying sufficient weapons and *matériel* to the Sandinistas to allow them to defend themselves without more direct Soviet help, and Washington refrained from direct intervention in Nicaragua to try to accomplish what clearly the Contras were unable to do – overthrow the Sandinista government.

Second, both superpowers have in some respects avoided policies that might have led to direct confrontation. Aware of US security sensitivity in its 'strategic backyard', the Soviets, for example, did not sign a Treaty of Friendship and Cooperation with Havana, as it had with so many other Third World clients, until April 1989. Even then, the new treaty did not include military cooperation as in so many other Soviet–Third World Treaties of this type.[41] Nor have Washington's policies been devoid of tacit cooperation. The US has preferred to work through the Contras in trying to unseat Nicaragua's Sandinistas, rather than directly intervening, and restricted the number of US military advisers in Central America.

Third, both sides have likely pursued Central American policies in the context of lessons drawn from the past, where experience has probably cautioned restraint. From the missile crisis, the USSR appears to have inferred that US security sensitivity precluded a preferred outcome of a greater Soviet military presence in Central America – as in Nicaragua or in directly aiding El Salvador's leftist insurgents during the early 1980s. Similarly, Moscow likely sensed the imperative of assuming a low profile posture in the face of US hostile action, as it did when the US intervened in the Dominican Republic in April 1965, in Grenada in October 1983 and when the US mined Nicaragua's harbors in 1984.

The United States, having agreed not to attack Cuba in exchange for the removal of Soviet missiles in 1962, eschewed direct intervention in Soviet-backed Cuba and Nicaragua to achieve its preferred outcome of unseating Castro and the Sandinistas – albeit for domestic political reasons as much as anything – and refrained from intervention in Grenada until Grenada's political infighting and possible threat to American medical students provided the opportunity to do so. In some respects, then, the US 'learned' that superpower confrontation, while unlikely, was not totally impossible – a 'lesson' that may have tempered its military interventionist tendencies. Overall, however, the US has pursued significantly more assertive policies in Central America, notably after the 1979 Sandinista victory, stemming from the Reagan Doctrine which held basically that Soviet gains in the Third World had to be resisted because they constituted losses for the US.[42]

Fourth, accepting non-preferred optimal outcomes and avoiding direct conflict situations have been managed by adhering to unwritten 'rules of the game.' The Soviets have centered decision-making on policies of caution and restraint, vividly illustrated by their approach to Nicaragua. Compared to Cuba's 7,500 personnel in Nicaragua, the Soviets restricted the number of Soviet advisers to around 250, concentrating instead on supplying the Sandinistas with military *matériel* to protect themselves.[43] Soviet economic aid, while making available needed oil supplies, fell far short of Sandinista economic needs, demonstrating that Moscow has no desire to create 'another Cuba' in Central America. Aid agreed to by the Soviets and their allies fell below Sandinista requests, and Soviet Latin American specialists made clear they did not wish to repeat the costs associated with supplying Cuba.[44] All in all, Moscow pursued a cautious policy in Sandinista Nicaragua, recognizing the geostrategic presence of the United States.

Moscow's approach to leftist movements in Central America also reflects a similar low-risk diplomacy. While the Soviets have demonstrated capabilities in bolstering leftist political elites once in power, they were reluctant to play a major role in directly supporting leftist revolutionaries with material aid *before* they assumed government control. Moscow failed to aid the Sandinista insurgents or Grenada's New Jewell Movement during their revolutionary struggles.[45] Once they were in power, Moscow gradually felt its way into closer relations with the new regimes – following low cost, low-risk, long-term opportunities to help them consolidate power.

Moscow's reluctance to support revolutionary movements with direct material assistance before they achieved power was repeated in Soviet policy toward leftist insurgents in El Salvador and Guatemala. Even in the euphoric days following the Sandinista victory in Nicaragua, when Moscow began to pay lip service to armed struggle as the wave of the future in Central America, the Soviets followed basically a low profile approach in terms of direct assistance to revolutionary movements outside Nicaragua. That Soviet theory of backing armed struggle departed from Soviet practice was made clear by Schafik Handel's frustration in Moscow in trying to arrange for Soviet air transport of weapons transfers to El Salvador for the ill-fated January 1981 guerrilla offensive.[46] Nor did documents captured in Grenada, following the US intervention of October 1983, provide conclusive evidence that Grenada had become a staging area for large concentrations of Soviet arms destined for future use.[47]

Following the failure of El Salvador's January 1981 'final offensive', Moscow adopted a more cautious and restrained view regarding revolutionary possibilities than it expressed during 1980–1. By 1982 – with guerrilla fortunes then fading in the region – Moscow's assessment of the nature of the present epoch shifted away from perceptions of 'regional upsurge' to the 'ebb and flow' of specific situations in specific countries.[48] The Soviets moved correspondingly toward consolidating their gains in Nicaragua, while playing peace-maker

elsewhere in countries like El Salvador.
Moscow's tacit cooperative efforts by no means indicated that the Soviets eschewed political competition with the USA. Active measures, party-to-party ties between the CPSU and pro-communist parties, and front organizations offered a variety of policy instruments for influence-seeking in Central America. Active measures included disinformation to undermine US policy, as in the frequent Soviet press releases declaring an imminent US invasion of Nicaragua, and classic KGB overt and covert deception operations, use of forged documents, agents of influence, and clandestine broadcasting.[49] Soviet front groups, for example, accused the USA of conducting chemical and biological warfare in Central America, while Moscow's Radio Peace and Progress, a known disinformation outlet, broadcast numerous inflammatory allegations, e.g. US brainwashing, torture, and murder.

Shifts since Gorbachev

A significant shift toward formal cooperation characterizes the Gorbachev era. Evidence for this thesis is found not only in the high-level regional talks on Central American issues that have been so pronounced since Gorbachev came to power, but in specific activities designed to advance Soviet–US cooperation in this part of the world. Gorbachev, for example, curtailed military aid to Nicaragua after 1988, pressured the Sandinistas to repudiate the FMLN in El Salvador and to hold elections in early 1990, and agreed with Washington to respect the results of a Nicaraguan election. As part of these activities, Moscow agreed with Washington on a mechanism to end Sandinista arms shipments to the FMLN in El Salvador – the UN Observer Group in Central America (ONUCA) that would monitor the Central American prohibition against using territory to aid guerrilla operations in neighboring states. President Chamorro's electoral victory brought a swift Soviet approval, a pledge to continue peaceful state-to-state relations with the new government, and cooperation with the UN to monitor the demilitarization of Nicaragua. These efforts were advanced by a close working relationship between US Secretary of States James Baker and Soviet Foreign Minister Eduard Shevardnadze at one level, and at another, Assistant Secretary of State for Inter-American Affairs, Bernard Aronson, and his Soviet counterpart, Yuri Pavlov.

Gorbachev's 'new political thinking', with its emphasis on East–West *détente* and political settlement of regional conflicts, has opened a new chapter in superpower cooperation. Gorbachev formally cooperated on Central America on the final day of the December 1987 summit in Washington when he proposed 'working together' to diminish the arms flow in this region.[50] The Reagan administration subsequently came to believe that Gorbachev was proposing a Soviet arms cutoff to Nicaragua in return for a US arms cutoff to El Salvador, Honduras and Guatemala, an unacceptable deal for the US.[51] Gorbachev stepped up his formal cooperation with the Bush administration when Soviet Ambassador Dubinin visited the State Department in February 1989 to deliver a positive statement regarding the recent Central American peace proposal and asserted Moscow's willingness to continue actively to promote the improvement of the situation in Central America.[52]

The Bush administration in turn began formally and informally to signal to the Soviets its attention to Moscow's activity in and around Managua – portraying Soviet–American relations globally as a function of Soviet actions in Nicaragua in hopes of persuading Moscow to halt military assistance to Managua.[53] In late March 1989 President Bush sent Gorbachev a letter urging him to use his influence to help end the Nicaraguan conflict by reducing support for the Sandinista regime – a pledge the Bush team believed should be made during Gorbachev's upcoming April visit to Cuba.[54]

Although Gorbachev failed to use his April trip to Cuba to heed Washington's urging, he reaffirmed Moscow's commitment to the peaceful settlement of regional conflicts. The Treaty of Friendship and Cooperation with Cuba, moreover, underscored reduced military spending to meet Soviet and Cuban economic development needs, rejected the use of force in inter-state relations, and pledged both parties to work toward global international security. These commitments, in effect, put pressure on Havana to ease back on military support of revolutionary regimes such as Nicaragua, and underscored Soviet cooperation in the Central America region. After the Cuban visit, Gorbachev replied in May to President Bush's original 30 March letter requesting a cutoff in Soviet arms to Nicaragua, stating that Moscow had stopped its arms supplies to Managua as of the end of 1988.[55] While Bush officials doubted Gorbachev's claims, formal communication and cooperation nevertheless were underway, marking a shift from the informal types so prevalent before Gorbachev.

Forces for change in the relationship

Transition toward formal cooperation was spawned by forces for change operating on both superpowers. First, Moscow and Washington learned that older policies were counterproductive. Gorbachev's 'new thinking' on East–West tension reduction, arms control, deideologized foreign policy and negotiated political settlements to regional conflicts stemmed in part from a realization that Moscow's entanglement in Third World conflicts had resulted in high economic costs, few political gains, and an arms race with the US – while its economy was failing. The USA learned that nearly a decade of using military power for quick and easy solutions to complex political and economic problems, notably Nicaragua, simply had not worked.

Second, pressure for change in superpower approaches to Central America comes from the Central American presidents. They have demonstrated a capacity to develop their own policy prescriptions for managing conflict that have frustrated the preferences of both superpowers. From 1986 onwards, Central America's presidents have attempted to negotiate their own solutions to regional conflict – from their first meeting in Esquipulas, Guatemala, when they issued a declaration affirming the commitment to 'peace and cooperation' to their 1989 meeting at Tesoro Beach, El Salvador, when they set a calendar for elections in Nicaragua and planned for the voluntary demobilization, repatriation, or relocation of the Contras.[56]

Third, the value of Cuba and Nicaragua in Soviet foreign policy is shifting under Gorbachev's 'new political thinking'. In Soviet–Cuban relations, Gorbachev's emphasis on political resolution of regional conflict – showcased by the negotiated Angola/Namibia settlement and projected withdrawal of Cuba's 50,000 troops – point toward a decreased role for Cuban military power and, hence, less Cuban leverage in dealing with the Soviets. This comes at a time of growing tensions in Soviet–Cuban relations, spawned by Moscow's rapidly deteriorating economy and foreign aid capabilities on the one hand, and on the other by Castro's lagging economy, lackluster management of productive processes, unwillingness to reform along the lines pursued by Gorbachev's *perestroika* and *glasnost*, a growing human rights movement inside Cuba looking toward Moscow for leadership in breaking Castro's tight centralized control and imprisonment of political dissidents. While publicly continuing to praise Cuba, privately Gorbachev likely will pressure Cuba to behave in ways more compatible with his 'new political thinking'.

Soviet economic relations with the Sandinistas reflect a similar trend – using economic aid to exert political pressure. Moscow's temporary suspension of oil deliveries in early 1987, leading Nicaragua's government to double the domestic price of fuel in 1988, and the 1989 reduction in Soviet-supplied oil to Nicaragua illustrate Gorbachev's effort to encourage Sandinista political negotiation.[57]

Gorbachev's economic influence on the Sandinistas is captured by the statement of newly-arrived Soviet Ambassador to Nicaragua, Valeri Nikolayenko, who in November 1988 made clear that Moscow's *perestroika* placed limits on how much help could be given to allies like Nicaragua. 'We just don't have as much anymore as we would like to give,' Nikolayenko said.[58] The new open Soviet profile – speaking on the record as they had not previously done – was consistent with Gorbachev's overall shift in foreign policy in Latin America, moving away from backing expensive rebel causes and toward improving relations with influential states and trading partners like Argentina and Brazil. In seeking to remove their image as conspirators in Nicaragua, the Soviets reportedly have told the Sandinistas that Soviet aid had reached its upper limits – as it had in Cuba – and scolded the Nicaraguan government for using much aid inefficiently in a notoriously deteriorating economy.[59] While Soviet aid to the Sandinistas ran at about $1 billion per year, divided equally between economic and military support, it was becoming clear by 1989 that Gorbachev's 'new thinking' had come to poverty-stricken Nicaragua – and with it the greater possibility of downscaling aid to an inefficient client in an effort to strengthen the process of East–West *détente* that might spawn more productive economic relations with the USA.

PROSPECTS FOR STRENGTHENING SUPERPOWER REGIONAL COOPERATION

Prospects for strengthening superpower regional cooperation in Central America may be approached from a three-scenario perspective. Scenario one proceeds on the assumption of linear development of trends now in place, with events marching toward more superpower formal cooperation based on Soviet and US interest in more negotiated settlements of Caribbean and Central American conflict, highlighting El Salvador, Soviet pressure on Cuba to cooperate in informal and formal negotiation, and movement toward rules of behavior or codes of conduct regarding crisis management. Such a scenario does not envision an end to Soviet–US competition in this region. The focus rather is on how to manage competition in ways to advance a cooperative relationship under conditions where no common government exists to enforce rules and where international institutions to channel cooperative behavior are less strong than might be desired.

Scenario two focuses on conditions that could speed cooperation more rapidly than implied in the first projected events. It suggests that dramatic changes in the USSR conceivably could move Soviet–US cooperation along path leading to rapid formal cooperation in bilateral and multilateral institutions – not only in Central America and the Caribbean, but also in other Third World regions.

Scenario three examines an alternative future based on conditions that could slow cooperative behavior. Scenario three suggests how superpower cooperation could break down – through unilateral decision-making that creates major obstacles to cooperation, uncontrollable third-party actions and regional trends producing increased anarchy and resurrected superpower competition. In examining potential obstacles slowing the cooperative process, this scenario considers how a reversal of positive outcomes might occur and underscores real and potential restraints on positive trends.

Scenario one

Scenario one suggests that cooperation in Central America could be strengthened. Methods include stepped-up confidence-building measures – signaling each side's interest in cooperation, strengthened perceptions of mutual trust, and allaying suspicions of hostile activities – to establish a more solid psychological foundation for cooperation. Examples of confidence-building measures include more Soviet–US dialogues and constructive communication to provide accurate information and avoid negative misperceptions – as in the January 1989 Moscow conference that brought together Soviet, US and Cuban officials who guided their countries through the 1962 Cuban missile crisis; revelations and a review of the crisis hopefully will help avoid a future crisis of a 1962 magnitude.[60] UN channels offer other routes to superpower cooperation, such as setting up a bilateral working group on Central America for the exchange of information and insights, and UN peacekeeping operations like monitoring military activities in Central America and verifying

Nicaragua's military demobilization. Soviet–US cooperation in bringing about the February 1990 Nicaraguan elections point toward such a scenario.

Scenario one depends on each superpower leaning on its clients to act in ways facilitating close superpower cooperation – elements of which are at work in Gorbachev's 'new political thinking' in Central America and in US policy.[61] Given Soviet economic dominance in Cuba, Gorbachev could exert greater pressure on Havana to work harder on improved relations with the US and publicly back away from the FMLN. As to the Nicaraguan connection, Soviet pledges to work cooperatively with the Chamorro government are a step in the right direction, as are the ongoing discussions with Washington regarding Cuba.

Counterpart US actions would entail decreasing activities that, in Cuban eyes, appear threatening – as in the celebrated TV Marti project that parallels Radio Marti – which for Havana and Moscow legitimizes Soviet weapons transfers to Cuba, applying more pressure on El Salvador's government to deal more authoritatively with military and paramilitary death squads, and working cooperatively with the Soviets in UN-related activities in the region.

Scenario two

Scenario two, pointing toward events that might speed Soviet–US cooperation, is based on forces at work in the Soviet Union and Cuba. Simply put, several factors could pressure Moscow to cut back sharply on aid commitments to Cuba, Leading Moscow and Havana to seek rapid cooperation with the US – out of Moscow's desire to maintain some type of Cuban connection and Havana's necessity to survive economically. Such events include escalated collapse of the Soviet economy, greater political pressure on Gorbachev to cut Soviet economic ties with Cuba, or disintegration of the USSR into independent states – including a Russia headed by someone like Boris Yeltsin who would be likely to do business with the Cubas of the world on a commercial basis. Moscow's moves toward a market economy and scheduled cuts in Soviet aid to Cuba – with possible drastic cuts ahead – point toward this scenario.[62]

Scenario three

Scenario three's stalemated cooperation is not difficult to identify.

Among more prominent obstacles are ongoing civil wars, as in El Salvador, where the presidential election of March 1989 produced a victory of the right-wing Nationalist Republican Alliance (Arena), which some observers marks the beginning of the end of efforts at economic and social reform. Given El Salvador's oligarchic land-holding pattern, massive poverty, and high population growth rate – matched against Arena's opposition to agrarian reform and extreme right-wing membership – civil war conditions are likely to increase rather than diminish in the years ahead. The issue is less one of Soviet assistance to guerrilla groups than Cuban assistance; Havana might be enticed to increase its direct support so long as Cuba remains committed to the principal of aiding revolutions.

Second, Cuban decision-makers may prove more resistant to Soviet pressure than expressed in scenarios one and two. Fidel Castro is known as an independent-minded foreign policy leader, who more than once has defined his difference with Moscow – as he did during the 1989 Gorbachev–Castro summit meeting in Havana. Castro is likely to resist any direct pressure from Moscow to change his behavior.

Third, some aspects of Moscow's traditional 'two-track' policy in Central America continue to undermine superpower cooperation. Soviet foreign policy in the past has operated along two tracks: (a) state-to-state relations to facilitate diplomatic ties, economic and commercial relations, and cultural exchanges between governments, and (b) party-to-party relations, combined with 'active measures', aimed at strengthening leftist forces and undermining US influence. Gorbachev's 'new political thinking' admittedly has affected both tracks in ways facilitating cooperation with the USA, but owing to the complexities of controlling all aspects of Soviet foreign policy and bureaucratic inertia, the weight of the past still drives considerable Soviet activity in Central America in ways detrimental to superpower cooperation.[63]

Fourth, US policy toward Central America, while adopting a more diplomatic profile under Bush administration leadership, retains a suspicious and sensitive problem-solving approach regarding FMLN activities in El Salvador, guerrilla leftism in Guatemala, and the nature of the Cuban threat in the Western Hemisphere. The Bush administration's reluctance to make diplomatic options more available regarding Cuba especially blocks the easing of Soviet military ties with Havana.

248 W. Raymond Duncan

Prospects

In assessing Soviet–US cooperative relations in Central America, one is struck by improving possibilities for widened informal and formal cooperative behavior, set against powerful limits to cooperation owing to the region's geographic proximity to the USA and historical legacy in US security perceptions. By 1990 Soviet–US cooperation had reached levels hardly dreamed of before Gorbachev rose to power in March 1985. The most remarkable set of cooperative events surrounded Nicaragua, where Moscow and Washington found common ground politically to manage a process leading to the elections of February 1990, which untied the Sandinista knot. Several factors combine with this record of collaboration on the Nicaraguan issue to point toward enhanced formal cooperation in the future:

- Moscow's need to continue a process of East–West *détente* in Third World regions like the Caribbean and Central America in order to stimulate more favorable trade and commercial relations in Soviet–US relations.
- Moscow's moves toward a market economy and away from Marxist–Leninist principles in foreign policy, coupled with rapidly declining foreign aid capabilities.
- Rising Soviet–Cuban strains, produced in part by disruptions in Soviet and East-European supplies – owing to decentralized trading practices and market forces at work in the Council for Mutual Economic Assistance (CMEA) – which pressure Cuba to think about the future of its Soviet ties and East European ties and consequent relations with the US for economic survival.
- Lessons learned by Soviet and American negotiators in the Nicaraguan case about how to politically manage Central American conflicts, as in El Salvador, and how to reach common ground on more thorny issues, as in Cuba.
- The increasingly important roles played by the OAS and UN in monitoring the peace process in Central America, Moscow's greater commitment to UN activities and to international law, and both Soviet and US acceptance on UN actions in Central America.
- FMLN movement toward a political settlement in El Salvador, stimulated in part by the ending of Nicaragua's role in providing a safe haven for FMLN guerrillas.
- The declining prestige and attraction power of Cuba as a model for other Latin American revolutionaries, owing to Cuba's sagging

economy and the dramatic shifts in Soviet domestic and foreign policy which will affect revolutionary regimes and movements in the future.

In the world of international politics where perceptions shape decision-makers' incoming information into pre-existing assumptions, images and expectations, however, Moscow's policies in Central America in many ways still trigger US security sensitivities and undermine cooperative relations. On this score Soviet relations with Cuba are the tightest knot of all. How long that knot will remain tied, however, is an open question.

NOTES

1. Evan Luard, 'Superpowers and Regional Conflicts', *Foreign Affairs*, vol. 64, no. 5 (Summer 1986), pp. 1013–16; and Luard, *Conflict and Peace in the Modern International System* (Albany: State University of New York Press, 1988), pp. 121–2.
2. For background reading on Soviet–United States adversarial relations in the Caribbean Basin and Central America, see Peter Calvert, *The Central American Security System: North–South or East–West?* (Cambridge: Cambridge University Press, 1988).
3. On the Reagan Doctrine, see Walter LaFeber, *The American Age: American Foreign Policy at Home and Abroad Since 1750* (New York: W. W. Norton, 1988), pp. 677 ff.; also James A. Nathan and James K. Oliver, *United States Foreign Policy and World Order* (Glenview, IL: Scott, Foresman, 1989, 4th edn), pp. 425 ff.
4. See Alexander L. George, 'Incentives for US–Soviet Security Cooperation and Mutual Adjustment', in Alexander L. George, Philip J. Farley and Alexander Dallin (eds), *US–Soviet Security Cooperation* (New York: Oxford University Press, 1988), pp. 641–54; and George, 'Factors Influencing Security Cooperation', op. cit., pp. 655–78.
5. Don Oberdorfer, 'Gorbachev Vows Halt of Arms to Managua', *The Washington Post*, 16 May 1989, pp. A1, A17.
6. Douglas Farah, 'El Salvador Civil War – New Tactics, Old Stalemate', *The Washington Post*, 23 July 1989, pp. A21, A25.
7. Luard, *Conflict and Peace in the Modern International System*, Chapter 4, p. 288 and Appendix I; and Luard, 'Superpowers and Regional Conflicts', pp. 1006–25.
8. See 'Early Decision to Counter Marxism Led to Nurturing Rebels', *The Washington Post*, 1 January 1987, p. A24.
9. Clifford Krauss and Robert S. Greenberger, 'Despite Fears of US, Soviet Aid to Nicaragua Appears to be Limited', *The Wall Street Journal*, 3 April 1985, p. 1.
10. William Branigan, 'Latins Reach Consensus on Contras', *The Washington Post*, 15 February 1989, pp. A1, A22.

11. Don Oberdorfer and Lee Hockstader, 'US–Moscow Global Ties Said Linked to Soviet Presence in Nicaragua', *The Washington Post*, 17 March 1989, pp. A45, A54.
12. Ibid. See also interview with V. V. Volskiy, Director of USSR Academy of Sciences, Latin American Institute, *Pravda* in Russian, 22 February 1989, second edition, p. 4.
13. *The Washington Post*, 17 March 1989.
14. See G. Pope Atkins, *Latin American in the International Political System* (New York: The Free Press, 1977), pp. 89–90; and Gordon Connell-Smith, *The United States and Latin America: An Historical Analysis of Inter-American Relations* (New York: John Wiley and Sons, 1974), pp. 2–6.
15. Atkins, op. cit. pp. 89 ff; Dexter Perkins, *A History of the Monroe Doctrine* (Boston: Little, Brown, 1955), pp. 28 ff.; Thomas A. Bailey, *A Diplomatic History of the American People* (New York: Appleton-Century-Crofts, 1950, 4th edn), Chapter 32.
16. John O'Laughlin, 'World-Power Competition in Local Conflicts in the Third World', in R. J. Johnston and P. J. Taylor (eds), *A World in Crisis* (London: Basil Blackwell, 1986), p. 260.
17. See Ronald M. Schneider, *Communism in Guatemala 1944–1954* (New York: Frederick A. Praeger, 1958); and Rollie Poppino, *International Communism in Latin America: A History of the Movement 1917–1963* (London: The Free Press of Glencoe, 1964), pp. 92–4, 133–4.
18. Schneider, op. cit., pp. 311–17.
19. Atkins, op. cit., pp. 231–2.
20. Ibid., p. 233.
21. Ibid.
22. Philip J. Farley, 'Strategic Arms Control, 1967–87', in George, Farley and Dallin, (eds), op. cit., p. 223.
23. US Department of State and Department of Defense, *The Soviet–Cuban Connection in Central America and the Caribbean* (Washington, DC: US Government Printing Office, March 1985), pp. 1–4.
24. Ibid.
25. Ibid.
26. See the discussion of this point in O'Laughlin, op. cit., pp. 259 ff.
27. Ibid.
28. See Richard H. Schultz, *The Soviet Union and Revolutionary Warfare: Principles, Practices, and Regional Comparisons* (Stanford University: The Hoover Institution, 1988), Chapter 6.
29. W. Raymond Duncan, *The Soviet Union and Cuba: Interests and Influence* (New York: Praeger, 1985), p. 157.
30. Stephen Clissold (ed.), *Soviet Relations with Latin America* (London: Oxford University Press, 1970); J. Gregory Oswald and Anthony J. Strover, *The Soviet Union and Latin America* (New York: Praeger, 1970); and Cole Blasier, *The Giant's Rival: The USSR and Latin America* (Pittsburgh: University of Pittsburgh Press, 1974).
31. US Department of State and Department of Defense, op. cit., pp. 1–2.
32. Ibid.
33. Havana Television Service in Spanish, 28 February 1988, FBIS-Latin America, 3 March 1988, p. 14.

34. See Duncan, op. cit., Chapter 7.
35. Oberdorfer, op. cit.
36. See 'Joint United States–Soviet Recommendations for Stable Coexistence', US Senate, Congressional Record, Proceedings and Debates of the 100th Congress, Second Session, vol. 134, no. 63, 9 May 1988.
37. Elaine Sciolino, 'Wrapping It Up: George Shultz Looks as His Tenure at State', *The New York Times*, 18 December 1988, p. 22.
38. Michael Dobbs, 'Document Details '62 Plans on Cuba', *The Washington Post*, 27 January 1989, pp. A14, A18.
39. Ibid.
40. George, 'US–Soviet Efforts to Cooperate in Crisis Management and Crisis Avoidance', in George, Farley and Dallin, op. cit., p. 583.
41. *Text of Soviet–Cuban Friendship Treaty*, Moscow TASS in English, 5 April 1989, in FBIS-Latin America, 5 April 1989, pp. 49–50.
42. See James C. C. Chace, *America Invulnerable: The Quest for Absolute Security From 1812 to Star Wars* (New York: Summit, 1988), p. 3.
43. US Department of Defense, *Soviet Military Power: An Assessment of the Threat 1988* (Washington: US Government Printing Office, 1988), p. 29.
44. Jiri and Virginia Valenta, 'Sandinistas in Power', *Problems of Communism*, vol. 34, no. 5 (September–October 1985), pp. 24–5.
45. Jiri and Virginia Valenta, 'Leninism in Grenada', *Problems of Communism*, vol. 33, no. 4 (July–August 1984), pp. 11–12.
46. See *The Wall Street Journal*, 8 June 1981.
47. Jiri and Virginia Valenta, 'Leninism in Grenada', p. 23.
48. Robert S. Leiken, 'Fantasies and Facts: The Soviet Union and Nicaragua', *Current History*, vol. 83 (October 1984), p. 317.
49. See *The Soviet–Cuban Connection*, p. 35.
50. Don Oberdorfer, 'US, Soviets Near Talks on Central America', *The Washington Post*, 3 March 1989, p. A32.
51. Ibid.
52. Ibid.
53. *The Washington Post*, 17 March 1989.
54. John M. Goshko and David Hoffman, 'Bush Urges Gorbachev to Aid Peace Effort', *The Washington Post*, 31 March 1989, p. A32.
55. *The Washington Post*, 16 May 1989.
56. *The New York Times*, 19 March 1989.
57. Jan S. Adams, 'Change and Continuity in Soviet Central American Politics', *Problems of Communism* (March–June 1989), p. 112.
58. Julia Preston, 'Soviets Raise Profile, But Not Aid, in Managua', *The Washington Post*, 6 November 1988, pp. A37, A42.
59. Ibid.
60. Michael Dobbs, 'Ex-Officials Meet in Moscow to Match Notes on Cuba Crisis', *The Washington Post*, 28 January 1989, pp. A15, A22.
61. Adams, op. cit., pp. 312–15.
62. A former senior Cuban official involved in recent negotiations with the Soviet Union, who deflected to the United States in July 1990, has stated that major cuts in Soviet aid to Cuba lie ahead. *The New York Times*, 13 September 1990.
63. Ibid.

10 Superpower Cooperation in South America

Howard J. Wiarda

THE END OF THE COLD WAR?

The United States has long been thought of, and has thought of itself, as *the* hegemonic power in Latin America. In the Western Hemisphere, since 1898 in the circum Caribbean and somewhat later in South America, the United States has been supreme – economically, politically, and militarily. A variety of popular images and metaphors convey the point: the United States is referred to, by the Latin Americans, as the 'colossus of the north', the great 'shark' as opposed to the Latin American 'sardines', the 'imperialists', or, more neutrally, 'the giant'. The metaphors used in the United States convey equally hegemonic images: Americans refer to the Latin American region as 'our backyard', the Caribbean as 'our lake', or, more kindly, 'close to home'. United States hegemony has been so dominant for so long and the image of the 'giant' so pervasive that when Cole Blasier wrote his path-breaking study of the Soviet Union in Latin America, it is significant that he chose also to emphasize the US role by titling his book *The Giant's Rival: The USSR and Latin America*.[1] Even a book dealing with the Soviet Union in Latin America was obliged to stress the US role first.

The United States has long been the dominant outside power in Latin America, and at least since World War II its primary goal in the region has been to keep out communist influences. This point is an indisputable one; it is elaborated and given historical context in the next section of this chapter. Less obvious have been the elements of cooperation that have come to mark the behavior of the superpowers in Latin America. By 'cooperation' we mean not some antiseptic sharing of values or papering over of differences but rather certain levels of agreement on the 'rules of the road'. 'Cooperation' may also mean acceptance or acquiescence by the superpowers of various outcomes with which they are not necessarily very pleased – e.g. of the agreements reached after the Cuban missile crisis of 1962, of the military pact by which the Soviets provide training to the Peruvian military, or of the Argentine–Soviet trade partnership. This is not the usual, notion of 'cooperation', therefore, but the game theory notion that even bitter rivals can arrive at certain understandings governing their behavior, some formal but most of them informal, and with many of the rules open for constant renegotiations as conditions in Latin America and the relative power balance between the superpowers change. Even within a context of often bitter rivalry, therefore, certain understandings have been arrived at as to what is permissible superpower behavior and what is not.[2] Hence the third section of the chapter explores what these operational rules of conduct are and what are the tolerable outcomes acceded to by the superpowers.

The fourth section of the chapter is more speculative. It seeks to assess what the implications of these trends, where rivalry and cooperation among the superpowers go hand in hand, might be. As the Soviet Union turns inward and concentrates more heavily on its domestic economy, are we likely to see greater cooperation between the superpowers in Latin America? Will the 'rules of the road' be further extended? How will the Soviet Union's re-emphasis on domestic matters affect the Big Power rivalry in Latin America? And for Latin America itself, what will be the effects of an end to, or at least a toning down of the Cold War? It seems unlikely that the thawing of the Cold War will provide a new opportunity for Latin America to receive greater foreign assistance but will add one more devasting blow to the region by likely making it uninteresting and unworthy of attention from either superpower. For if it is true that the only reason the United States is interested in Latin America is because of the Cold War (which *is* in fact the case – or mostly so), then as the Cold War winds down it seems likely the US will not be very much interested in Latin America at all. We explore the dimensions of this problem in the conclusion.

THE UNITED STATES, THE SOVIET UNION, AND THE COLD WAR IN LATIN AMERICA

The United States has certain bedrock interests in Latin America.[3] These interests have remained largely the same since the Spanish–American War of 1898 and the emergence of the US as a major global power. US interests in the area were given intellectual formation about that same time in the writings of Admiral Alfred Thayer

Mahan. Some analysts would go so far as to say that US interests in Latin America have not changed in their essentials from the time of James Monroe and the famous doctrine that bears his name – although in 1823 the United States was not in a position to back up the sweeping foreign policy claims contained in the Monroe Doctrine with much in the way of military force.

Among the basic interests of the United States are:

(a) First and foremost, keep out hostile foreign powers. In the nineteenth century that meant diverse actions directed against France, Spain, Britain, and Czarist Russia; during the periods of World Wars I and II it meant efforts to monitor the actions of the sizable German colonies in Latin America and to reduce German influence throughout the region. Since World War II and the onset of the Cold War, American policy has been mainly directed at keeping out Soviet influences and preventing the possibility of communist takeovers.

(b) Complementary to this first-order goal, the United States has consistently sought to keep open and friendly the sea lanes into the area, to guard the Panama Canal and the approaches to it, and to acquire a string of bases and listening posts in that critical archipelago of Caribbean islands that stretches from Key West to Venezuela.

(c) The United States has always had stability as a high priority for the region. The US fears that the historic, endemic instability of these generally small and weak states will enable some foreign predator to take advantage of the conditions to establish bases or a beachhead – again, top priority. In the past the US often believed that the best way to preserve stability was to support authoritarian dictators, but since the Batista–Castro experience in Cuba we have, for the most part, come to believe that democracy preserves stability better than dictators.

(d) Since the US interest in Latin America has historically been not so much with the area itself but with outside powers securing beachheads there, US policy toward the area has mainly been *derivative*. That is, the main interests historically have been Spain, Britain, France, Germany, and now the Soviet Union; Latin America only achieves importance as these other powers and threats loom more imminent. Latin America's strategic importance has mainly derived from its *potential* to become a setting for superpower conflict. And since Latin America is not thought of as the main theater, the assumption has long been strategically that it can be dealt with through an 'economy of force'. The principal theaters are presumed to be Central Europe or perhaps the Middle East; so long as Latin America is not a main theater, little attention needs to be paid to it. 'Benign neglect' in the political and diplomatic spheres is the counterpart to 'economy of force' in the strategic arena.

(e) The United States has some, limited economic interests in Latin America: trade, investments, markets for its products, a source of raw materials and of labor supplies, and some agricultural products (sugar, coffee, bananas), and now, increasingly, manufactured goods. These trade relations are valued both for their contributions to the US economy and because we assume they also help bring prosperity and hence stability to Latin America – again the first-order strategic consideration.

(f) The US has long been interested in democracy and human rights in Latin America, for its own sake, because such a policy fits the American historic sense of being a special nation with a particular missionary purpose, *and* because democracy and human rights, once again, serve US higher-order strategic priorities of maintaining stability and keeping out hostile foreign powers. When the democracy and strategic considerations came in conflict, the USA usually chose the 'lesser evil' of its strategic imperative. Now, Americans tend to see democracy as also maintaining their strategic objectives: democracies do not usually support guerrilla groups in neighboring countries, do not interfere in their neighbors' internal affairs, do not get involved in international wars (Argentina in the Falklands), tend to be more stable than other kinds of regimes, and make it far easier for the US to defend its policies domestically.

(g) More recently other, non-strategic interests have gained prominence: drug traffic, immigration, the international debt, greater economic interdependence with Latin America. Some of these new issues obviously relate to strategic concerns; others are non-strategic, but nevertheless touch some basic issues in domestic US politics and society. In this way Latin America may come to have greater salience for the US even though its strategic importance may no longer be seen as very high.

These are the basic foundations of US policy in Latin America. These priorities must now be set against another, generally negative but nevertheless realistic, set of conditions and attitudes toward Latin America that also affects US policy there:

(a) Latin America ranks low on the US list of regional priorities, below the Soviet Union, Western Europe, East Asia, the Middle East and Eastern Europe. It may rank above sub-Saharan Africa in importance but perhaps at about the same level as South Asia (India, Pakistan) or North Africa.

(b) The US does not always understand Latin America very well, and what the US does understand it doesn't like very much. Surveys show that most Americans think of Latin America as corrupt, backward, violent, inefficient, and unfriendly toward the United States.

(c) Not only do Americans not understand Latin America very well but they often do not wish to understand it better. The US tends to be condescending and patronizing toward the area. The attitude is, with Hegel, that Latin America has 'no history', or with Henry Kissinger that it is peripheral to the world axis of power. The models and formulas that the US uses to try to reform Latin America are also derived ethnocentrically from the US's own developmental experience and frequently have little to do with Latin American realities. Americans fail to read about Latin America or try to comprehend it on its own terms because fundamentally they believe that Latin America has nothing to teach us.

US policy toward Latin America, shaped by basic strategic interests on the one hand and by strongly-held biases and sentiments on the other, has long gone through a variety of ups and downs. While the United States has been consistent in the goals sought (no foreign bases, stability, anti-communism), the means used (aid to dictators versus aid to democrats) have often gyrated. The US has alternated between dramatic interventions and periods of benign neglect. It has often allowed small problems to fester into large ones (Nicaragua, Guatemala, and El Salvador during the decade of the 1970s) until they explode onto America television screens, if not always into the American consciousness, occasioning a new round of interventions or, in its softer forms, pro-consularism. *Never* has the US developed the sustained, steady, normal, and mature relations with Latin

America that it has long maintained with Western Europe and now increasingly with China and Japan. The reason is the low ranking the area has in the US list of foreign policy priorities, coupled with the attitudes and prejudices Americans harbor about the area, plus the strategic doctrine of economy of force.[4]

THE COLD WAR IN LATIN AMERICA

The internal conditions in Latin America in the 1940s and early 1950s did not seem ripe for revolution. None of the groups that one thinks of as constituting a potential base for communist revolution seemed in Latin America to offer very many strong opportunities. The peasantry remained illiterate, backward, unmobilized, unorganized, and not a fertile territory for Marxist-Leninist proselytizing. The trade union movement was similarly weak and unorganized; even in the advanced countries the percentage of the population unionized seldom numbered more than 5–10 per cent of the population. The intellectuals were often on the left but were disorganized, undisciplined, and usually thought of themselves as independent Marxists rather than full-fledged communists. Nor did the local communist parties, which in most countries dated from the interwar period, constitute much of a threat. They were poorly organized, poorly led, poorly financed, and without strong roots in the area.[5] They consisted mostly, in Luis Mercier Vega's words, of 'tired bureaucracies' led by old men with little hope of coming to power.[6]

The US worry about the possibilities for communist encroachments in Latin America grew slowly. In 1948 there was a bloody uprising in Bogotá, Colombia (known as the '*bogotazo*'), in which a number of communists and others (including the young Fidel Castro) participated. That same year a social-democratic revolution took place in Costa Rica, an event that in later years in other countries would call forth US warships; but fortunately for the Costa Rican revolution the local communists, still operating on the basis of older directives from Moscow, were on the other side. The US therefore stood by while Costa Rica's brief but bloody civil war ended in a democratic victory. In Bolivia in 1952 there was also a revolution that included communist and Trotskyite support and participation, and the USA began to worry. But US Ambassador Ben Stefansky succeeded in persuading Washington that the revolution was primarily social-democratic rather than communist, and even secured for a time sizable US assistance to support the revolution and prevent the communists from seizing control of it.

That is precisely what the US feared was happening in Guatemala in the early 1950s, which constituted the first postwar US intervention in a Latin American country to prevent a possible communist takeover. Not all the details of those familiar events need to be repeated here. Suffice it to say that in 1944 a revolutionary and vaguely socialist process began in Guatemala, that after 1950 the revolution went further to the left, and that by 1953–4 communists had cemented their hold in three major government agencies: the labor ministry, the agrarian reform institute, and the social welfare ministry. It needs to be emphasized that the Guatemalan communist party was not like the others previously discussed; rather it was well organized and led, tough, disciplined, sizable and with strong roots in the country's largest labor organization, the banana workers' union. Though most existing analyses have emphasized that the US intervened in the revolution to protect the threatened lands of the United Fruit Company, in fact the evidence is overwhelming that the US motivation was strategic and not economic. That is, US leaders wished to prevent a potential communist takeover of Guatemala, not necessarily or primarily come to the defense of the United Fruit Company. Hence in 1954 the CIA found an obscure, exiled, Guatemalan colonel, armed his followers, and assisted them in invading Guatemala. Guatemala's revolutionary government, by then no longer popular, quickly fell and, significantly, no one rose up to defend it. This was the first US intervention in Latin America since the Good Neighbor Policy of Franklin Delano Roosevelt; its success resulted in the CIA's using the Guatemala experience as a model for other, future interventions.[7]

For a few more years things were relatively quiet on the Latin American front, but then came the Cuban revolution. Cuba changed everything. Cuba was the first avowedly Marxist-Leninist state in the history of the hemisphere; it was the first Latin American country to ally itself with the Soviet Union and to join the socialist camp; it became a Soviet military, intelligence, and guerrilla training base (thus violating all the hallowed precepts of US policy in Latin America since the Monroe Doctrine); and it enormously complicated the development process in Latin America and US policy there. For, instead of the older two-part struggle between the advocates of change and the defenders of the status quo, now a powerful third force was added to the situation: one which favored radical change, nationalism, and anti-Americanism (all popular themes in Latin America), but opted for Marxist-Leninist methods and an alliance with the Soviet Union in order to carry them out. Henceforth whenever there was upheaval in Latin America or a revolutionary movement, the United States would be obliged, since that is its primary interest in the area, to think first about the possibilities of a communist takeover. The history of future US interventions in the area (the Dominican Republic in 1965, Chile in 1973, Grenada in 1983, and Central America in various forms from 1979 on) all followed from the experience of and policy assessments drawn from the Cuban revolution.

Following the Cuban revolution the United States fashioned the Peace Corps, the Alliance for Progress, and other programs to try to prevent more Cubas from happening. The leitmotif of policy then and since was: no second Cubas. For its part, the Soviet Union also reassessed its possibilities in Latin America. Heretofore it had thought of Latin America as backward and non-revolutionary, and in any case part of the US sphere of influence. But now, with Cuba serving as a guide and teacher, the Soviets began to consider that maybe Latin America was ripe for revolutionary plucking after all. Hence with Cuba leading the way, the Soviets began to aid other guerrilla movements and revolutionary groups in Latin America. In Guatemala, Venezuela, Colombia, Peru, the Dominican Republic, El Salvador, Nicaragua, Bolivia, Brazil, and elsewhere, new guerrilla movements were organized. Because Cuba played such a leading role in these struggles and served as the Soviets' mentor, the image of the Cubans often popularized during this period as a simple proxy for the Soviet Union is far too simple.[8]

The strategy employed at this time was known as the '*foco* theory'. Derived from French Marxist Régis Debray,[9] the *foco* theory suggested the organization initially of a rural nucleus of dedicated guerrillas – presumably as in the Cuban model. From this nucleus the guerrilla movement would spread out to encompass peasants, workers, and increasing areas of the national territory. Eventually the revolution, launched in the countryside, would surround and absorb the cities as well, including the capital. The plan and pattern stemmed from Ché Guevara's book, *On Guerrilla Warfare*,[10] a popular tome among revolutionaries but one based on a romantic and erroneous reading of the Cuban revolution itself – i.e. that the Cuban revolution had been a peasant-led revolution; in fact it was a broad-based revolution encompassing all classes.

By the late 1960s, however, virtually all the guerrilla movements that had sprung up in the early 1960s had faded away, atrophied, or been snuffed out. Guevara himself died in Bolivia in an attempt to spread the revolution to the peasants of that country – apparently Guevara believed the myths contained in his own book. But actually, the reasons for the failure of the guerrilla campaigns and of the *foco* theory were several: the Latin America countryside proved to not be very revolutionary, the workers also proved not to be radical, the guerrillas were unpopular, the Latin American armed forces proved more efficient than expected, and the Latin American societies and polities proved more viable and functional than many had conceived.

The failure of the guerrilla/*foco* strategy led both the Soviet Union and the United States to reassess their strategic policies for Latin America. With the failure of the guerrilla movements, the United States decided – in contrast to what it had believed since the Cuban revolution – that maybe Latin America was not so susceptible to Marxist-Leninist takeovers after all. The result was the *de facto* end of the Alliance for Progress and a new era of benign neglect that ended only in 1979 with the Nicaraguan, Grenadan, and Salvadoran revolutions. For the Soviet Union, disillusionment and reassessment similarly set in, with the conclusion reached remarkably parallel to that arrived at by the United States: that Latin America was not as immediately revolutionary as the Cubans had led them to believe, that the gains registered for all their efforts were meager, and that they should not waste their resources pursuing chimeras.

The Soviets, over the objections of the Cubans, then determined on a new course during the 1970s. That involved pursuing a long-term strategy for Latin America, as distinct from the failed short-term revolutionary strategy of the previous decade. The long-term strategy was aimed at gradually building up Soviet contacts, credibility, and presence in the area. This was done through the expansion of normal state-to-state relations, cultural exchanges, expanded trade, diplomacy, even military training programs in the case of Peru. The Soviets tried to present themselves as a reasonable, serious, trustworthy partner, as distinct from their negative, destabilizing reputation left over from the 1960s. In pursuing this tactic, the Soviets were playing for long-range advantage and no longer just immediate conquests.

The revolutions in Central America and the Caribbean culminating in 1979 forced a new reassessment. Again with Cuba taking the lead, the Soviets concluded that maybe the area was ripe for revolution after all. A new strategy was devised that sought to combine both short-term and long-term aspects, both the revolutionary tactics of the 1960s and the peaceful, accommodative strategy of the 1970s. Thus, the Soviets continued their policy of expanding normal diplomatic relations, increasing their trade, and continuing their student and other exchanges. But now they began again to assist the guerrilla movements at the same time. The Soviets brought the often feuding guerrilla groups in Nicaragua and then El Salvador together to forge a common front and strategy, they provided greater funds and arms, they then assisted the Nicaraguan Sandinista government on a large scale, and in Nicaragua they brought in their Eastern European allies in an interesting socialist division of labor: the Soviets provided overall guidance, the Cubans did the guerrilla and other training, the Bulgarians trained the secret police, the East Germans taught torture techniques, and the Czechs supplied the guns.

Far more than in the past, the Soviets began to distinguish between the various Latin American regimes: military-authoritarian regimes, mixed civilian/military regimes, populist regimes, social-democratic regimes that are also intensely nationalistic (and often anti-American), and genuinely socialist regimes. The Soviets devised a separate strategy for each type of regime, indeed for each country. In some countries (the social-democratic ones) the Soviet Union tried to have cordial relations with the government in power, and played on their nationalism and existing anti-Americanism – while sometimes assisting the opposition guerrilla groups at the same time. The Soviet strategy in the 1980s was thus far more complex, sophisticated and differentiated than it was before. And in some countries (Costa Rica, Peru, Venezuela) it has actually been two-faced, cozying up to democratic governments on the one hand and seeking to destabilize them on the other.

By 1989 the Soviets once again concluded that the revolutionary potential that seemed great in 1959 and then again in 1979 had in all likelihood been exaggerated. The United States during the 1980s proved more willing to defend its interests in Latin American than it had been in the 1970s. And once more, Latin American society, its armed forces, and its governments proved more resilient to revolutionary challenges than appeared likely in 1979. In addition, with the Soviet economy performing poorly, with the need to concentrate on domestic reform, and with the renewed realization of how little strategic value Latin America has to the Soviet Union, the Soviets appear likely in the future to diminish their activist and expansionist role in Latin America. But if the Soviets reduce their presence in Latin America, it seems likely that the United States will enter into a new era of 'benign neglect' as well.

SUPERPOWER RULES OF THE ROAD AND CODES OF CONDUCT

On the surface, the United States and the Soviet Union would appear to have been mortal rivals in Latin America over the past forty years of the Cold War. While in no way minimizing the rivalry, it needs also to be emphasized that, within this conflict, elements of cooperation have also been present. 'Cooperation', recall, here refers to rules of the road or codes of conduct between the superpowers, not mutual friendship or necessarily a meeting of the minds. Such cooperation can be either formal or informal, and it can obviously change with the circumstances.

During the 1950s, particularly after the Soviets' explosion of a nuclear device, a certain 'gentleman's agreement' appeared to govern the relations between the superpowers. The acquisition of 'the bomb' meant that henceforth the Soviet Union would have to be treated as a more-or-less equal with the United States, whatever the marginal superiority the US had in certain military areas. The informal understanding that had developed, by 1956 and quite clearly thereafter, was that: we will not interfere in your sphere of influence and you had better not interfere in ours. The Soviet sphere of influence encompassed Eastern Europe, which helps explain why the US did not intervene to assist the freedom fighters in the 1956 uprisings. In turn, it was understood that the Soviet Union would not interfere in the US sphere of influence, Latin America. Hence the Soviets could put down the Eastern European uprisings militarily and the USA could intervene in Guatemala in 1954 without fear of retaliation. World public opinion might be condemnatory of both of these actions, but at least neither superpower had to fear action from the other within its own sphere of influence. The superpowers had also agreed informally not to allow Latin America to become a center of potential nuclear confrontation.

The Cuban revolution changed the givens of this understanding in all kinds of complex ways; it could be said that the superpowers have still not worked out a new satisfactory understanding concerning the particulars of their relationship in Latin America since that time. It should be remembered, however, that Cuba was not really a conquest, in any military sense, on the Soviet Union's part. The Soviets sent no army to Cuba, did not aid the revolution until the very end, and had denounced Castro and his 26th of July Movement as 'petite bourgeois reformers'. Rather than representing a conquest of Soviet foreign policy, Cuba was instead an accidental acquisition for the Soviets. They did not expect Cuba to become a Marxist-Leninist state nor had they done anything to abet the revolution. So the Soviets could still claim that they had done nothing to violate the earlier gentleman's agreement; the US was not so certain.

With Castro's declaration of Marxism-Leninism and Cuba's alliance with Moscow rapidly being cemented, the US devised a series of plots to oust the regime and restore American hegemony. The Soviet–Cuban ties violated the precepts of the Monroe Doctrine, which among other things prohibited outside involvement in Latin America. At stake was *the* primary goal of US foreign policy in the region: keeping out hostile foreign powers. The steps the US took to rid Cuba of Castro are now the 'stuff' of congressional and CIA investigations and of legend: explosives or poison in his cigars, more poison in his beard, assassination attempts and mob hit squads. The culmination of these events was the 1961 attempt at the Bay of Pigs to overthrow the Castro regime, à la Guatemala in 1954, by sponsoring an invasion of the island by Cuban exiles backed by the US. The effort ended in defeat, disaster and ignomy, what one book called a 'perfect failure'.[11]

The next year, 1962, and in part as a response to the Bay of Pigs invasion, the Soviet Union implanted intercontinental ballistic missiles in Cuba, armed with nuclear warheads, and capable of reaching most US east coast cities. Whatever our earlier assessment of whether a Marxist-Leninist Cuban regime allied with the Soviet Union violated the gentleman's agreement between the superpowers over respect for each other's spheres of influence, it is clear that the implantation of offensive ICBMs *did* violate those understandings – certainly as the US understood them. The precise motive for the sending of such missiles to Cuba remains obscure. We do not know if Khrushchev aimed to test President Kennedy, wished to protect Cuba from some presumed future US invasion, was acceding to the wishes of Castro, or perhaps all three. In any case, the showdown over the missiles in October 1962 was probably the closest the US and the Soviets have come to escalating the Cold War into a hot war.

The Soviets were the ones to blink first, by turning their other missile-carrying ships around and agreeing to remove their missiles from Cuba. But under a secret agreement worked out at the time, the US also agreed (a) not to invade Cuba, and (b) gradually to remove its missiles from Turkey which, lying on the border of the Soviet Union, was viewed as analogous to the presence of Soviet missiles in Cuba. No clearer or better example of superpower cooperation, in the rules-of-the-road definition here used, could be found. Though the 1962 missile crisis has usually been viewed as a US victory (the missiles were removed), in fact the secret accord implied severe costs to the USA: its hegemony in Latin America had been broken, the Monroe Doctrine had been violated, it was obliged to accept a Marxist-Leninist state 'only ninety miles from home', and the Cuban revolution was now free from external threats. This was perhaps the major 'agreement on outcomes' in Latin America, defined earlier as a sign of Cold War cooperation.

The Cuban missile crisis 'solved' the problem of the actual presence of the missiles in Cuba and led to their removal – the overriding goal of US policy – but it left other issues unsettled. Unresolved were the questions of how large the Soviet non-missile military presence would be in Cuba, to what extent Cuba would become a Soviet military base, how many Soviet troops could be stationed in Cuba, the extent to which the Cubans and their Soviet sponsors could spread subversion throughout the Americas, Cuba's function as a guerrilla training base for Marxists from other countries, and so on. None of these critical issues were resolved by the US–Soviet missile agreement of 1962; all would prove to be hotly contested issues in future years.

Although the Cuba issue had been 'settled' in a limited sense (no missiles in return for no invasion), no other issues in Latin America had been; and the rest of the 1960s (the period ends in 1973 with the overthrow of Allende in Chile) turned into a free-for-all in the US–Soviet competition. Working through Cuba, the Soviet Union began assisting anti-American guerrilla movements in a variety of countries. The campaign was waged hemisphere-wide, encompassing not just the historic bones of contention in the Caribbean (Guatemala, Nicaragua, El Salvador, Panama, Puerto Rico, the Dominican Republic) but the larger South American countries as well (Venezuela, Colombia, Brazil, Argentina, Uruguay, Chile, Peru, Ecuador, Bolivia), which neither the US nor the Soviets had ever paid much strategic attention to before. Subversion of established governments, the fomenting of violence and riots, the support of anti-regime guerrilla movements – these were the tactics used by the Soviets, their Cuban allies, and the local revolutionary forces. With guns, money, and agents now flowing into the area, the stakes had clearly been altered and the ante upped. The United States feared that unless it responded, all of Latin America might go the way of Castro's Cuba. It is now clear that those fears were considerably exaggerated, but in the context of the early-to-mid-1960s they seemed very real to US policy-makers. Hence the US developed the Alliance for Progress, the Peace Corps, the Inter-American Development Bank, and a whole host of programs (agrarian reform, community Development, family planning, technical assistance, political party and labor union development, farm cooperatives, peasant leagues, etc.) – all to counter the Soviet/ Cuban threat. In 1965 the United States sent in 23,000 troops to the Dominican Republic to put down what it thought was an attempted Castro/communist takeover. But the Dominican invasion was aimed not just at that country, it had larger foreign policy goals. It was also aimed at Hanoi, in a demonstration of what the US would do if North Vietnam continued to try to subvert and conquer South Vietnam. It was meant further to demonstrate to the Soviets (as were the CIA machinations in Chile in 1973) that there were limits beyond which the Soviets ought not go in Latin America and that the United States was willing to go to considerable lengths to defend its interests there, including the use of military force.[12]

These elliptical messages, sent from Latin America, apparently had very little effect on Hanoi. They did have some effect on the Soviet Union, however. By the late 1960s the guerrilla movements sponsored by Cuba and the Soviets were sputtering out. Guerrilla movements are seldom completely defeated but they do atrophy and become less threatening. As the Latin America area proved less revolutionary than the Soviets had thought, the Soviets lost interest in it. The last gasp in this effort was the Socialist-communist alliance in Chile that had brought Salvador Allende to power; and after he was overthrown in 1973 the continent was all but completely dominated by bureaucratic-authoritarian military regimes which offered few openings to Soviet activities. Hence for a time the Soviets all but abandoned the Latin American playing fields and reassessed their tactics.

The two exceptions were Peru and Panama. Both these countries were also under military rule after 1968, but they were military regimes of the left (reformist, nationalist, anti-imperialist) rather than the usual rightist types. They were sometimes known as 'Nasserist' regimes,[13] and therefore offered certain attractions to the Soviet Union. The Soviets ordered the local communist parties in each country to support the government and gave them the designation as 'progressive'. A new departure for the Soviets in Peru, after US military training was cut off following the US refusal to sell the country advanced fighter planes, was the signing of an agreement to provide training and equipment to the armed forces – the first time the Soviets had made important inroads into that critical institution. In Panama there was apparently some agreement to share intelligence information – although the United States also had its own arrangements with the Panamanian intelligence services.

It is hard to discern very many rules of the road operating during this period, 1962–73. Obviously some agreement had been reached at the most fundamental level: there were to be no more missiles in Cuba. But below that level there was intense competition. The Soviets aided and abetted guerrilla movements throughout the region aimed at destabilizing existing regimes, while the US sought strenuously to prevent any more Cubas. The US eventually won out, as the guerrilla movements petered out or were defeated and the Soviets lost interest in the area. But this was the product of vigorous competition, not the result of cooperative arrangements.

It is interesting also – and has implications for the present context – that as the Soviets lost interest in the area, so did the United States. The Alliance for Progress, after all, had been a new way of resisting communism but it was still, in its fundamental premises, an anticommunist strategy. As the communist threat loomed smaller by the end of the 1960s, however, so did the Alliance. US interest in the area also flagged, which supports the earlier contention that the predominant US concern in Latin America is strategic. As the strategic threat lessened, so did US concern for the area. Hence under Nixon the Alliance was allowed to die; benign neglect was back. One of the rules of the road that does seem to prevail, therefore, is this: when Cuban/Soviet machinations are vigorous, so will be the US response; but when the Cuban/Soviet interest or efforts at subversion flag, the US primarily reverts to benign neglect.

The mid-1970s, more or less corresponding to the era known globally as *détente*, was generally a period of peaceful competition between the superpowers in Latin America. The Soviet Union had largely abandoned its strategy of stirring up guerrilla movements in favor of a more broad-based policy. The new policy emphasized expanding its normal state-to-state relations, to the point where the Soviet Union now has diplomatic relations with sixteen of the twenty-one Latin American countries. The Soviets also considerably expanded their trade relations, particularly with Mexico and the larger countries of South America. Cultural exchanges and fellowship were also vastly expanded to the point where in many countries they outnumbered those of the United States. In addition, the Soviets expanded their overall *presence* in Latin America through diplomatic initiatives, more visits by Soviet officials, an expansion of the Latin American studies programs in the Soviet Union, and efforts to be 'friendly' (as compared with the earlier efforts at fomenting guerrilla war and destabilization, which did not endear the Soviets to very many Latin American officials).

These efforts obviously required time before the results began to be visible. But by the early 1980s Soviet trade with Latin America had increased *twelve-fold* over what it had been previously (admittedly quite low). The fellowship programs were paying huge dividends in terms of thousands of young Latin Americans receiving travel grants or a free education in the Soviet Union. The diplomatic initiatives succeeded in convincing many Latin Americans that the Soviet Union was a serious, responsible power, bent on avoiding war and conceivably an alternative to the United States. The military training program that brought Peruvian officers to Moscow did not necessarily convert them into dedicated Marxist-Leninists, but it did teach them the logic and rationality of Soviet defense policy, equipment, training, and their military *system*, and therefore brought the Soviets several degrees of legitimacy and acceptance. In commercial relations the big breakthrough came when President Jimmy Carter cut off US grain sales to the Soviet Union as a response to the Soviets' invasion of Afghanistan in 1980, whereupon the Soviets turned to Argentina (and other countries) for their grain. Today in critical Argentina, the Soviet Union has become that country's largest trading partner.

Meanwhile, the Soviet Union kept bumping up against the superpower rules of the road – both those established by the 1962 missile accord and those left unstated in the accord but presumably governed by *détente*. During the course of the 1970s the Soviet Union continued to build up its military bases and facilities in Cuba until the island was almost literally a floating military base, bristling with weaponry. ICBMs were not involved but modern MiG fighter planes were – did that violate either the informal or formal codes of conduct? The Soviets used Cuba as a base for missile-carrying nuclear submarines – did that violate the rules of the road? Soviet bombers and reconnaissance aircraft based in Cuba regularly travelled up and down the US east coast – was that a violation of the rules? Cuba had also converted itself into a vast training center for political indoctrination, guerrilla activities, and terrorism -- did this violate the understandings? The problem was that the rules that existed were very few, they were imprecise, the superpowers had different ideas of what they meant, they were being continuously tested and stretched, and they did not cover any of the most immediate contingencies.

But now matters began to escalate even further. In 1975, using weapons and transport planes provided by the Soviet Union, Cuba sent its troops to Angola to defend a wobbly Marxist-Leninist regime recently come to power. Soon Cuban troops, advisers, and paramilitary personnel were in 25–30 countries, from Vietnam and Kanpuchea, to the Yemens, to the Middle East, to the Horn of Africa, East as well as West Africa, the Caribbean and Central America. Cuba was taking on the role of a global power; and having fought in so many conflicts, the Cuban troops were garnering a reputation as the best, most experienced fighters in the world. The Soviets built up their own troops in Cuba to the point where they constituted a full 'brigade', and hence there was a considerable flap in the United States over whether this brigade violated the 1962 agreement and therefore ought to be removed. *Détente* was about to come to an end.

Further escalation came when, as Cuba twenty years earlier, Nicaragua and Grenada experienced revolutions in 1979 and gravitated toward the Soviet orbit. The Soviet Union was not overtly or directly involved in these two revolutions, but Cuba certainly was.[14] At the same time, revolutionary situations seemed to be developing in Guatemala and El Salvador. Once again the Soviets reassessed and concluded that the potential for revolutionary seizures of power in Latin America might be greater than they had thought. But based on the 1960s experience, the Soviets no longer trusted the Cubans entirely to serve as their guides and mentors. They therefore took the lead themselves in deciding revolutionary strategy, providing overall coordination, and welding the guerrilla forces into coordinated movements.

Meanwhile, in South America, other shifts were under way. Virtually all of the South American countries began by the late 1970s to follow new, more independent, more neutralist foreign policies. One after the other they began to re-establish diplomatic and commercial relations with Cuba, which had been severed in 1961 at

US insistence. The South Americans began to look more benignly on the Soviet Union and often accepted the position that the superpowers were morally equivalent. They expanded their trade, diplomatic, and cultural relations with the Soviets. This was also the time when anti-American dependency theory, which blamed the United States for all of Latin America's problems and absolved Latin America of any responsibility, was at the height of its fashion.

In addition, by the late 1970s, the United States was widely perceived in Latin America and elsewhere to be a nation in decline. Its political system seemed to be unraveling (Watergate), the US had been defeated in Vietnam, OPEC had devastated the US economy, the Soviets seemed to be surpassing the US militarily, and ineffectual leadership was in the White House. Nicaragua and Grenada had just 'fallen' and El Salvador seemed about to. The Soviet Union was vastly building up its military capacity and seemed to be a nation on the march. Throughout South America during this period, according to several analysts, one could almost *feel* the United States slowly give way and the Soviet Union gain ascendancy.

But then came the dramatic about-face of the 1980s. The US economy recovered and began again to expand. The military build-up was dramatic. President Reagan, for all his leadership faults, helped the nation recover its jaunty self-confidence. America was often admired and emulated once again. The *malaise* of the 1970s ended; America was 'back'. As the US recovered, the Soviet Union slumped. Its economy was a disaster, it could not keep up technologically, it faced crises in its leadership, in its institutions, in society, between the generations, in its ideology, among the nationality groups, seemingly everywhere.[15] Crisis at home seemed to forbode retrenchment abroad. And since Latin America is among the least important regions strategically for the Soviet Union, the possibility loomed of a considerable Soviet retreat from the Latin American theater.

Let us at this point sum up the rules of the road in superpower relations in Latin America, as they appeared to exist in the mid-1980s. These rules are not clear-cut, and as we have seen they are subject to constant renegotiation. But there are rules nonetheless. For example, on Sandinista Nicaragua the United States had made it very clear to the Soviets as well as to the Nicaraguans that there were to be no Soviet military bases, no MiG fighter planes, and no subversion of Nicaragua's neighbors. That is the price that had to be paid for the US allowing Nicaragua's revolution to survive. At issue still were what to do about the other sophisticated military equipment (tanks and attack helicopters) that Nicaragua had recently imported, and the degree to which Nicaragua had to democratize. These issues of course left the future of Nicaragua open-ended. It was open-ended not just because of the interplay of the superpowers but because it was also subject to the vagaries of the US political process (whether to continue funding the Contras, for example) and, increasingly, to the vagaries of the Soviet political process as well. Whether the Soviet Union would at some stage be cooperative in pressing Cuba, Nicaragua, or the several guerrilla groups in the Central American isthmus to arrive at a peaceful settlement of the several interlocking disputes there remained for the future to tell. But on the basis of 1989–90 negotiations regarding Nicaragua, an unprecedented degree of cooperation was achieved, and the 1990 election drove the Sandinistas from power.

In South America, where the superpowers have not been so heavily committed (even though the geostrategic stakes are considerably higher than in Central America), the situation of superpower relations is even more open-ended. The South American countries are now free to have diplomatic relations with the Soviet Union, to trade with the Soviet Union, to have exchanges with the Soviet Union, to assume neutralist positions in the UN and elsewhere, and to restore relations with Cuba – all steps that would not have been possible at the height of the Cold War and of US hegemony in the region twenty-five years ago. The South American countries can criticize the US with impunity, pursue independent foreign policies, refuse to pay their international debts, turn down US requests for the extradition of drug traffickers – do almost anything that they want without fear of US disapproval or retribution.

South America has become increasingly more independent of the US, and believes that it can go its own way regardless of the US.[16] In part this results from the new power and assertiveness of several of the Latin American NICs (Argentina, Brazil, Mexico, Venezuela); in part, also, it derives from the new presence of several other actors in the continent (West Germany, Japan, Spain, China, as well as the Soviet Union), which provides more options and leaves the Latin Americans somewhat freer (or at least they see it that way) to pursue their own foreign policies *between* the superpowers; and in part it is due to a significantly smaller US presence in the region now as compared with the 1960s.

The United States and the Soviet Union seemed to have reached a certain *modus operandi* in the mid-1980s. The relationship had moved a long way from the hostility and opposition (including armed opposition) on the part of the United States in past decades to *any* Soviet activities in the Americas, to one of more or less peaceful coexistence. 'Peaceful coexistence' as used here means a continuation of the rivalry, but with some, to this point vague and imprecise rules of the game which are almost constantly being changed as both the situation in Latin America and the situation between the superpowers change. But now, under Gorbachev, whatever rules did exist are being altered once again; clearly we are in a new era. The next section speculates on what these changed circumstances might imply for all the parties concerned: the US, the USSR, and the Latin American countries.

THE NEW CONTEXT AND SUPERPOWER RELATIONS IN LATIN AMERICA

The fact with which we begin this section is that the Cold War is now declining in intensity. The Soviet Union is not very interested in Latin America and to the Soviets the area is not of significant strategic value. But, if the Soviets are uninterested, US disinterest will surely follow. Here is where many hopeful Latin Americans are wrong. They think the ending of the Cold War will free up large amounts of Department of Defense funding that will now go to them, so that the United States will not only forgive their foreign debts but that the US can pay them to have their independent foreign policies. But this is unlikely to happen. The ending of the Cold War will not free up a large amount of US dollars for Latin America, and certainly not to finance an 'independent' (read 'anti-American') foreign policy. The United States has its own domestic priorities to which it will give initial attention; and in the US Congress and among the public at large, the reputation of Latin America has never been worse.[17] Among congressmen the sense is strong today that Latin America is a 'black hole' into which they pour billions; nothing happens; the money disappears; and the United States is criticized besides. It used to be said by perceptive South American diplomats that the trouble for their continent was that the US believed Latin America ended at the Panama Canal. Now it is fair to conclude that, so far as Americans are concerned, Latin America ends at Mexico. Few others get much attention.

Actually, there are two possible readings, two possible logics and

Howard J. Wiarda

scenarios, that grow out of the recent changes in the Soviet Union. The first, which is currently the most in vogue, suggests that since the Soviet Union is in a desperate economic crisis, is oriented toward internal reform, has flagging technology and agriculture, and faces severe crises, it will reduce its foreign policy commitments, especially in the Third World, turn inward, and cease its adventurism in far-flung areas of the globe. In this scenario, not only is the Cold War over but it is the West that emerged victorious. The Soviet Union, in this reading, will no longer continue to be a challenge to the United States in Latin America or elsewhere.

The second logic and scenario is as follows: yes, the Soviet Union is facing a series of crises but: (a) in the past it has been very successful in passing many of the costs of its empire onto its ideological allies; (b) it can easily run its empire on inertia or automatic pilot for a while; (c) while its economy is not robust, it can still provide ample military equipment to allies and guerrilla groups; (d) the Soviets can continue to rely on their Cuban allies to serve as their proxy in Latin America; (e) the Soviets still have other things going for them: ideology, fifth columns, local communist parties and labor organizations, intellectual networks, a formula for seizing and holding power, active guerrilla groups; (f) while the Soviet Union may not undertake new offensive actions in the present circumstances, it is likely to do everything possible to avoid retreat; (g) the Soviets' allies, especially Cuba, do not at this time seem threatened and are in fact consolidating themselves; (h) seemingly unlike the US, the Soviets do not always need a lot of money to be successful internationally; and (i) while the Soviets may shift their priorities (less financial aid) they may still play an active role in the area.[18]

In short, from the viewpoint of this second scenario, the prognosis that sees the Cold War as over may well be premature. Worse, it is dangerous because it results in the US letting its guard down, pressures premature reductions in the defense budget, gives further impetus to the unilateral disarmament forces, and may even allow the Soviets to recover. Hence this logic suggests for policy purposes that the US follow a cautious and prudent approach, maintain its strong defense position, wait for the Soviets to follow up their words with deeds, and continue to maintain a posture of peace through strength.

The truth probably lies somewhere between these two scenarios. The trouble with the first one is that the American people so much *want* the Cold War to be over that wishful and overly optimistic thinking may get in the way of hard analysis. The trouble with the second is that it is *so* skeptical of Soviet intentions that it may miss the opportunity to exploit the real changes that are in fact occurring in the Soviet Union.

It seems unlikely that the Soviets will soon withdraw entirely from Latin America, abandon the access and relations they have built up over the years, or give up on such clients as Cuba. In fact the evidence was overwhelming that until 1989 the Soviets were increasing their military aid (economic aid may be another matter) to Nicaragua, not reducing it. There is no evidence that the Soviets are reducing their commercial ties with Argentina, their military ties with Peru, or their political and diplomatic ties with all the other South American countries. Cuba is successfully breaking out of its diplomatic isolation as well. Moreover, in such unstable countries as El Salvador, Guatemala, and now perhaps Peru, the possibilities for the guerrilla groups to take power and hence for the Soviet Union to *expand* its network of Marxist-Leninist clients are quite good – even without any significant expenditures. The scenario of the Soviet Union, precipitously or over the long term, abandoning its empire is probably premature at best, dangerous at worst, and simply not very likely to happen.

On the other hand, the view that sees the Soviet Union as entirely aggressive, bellicose, and expansionist as before is probably wrong too. The Soviet Union is changing very rapidly. Some of these changes may not be controllable. They may get out of hand. Like other Third World NICs who suddenly face hard times and new pressures, the Soviet Union could unravel. Or if not unravel, then likely fragment. None of these trends augur well for the kind of aggressive, expansionist foreign policy that the Soviets carried out in Latin America in the 1960s and 1970s.

Where does all this leave the possibilities for greater superpower cooperation in Latin America? With one exception, greater cooperation seems destined not to go much beyond what it already has been. The historical record surveyed here shows that the times of greatest cooperation and 'understandings' between the US and the USSR in Latin America were when they were at and had achieved approximate parity of power. When one or the other superpower is rising or falling in power, in contrast, that is when the rules of the road are most in flux, when the 'gentlemen's agreements' are most subject to renegotiation, to pushing up against and often beyond the boundaries of previously acceptable behavior. Today is one of those eras of change and flux; hence only limited areas of cooperation can be expected to develop.

It seems likely that the South American countries will continue to pursue their more independent and non-aligned foreign policies. They will continue to trade and have diplomatic relations with the Soviet Union, vote as they please in international bodies, even work out military assistance programs with the Soviets. They will continue publicly to criticize the United States and to pursue their nationalistic designs. The United States cannot do very much about this situation, nor is it very much inclined to. US relations with Latin America will likely be based not so much on a mutuality of interests (the Pan-American ideal) but on pragmatism and self-interest.[19]

The Soviet Union will try to hand onto its enclaves in Latin America and may even expand them. While it is true that the Soviets cannot afford to support very many new insolvent regimes in Latin America, they seem unlikely to refuse any plums that drop into their lap – maybe to the extent even of hastening the ripening process a little. For its part, the United States seems likely to continue its democracy-human rights-development strategy as the best means to preserve stability and protect US interests. But it will likely do so with somewhat less enthusiasm than did President Bush's predecessor, with less funds available; and it is unlikely to intervene militarily or even very strongly diplomatically (such as suspending relations or aid) for the sake of keeping some wobbly democrat in power. Every president has his foreign policy 'thing'; and while democracy was clearly one of President Reagan's major interests, a program he initiated in his British Parliament speech, carried through in the Democracy Project and the National Endowment for Democracy, and in which he truly believed, President Bush will certainly establish his own priorities. He will continue the Reagan pro-democracy foreign policy but he may not feel so strongly about it as did Reagan.

The areas where greater cooperation between the superpowers is likely are Central America and the Caribbean. There is no doubt that the United States had been relying on the Soviet Union to help put pressure on the Cubans and the Nicaraguans to resolve the Nicaragua crisis. In part because the Soviets had already told the Nicaraguans that they should not expect more in Eastern bloc economic aid, it became incumbent on Nicaragua to end its war with the Contras, get the trade embargo imposed by the US relaxed, and regain access to US markets. Obviously some political/diplomatic cooperation between the superpowers was required to achieve those goals. The culmination of that process, from the US viewpoint, was the electoral defeat of the Sandinistas in February 1990.

In 1987, concurrent with the Central American peace accords proposed by the Contadora countries (Mexico, Colombia, Venezuela, and Panama) and later amplified by President Oscar Arias of Costa Rica, the Soviet Union had proposed that *both* superpowers cease funding their clients in the region. The proposal was rejected at the time by the United States because it implied that the Soviet Union had equal status in Central America as the US. But by 1989 Secretary of State James Baker had apparently concluded that any chances for success for US policy in the region must include an end to Soviet financial support to the Sandinistas in Nicaragua and the Farabundo Martí National Liberation Front (FMLN – the guerrillas) in El Salvador. He, therefore, expressed an interest in reviving this proposal, which Washington continued to view publicly (and non-committally) as the 'starting point for negotiations'. Through various channels the US conveyed to Soviet President Mikhail Gorbachev the suggestion that he use his visit to Cuba in April 1989 to signal a willingness to cut aid to Nicaragua, push the Managua regime toward greater democratization, and curtail support for guerrilla groups in El Salvador and elsewhere. But Foreign Minister Eduard Shevardnadze had already told Baker that the Soviets would only consider such a move if the US also cut military assistance to its allies in the region – the 'equivalency' position that the US had rejected earlier. Nevertheless the fact that the US was now willing to respond constructively to the Soviet initiative, was making proposals of its own and seeking to get Gorbachev to intervene with the Cubans, and had at the same time moved to settle the divisive Contra issue and work out a bipartisan policy between the White House and Congress, suggested that US–Soviet cooperation on resolving the difficult Central America issues was farther along by late 1989 than had to that point been made public. But again, it was the February 1990 election that was decisive.

Other areas of *possible* future cooperation include the domestic situation inside El Salvador and relations with Cuba itself. It may be that the Soviet Union will put pressure on (and is apparently already doing so) the Salvadoran guerrillas to reach an accommodation with the government there – although given the bitterness of the conflict in El Salvador, a happy, peaceful outcome seems unlikely. Other guerrilla struggles – in Peru or Colombia – may continue to drag on because they cost the Soviets next to nothing while causing great concern for US policy; in addition they operate quite independently of Soviet finances and often even influence. Finally, we may see eventually, with Soviet blessing obviously, some growing *rapprochement* between the United States and Cuba. Some movement in this direction on smaller issues (immigration, the straits of Florida and boat people, the Mariel prisoners, radio broadcasts) has already occurred; but full normalization is very complicated and it is not certain that the main parties, the United States and Cuba, can reach accommodation or want it all that much.[20]

CONCLUSIONS AND IMPLICATIONS

It appears at this stage that both superpowers are tired of the Cold War. The Soviet Union has to live with the legacy of Afghanistan; with the knowledge that its social, economic, and political model is inefficient at home and unattractive abroad; that Singapore, Hong Kong, and other free-market NICs represent the wave of the future in the Third World and not Ethiopia or Angola; and that Latin America is far away and not of great strategic value to the Soviets. The United States has the legacy of Vietnam with which it still lives, considerable disillusionment with the Third World, and the growing realization that Latin America is becoming like Africa – hopeless, with few interests that we both share, a perpetual drain on our resources as well as constantly causing difficulties. There has been on the part of both superpowers, in the words of Iranian-born political scientist Shahram Chubin, a 'symmetrical disillusionment with globalism' – and particularly with globalism's Third World obligations.[21]

While disillusionment with Latin America on the part of both superpowers is great, that does not necessarily mean an end to their Big Power conflicts in that part of the world. The Soviets still have Cuba, various active guerrilla movements, and numerous opportunities to embarrass and use up US resources in Latin America. At the same time the US cannot allow Latin America to go broke under the burden of its enormous foreign debts, for its fledgling democracies to go under, or to collapse and disintegrate – especially if that gives rise to the renewed possibilities of Marxist-Leninist takeovers. Latin America may be 'hopeless', but the US will still be obligated to try to prop it up – in Mexico, in Central America, in Brazil, in virtually every country of the area. Since the Alliance for Progress, the US commitment to Latin America is such that we cannot just give up on the area and allow it to remain poor and unstable. Moreover, even though our strategic interests in Latin America may decrease, other interests – drugs, debt, immigration, trade – will not allow us to abandon or ignore the rest of the hemisphere. Nor will the various special interest lobbies that have sprung up in recent decades – human rights groups, religious lobbies, committees in solidarity with the peoples of Chile, El Salvador, and others – allow us to do so. We are involved in Latin America whether we want to be or not and whether or not it is rational from a foreign policy viewpoint to continue committing so many resources to the area.

Latin America may be one of the areas treated in this study in which, prior to 1989, the *least* amount of Soviet–US cooperation had so far taken place. The Soviets had demonstrated at least some flexibility in working with the US to resolve regional crises in the Middle East, Southern Africa, and Afghanistan. But very little of the cooperative 'new thinking' in Soviet policy had been visible in Latin America. As a US official put it, 'We have to let them know that if they really want to impress people here with their "new thinking", the best place to start is by using their influence with the Sandinistas.' The same official added, 'We've shown our "new thinking" on Central America, now let's see their's.'[22] Meanwhile, the politics of the issue involved the facts that since the US had already cut off its military aid to the Contras, now if the Soviets failed to end their military assistance they would look bad before the Central Americans and the Democrats in the US Congress, who had insisted on the Contra aid cut-off in the first place. Once again, the international and the domestic dimensions of this foreign policy issue were both present in all their complexities. During 1989 and early 1990, however, superpower cooperation to resolve the series of Central American issues was accelerated.

It seems likely that the Cold War will continue in Latin America but in somewhat diminished form and intensity. Numerous direct armed interventions by either superpower seem very unlikely, though their proxies (especially the Soviet Union's guerrilla groups, which in any case are quite independent of Soviet financial support) will continue to operate. There will be fewer resources committed and less interest by both parties in the region, as on both sides Latin America is seen chiefly in terms of its nuisance value and its capacity to serve as a graveyard of lost hopes and frustrated, failed social and political experiments. There may even be further cooperation between the superpowers, especially on Central America and Cuba as the Soviet Union seeks to avoid having to support economically any more shaky Marxist-Leninist regimes and the USA looks to the Soviets to help resolve the regional imbroglios. But how far either superpower can pressure or control its own clients remains a very large and unanswered question.

Latin America will, meanwhile, likely continue to slide downhill; as it does so, it will be of less and less interest to either superpower. Since there is still some lingering, residual interest in the area on the part of both superpowers, however, Latin America will probably not be completely abandoned as sub-Saharan Africa has been. Rather Latin America will remain rather like North Africa, a peripheral area not of major superpower interest, an area that sometimes gives rise to problems and frustrations but that will not lead to superpower confrontation. Nevertheless, Latin America is also the area in which the United States remains the overwhelmingly preponderant power, and the Soviet Union sees it chiefly as an area to cause grief and embarrassment to the United States.

EPILOGUE

The unexpected electoral victory of oppositionist Violeta Chamorro over Daniel Ortega and the ousting of the Sandinistas in early 1990 changed significantly the superpower equation in Central America, and perhaps in all of Latin America. The shift in power in Nicaragua away from a Marxist regime deprived the guerrillas in El Salvador of their ideological inspiration, training base, and source of arms. Added pressure has therefore been put on the guerrillas to come to terms with the El Salvadoran government and sign a peace treaty. Without Nicaragua, Fidel Castro in Cuba is similarly more isolated; that plus the internal fissures in Castro's regime increase the pressures in Cuba. In fact, throughout the hemisphere, guerrilla groups and communist parties are all reassessing their strategies, particularly in the light of the Soviet Union's decreasing support and interest in the area.

The turnaround in Nicaragua was in part the product of unprecedented superpower cooperation on these regional issues. Both superpowers, for different reasons, had come to accept the Central American peace accords as offering a way out of the regional impasse, although the United States also kept up the military, economic, political, and diplomatic pressure on Nicaragua. In 1989 the Soviets were persuaded to stop arms shipments to Nicaragua and to pressure their East European and Cuban allies to curtail their assistance also. Assuming that the Sandinistas would win, the Soviets put pressure on Nicaragua to go through with the elections and respect the results, which proved to be a trap when in fact the opposition won. The Soviets demonstrated greater cooperation on Central America than Secretary of State James Baker had expected when he began these negotiations. The result seems to be a trend toward a declining Soviet presence in Latin America. But if the Soviets are not interested, the United States' strategic interest in the region will wane as well. The US will still be involved in Latin America because of drugs, debt, and human rights concerns; but those are not as powerful motivating factors as the overweening strategic one (anti-communist containment) that has dominated since the 1950s. Hence Latin America may well go back to being what it was in the nineteenth century: a poor and underdeveloped area of only secondary interest to any of the powers.

NOTES

1. C. Blasier, *The Giant's Rival: The U.S.S.R. and Latin America* (Pittsburgh, PA: University of Pittsburgh Press, 1983).
2. The definitions and assessments are provided in the materials prepared by Kanet and Kolodziej for this research project and included in the books' introductory materials.
3. See the analyses provided in Howard J. Wiarda, *In Search of Policy: The United States and Latin America* (Washington, DC: American Enterprise Institute for Public Policy Research, 1984); and *Finding Our Way? Toward Maturity in US–Latin American Relations* (Washington, DC: AEI, 1987).
4. See the discussion in Terry L. Deibel and John Lewis Gaddis (eds), *Containment: Concept and Policy* (Washington, DC: National Defense University Press, 1986), especially Chapter 24.
5. For background see Blasier, op. cit.; 'The Rising Soviet Presence in Latin America', a special issue of *World Affairs*, vol. 149 (Fall, 1986); and Howard J. Wiarda and Mark Falcoff, *The Communist Challenge in the Caribbean and Central America* (Washington, DC: American Enterprise Institute for Public Policy Research, 1987).
6. Mercier Vega, *Roads to Power inLatin America* (New York: Praeger, 1969).
7. The best study is Ronald C. Schneider, *Communism in Guatemala, 1944–54* (New York: Praeger, 1959).
8. See the chapters by Juan del Aguila and Raymond Duncan in Edward A. Kolodziej and Roger E. Kanet (eds), *The Limits of Soviet Power in*

280 Howard J. Wiarda

the *Developing World: Thermidor in the Revolutionary Struggle* (London: Macmillan, 1989).

9. R. Debray, 'Revolution in the Revolution', in Walter Laqueur (ed.), *The Guerrilla Reader* (New York: Meridian Books, 1977).

10. Ché Guevara, *Guerrilla Warfare* (New York: Vintage Books, 1961).

11. Karl Meyer and Tad Szulc, *The Cuban Invasion: Chronicle of a Disaster* (New York: Praeger, 1962).

12. See Howard J. Wiarda, 'The United States and the Dominican Republic: Intervention, Dependency, and Tyrannicide', *Journal of Interamerican Studies and World Affairs*, vol. 22 (May 1980), pp. 247–60; based also on interviews with Johnson Administration officials during this period.

13. See 'The Latin American Development Process and the New Developmental Alternatives: Military "Nasserism" and "Dictatorship with Popular Support"', *Western Political Quarterly*, vol. XXV (September 1972), pp. 646–90, by the present author.

14. Wiarda, 'The Soviet Union, the Caribbean, and Central America: Toward a New Correlation of Forces', in Kolodziej and Kanet (eds), op. cit.

15. See the book-length project being carried out at the Foreign Policy Research Institute, directed by Vladimir Tismaneanu and Howard J. Wiarda, on 'The Crises in Communist Regimes'; see also the special issue of *World Affairs*, vol. 150, no. 3 (Winter 1987–8), devoted to this same subject.

16. G. Pope Atkins and George Fauriol (eds), *South America into the 1990s: Evolving International Relationships in a New Era* (New York: Praeger, 1989).

17. For elaboration on the reasons to be pessimistic, see Howard J. Wiarda, 'The United States and Latin America: Toward the 1990s', *The Five College International Forum*, vol. 2 (Fall 1988), pp. 24–31.

18. See the debate on Latin America and other areas, in Jiri Valenta and M. Rageretnam (eds), *Gorbachev's 'New Thinking' and Regional Conflicts in the Third World* (New Brunswick, NJ: Transaction Books, 1989).

19. Based on widespread interviews by the author with officials in the US government responsible for Latin America policy, Washington, DC, March 1989.

20. Jorge Domínguez (ed.), *US–Cuban Relations in the 1990s* (Boulder, CO: Westview Press, 1989).

21. Quoted in James M. Markham, 'The Idea that Democracy Pays Helps Reshape East–West Ties', *New York Times*, 25 September 1988, p. C1.

22. Quoted in *New York Times*, 30 March 1989, pp. 1 ff.

11 Superpower Cooperation in South Asia
Stephen P. Cohen

INTRODUCTION

South Asia is often thought to be one region where the United States
and the Soviet Union have cooperated even as they have pursued
their own – sometimes conflicting – Cold War objectives. Their
support for New Delhi in the 1962 Sino–Indian war, their large-scale
economic aid projects in India (and their smaller, but important
programs in other regional states) and their de facto willingness to let
one side or the other broker regional conflicts are frequently mentioned in this context. Further, US–Soviet discussions on non-
proliferation – now regularly conducted at a high level – often deal
with South Asia, since the region contains the two most likely
candidates for the title of newest nuclear weapon state.[1]

The characterization of South Asia as a region where Washington
and Moscow have engaged in significant cooperation is both superficial and misleading. It is superficial in that it omits many important
cases where the two did not cooperate in any sense of the word (and,
we will note below, there are several senses to this word), and it is
misleading in that their policies in any region cannot, as the editors of
this volume suggest, be characterized neatly along a cooperation–
conflict dimension. Regions can themselves be defined in part by the
existence of conflictual relations, the act of defining a conflict is itself
a 'cooperative' act in that it takes two (or three, or four) to make a
quarrel.[2] Conflict is thus a paradoxical but significant form of
cooperation, as the title of this book suggests.

Further, conflict (or cooperation) resonates: when two states such
as the US and the Soviet Union pursue their interests in a regional
context, the prospects of 'cooperation' may be viewed differently by
others. For example, the presumably conflictual Cold War provided
significant opportunities for several South Asian states to cooperate
with one or both of these two outside states and with nearby China;
cooperation between the US, the Soviet Union, and India (especially
when all three were in agreement) affected the likelihood that other

regional states would cooperate with each other or seek other outside partners. Conversely, regional cooperative mechanisms, such as the South Asian Association for Regional Cooperation (SAARC) can influence and shape the way in which outside states perceive the region and become engaged in it.

We will return to this theme when we consider the consequences as well as the causes of US–Soviet cooperation in South Asia. First, however, we shall summarize the record of cooperation between Washington and Moscow, beginning with the most publicized and visible military and security-related episodes, but not neglecting economic, political, and ideological concerns. We will see that while there have been trends and movements in certain directions, these are to some extent overshadowed by the increasing complexity of American and Soviet regional interests, the increasing difficulty of managing and pursuing those interests, and a general decline in the significance (for the US and the USSR) of South Asia compared with other regions. We will then examine, in more nuanced fashion, the ways in which Moscow and Washington have determined their regional interests, and whether cooperation with the other side advances or retards them; we will also look at this from the perspective of regional states, acting out their own competitive and cooperative drama, and will note that the interaction between the two sets is persistent and significant. The final section will apply what we have learned to problems that will engage both regional and non-regional powers for a number of years to come: the task of adapting to India's expanding military power, the dilemma of regional nuclearization, and a host of political and ideological concerns that will become accentuated as we move into the next century.

PATTERNS OF SOVIET AND AMERICAN POLICY

Most of the interaction between American and Soviet policies in South Asia has taken place as an extension of their broader competition to influence the region, often in the context of regional wars. We address these first, and then turn to their non-proliferation, economic and ideological goals.

Strategic and military objectives

There have been four South Asian wars and several crises where the region teetered on the edge of war.[3] Overall, there has been a pattern of American and Soviet withdrawal from involvement in these crises, but no clear pattern that indicates an increase or decrease in their willingness to cooperate with each other in resolving regional strategic crises.

The US: early involvement

The first regional war (the India–Pakistan conflict in Kashmir in 1947–8) led to a persistent and intrusive American effort to bring the two parties to the negotiating table, and to establish a mechanism to keep them from fighting with each other again. This was really a continuation of America's decision to preserve the strategic unity of South Asia against external (seen largely as Soviet) threats by bringing India and Pakistan into some form of cooperative arrangement. Indeed, at this time both India and Pakistan were willing to play a Soviet 'card', and appealed for assistance to Washington on the grounds that each was threatened by Soviet communism.

The US refused to be drawn into the contest and suspended arms shipments to both. Subsequently, American diplomats were active in getting both sides to accept United Nations observer teams on their territory, and an American admiral was appointed to administer a plebiscite in Kashmir.[4] These UN observers still patrol the cease-fire line in Kashmir. In all of this, the Soviets played no role. They had neither the interest nor the resources to become a factor in the dispute, and there is no evidence of US–Soviet discussions on postwar regional developments.

Pakistan's entry into the Baghdad Pact in 1954 (later CENTO) led to a close military relationship with Washington.[5] It also contributed to a change in Soviet policy. When Nikita Khrushchev and Nikolai Bulganin came to India in 1955, they joined the regional strategic game by proclaiming their support for India's position on Kashmir (although even today Soviet maps do not show all of this territory to be under Indian control).[6] However, the Soviets did not provide across-the-board support for India, which enabled them, in 1965, to play an important mediating role between Islamabad and Delhi.

1962: shared policies?

The 1962 war between India and China found both Moscow and

Washington more or less on the same side. For a number of years Americans had been warning India of the threat from China, and after 1959 the two began to collaborate in various ways. After the war this collaboration was intensified. The US rushed a large quantity of weapons to India during and after the 1962 war on a sale and grant basis, and US air force units actually came to India and participated in joint Indian, Commonwealth and US air defense exercises. America had approached this war with the same policy premises that had guided it in 1947. The war threatened India, but Pakistan was also part of the regional strategic equation; as long as Indo–Pakistani conflict persisted, New Delhi could not devote adequate resources to coping with the Chinese challenge. Thus, the US and Britain made their aid to India contingent upon the resumption of negotiations between India and Pakistan. These failed for reasons which are still instructive: both India and Pakistan regarded the other as a greater threat than outside communist powers, and both found, in these outside communist powers, a willing supplier of military hardware and political support that could, to some extent, replace Western sources.

For the Soviets the war presented a different set of problems. They were torn, in their words, between 'brothers' (the Chinese) and 'friends' (the Indians); they had agreed to supply India with high altitude helicopters before the beginning of hostilities, and did so, and after the war was over they followed through on their promise to offer advanced aircraft, the MiG-21, when the US itself began to hesitate. While India and Pakistan (the former before the latter) were able to take advantage of divergence in US–Soviet policy (that is, they both supported India in 1962) the Chinese concluded that there was 'collusion' between the two. From the early 1960s onward they blamed both for Indian aggressiveness, and, drawing upon a remarkable talent for invective, labeled India as the stooge of both the imperialists and the 'social imperialists'. And, like the Soviets a decade earlier, they became a South Asian power – in this case by providing support to Pakistan when America withdrew from the region in 1965–6.

1965: America abstains

The India–Pakistan war of 1965 was a turning point for American regional policy, and provided a significant opportunity for the Soviets. At the conclusion of the war the Soviets offered their services as mediators, and put considerable pressure on Ayub Khan and Lal Bahadur Shastri to conclude a peace treaty in Tashkent. The United States not only stood back but offered positive encouragement to the Soviet effort at mediation. Americans were both disillusioned with nearly twenty years of regional engagement in South Asia (the spectacle of India and Pakistan each using American weapons against the other was too much for the US Congress), and were becoming deeply engaged in Vietnam. South Asia was seen as a sideshow; the Soviet threat to this region was deemed to have faded and Dean Rusk and others (especially the 'China hands') regarded Indian fears of Beijing as hysterical and exaggerated; Vietnam was the most vulnerable 'domino'.[7]

1971: Internationalization of war, regionalization of peace
The Soviets had fared no better than the US in their attempt to maintain close ties with both India and Pakistan. The efforts to get India and Pakistan to settle the Kashmir dispute met with exactly the same fate as the Anglo-American effort of 1963–5. The 1965 war so destabilized Pakistan that by 1970 it was in chaos, and India's intervention in 1971 led to a full-scale war between the two. By coincidence, Pakistan had played an important role in the 'opening' to China – Henry Kissinger had flown to Beijing from Islamabad – and Kissinger and Nixon wanted to demonstrate to their new Chinese interlocutors that the US was a steady supporter of old friends, namely Pakistan. Thus, the 'tilt' policy provided a small amount of military equipment for Pakistan, strong verbal and diplomatic support, and a last-minute foray by the USS *Enterprise*.

This did not come close to matching massive Soviet support for New Delhi provided under the umbrella of a treaty of Peace and Friendship that had been hastily signed in early 1971. The Soviets had given up on Pakistan, and by 1969–70 saw an opportunity to pursue their larger strategic objective (the containment of China) and to damage Pakistan and the US in the process. Although there have been claims that the Soviets did not want Delhi to invade Pakistan and would have preferred a negotiated settlement, there is no evidence that Moscow ever approached Washington (or vice versa) to push events in this direction.

At least Beijing was partly pleased by these events. Although China's friend, Pakistan, had been carved up, the unity of its two chief strategic rivals had been broken, and the Americans had come over to 'their' side by supporting Pakistan. And, in a sense, India was also pleased by the breakdown of US–Soviet regional cooperation that had begun in 1962 and continued through 1965–6. Together, they might be able to impose unacceptable conditions on New Delhi; separately, they could not as long as Delhi remained strong. Only Pakistan was left out: the Soviets and the Indians were hostile, China was supportive but ineffective, and the US was worse than ineffective since its vague promises of support had led the generals in Islamabad to expect help that never came. Pakistanis came to the conclusion that only a nuclear weapon would ever provide full protection for their country should it again be faced with a similar threat, and the Pakistani bomb program was launched shortly after the war ended.

Both the Soviets and the Americans were excluded from the bilateral regional peace talks after the war. These culminated in the successful meeting between Indira Gandhi and Zulfiqar Ali Bhutto at Simla (India) in 1972. This summit meeting established a set of ground rules for handling India–Pakistan disputes, Simla explicitly rules out resort to third-party mediation or outside fora as a method of solving regional conflict. The era of external involvement in regional disputes appeared to have come to an end, partly because of India's emergence as the region's dominant power, partly because all sides had been disappointed with the results of such involvement, and partly because the emergence of regional nuclear programs began to replace regional conventional war as a chief concern of Washington and Moscow.

The crises of 1987

While there have been no further regional wars since 1971, there was a war scare in 1987. This found Washington and Moscow on the same side at one moment, and opposites sides at the next. The crisis began with a series of grand Indian military exercises (Operation Brass Tacks) along the Pakistani border in Rajasthan and Punjab. These may have been the largest military maneuvers held in peacetime since World War II, and involved virtually every armor unit of the Indian army. It generated a real war scare since the Indian forces could have easily shifted direction and crossed into Pakistan (the Pakistanis had just concluded their own annual winter exercises). There is speculation that senior Indian officials intended to provoke Pakistan into a move that would have justified a forceful Indian response, or that they had planned to attack Pakistan in the north.[8] The crisis was instead resolved by Zia's sudden and dramatic flight to New Delhi (ostensibly to attend a hockey match) and direct Zia–Raijiv discussions. However, the Indians had also begun another exercise –

Checkerboard – far to the northeast, along the disputed MacMahon line with China and were planning operation Pawan – the occupation of northern Sri Lanka. Washington and Moscow split down the middle. The Soviets would have been delighted if India had pressured Pakistan, since the latter was the chief foreign base for Mujahedin forces operating in Afghanistan. The war was going very badly for Moscow, and 1987 was a pivotal year. The Russians had escalated the air and ground war to attacks on Pakistan itself, and they had actually threatened Pakistan on several occasions. Indian pressure on Pakistan would have presented the US with a terrible dilemma, since American commitments to Islamabad did not extend to a war with Delhi (but if this could be interpreted as a Soviet-sponsored operation, then there might well have been American help).

For whatever reason, India backed down and Operation Brass Tacks fizzled out. However, by February 1987, Delhi had also built up its forces against China. This found both Washington and Moscow on the same side of the fence, but for very different reasons. A Sino–Indian war would have forced Washington to reconsider its 1962 declaration of support for India with regard to the border dispute, and no country likes to repeal strongly held public positions. So, Washington urged both Beijing and Delhi to withdraw their forces and avoid provocative actions. At the same time, Moscow was telling New Delhi the same thing. Even under Brezhnev the Soviets had begun to shed their Sinophobia. A Chinese–Indian conflict would have forced the Russians to again choose between friends and brothers, and the normalization process with China had reached a point where any significant support to Delhi would have hurt this process. In any case, it was the Indians, not the Chinese, who were being provocative, and Moscow would have much preferred Indian action against Pakistan than China.

The crisis evaporated when India withdrew its forces. China had refrained from public gestures of defiance, making it easy for Delhi to back down. However, what probably tipped the balance was Delhi's discovery that neither the US nor the Soviets were enthusiastic about their Himalayan adventure; my own theory is that the operation was planned, in part, to test exactly how much support Delhi did have from both. The answer: not much.

Non-proliferation interests

For both the US and the Soviet Union non-proliferation began to replace more regional-specific interests after India's nuclear test. The discovery of Pakistan's clandestine military program a few years later accelerated their concern. Their joint interest in non-proliferation had begun in the mid-1960s, and culminated in the 1968 Non-Proliferation Treaty. In recent years, experts of both countries have met every six months (for several days) in intensive discussions of current non-proliferation matters. These discussions usually include South Asia.

Over the past eight years events in South Asia have revealed both the limits of such cooperation and the similarity of their approach to the issue. While both Moscow and Washington have adhered to the letter of the NPT both have separately tried to accommodate the regional near-nuclears, India and Pakistan, in a way that served both non-proliferation interests and their other strategic interests.

The Soviets led the way in South Asia as they moved away from technology denial as a way of halting proliferation to a policy of offering security guarantees. The Soviet–Indian treaty of Peace and Friendship had clear implications for India *vis-à-vis* the latter's nuclear vulnerability to China; Indian leaders had been seeking a nuclear 'umbrella' from both East and West, and by 1971, after Kissinger's trip to Beijing, the Soviets were the only state willing to provide one. There is no evidence that Moscow has offered *explicit* nuclear guarantees against Chinese nuclear threats, but the relationship is close enough, and formal enough, to serve as a modest nuclear deterrent. Indeed, the Chinese have been careful not to rattle nuclear weapons when dealing with Delhi. Further, the massive supply of Soviet conventional weapons to India (and, most recently, the lease of a nuclear-powered attack submarine) clearly had the result of enhancing Delhi's overall security, and thus reducing the need for an Indian nuclear weapon.

The Reagan administration adopted this strategy in 1981, when it linked the sale of conventional weapons to Pakistan's overall feeling of security and, hence, Pakistan's need to go nuclear.[9] While still keeping an eye on the flow of nuclear technology and materials to India and Pakistan, and moving in courts and other fora to stop that flow whenever possible, the US has joined the Soviet Union in an essentially political strategy of non-proliferation. But this has not extended to discussions of *regional* security arrangements, e.g. a collaborative effort to reduce Indo–Pakistani conflict, Sino–Indian conflict, or even collaboration on a regional non-proliferation regime. While it may be too late for such steps, they will be discussed further in the final section.

Economic ties

Perhaps the first (and possibly the last) discussion between high level Soviet and American leaders about economic prospects for India took place between Joseph Stalin and Franklin Delano Roosevelt in Teheran in 1944. Waiting until Winston Churchill was absent (he strongly objected to any discussions about Britain's imperial jewel), the two leaders traded ideas about India's future. Roosevelt suggested that 'reform from the bottom, somewhat on the Soviet line', was the best solution to India's poverty. Stalin, perhaps better informed about the subcontinent, demurred: he pointed out that this would mean 'revolution', but that India was a complicated society 'with different levels of culture and the absence of relationship [between] the castes.'[10]

This fragmentary conversation turned out to be a good guide to subsequent American and Soviet economic policies. Both powers initially saw economic development and economic assistance through ideological and political lenses. For the United States, the region's poverty opened the gates for revolution, and required a revolution of sorts to bring about the massive changes necessary for rapid economic growth. Later, Americans were to argue that India's continuing poverty opened the gates to communist subversion, but retained the assumption that dramatic economic and social change was not only desirable but possible. Further, the simple association between wealth and democracy was rarely, if ever challenged, and still dominates American thinking on the subject in spite of impressive evidence to the contrary, much of it from India). The result was an early and massive American assistance program to India, which still continues, and for many years was the largest American program in the world. It concentrated upon agricultural reform and the provision of basic necessities, including the largest PL480 food program in history.

For the Soviets, India's poverty was baffling. As Stalin recognized, Indian society did not fit any of Lenin's or Marx's theories (or his own), and Soviet theoreticians have been grappling with the question of reform and revolution in India for decades.[11] We are less interested in that debate than in the actual policies pursued by the Soviets.

By the 1950s (even before Stalin's death) the Soviets saw a chance to make inroads in India by providing certain kinds of economic assistance highly desired by New Delhi. Repressing their puzzlement over the caste system and a bourgeoisie government, they began their own massive aid program to India. Soviet technicians built a number of heavy engineering projects, provided India with its first public sector steel mill, and its first aircraft production line. All of these were high profile projects, much favored by the Indian elite, and it was clear from the outset that the Soviets saw their aid projects in political terms. They tended to provide what the Indians (and, later, the Pakistanis) asked for, which often was what had been denied by more development-oriented Western governments.

This pattern continues today. Moscow has specialized in projects that Western countries would not support. Since most of these are now in the defense sector, the Soviet Union has become closely associated with India's defense and security. Most recently, the Soviets have provided very advanced aircraft and nuclear powered attack submarines and civilian nuclear reactors.

At no time could Washington and Moscow be said to have cooperated in their economic policies toward South Asia, but, as was the case from time to time in their strategic policies, their actions had the same consequence for regional states as if they had. With the US providing massive shipments of food, developing India's agricultural base, and offering other forms of prosaic but basic assistance, and the Soviets providing the (then) high-tech and defense-related help, India at least benefitted greatly. Pakistan also began to play the two powers off against each other and later acquired the additional ability to play its own Chinese card when the PRC began a number of developmental projects in Pakistan. Sometimes this hurt Pakistan's relations with Washington (aid was suspended when the Pakistanis had Beijing build an airport at Dhaka), but Pakistan, Sri Lanka, Nepal, and now Bangladesh have all been able to extract economic assistance from Washington, Beijing, and Moscow, exploiting this three-cornered competition for their own purposes.[12]

In the past ten years India's economic ties to both the US and the Soviet Union have changed significantly, and, for our purposes, this has led to a new form of cooperation. India set itself the goal of becoming a supplier to the Soviet Union of medium technology.

Indian factories have provided massive quantities of shoes, clothing, and traditional goods to Moscow, but have also shipped quantities of consumer goods and other manufactured items. Some of this technology is fairly advanced; it was introduced to India by Western corporations eager to sell in the Indian market, and also as a way to bypass COCOM restrictions. Duplication and computer technologies (software and hardware), managerial skills, construction and design services, have all become a significant factor in Indo–Soviet relations. Thus, there is a tacit – sometimes quite explicit – flow of Western technology, skills, and goods to India, which is then absorbed and 'Indianized' and sold to the Soviet Union. The arrangement suits the Soviets and the Indians; it has, however, produced severe strains between some Western governments (especially the US) and India, when the latter is believed to be providing the Soviets with sensitive technology.

Political and ideological engagement

Finally, we should note the degree of convergence, or cooperation, between Washington and Moscow as they have attempted to influence or support various political forces in South Asia, especially India. Both states have faced the same dilemma: what principles should govern their relationship with governments in power when groups that they favor are out of power? For the Soviets, this has always meant squaring their support for Congress governments in India with the self-evident claim of India's communists. For the Americans, this has meant reconciling their support for various military dictatorships in Pakistan and Bangladesh with the claims of more truly democratic groups in both countries. And, both the US and the Soviet Union were thrown off balance between 1975 and 1977 by the 'Emergency' rule of Indira Gandhi.

Other than a shared interest in predictability and stability there is no evidence that the two countries ever coordinated their support for regional political groups. At times, both found themselves supporting the same side (most often in India, where there were rarely any alternatives to Congress). But neither state has been able to anticipate or influence the twists and turns of Indian or Pakistani national politics, and neither has apparently shown any interest in influencing the politics of other regional states (Afghanistan excepted). Both, however, have tried to hedge their bets (the US perhaps more successfully than the Soviets) by courting opposition groups; the US, for example, had good ties with Benazir Bhutto during the recent spell of military rule in Pakistan and maintains cordial ties with opposition groups in Bangladesh and India. These ties (and similar Soviet ties with various communist and left-wing groups in all regional states) are not cost free, since they make both the outside powers and their regional friends vulnerable to the charge of 'destabilization'. Indeed, while the two outside powers have not seriously meddled in the internal politics of any regional country, it is widely believed in South Asia that they do. But this is seen as a separate and competitive, not a cooperative or shared, form of meddling.[13]

Trends and patterns

This overview of American and Soviet cooperative, collaborative, and competitive policies in South Asia yields three important conclusions.

First, there has been an overall decline in the involvement of both powers in the region. From very intensive, highly intrusive American and Soviet attempts to mediate regional conflicts (in 1948 and 1965, respectively), both have come to a stand-off position with regard to such disputes. The Soviets wanted the Indians to pressure Pakistan in 1987, but they certainly urged restraint upon India when the border conflict with China flared up. Since the Soviets are out of Afghanistan, we can expect further disengagement from such regional issues. The same is true of American and Soviet economic and political involvement in South Asia: it is diminishing in scope and intensity. To the degree that economic ties with India are likely to grow, they will be on a self-sustaining, commercial basis.

Second, both the US and the Soviet Union have concluded that South Asia is not as important now as it was in the 1950s or 1960s. Both have relaxed their interest in the fate of regional communists, in regional economic prospects, as well as regional strategic issues. Even their own strategic and global interests (in their regional incarnation) seem less important now than ten, twenty, or forty years ago. South Asia (with the important exception of the Afghanistan episode) is no longer viewed as relevant to America's containment strategy, the Soviets no longer see it as critical to their larger strategic problems, namely preventing the US from gaining a regional foothold and countering Chinese power. The chief concern of both states is that India and Pakistan do nothing that might unsettle Washington's and Moscow's own strategic dialogue with Beijing: to this extent, they will retain a residual, indirect, shared, but uncoordinated regional strategic interest. But, it is based upon a relatively low evaluation of the importance of South Asia *per se*, especially when compared with China. The only area where American and Soviet interests might be said to have increased is in India's emergence as a significant importer and exporter of medium to high technology. In the case of the United States a large ethnic South Asian community may, eventually, have some impact of policy-making.

Third, a very wide range of issues has engaged the US and the USSR in South Asia. As a result, the policies of both states have a layered appearance: more recent concerns are stacked upon older ones; the latter may sometimes disappear from sight, but can suddenly re-emerge. This was made vividly clear in 1987 when Indian pressure on China painfully reminded both the US and the Soviet Union of their previous support for New Delhi. A future Sino–Indian conflict, or an India–Pakistan conflict could embarrass both powers, but the uncertainty of their response – that they might not be the most reliable of allies – has itself acted as a brake on Indian and Pakistani policy-makers.

This shared Soviet–American concern about defusing regional conflicts does not extend to lesser disputes. Both states offered their encouragement to India in its recent operations in Sri Lanka and the Maldives. Here there were no strategic implications, nor were there close US or Soviet ties to rebels in either state. The Soviets were pleased to see a friend, India, displaying the effectiveness of Soviet equipment and airplanes. Washington concluded that there was little to gain and much to lose by challenging India's dominance over its weakest neighbors. Thus, while both supported India, they did so for somewhat different reasons. One important future unknown is how each will accommodate India's regional ambitions and whether they will come to a shared understanding of India's regional dominance.

DETERMINANTS AND CONSEQUENCES OF AMERICAN AND SOVIET POLICY

Two larger questions are suggested by the previous discussion. The first is whether cooperative behavior displayed by the Soviet Union and the United States stems from 'rules' or from 'codes'. The former implies behavior constrained by external circumstances, the latter, behavior prompted by internal guidelines. Do American and Soviet policy-makers behave in the region according to their understanding of regional opportunities and limitations, or do they behave according to prompting from some inner list of objectives and standards? This is a question with very broad implications. It sets out the difference between an *ordinary* and a *great* power. The former proceeds carefully, testing the opposition and the responses of other states; the latter, confident of its own objectives and capabilities, need not pay much attention to other states, especially regional states.

The second analytical question asks what we mean by 'cooperation' in the South Asian context. Does identical behavior imply cooperation, or does there have to be a set of shared objectives as well – and do both parties have to be aware that they share these objectives and do they have to collaborate, or coordinate their policies in pursuing such objectives? Finally, what about the impact of outside powers on regional states? We have pointed out several examples where conflicts between the US and the Soviet Union expanded cooperative possibilities for such states. Is there also an inverse relationship between external and regional cooperative behavior?

Cooperation in South Asia: past imperfect

Our brief history has revealed four forms of US–Soviet 'cooperation' in South Asia. The first three relate to these states alone, the last incorporates a regional perspective.

Full cooperation
There have been very few, if any, instances where both Washington and Moscow have consciously agreed to pursue a common regional objective with common means. About the only issue where the two states consciously share the same policy goal, and have consulted over this goal, is non-proliferation. Further, although they have both subscribed to the Non-Proliferation Treaty and cooperate with each other, other NPT signatories, and the IAEA with regard to technology transfer, they have supplemented this with their own versions of 'security guarantees' as an instrument of non-proliferation policy. Since, in both cases (the USSR and India, and the US and Pakistan),

other strategic considerations really drive these guarantees, the common non-proliferation objectives of both states have been somewhat undercut. Further, non-proliferation is not a regional (i.e. South Asian) policy, but stems from broader Soviet and American concerns about the addition of new nuclear states, nuclear terrorism, and threats to allies and friends. While the two states can thus be said to be fully and actively cooperating on South Asian proliferation problems, this cooperation is somewhat qualified; it has not extended to a concrete, joint, US–Soviet plan to prevent or contain regional proliferation in South Asia, and the Soviet Union has been particularly vocal in accusing the US of breaking ranks by its tacit acceptance of the Pakistani nuclear program.

Parallel cooperation

There have been more cases where Moscow and Washington have pursued parallel objectives in South Asia, and where they might have had a *tacit* understanding that neither would disrupt the plans of the other. This was the case in 1965, when the US stood aside and let the Soviets broker an Indo–Pakistani peace agreement. It was partly the case in 1962 when both powers found themselves supporting India *vis-à-vis* China (although the US was still very critical of Indian acceptance of Soviet arms, and its own aid program was stimulated by the prospect of Indo–Soviet cooperation; we do not know whether the Soviets were more relaxed about India receiving help from Britain and America). Finally, it appears that in 1987 both sides separately, but in similar language, warned India (and China) that they would not intervene in the conflict, and urged both sides to reach a peaceful settlement of their mini-crisis. To my knowledge there was no formal consultation between Moscow and Washington on these issues, but each side must have been able to figure out the other's policies from their public statements, from their own conversations with India and China, and from third parties.

Different policies, same consequences

There have been a number of cases where Washington and Moscow have pursued quite different policies, even competing policies, but employed instruments which sometimes made it appear as if they were cooperating, or in policy concordance. The most important example of this comprised their economic assistance programs to various South Asian states, especially India. It is quite clear that these aid programs had different objectives: the US took seriously its rhetorical linkage of economic and democratic development; the Soviets always saw economic aid as a political instrument, and had very low expectations concerning the impact of such programs on the fundamental social, political, and economic problems of the region.[14]

Regional consequences of cooperation
Finally, we should note several sets of calculations which are triggered by even the suggestion of cooperation between the US and the Soviet Union – and between either or both of them and the region's dominant power. India.

Pakistan. It is clear that when both Washington and Moscow have backed India (as in 1962 and, more recently, in India's operations in Sri Lanka and the Maldives), this has set off a predictable reaction in Pakistan and often in the weaker regional states. China has filled the important role of third outsider: the Pakistan–China relationship goes back to exactly the period when both Moscow and Washington came to realize that they had a common strategic interest in backing India against Beijing. The relationship grew stronger when Washington found its own path to Beijing, since the Soviets remained a threat to both China and Pakistan; Islamabad is understandably nervous about the prospect of *both* Moscow and Washington normalizing their ties to China, not because of the loss of American support, but because of the loss of Chinese support, since there remains some question as to whether China regards India as a serious strategic threat on its own (i.e. without Soviet or American backing).

India. Indians bristle when any mention is made of US–Soviet cooperation, and raise the specter of a new 'Yalta'. They invented and have perfected the art of exploiting the competitive relationship between Moscow and Washington and, despite considerable rhetoric about wanting to end the Cold War, every Indian strategist knows that the security of a struggling middle-power depends on preventing larger powers from 'ganging up' and imposing regional solutions. The present situation, of limited alignment with one outside power (Moscow) against an alignment involving a regional power, Pakistan, and two outside powers (China and the US) is less advantageous than having India as the only dominant regional power, but more advantageous than outright cooperation between Moscow, Washington, and Beijing, or even any two of these states (if the third were to drop out of the regional strategic competition).

Other regional states. From the perspective of Dhaka, Kathmandu, or Colombo, cooperation between Washington and Moscow is disastrous. While they have benefitted from 'competitive' cooperation (in that all have received some assistance from the US and the USSR) this is increasingly marginal to their overall aid requirements, and in any case Japan has emerged as the most important foreign donor. The real fear of these states is that the Soviets and the Americans will agree to support India as the regional dominant power, giving New Delhi a free hand in its dealings with its smaller neighbors. For them, such cooperation is really collusion since it encourages Delhi's hegemonic ambitions. These fears have prompted some increased cooperation between these states, and was certainly a factor in the creation of SAARC. SAARC may be one device by which the weaker states of the region can bring one or more superpowers back into the area under favorable terms; this has already happened in the areas of terrorism and narcotics; a number of regional states have accepted contingents of DEA agents who provide *de facto* regional coordination.

For their part, the Soviets and Americans now speak freely of the desirability of their cooperation on regional matters. They have been engaged in formal talks at the highest level on regional issues since the mid-1980s, and even Soviet scholars will stoutly defend the principle of 'Yalta' against Indian critics.[15] Of course, from the Soviet perspective, such an equation elevates them to a status equal to that of the US, which has been a longstanding Soviet goal.

Rules or codes?

The test of a 'great state' is that it will pursue foreign policy objectives without much regard to other states. Such powers have a vision of a new emergent world and a belief in their own omnicompetence; they become 'great' when they put the two together. Of course, such states eventually collide with reality, but the true measure of a great state is its ability to keep on pursuing its broad vision even after such setbacks as Vietnam and Afghanistan. Lesser powers will collapse, rationalizing their decline in a number of ways, and seek to hang on to the shreds (or at least the trappings) of influence and power. Such 'smaller' states) (who, in fact, may be relatively powerful in material terms but still lack either self-confidence or a driving vision) are utterly realistic about the outside world. They know that an error can be fatal to their state or to its ruling regime. They are acutely sensitive to their environment – they are driven entirely by it, they make no pretense at shaping or changing it.

Our brief survey of American and Soviet policies in South Asia indicates that (leaving aside the question of Afghanistan) they began their regional involvement as 'superpowers' and have now come to see themselves as 'lesser' powers, at least in this regional context. Not only have their interests shriveled, they have both become acutely aware of limitations on their ability to exert influence in the region. In the case of the Soviets this was traumatically driven home in Afghanistan, and the lesson is likely to stick for a number of years. Frustration, impatience, anger, and disillusionment with regional 'friends' has become the shared experience of both states, it has led them to behave in South Asia as if they were themselves ordinary, not great, states.

We will consider this question further in the next section, but an additional factor in the declining direct role of the US and the Soviets in South Asia has been the growing power of the region's two military powers, India and Pakistan. The 1972 Simla Summit between Indira Gandhi and Zulfiqar Ali Bhutto effectively barred outsiders from mediating regional disputes; India's and Pakistan's increasing power, epitomized by their nuclear programs, and their displays of conventional military competence, have made them both attractive partners. Indian is emerging as a regional 'peacekeeper', i.e. it is prepared to use force and other forms of persuasion to ensure that smaller regional states do not stray too far; it is not worth the effort of either Moscow or Washington to challenge India on its own turf. Pakistan's role in supporting the Mujahedin against the Soviets was vital, it is now a *de facto* participant in the Afghan civil war. Pakistan is also seen as something of a Middle Eastern power, as India is seen as a prospective Indian Ocean power. Both are thus candidates for extra-regional cooperation with one (or perhaps, both) outside powers and, in the case of Pakistan, China.[16]

To summarize, both Moscow and Washington no longer see themselves as 'super' powers as far as South Asia is concerned – they are merely participants in a complex, five-sided strategic game, where alliances and friendships are all temporary, where all of the players are armed with nuclear weapons and where there is very little gain and quite a lot to lose by miscalculation. They are driven by regional rules, not their own vision of a South Asian order. Their policies have become more cautious, their rhetoric more restrained. Ironically, this suggests that as their own competition in South Asia has faded away, and as their regional interests have diminished, they may move toward greater cooperation on certain regional issues; it also suggests that such cooperation will be a delaying and defensive tactic (even in the important case of nuclear proliferation), not likely to significantly increase their collective or separate influence. We now turn to a closer examination of the prospects for such cooperation over a range of current and emerging issues.

COOPERATION IN SOUTH ASIA: FUTURE IMPERATIVE?

The regional involvement of both the US and the USSR has, in the past, been shaped by their shifting interests and, as we have seen, these interests have not moved in the same (or even opposite) direction for both powers at the same time. First one, then both, then the other have been engaged in regional strategic disputes, now neither is likely to play an active role. Their regional economic involvement has waxed and (mostly, now) waned, and in any case was based upon quite different premises. Both powers have also sought to ally themselves with reliable and stable leaders in India and Pakistan; this, too, has rarely met with success. All in all, one might predict a decline over the next decade of American and Soviet interest and involvement in the region – conceivably leading to greater cooperation between them, but such cooperation being of relatively minor significance.

Four qualifying factors

However, four emerging factors affect such a general assessment. They might even reverse the trend of lessening Soviet and American interest in South Asia.

First, the growth of internal regional capabilities is likely to have extra-regional consequences. This is self-evident in the case of nuclear proliferation, but it also applies to India's expanded Indian Ocean role and Pakistan's attempts to become strategically the most advanced state in the Islamic world. It also applies to the emergence of India as a middling economic power, part of the global electronics and software revolution. Even if India's ambitious arms export

projects fail and it cannot move to the manufacture of indigenous
armor and air systems, Delhi has already carved a niche as a supplier
of managerial talent, construction, and consumer goods. India has
built a number of airports and railways in Africa and the Middle East
and Indian firms are important subcontractors in the Gulf region.
South Asia will, in the future, have two significant powers whose
resources and reach are different, but in some ways complementary
as well as competitive. Both the US and the Soviet Union will have to
pay greater attention to these powers.

Second, it may become easier for Washington and Moscow to
project their economic and technological influence *into* the region.
While their services as mediators in regional strategic conflicts will
not be in demand, their technology, their markets, and their influence on other states (notably China and Japan) make them
important factors in the calculations of India and Pakistan.

Third, there are new direct links between the two regional powers
and Moscow and Washington. India and Pakistan have become
consumers of advanced Western technology, and India at least has
tried to absorb that technology and transfer it to the Soviet Union for
a profit. India has also won contracts to construct and manage hotels
in the Soviet Union, and is a major supplier of consumer goods as
well. India and Pakistan have been courted by both Moscow and
Washington for their services as mediators in other regions (Pakistan
with Iran, India with Vietnam and Cambodia). As we have noted,
there are going to be nearly a million Americans of South Asian
origin early in the next century, and they will serve as a new,
complicating factor in Washington's relations with Delhi.

Finally, we can expect that Japan, and to a lesser degree, China,
will increase their influence in South Asia largely through an expansion of economic investment and trade, but also as suppliers and
producers of dual-use technology.

These 'new' factors (some of them merely being the intensification
of current trends) do not imply enhanced American/Soviet cooperation, but neither do they appear to be barriers to such cooperation.
This conclusion is strengthened when we examine the specific issues
of the 1990s which are likely to face both Moscow and Washington as
they pursue their South Asian interests.

Issues

India as a great power
By far the biggest challenge to American and Soviet diplomacy, with direct implications for their own relations, will be the degree of support they offer to India's regional ambitions. It is still too early to draw conclusions about their likely India-related policies, since both states are still preoccupied with events in Afghanistan. After that, however, it is an open question as to whether the US or the Soviets will back all of New Delhi's regional policies. Indeed, this will depend greatly upon a number of considerations, not least of which will be the extent to which New Delhi is seen as acting on behalf of the Soviets by Washington, or acting as an ungrateful, expensive, or even hostile state by Moscow. It is not beyond the realm of imagination that India will wind up alienating both outside powers. However, recent events would seem to indicate that Washington is likely to offer modest backing for New Delhi's regional ambitions, since it accepted Indian actions in Sri Lanka, the Maldives, and now Nepal, without demur. It would appear likely that the Soviets, also, will continue to accept India's claim to be South Asia's regional dominant power.

What remains an open question is the degree of support both outside powers would provide to India in case of a conflict with China, or (for the US), Pakistan, and the degree to which they will see Pakistan or China as a legitimate alternative to support for India. India may be the regional dominant power, and all parties in the region and outside it will acknowledge this, but they will still have to include a nuclear or near-nuclear Pakistan in their calculations. Neither Washington or Moscow seem to have thought through the meaning of 'dominance' in the South Asian context. Will this mean *carte blanche*, a willingness to look at alternatives, or withdrawal from regional issues altogether? I suspect the Soviet Union will choose the first course, the United States the second or the third; the two states will not cooperate in supporting India, but neither will they allow themselves to be placed in a confrontational position regarding India or allow Indian actions to lead them into conflict.

Non-proliferation
The second great issue that the two outside powers will face is nuclear proliferation. By and large, the die appears to be cast. Neither has taken the initiative (let alone sought the cooperation of the other) in

formulating an effective regional non-proliferation regime. Both seem content to let the other handle its 'friend', both seem aware that this will not be sufficient to prevent India and Pakistan from crossing the military nuclear threshold. All of this applies to constraints on the development of ballistic missiles. The technology denial strategy adopted by the US in recent years is identical to that of the Carter administration's approach to nuclear proliferation. At best it is a way of buying time, but unless root causes are addressed it will only be a matter of time before Indian ambitions and Delhi's competition with Islamabad and Beijing yield up a full-scale IRBM and ICBM program – India successfully tested a sophisticated IRBM as a 'technology demonstrator' in May 1989. Much the same is true, on a smaller scale, for Pakistan. While future American/Soviet cooperation on the NPT and related issues may continue, it is likely to have only a marginal impact on regional nuclear programs and less than that on missile systems.

Regional economic development

Ironically, the one area where cooperation of a sort has existed, although the purposes behind such cooperation were very different, has been in aid and economic developmental projects. American and Soviet programs had different objectives but similar consequences. Now, it appears that a new form of cooperation is emerging. With different objectives, and different means, a relationship is being established in which the West (especially America) will provide various advanced technologies, and the Soviet Union will acquire those technologies, via India.

Of course, this form of 'cooperation' is highly vulnerable and is not likely to last. First, as the Soviet Union opens up its economy to outside investors, American and Western corporations will deal directly with Soviet buyers. Second, very advanced technologies and dual-use technologies are now being more carefully monitored. If the restraints put upon the first American supercomputer sold to India are any indication, future high-tech transfers will not seep out of India.

If Moscow and Washington *were* looking for regional economic cooperative projects, there are several at hand. Chief among these are the development of South Asia's complex and vital water system. The Himalayan waters flow through China, Nepal, Bangladesh, India, and Pakistan; their efficient exploitation will require multinational cooperation and lavish outside funding. Neither seems likely.

India wants to deal with other regional states on a bilateral basis, and refuses to bring China into any agreement. Past American efforts in this direction have been met with grudging acceptance (the Indus Waters treaty between India and Pakistan) or outright rejection (Jimmy Carter's proposal for an eastern waters arrangement between Nepal, Bangladesh, and India). The Soviets have never been part of these discussions.

Finally, a paradox. From the perspective of many regional states, the decline in Soviet–American competition engendered by the Cold War will damage their own ability to forge ties with one or both of the outside great powers, to protect themselves against India's regional dominant position. And, to the degree that the US and the Soviet Union come to overt cooperation in the region (admittedly, an unlikely step), then certain regional states (especially India and Pakistan) will be positively fearful of a new Yalta. The Cold War did not yield much in the way of cooperation in South Asia, but the Cold War as competition provided breathing space for a number of regional states.

The future of cooperation

Imagine a combination lock with three numbers. One each is held by two parties; the third number may, or may not, be held by one or more of several other parties, or it may not be known to them at all.

This is the situation that the US and the Soviet Union face with regard to cooperation in South Asia. Together, they can solve two-thirds of many problems, but the remaining third of any solution may or may not exist, and if it does, it may not be within their power (or overall self-interest) to induce cooperation from third, fourth, or fifth parties.

Occasionally, of course, cooperation seems to work. However, this generally tends to happen on occasions when only two numbers are needed to open a lock – to shift metaphors for a moment, when outside states are pushing on an open door. In the case of non-proliferation, the issue most often cited as an example of cooperation, the US, other Western powers, and the Soviets have been able to restrict the flow of some sensitive materials and items to India and Pakistan but they cannot – or perhaps will not – use technology restraint to bring about anything approximating a permanent halt to regional proliferation.

This situation does not suggest defeatism, but it does counsel restrained enthusiasm for the prospects of cooperation between Moscow and Washington as far as South Asia is concerned. This is a region with many problems – many 'locks'. Some of them are quite peculiar to the area, others are merely regional variants on global themes. Non-proliferation falls into the latter category.[17] There are also problems for which neither state holds a key or a number. There are a number of important (to regional states, *vital*) issues on which outsiders can have little influence.

Regional qualities

While this chapter is somewhat pessimistic about the prospects for any form of Soviet–American cooperation in South Asia, there are certain regional qualities that make such cooperation less important than might be the case elsewhere. I have once compared India–Pakistan relations to a half-filled glass – it can be described pessimistically as half-empty, optimistically as half-full.[18] But when we look elsewhere we find that there are many features of South Asia which suggest even greater optimism than would be implied by 'half-full'. The region has far greater coherence and stability than the Middle East, the Persian Gulf, or most of Africa. Even the much vaunted ASEAN covers only half of Southeast Asia, the other half remaining sullen under Vietnamese rule, and the entire region remaining quite vulnerable economically and politically to Soviet, Chinese, American, and Japanese influence, and to its own regional dominant powers. Vietnam and Indonesia. Our answer to the central theme of this book has been that the Cold War did not breed much cooperation between Moscow and Washington, and the end of the Cold War is unlikely to breed more; but a fuller answer would also add that compared with many other parts of the world South Asia itself may do quite well without the kindness of strangers.

American policy

In the approaching era of reduced overt hostility between Washington and Moscow certain weaknesses of each state will become more apparent. In the case of the Soviet Union, its economic incoherence and its unnerving opportunism will hurt it in many regions of the world. This may be less of a handicap in the poorest states of South Asia (notably Afghanistan, where it will continue to play a role), but

Russia will not be the country of first choice for those developing
regional states looking for economic, strategic, or technical partners
(but, as the Indo–Soviet relationship has demonstrated beyond any
doubt, the Soviet Union can make an excellent country of *second*
choice in each sphere). India and Pakistan will first turn to the USA,
Japan, China, and Western Europe.

American policy-makers will have to demonstrate extraordinary
patience and flexibility if the USA is to play a significant role in either
the economics or politics of South Asia. Can the USA demonstrate
such patience and flexibility? To the extent that America's regional
engagement has been successful it has flowed directly from a sense of
competition with the Soviet Union. The US did not imagine or create
the Soviet (or the Chinese) threat to the region, but several generations of policy-makers and politicians used those threats to build
sustaining coalitions within the American policy process. Such coalitions were formed around economic aid to India and military aid to
Pakistan in the 1950s, and military aid to India from 1962–4. Later
coalitions were built around a regional non-proliferation policy, a
regional human rights policy, and, more recently, a return to
containment via a massive economic and military program for
Islamabad.

What threat *to* the region might again mobilize a significant sector
of the American policy community? What vital American interests *in*
the region would lead to a coalition between Congress and the
executive that would sustain American intervention in South Asia?
As for the former I cannot see any American administration becoming involved in a future India–China conflict, the Soviets seem to
have decided to cut their losses in Afghanistan, and while Iran
presents an ideological threat to both India and Pakistan no form of
American support could help those two states to meet it. Indeed, it
would not be welcomed by either.

As for the latter, there are no vital American interests in South
Asia, if one defines vital as a cause which threatens deeply held
American values and for which American policy-makers are prepared to use force. There are signs that the American policy
community is beginning to see India as an 'emergent', or 'awakening'
regional power, and there is some apprehension at this, but my
judgement is that India will move cautiously and avoid direct
confrontation with what American interests remain in the area. Even
if Indian actions raised American hackles, the US is not likely to do
any more than it did in 1971 when it failed to provide serious support

for Pakistan; and in any case India is in a far better position now to
resist American pressure.

For both America and Russia, the lesson seems to be that as far as
South Asia is concerned, they are 'great' powers, not 'super' powers.
While it is true that their military and economic presence has
increased in recent years, and that their concern over issues such as
human rights (for the US) and the fate of revolutionary friends (for
the Soviets) continues, these two states now find themselves operating in a region which contains two significant local powers as well as a
fast growing Japanese, Chinese, and European presence.

What has in the past set America and Russia off from these other
states has been the interconnectivity of their interests. Actions that
they take in South Asia may (and I would emphasize the conditional-
ity of this 'may') have had implications for their policies and stature
elsewhere. But, increasingly, no one will care. Increasingly, it will be
harder to identify the tradeoffs being made *between* regions when
many of the world's great powers are operating in a number of
regions as strategic, economic, and political partners. It will simply be
too hard to keep track of who is ahead, who is behind. In a complex,
global system composed of a number of significant regional balances
of power, real gains and losses will take place in the regions, not on
some global scoreboard.

Perhaps this is the way things have always been, anyway. If this is
the case, then America will have as much to learn from studying the
successes of regional great powers (China, Japan, France, the great
European states of the nineteenth century) as the regional dominant
powers can learn from the mistakes of the 'superpowers'. The former
will learn that a flexible policy of multiple alignments, based on
different issues and different interests, is absolutely necessary. Cooperation between the United States and the Soviet Union will be useful
on some issues, less so on others; the idea of cooperation should not
get the blood pounding, the two states only have a limited number of
shared regional interests in South Asia. Both would be advised to
seek out other regional and non-regional partners in their search for
shared policy perspectives.[19] They will learn also that it is very
difficult to conduct such a policy. It requires an adept foreign service,
limited popular involvement in the policy-making process, a certain
degree of tolerance for distasteful partners and a good sense of what
one's regional interests are. As for the 'new' or 'emerging' or
'awakening' regional powers in South Asia, they will learn that there
are no workable plans to remake the world, or even their region, in
their own image.

NOTES

1. Reports from New Delhi indicate renewed Soviet pressure on India to sign the NPT, partly as a result of American–Soviet conversations. Kuldip Nayar, *India Abroad*, 20 April 1989.
2. Barry Buzan has developed the concept of 'security complex'. See Buzan, 'A Framework for Regional Security Analysis', in Buzan and Gowher Rizvi, *South Asian Insecurity and the Great Powers* (New York: St. Martin's Press, 1986). Buzan argues that the India–Pakistan dispute forms one such important security complex, I would add that the extension of the US–Soviet conflict to South Asia affected this complex.
3. We exclude the Soviet war in Afghanistan from the following discussion. The Soviets viewed Afghanistan as part West or Central Asia, not as part of 'Hindustan', i.e. South Asia. Similarly, the US never saw Afghanistan as a threat to South Asia, *per se*; its implications for US–Soviet relations and for Soviet policy towards Iran were always far more important in American calculations. Pakistan was a key player for both major powers since it was willing to serve as a base for Mujahedin forces, not because Pakistan itself contained any resources or objectives treasured by either state.
4. See Josef Korbel, *Danger in Kashmir* (Princeton: Princeton University Press, 1966), p. 156.
5. For a survey of the evolution of American policy see Devin T. Hagerty, 'The Development of American Defense Policy Toward Pakistan, 1947–1954', *The Fletcher Forum*, September 1986. Indians claim that American support for Pakistan exacerbated Indo–Pakistan conflict (thus dividing the region), while Pakistanis argue that American (and later, Chinese) support made it possible for the smaller regional powers to negotiate on more equal terms with India (thus preserving the unity of the region). Of course, America's intention was neither to divide India and Pakistan nor to make it easier for Pakistan to stand up to India; however, Washington's effort to bring the two together against threats to the region (as perceived by Washington) had the latter consequence.
6. For a skeptical history of Indo–Soviet relations see S. Nihal Singh, *The Yogi and the Bear* (New Delhi: Allied, 1986).
7. India figured prominently in the domino theory, at least for such key advisors as Walt Rostow. He argued that if Viernam was lost then the other dominoes would fall, the last one being the real prize, India. Indian diplomats were astonished at this, but Rostow always had a soft-spot for India and wanted to fit the world's largest democracy somewhere into his Vietnam obsession.
8. See Ravi Rikhye, *The War That Never Was* (New Delhi: Lancers International, 1988).
9. Of course, the chief justification for the aid package was to support Pakistan against Soviet and Afghan pressure from the northwest, but the nuclear issue was taken seriously by policy-makers at the time and is now a principal basis for the relationship. There are some parallels between it and between US–Israel strategic ties.

10. These remarks were recorded by Averell Harriman. See W. Averell Harriman and Elie Abel, *Special Envoy to Churchill and Stalin, 1941-1946* (New York: Random House, 1975), p. 266. I am grateful to Professor R. V. R. C. Rao for bringing this reference to my attention.

11. For two excellent studies see Jerry F. Hough, *The Struggle for the Third World: Soviet Debates and American Options* (Washington: Brookings, 1986) and Rajan Menon, *Soviet Power and the Third World* (New Haven: Yale University Press, 1986). The original Soviet policy toward South Asia combined support for local revolutionary forces (and some expectation of their success?) with an attempt to undercut the strong Western presence. The former policy gave way to the latter as it became clear that revolutionary communist parties were not going to flourish and that bourgeois ruling elites were firmly in control. Hough points out that the Institute of Oriental Studies in Moscow was heavily weighted with Indian specialists; their influence and perspective may have anticipated Gorbachev's attempt to improve Soviet ties with the more moderate, India-like states of the non-Western world. See Hough, pp. 231-2.

12. Some of the regional states (especially Nepal and Bangladesh) have received substantial amounts of Indian aid; India is especially sensitive to Chinese support for these two countries.

13. When Corazon Aquino came to power in the Philippines individuals claiming to represent important women politicians throughout the subcontinent (as well as most other regions of the less developed world) contacted American officials, asking whether their country was 'next' – when the US would put their leader in power. And, the dictators of some of these states took this seriously enough to seek assurances of continued American support.

14. We might refine this somewhat: American expectations concerning the democratization of Nepal, Bangladesh, and (for some) Pakistan were very low; in these cases aid was seen largely as a political instrument, not a developmental one; however, the US has taken seriously the prospect of development/democracy in India, and in recent years, the Soviets have come to benefit from Western investments in that country.

15. See the vigorous defense of Yalta by Soviet scholars in K. Subrahmanyam and Jasjit Singh, (eds), *Security Without Nuclear Weapons: Indo–Soviet Dialogue* (New Delhi: Lancer International, 1986), p. 212.

16. This happens to be exactly the position that India and Pakistan want to be in: they retain control over their own regional dispute, but they receive resources from outside powers for other purposes (and these resources can be easily diverted to their own bilateral conflict).

17. It may be worthwhile pursuing an ineffective collaborative effort in South Asia for the sake of non-proliferation interests elsewhere in the world, but that raises issues and problems beyond the scope of this chapter.

18. In the conclusion to Stephen P. Cohen (ed.), *The Security of South Asia: Asian and American Perspectives* (Urbana: University of Illinois Press, 1987).

19. In the Middle East and other regions the US has long since shared information on terrorism and narcotics with regional states and its Western European allies; the latter have joined America and Russia on non-proliferation issues, and Japan is a critical partner when it comes to developmental assistance. As far as South Asia is concerned, the US should immediately begin the kind of high-level policy discussions with India and China that it already has with the Soviet Union, and Japan would make a better long-range partner on non-proliferation matters than the Soviet Union.

12 Superpower Cooperation in Southwest Asia

Marvin G. Weinbaum

Southwest Asia provides an excellent focal point at which to study the course and pace of global US–Soviet relations. In Iran and Afghanistan, superpower strategies and commitments have regularly intersected over the last half century. Moscow's security and commercial interests have continuously assured the area more careful attention and higher valuation. In the Cold War competition of the superpowers, the high stakes for one prompted involvement by the other. Motivated above all by geopolitical concerns, the United States assumed in Iran and to a lesser extent in Afghanistan prominent political and economic obligations.

Iran and Afghanistan are dissimilar in their natural and human resources. Iran is the more richly endowed, more developed state and, given its access to the Persian Gulf, the more strategically located. The postwar experiences of both countries with the United States and the Soviet Union, including trade and aid, are also contrasting. As this chapter describes, Iran has for a longer time been a potential setting for confrontation between Moscow and Washington. Only with the Marxist coup of 1978 and Soviet invasion of 1979 did Afghanistan become a flash point in superpower relations. These discussions also find that Iran and Afghanistan offer instructive, sometimes contrasting, cases of superpower cooperation, both tacit and explicit. The potential that available and newer codes governing superpower engagement may influence the region during coming years frames much of the analysis here.

The central thesis of this chapter is that the larger global setting of superpower relations normally drives policies in Southwest Asia, as in other Third World areas, and colors American and Soviet regional interactions. But it makes a strong difference whether the prevailing global interests and goals of Washington and Moscow are essentially convergent or divergent. When the relationship is more antagonistic, Iran, Afghanistan and the region loom larger for the US and the Soviet Union, and local regimes are often able skillfully to play off one superpower against the other. Domestic politics in these countries can carry salience and criticality for American and Soviet decision-makers. The mechanisms of cooperation as well as the modes of competition are affected by the dominance of particular elites or groups and how they define their interests. Locally ascendant ideologies and national policies figure importantly in the ability of the superpowers to realize their objectives, competitively or cooperatively, singularly or mutually.

By contrast, when the state of global relations between Washington and Moscow is more harmonious, the influence of Iran and Afghanistan is diminished, and agreements between the US and Soviet Union may come at the expense of these countries, or at least be perceived by them as detrimental to their interests. With improved relations between the superpowers there is less need for policies of penetration and involvement, and greater incentive to disengage unilaterally and bilaterally. The levels of military and economic aid will predictably fall. Where the superpowers seek a less active, smaller role, surrogates or clients in the Third World become more dispensible. Similarly, domestic politics in these countries are likely to be of more marginal concern. As both major powers experience financial constraints, the value of investment in the conflicts of others seems less justified. At the same time, under contemporary conditions of emerging global superpower trust and mutual confidence, new modes of superpower interaction, cooperative and competitive, may be introduced.

Some of the earliest and best tests of earnestness and success by the US and Soviet Union in reducing regional conflicts may come in Iran and Afghanistan. The outcomes of recent military and political developments in the two countries have already had a direct bearing on the state of East–West relations. Cooperative patterns in superpower relations that succeed in these countries could provide models for American and Soviet policies that would contribute to resolving conflicts in southern Africa and Central America, as well as the broader Middle East.

IRAN: A LEGACY OF CONFLICT AND COOPERATION

Iran has always been of strategic interest to the Soviet Union for its oil resources, geographical proximity, and as a gateway to the Middle East and South Asia through the Persian Gulf and Indian Ocean. Despite the wartime cooperation between the US and Soviet Union that centered on lend-lease shipments through Iran, Stalin was 'obsessed with the idea' that after the war northern Iran would be used by the Americans and/or the British as a base of attack against the Soviet Union as part of their policies of encirclement.[1]

The postwar breakdown of collaboration in Iran is often cited as marking the beginning of the Cold War. The Soviets refused to withdraw from the northwest province of Azerbaijan, giving protection to their protégés who installed an independent regime. A case can be made that the Soviets were reacting defensively against what they perceived to be an attempt, likely by the British, to dominate a weak Iran. In any event, American firmness is usually credited when, in 1946, the Soviets backed down in Azerbaijan, withdrawing their troops and allowing the revolutionary government to be ousted by central government forces. The Azerbaijan crisis was probably the closest that the US and Soviet Union have come to direct superpower military conflict in Southwest Asia. However intense the Cold War was to become over the following decades, and despite the Shah's close alignment with the West, the US was never to use Iran as a forward base from which to threaten the Soviet Union.

It was the East–West struggle that, above all, accounted for superpower motives and shaped their policies toward Iran. With the emergence of the US as a major player after the Shah's exile and return in 1953, oil continued to be important, but Iran also became a player in a larger strategy of containment of the Soviet Union. The Shah's governments were willing to participate in exchange for generous development and military assistance. The US stake also increased with agreements that replaced the British with major American oil companies. The Soviets could not hope to undo the US's links with the Iranian regime with threats or pressures. They sought instead to concede an American advantage and to minimize its implications. At best, the Soviets hoped to keep their southern neighbor from signing on with the US to any policies overtly aggressive in intent toward the Soviet Union. And this they accomplished mainly through their own economic assistance and commercial activities.

In an agreement reached with the Shah in 1956, the Soviets became one of Iran's best customers in world trade, the largest single market for manufactured Iranian goods. Accordingly, the Soviet propaganda line against the Shah assumed a muted tone and, in fact, became flattering toward him. Only in March 1959, after the bilateral defense agreement with the US, did the Soviets again attack the Shah in vitriolic terms. The Soviets took the accord, even more than the earlier Baghdad Pact, as a menace, designed to encircle them and increase American influence in the region. For three years the Soviets mounted verbal attacks on the monarchy, years of Soviet diplomacy characterized by J. C. Hurowitz as 'bludgeon and bluster toward Iran'.[2]

Soviet policies toward Iran reversed sharply in 1962. The change followed the Shah's pledge on 15 September to keep US missiles off Iranian soil and to refrain from any actions directed against the Soviet Union. In addition to the pledge, Moscow accepted Iran's definition of foreign military activity in the country. Ramazani argues that after the Cuban missile crisis, a greater flexibility in the Soviet attitude toward the West helped to produce the more conciliatory attitude toward Iran. A temporary thaw in Soviet–US relations also brought a more relaxed attitude on Iran's part toward the Soviet Union.[3]

The Shah's missile pledge paved the way for him to exploit the Soviets' offer to become a significant new source of economic and technical assistance. It was a time of deteriorating economic conditions in Iran and coincided with the reluctance of the Kennedy administration to provide additional budgetary support and its insistence on pressing the Shah for basic social and economic reforms.[4] New transit and trade agreements were signed between the Soviet Union and Iran in July 1963. Diplomatic visits followed. The Soviets could claim and many Iranians agreed that the Soviet role in the economy was more helpful than the West's since they were willing to import Iranian goods other than oil. The barter was considered to be based on favorable terms for Iran. The Soviets would also build a steel mill, something that the West had been reluctant to do. Most notable in the economic-technical area was the January 1966 agreement that called for the construction of a steel plant and mechanical engineering plant in Iran by the Soviets and a pipeline to carry natural gas across the border.

Arms purchases from the Soviets, worth $110 million, were agreed to in January 1967. The rather unsophisticated nature of the arms made large numbers of Soviet technicians or training unnecessary and assured that the Soviets would be unable to penetrate the military establishment, as was occurring in Afghanistan. Although initially Washington was apprehensive over Iran's military purchases from the Soviet Union, it did not take long for US policy-makers to recognize that the Shah was merely maneuvering for leverage with the US and was not seeking to loosen military or political links. In exchange for

Iran's friendship with the West, the Shah always expected large-scale military and economic aid, and he was prepared to play off the superpowers whenever necessary. In 1959, he had threatened to sign a non-aggression treaty with Moscow in an effort to gain greater economic and military assistance from the US. The ploy worked.

At least during the Kennedy administration a coincidence of interests emerged between the US and the Soviet Union as Washington was resistant to agreeing to the Shah's requests for a massive build-up of his military. The US saw no logic in supporting the size army envisioned by the Shah. This point of view disappeared in the Johnson administration with a 1964 accord that enabled Iran to buy $200 million in military equipment. By the late 1960s all restraints were off, as the US backed Iran's ambitions to assume from the British the role of protector in the Persian Gulf. Moscow made no serious attempt to compete with the West in the arming of Iran. In June 1966 the Soviets had refused an Iranian request for surface-to-air missiles, very likely in the expectation that these might be used against Soviet clients in the Arab countries. The Soviet Union's pursuit of close diplomatic and economic ties with Iraq, resulting in the treaty of friendship of 1972, severely limited the possible areas of cooperation with Iran, particularly in the sale of arms.

The Persian Gulf was the expected focal point of US and Soviet competition in the region during the late 1960s and early 1970s. The Shah was anxious to keep the Gulf free of superpower hegemony and volunteered his regime as a bulwark against Soviet imperialism.[5] Some government officials in Tehran argued that more balanced policies toward the US and Soviet Union could have the superpowers competing with material support for influence in Iran. But the Shah remained suspicious of Soviet foreign policy and his views prevailed. At the same time the Shah was always careful to avoid provoking the Soviets, and his public statements were crafted so as not to be seen as offensive in Moscow.

When US–Soviet relations on a global level improved in the *détente* of the early 1970s, the effects were registered on the region. While concerns about subversion by the Soviets did not entirely disappear, Iran was encouraged to enter into close economic relations with the Soviets and further pursue barter agreements with countries in Eastern Europe. The Iranian regime meanwhile worried that agreements reached between the superpowers would be at the expense of their country.[6] Improving Soviet–American relations together with increased oil revenues no doubt hastened the phasing out of US economic aid to Iran. Iran was more concerned, however, about the meaning of *rapprochement* between the superpowers for further military arms sales. Nixon visited Iran in May 1972 to assure Iran that it had nothing to fear. Particularly after the oil price increases in late 1973, he promised that Iran could purchase for dollars all the military equipment the Shah believed necessary to become policeman of the Gulf. The offer also suited the American concerns that a way be found to recycle the region's massive oil revenues.

The Soviets gave little indication that they felt threatened by the Iranian military build-up beginning in the early 1970s. Civility in relations with the Soviets were maintained despite the fact that Iran improved ties with China and allowed the US to locate listening-posts near the Soviet border. Moscow sold the Shah artillery and ground transport equipment, and the Soviets applauded and encouraged the vigorous trade that developed with Eastern Europe.[7] And throughout this period, notwithstanding their earlier complaints, the Soviets did not allow Iran's membership in CENTO, the Baghdad Pact's successor, to become an obstacle to relations.

From the mid-1950s through the late 1970s the Soviets took little interest in influencing Iranian domestic politics. Even as the monarchy was crumbling, Moscow was reluctant to turn against the Shah. Not until September 1978 did the Shah and his government suffer criticism.[8] Once the Shah's position had become untenable, the communist Tudeh party received the green light to join the broad coalition of the left and the clerical right against the Shah. Only in the aftermath of the revolution, and in a period of deteriorating US–Soviet global relations, did the Soviets adopt a more aggressive, risky approach to Iranian domestic politics. Taking advantage of Iran's anti-American, anti-imperialist policies, Moscow sought to establish a good working relationship with the Islamic Republic while local communists infiltrated the power structure. In the wake of the defeat of liberal revolutionaries and brutal repression of the Islamic left by Iran's ruling clerics, the Tudeh hoped to inherit the left's mass base of support.[9]

In 1983, the theocratic government finally cracked down on the Tudeh party. In a strategy orchestrated in Moscow, the Tudeh had overplayed its hand. The Soviets were now subject to much of the same bitter rhetoric aimed at the Americans. Yet they succeeded in juggling policies that kept alive many commercial ties with Iran, including military sales, even as they were engaged in battle with resistance forces in Afghanistan and were continuing aid to the

Baghdad government that had invaded Iran in September 1980. Driven by ideology, the Islamic Republic meanwhile passed up opportunities presumably created in a period of heightened tensions between the superpowers.

AFGHANISTAN: A LEGACY OF CONFLICT AND COOPERATION

Throughout most of the postwar era, Afghanistan was in the enviable position of being materially the beneficiary of superpower competition. In substantial development assistance programs, the United States and Soviet Union also agreed to define the nature of their competition in a fashion that, in effect, produced coordinated aid. In the tradition of the Great Game, Afghanistan was considered too important to leave entirely to one imperial power or another but not worth the price of trying to dominate militarily. As Dupree wrote, the country served, beginning in the 1950s, 'as a guinea pig for Soviet economic penetration and American counter-moves, and forced both countries to evolve tacit policies of mutual cooperation in helping Afghanistan to develop.'[10] Despite the Afghan government's heavy Soviet and East European dependence in the form of loans and trade and, most important, military training, the Kabul government considered its US and Western economic links an important counterbalance, assurance against future Soviet demands and compromise of Afghan independence.

The Soviets had held a favored position in Afghanistan during the 1920s, under the regime of the reformer King Amanullah. The monarch's fall and a usurper's subsequent overthrow by the pro-British Nadir Shah brought the dismissal of the Soviets in the name of Afghan neutrality and independence. Following World War II, the Soviets worked to regain their favored position. Pakistan's running dispute with Afghanistan over the creation of a state for ethnic Pushtuns promoted the Soviet Union as an alternative to transit trade through Karachi's port. Beginning in 1950, the Afghans signed trade agreements with the Soviets and assured that Afghanistan would have petroleum products and cotton cloth, and opened the way for the exchange of a wide range of other commodities.[11]

The first direct Soviet loans were made in 1954. Several others soon followed. In an agreement signed in January 1956, the Soviets granted Afghanistan a $100 million long-term development loan. By

1965, between 35 and 40 per cent of Afghanistan's foreign trade was with the Soviet bloc.[12] Arms agreements were reached in August 1956 with the Soviet Union and several East European countries. They followed US refusals between 1953 and 1955 to aid Afghanistan militarily. Afghan leaders had become interested in US arms and made several requests of Washington, particularly after the US approved an arms aid agreement with Pakistan in 1954. Afghanistan was denied arms because it was unwilling to sign a mutual security pact, as had Pakistan. In any case, Washington considered links with Pakistan more valuable. By comparison with American policy, Moscow and its allies gave the arms without any written or verbal political pledges. It was satisfied with a commitment that came with dependence on military training and spare parts. The US and others underestimated the degree of influence that the Soviets would eventually come to have through the indoctrination of Afghan officers.

The major Soviet aid agreements with Afghanistan were notable at first because they represented the beginning of an era of competition with the US for influence in the Third World. Previously, while Stalin lived, the Soviets had refused to offer assistance to neutral countries. Soviet aid was essentially for ideologically correct allies and for political ends. Khrushchev extended assistance to Afghanistan; but not until the Brezhnev era was aid and trade with Afghanistan and other neutral countries also viewed as bringing economic returns for the Soviet Union.[13] Dupree found that the Soviets became aware that 'economic penetration is the easiest and most logical way to influence all institutions in a society.'[14]

During the 1950s and 1960s, the US encouraged Afghan neutrality, keeping Afghanistan free of regional military pacts, and stressed education in its aid program as a means of contributing to Afghanistan's ability to retain its independence. Though Washington seemed resigned to playing a subordinate role in Afghanistan, it was by no means ready to cede to Moscow full influence over the country. US policy-makers believed that the government in Kabul could be kept from total dependence as long as the US and its Western allies were willing to maintain, not necessarily match, economic assistance. Soviet inroads into the Afghan economy and society were not in themselves deemed threatening to Western interests. Afghanistan, it was assumed, would naturally tilt to the north. Trade with the Soviets necessarily figured in the economic development of Afghanistan, especially since transit trade through Pakistan remained problematic.

318   *Marvin G. Weinbaum*

Among the major US projects was an extensive irrigation project in the Helmand River Valley in the southwest and the building of an international airport in Kandahar, the second largest city. Most conspicuous was a road building program that complemented a Soviet effort. Although no joint construction occurred, the projects were coordinated by the superpowers in that feeder road construction and maintenance were financed by the US and the Soviet Union. The major road net was completed in the mid-1960s. What may have looked at first like a competition, albeit unequal, to develop Afghanistan became so routinized in time that it more closely resembled a collaborative effort to build the Afghan physical infrastructure.

Until the 1970s, the Soviets seemed satisfied with the status quo, as they were in Iran. They appeared to have little to gain from trying to undermine either the Afghan economy or its political system. Socially and economically, the country was judged to be at too primitive a stage for socialist revolution. In a campaign to woo other Third World governments, the Soviet leadership had accepted the degree of penetration in Afghan public life attained and the level of economic dependence created. Even if Afghanistan fell far short of a satellite in the East European sense, its antagonism to Pakistan made it useful. Perhaps most importantly, as early as 1960, Moscow recognized that a Soviet-dominated Afghanistan would be rebellious, and that the Afghans would never submit peacefully to foreign or puppet rule.[15]

Yet the Soviets felt unrestrained in backing the Marxist coup of 1978 and then, in December 1979, embarking on a military campaign in Afghanistan. Plainly, by the 1970s, Soviet policy-makers had begun to become more directly involved in the country's domestic politics. They found themselves obliged to support in July 1973 the ousting of the king, Zahir Shah, by leftist military officers, and for the rest of the decade allowed the pace of change to be set by local communists. Mohammed Daoud, installed by the military as President of the new Republic, angered the communists by easing them from power and disappointed Moscow by establishing cordial relations with pro-American, conservative Middle East states, including Iran. Promised financial support together with signs of reconciliation with Pakistan, first with Prime Minister Ali Bhutto and then with his successor President Zia ul-Haq, pointed to a future Afghanistan less economically reliant on the Soviet Union.[16] Indeed, the US encouraged the Daoud regime to cultivate closer ties with Iran and countries of the Middle East and to become 'truly non-aligned'.[17]

Daoud's policies did not openly challenge the Soviet role as the prime source of military supplies or give reason to suppose a security threat for the Soviets. But when Daoud's former communist allies plotted his overthrow in April 1978, the Soviets apparently gave their blessing and may have participated. The new regime, headed by communists Mohammad Taraki and Hafizullah Amin, welcomed continued US development aid, giving the Marxist regime wanted leverage with Moscow. Washington was willing to continue a modest aid program, ending it only after what appeared to be government mishandling or complicity in the kidnapping and killing of the US ambassador, Adolph Dubs. With the US aid program withdrawn, any parallel superpower interests that still existed in the country's economic development disappeared.

The Soviet Union's December 1979 armed intervention that so grossly underestimated US and global reaction took place in the mistaken belief that rising opposition in the countryside to the communist regime could be quickly snuffed out and a more reliable and popularly acceptable, though still communist, leadership could be installed in Kabul. In response to the Soviet's invasion, as Sen Gupta writes, 'The Carter Administration systematically dismantled the confidence-building mechanisms that had been built between Washington and Moscow by Nixon, Kissinger and Ford.'[18] While miscalculation certainly played a part in the Soviet invasion and a great deal of *ad hoc* defensive policy motivated Moscow's leadership, the decision was also based on a conclusion that the global correlation of forces had turned against the US, and that the Soviets had emerged as the military equal.

THE RULES AND CODES OF COOPERATION

Policies defined as competitive and cooperative have variously been employed by the superpowers in Iran and Afghanistan. The competitive has clearly predominated over the last four decades. Modes of competition involving economic and military aid are the most salient. The competition has remained largely indirect, usually reactive. With the notable exception of surrogates in the Afghan war, it has not been lethal. Policies that qualify as cooperative have often been little more than regulated competition. Tacitly managed conflict has naturally been more feasible than more formal forms since it involves few changes in perceptions and behavior, and does not require that the superpowers have shared interests.[19]

Mutual constraint in highly conflictual circumstances is the most familiar form of regulated competition. Regulated competition also occurs when, in effect, the US and Soviet Union compromise, agreeing informally to limit their gains and, tacitly to be sure, settle for 'satisficing' outcomes. But the superpower rivalry in Afghanistan and to a lesser degree in Iran has also seen occasions of US and Soviet informal understanding that included coordinated actions. Despite different objectives, policies involving aid and trade were at times consciously parallel and complementary.

More overt forms of cooperative behavior require each side to allow the other to benefit from the outcome, including a willingness to tolerate asymmetrical gains. Strained US–Soviet global relations over most of the last 45 years obviously discouraged this. There is little room for cooperation where a zero-sum game is assumed. If the Geneva accords that led to the Soviet withdrawal from Afghanistan are any indication, it is also clear that agreements between the superpowers must occur at both the diplomatic and informal political levels, often using back channels. Similarly, the conclusion of hostilities in the Iran–Iraq war owed much to determination of both superpowers to join multinational efforts aimed at a cease-fire resolution. Although in direct bilateral relations involving such areas as disarmament, trade and cultural policies the US and Soviet Union negotiate directly, in their regional interactions the use of intermediaries, namely United Nations representatives, may facilitate agreements. Mediated discussions can be especially useful as a means of relieving the anxieties of local regimes that fear superpower collusion aimed at their vital interests. Still, whereas in the past openly agreed goals might have proved a political liability to either superpower, the US and Soviet Union may find fewer obstacles in post-revolutionary and postwar eras in Iran and Afghanistan to identifying like or at least parallel objectives.

Several motives or incentives have induced cooperation between the US and the Soviets. Perhaps the most impelling is where there has existed a common adversary, as occurred during World War II. In the present period, the mutual perception of Islamic fundamentalism as challenging superpower interests within and even outside the Middle East could offer the basis for cooperative actions. The issue may be one of terrorism. For example, concern over the export of the Iranian revolution could serve to bring dual pressures on the Islamic government. It is conceivable that the superpowers would act in concert to thwart Iranian policies that pressure Arab regimes along the Persian Gulf.

A second category is when there have been goals, whether separate or common, that can be reached or solutions found only through mutually arrived at policies. High on the list of possible areas of cooperation are efforts by both the US and Soviet Union to reduce, in each case for domestic financial reasons, their commitments in the Third World. Force reductions or the contraction of military and economic aid can occur in response to the actions of the other power, as well as in understandings requiring coordinated policies. Curbing the production and transit of drugs, halting the spread of chemical and nuclear weapons, and addressing common threats to the environment also require some measure of mutual action. As in the first category, the cooperative behavior that occurs is not necessarily the preferred option by US or Soviet decision-makers but may be perceived as rational choices once the costs, risks, and potential benefits are weighed.

A third category is where cooperation between the superpowers derives from the desire to sustain or build upon a positive relationship. With the realization of tangible gains over time and confidence building, the incentive exists to work together to avoid jeopardizing what has been accomplished. This may at times involve sacrifices and even some compromise of national interest. Tradeoffs not infrequently occur within the Western alliance and are possible in the atmosphere of improving East–West relations, especially under conditions of military parity. Incentives of this kind are already apparent in Soviet offers for strategic and conventional disarmament and the decision to withdraw militarily from Afghanistan.

From the mid-1950s through the early 1970s there was an agreement of sorts that each superpower could realize its legitimate interest in recognizing the other's presence in Afghanistan. Even during the nine years of Soviet military engagement in the country there evolved a set of rules that allowed containment of the conflict; the understanding precluded Soviet aggression aimed at Pakistan and Iran, and direct US military involvement, including a possible US military move into Iran that many Soviet strategists expected. At the time of the Soviet invasion, Brezhnev, while justifying his action, conceded that the American and West European concern over the uninterrupted flow of oil from the Gulf was partially legitimate.[20] American assistance, mainly to satisfy Pakistan and the mujahideen, was kept covert. In what was, in effect, a tacit accord, the Soviets would not increase their level of troop commitment and lethal power and the USA would refrain from giving the Afghan resistance the most sophisticated weapons. Other reasons for restraint existed on both sides, of course, but there was joint interest in not raising the level of superpower commitments. It took revised Soviet military tactics during 1985 and 1986, making the position of the resistance more tenuous, to help induce Washington to provide Stinger ground-to-air missiles and to raise the dollar value and effectiveness of aid to the resistance.

Soviet negotiations with the USA in the weeks prior to their armed forces' departure from Afghanistan and in the months thereafter indicated a mutual interest in reaching a political settlement that would avert a bloody civil war. One of the major stumbling blocks to a Soviet pull-out involved the resolution of arms deliveries to the contending sides. The compromise, reached in a tacit agreement that permitted both superpowers to continue aiding their clients, provided a politically acceptable way out for Moscow and Washington. The Soviets did not have to appear to be abandoning their Kabul allies, and the Reagan administration could quiet its critics who feared that the US would prematurely cut off the delivery of weapons. The agreement signaled an ability of the superpowers to find mutually acceptable solutions, at some sacrifice of their long-held objectives. The flexibility shown on both sides suggests mechanisms for problem-solving that could also be applicable to finding a compromise interim government and superpower codes possibly applicable beyond the Afghan conflict.

The invasion of Afghanistan was traumatic simply because it occurred in a country that featured a code of modulated cooperation and relatively low commitment. Iran, as an arena for the superpowers, presents a rather different case: a country that joined superpower ambitions and strategic concerns. The Soviet policies toward the Shah are noteworthy for how Moscow accepted the country's Western orientation without conceiving it as a threat to security. Just the same, there is very little over the postwar period that represents direct US–Soviet cooperation in Iran. It was a competitive relationship, albeit one that sought to avoid confrontation. Even though the Baghdad Pact (later CENTO) was characterized as having hostile intent, the fact that the US remained outside softened its potential hostility in Soviet perceptions and, in any case, the members came to see the alliance more for its diplomatic and economic ties than its military potential. The failure to formalize competitive positions, if nothing else, enhanced chances for mutual restraint.

There was also a measure of understanding in the early 1960s within a competitive relationship. In accepting the Shah's 1962 pledge that Iran would not accept US missiles, the Soviets gave an interpretation of 'military bases' that permitted the US to maintain its military operations in Iran. Earlier, the Soviet Union had insisted on the dismantling of all bases, not simply missile installations.[21] With the notification by the US that it was removing missiles from Turkey, the northern tier became part of the broader understanding that resolved the Cuban missile crisis. It said in effect that neither side would place these offensive weapons at the doorstep of the other. The key was of course reciprocity, not necessarily parity but the indication of a willingness to understand the need for some face-saving on each side.

In devising policies for Iran and Afghanistan before the late 1970s, Washington and Moscow followed a code of respect for one another's spheres of interest that obviously allowed some latitude for the pleas and demands of political elites in Tehran and Kabul. Of the two, Iran was more successful in exerting its influence. Under the Shah's rule, despite the pro-Western connections, Tehran exercised considerable latitude, not always pleasing to the US or the Soviets. With the ascent of a revolutionary government, Iran has been able to set much of the agenda in relations with the Soviet Union and stubbornly resisted Moscow's attempted intrusions in domestic politics. Even more regularly, the revolutionary leaders have frustrated US foreign policy. In Afghanistan, by some contrast, governments were typically circumscribed and watched carefully, especially by Moscow, for signs of too great independence. After the Marxist coup and Soviet armed intervention, little remained of national sovereignty. Ultimately, the difference between the two countries has involved the superpowers' mutual recognition of the relative weights of Iran and Afghanistan in regional politics and the larger bilateral rivalry. By virtue of Iran's oil and gas reserves, its geography and population, and its often formidable leadership, the US and the Soviet Union felt constrained to negotiate with Tehran, rarely to try to dictate.

A major obstacle to codes of cooperation has been the considerable ignorance demonstrated by the superpowers about Iran and Afghanistan, the US more so in Iran, the Soviet Union in Afghanistan. The lack of useable information is well known in Iran. As a result, there was a little ability on either side to predict domestic developments. Neither superpower has had much success in understanding revolutionary changes, especially those motivated in large part by religion. Both exhibited excesses in their policy.

In each country the superpowers have tended to see events through their separate prisms. A high degree of wishful thinking occurred in Washington and Moscow. The superpowers tended to devise policy to fit their own values and desired outcomes. They tended to accept what fitted preconceptions, often by ignoring what did not. Also, each showed a patronizing, even contemptuous attitude toward the two countries.[22] The parallels in superpower misperceptions and actions in the past in Iran and Afghanistan did not of course bring the USA and the Soviet Union any common frames of reference. To the contrary, they tended to intensify misunderstandings of their intentions and capabilities.

Rather than dealing with new leaders and policies on their own terms, the tendency, particularly among American policy-makers, has been to see external forces at work, and to perceive, particularly for Iran, the country readily becoming a pawn in Soviet hands. There has persisted the belief that in the absence of an active US role, Iran would inevitably have to submit to the Soviet Union. This has been apparent in the US military presence in the Persian Gulf where the major concern has turned on American credibility with both friendly Arab governments and the Soviet Union. An indication of a superpower global rethinking in Southwest Asia as elsewhere would be signaled by a reluctance to see actions of the other as a challenge to their resolve or necessarily in terms of a regional domino theory. More realistic, informed views of Iran and Afghanistan will be more likely to produce the basis for superpower cooperation in the region.

At least relative to Europe and the Arab–Israel conflict, the lines of competition between the superpowers in Iran and Afghanistan have been only roughly delineated. In theory, this could be expected to allow the US and the Soviet Union to pursue policies in Southwest Asia that avoid being perceived as coming at the expense of the other party. There is another side, however. Because the interests of the two parties have not been so precisely defined, their differences clearly drawn, the dangers of miscalculation are greater. Miscalculation no doubt helps to account for the Soviets' decision to invade Afghanistan in 1979. The American hostage crisis and naval intervention in the Persian Gulf revealed uncertainties over mutual intentions and the potential for escalation. Yet, because the stakes in Iran have always been perceived higher, there is perhaps greater recognition of the limits of the other's tolerance in accepting setbacks. These understandings may have acted to help avoid direct confrontation, but one has to ask how useful they can be in facilitating cooperation. After all, cooperation may not be simply the other side of the coin from competition. To some extent it may require its own set of behavioral codes.

A question remains as to how well global perspectives on US–Soviet relations apply to Southwest Asia. Is there much that is distinctive about the history, culture, politics, and society of Iran and Afghanistan that makes it difficult to extrapolate easily from the experience in other areas to these two countries. And, for example, because of an Islamic dimension, can theories and generalizations from other regions be entirely applicable?[23] Soviet policy-makers have demonstrated the pitfalls as they tried to apply modes of analysis of Marxism, involving socialist transformation and the class struggle. The USA had its preconceptions of socialist imperialism, most of all of the Russian march toward warm water ports. Both powers have already been surprised by events in these regions, which contradicted their preconceptions at considerable cost to both states. The use of analytic categories by political scientists dealing with the region have also at times had little application or may have been misleading. At the same time, there are dangers in becoming too regionalist in approach. Southwest Asia encompasses many of the same issues and interests and evokes often similar goals and strategies for the superpowers as are found in Latin America and Africa. In turn, political leaders in Iran and Afghanistan will take into account what they perceive are the trends in superpower foreign policies occurring outside the region.

The operational rules and codes likely to govern policies toward Iran and Afghanistan will be influenced by the recent and distant past. However different are the new ways of thinking in foreign policy in Moscow and Washington, the legacy of their relations with governments and people in Iran and Afghanistan will help determine both the future bilateral relations with these countries and also the range of cooperative actions that can be undertaken between Soviets and Americans. This may be even more the case for Iran and Afghanistan than is the case anywhere else in the Third World. For, as has been described, there has been over a longer period of time a structured, even institutionalized bilateral relationship with these two northern tier countries. While the relationships between the Soviets and their southern neighbors have altered considerably since the late 1970s, they still rest on certain fundamental interests and concerns that do not quickly or easily change.

Although real obstacles of ideology and national interest will remain, new mechanisms of coordinated behavior may be evolving.

The sharing of intelligence data in the combatting of terrorism, drug traffic, and the spread of missiles would be ground-breaking as it would tend to reveal mutual intelligence abilities and sources.[24] Even military cooperation is conceivable. In the guise of peacekeeping, Western and Soviet forces might, as occurred twice in this century, pursue parallel interventionary policies in the region in the name of stability and order. Joint naval operations were contemplated to enforce an arms embargo had the Iran–Iraq war dragged on, and US and Soviet ships engaged in limited cooperation involving mine detection in the Gulf. Leaders in Iran and Afghanistan will attempt to revive a kind of regulated competition, where both the US and the Soviet Union are invited to compete against one another through economic assistance. This chapter next examines the likelihood of these developments as well as other obstacles and the opportunities for the superpowers in Iran and Afghanistan as we begin the 1990s.

THE PROSPECTS FOR IRAN

Over most of the postwar, pre-revolutionary period American policy toward Iran was premised on the view that close ties and support for Iran were essential because of Soviet designs. Whether the Soviets would threaten it militarily or through subversion, anything less than full backing for the Shah's regime's ability to fend off the Soviets would leave Iran vulnerable. At the same time, the Soviets saw American ties with governments in Tehran as part of the policy of encirclement, intended to place unfriendly forces close to the Soviet borders and enlist Iran as a surrogate force for American interests in the region. Improved relations with the government in Tehran was seen as a way of balancing if not neutralizing Western and especially US influence. Since Moscow could not expect to reverse this dependence on the US, it engaged in few direct attempts to undermine the Shah's regime and instead sought to lessen suspicions in Tehran and create symbolic debts through economic assistance. This left very little room for cooperation between the superpowers, although at times, as in the preference for the Shah's regime over alternatives, there was a convergence of interests.

The fond hope of American administrations during much of the last decade had been that the regime in Tehran and the revolution would sooner or later exhaust themselves. The Islamic leadership was felt to be instinctively anti-communist and would therefore eventually seek accommodation with the West.[25] Whatever its feelings toward the US, the Islamic Republic in fact did stand as an impediment to deep Soviet penetration and subversion of the country's politics. Moreover, the Afghan intervention undoubtedly cooled whatever ardor there might have been for a forward policy in Iran. The Soviets also no doubt appreciated that an armed attack on Iran would threaten a direct conflict with the US on a global scale.

Yet policies devised by the Reagan administration for Iran did not always change with Soviet intentions and capabilities or the unalterable facts of the Iranian revolution. Policy in Washington was directed not at overcoming the wide differences that separated the two countries but at finding, somehow, those who might represent a deviation from the hard-line policies stated by the leadership; it was the search for the so-called moderates. This view shared the dominant Israeli perspective that, while the cast of characters had changed in Iran, you could do business on much the same terms with the revolutionary government as with its predecessor. There is no evidence that the Soviets had similar illusions.

In the post-Khomeini era the superpowers can expect changes in the constraints and opportunities that govern their policies in Iran. Although the ascendance of a more pragmatic, less insular set of leaders in Tehran seems probable, internal challenges and external events could delay more open, realistic foreign policies. Even a normalization with strict limits would be welcomed, however. The US can settle for an Iran that offers little more than non-belligerency against the moderate Arab states, cooperation in getting hostages in Lebanon released, and the eventual opening of Iran's markets to American goods.

The Soviets share with the US frustrations about the unpredictability of the Islamic government. They also recognize the potentially disruptive effects that catering to Iran could have on the broader scope of superpower relations. The US and the Soviet Union can more openly signal their intentions in Iran so as to minimize suspicions. Even through the 1980s, the Soviets showed little will or, alternatively, lacked the means to increase their influence in Iran at the expense of the US. Despite the deeper bitterness in Iran toward American leaders and policies, Moscow appears to have acted with some restraint politically. Of course, the potential for taking advantage of the circumstances was limited, with many of the same elements that portrayed the US in satanic terms also expressing their antipathies toward the Soviet Union. In the light of the Soviet

Union's present global outlook that shows a reluctance to support liberation movements or, for that matter, most radical groups, it is highly improbable that Moscow would now encourage adventurous policies in Tehran.

The approaching superpower competition will be primarily economic. Current indications are that while US–Iranian relations remain in the deep freeze, the Soviets will move to strengthen economic ties. There are bilateral trade agreements and contracts for petrochemical, power, transportation and industrial projects that have been negotiated between Iran and the Soviet Union. A measure of the new thinking in Tehran is the fact that the Soviet Union and Iran have agreed to the resumption of the export of natural gas. There had been no deliveries to the Soviet Union since immediately after the 1979 revolution. By the time that US diplomatic relations warm up, the opportunities for the US may be few.[26] The US, aware of its difficulties in gaining a foothold in Iran, will encourage its NATO and Arab allies to take the lead in bringing Iran back into the Western fold.[27]

Both the East and West will be accorded a role in the reconstruction and invigoration of the economy. By one estimate Iran will have to spend $28 billion for the rebuilding of destroyed oil and industrial facilities.[28] The West will be an obvious source of loans, and it is an area where the Soviets will have more difficulty competing since they are themselves in the market for credits in Western Europe. Even if Iran chooses to become more reliant on the West and the US in time, this does not mean that leaders in Tehran will be any more anxious to mortgage their country's economic future than they were during the war with Iraq when the regime was able to avoid accumulating a foreign debt. Also, those elements in Iran which want to end the country's economic isolation by looking for economic assistance in the West are likely to remain no less determined to protect the country's political independence.

For domestic political reasons in Iran, the US will move cautiously to prove its good will toward an Islamic government. The failure to date to gain the release of hostages in Lebanon poses a formidable barrier to an improvement in US–Iranian relations. For the time being, Iran's definition of a show of goodwill is the delivery of those still undelivered weapons and spare parts paid for by the Shah. Tehran's leaders also demand the return of assets frozen after the American Embassy was overrun in November 1979. The 1987 trade embargo is also still in effect. Compensation for the Iran Air jet downed by American missiles over the Gulf will also be part of any reconciliation. While these issues remain unresolved, about 400 cases of disputes between Iran and the US have been settled since 1981, and claimants on both sides have been paid more than $1 billion.[29] In all likelihood, a commercial relationship, with the relaxing of export restrictions, will develop before a political one, although some easing on the latter will also bring progress in the former.

It is important for the future of US relations with Iran as well as the potential for cooperation with the Soviet Union that although Washington intervened in the war with Iraq through its naval presence in the Persian Gulf, it did not succumb to pressures to invade Iran nor sponsor a resistance group (as in Afghanistan) that sought to overthrow the Khomeini regime. Despite the introduction of naval warships to protect shipping lanes in the Gulf, the US escaped having to defend militarily against a major Iranian effort to export its revolution to pro-Western Middle East states. However difficult the future relationship may be to re-establish, this fact makes reconciliation somewhat easier. Despite US naval forces in the Persian Gulf, the restraint shown with Iran creates less apprehension by the Soviets over US designs in the region and better chances for superpower understandings.

Better relations between the US and Soviet Union on a regional and global level will obviously mean that there will be less effort to seek advantages in Iran at the expense of the other superpower. The need for US–Soviet cooperation may increase if it turns out that Iran tries to play a more active role in Afghanistan now that the war with Iraq has concluded. No doubt, Tehran's preferred political solution in Kabul is at some variance with the perceived interests of both Washington and Moscow. Yet from the Iranian perspective, any set of superpower understandings is evidence of the USA and the Soviets pursuing their individual goals at Iran's expense. Past events make it easy for the Iranian leadership to believe that the US and Soviet Union continue to play a behind the scene role inside Iran. Through the 1980s, the Islamic regime regularly complained that the US was working actively to undo the revolution and restore the monarchy, and that the Soviets too were engaged in trying to bolster the domestic opposition and undermine the authority of the mullahs. As a wartime adversary, Iraq was portrayed as an instrument of both the Soviets and the Americans.

There always remains the danger of wishful thinking by the superpowers, of anticipating too much from signs of progress, and even of overplaying their hands. If either of the superpowers tries for a full breakthrough in relations with Iran, it will no doubt be disappointed. Understandings between Washington and Moscow involving Iran are likely to be informal and non-specific. Anything approaching a condominium is improbable. However, should Iran take a more radical course, the superpowers could seek, either through tacit agreement or in more explicit coordination of policies to quarantine the Islamic regime, reducing its capacity to export its ideas and wage war.

THE PROSPECTS FOR AFGHANISTAN

The ability of either the US or the Soviet Union to find a role in a postwar Afghanistan will naturally depend on the future configuration of power. Both Moscow and Washington will probably be better served if the outcome is a compromise among forces, one that denies the more radical political elements a pre-eminent position. On the whole, both the US and Soviet Union will gain from a stable political system that is not drastically decentralized. By contrast, Pakistan and Iran may determine that if they cannot have a government in Kabul entirely to their liking, they would be better served by a diffusion of authority, giving rise to autonomous provincial groups that look to Islamabad or Tehran for assistance.

In international affairs, Afghanistan can be expected to avoid any military pacts and to re-position itself among the non-aligned. A strong US or Soviet tilt is doubtful, and if any orientation strengthens it is most likely to be one that places the country more firmly in the community of Muslim states. A postwar Afghan government will also no doubt attempt to restore the kind of neutral policies of the 1960s that permitted a pre-war Kabul government to draw financial and development assistance from the East and West. But as in Iran, the Afghans will be more sensitive to the need to preserve their political independence – while appreciating their economic dependence. In accepting foreign economic assistance, a postwar generation of leaders is less likely to make Afghanistan's past mistake in failing, as Newell describes it, 'to root institutional and political change in the human resources and social institutions integral to its indigenous culture.'[30]

Washington policy-makers are sensitive over the issue of self-determination. Some still believe that the US can play a role in helping to create a broadly popular regime, one better able to undertake the job of rebuilding the country. There may be a commonality of interests between the US and the Soviet Union in encouraging a moderate government; an Islamic radical regime that would be contemptuous of the US and its allies would also be more likely to intensify ferment among Muslim populations in the Soviet Union. In the spirit of saving the Afghans from themselves, there are calls for US–Soviet talks aimed at mutual arms cutoffs to the combatants intended to exclude Marxist leaders and Islamic radicals in a regime of reconciliation in Kabul.[31]

Efforts to use economic as well as military aid to try to influence institution building and the factional ascendance of moderates in Afghanistan could backfire, however, and result in a regime in Kabul that feels resentful of the Americans as well as the Soviets. Whatever leverage past military and economic assistance provided, the US cannot determine where power eventually comes to rest in domestic struggles and would be unwise to try. Once the Soviets end their supply of weapons to the Kabul regime, American strategic and political interest in Afghanistan, already diminished, should recede further. This, in turn, will ease the fears felt in Moscow and Tehran that a mujahideen led government in Kabul will be under the tutelage of the US. If one of the reasons for the Soviets' invasion of Afghanistan was their belief that the US and China were about to establish, with the Amin government's defeat, outposts across the Soviet Union's southern frontier, there seems little reason to be concerned now. The US is not expected to capitalize on Soviet policies by trying to align Afghanistan with the West strategically.

The US has eventually to determine to what degree it will convert its military aid to rehabilitation, either directly or through the United Nations' programs. In all probability, not all of the financing of military equipment to the Afghan resistance will be transferred to the reconstruction process. The decision involves as well the issue of how much the US should continue to funnel its assistance through Pakistan, especially Islamabad's intelligence service. (Improved US–Soviet relations might be most immediately apparent in reduced US military and then economic support for Pakistan, and also in a more vigorous scrutiny of the country's nuclear program.) There exists concern in Washington that unless the US is prepared to renew its economic aid program, bilaterally as well as through international agencies, Afghanistan will be pushed toward re-establishing in many areas economic dependence on the Soviets – of an unhealthy kind.

Yet the US is not likely to get drawn into a competition with the Soviets, particularly at a time when foreign aid continues to be trimmed in the American Congress. For that matter, it is doubtful given recent experiences and their current budgetary problems that either superpower will be as ready to have an Afghanistan government play off one against the other.

Whatever informal superpower understandings are reached involving Afghanistan, the Soviet economic presence is bound to be the more prominent. Moscow will probably be prepared to offer barter agreements for a hard currency-strapped Kabul government. The Soviets will also offer transit routes through Soviet territory and, most important, be the sole market for the sale of Afghanistan's natural gas, though at far better terms than was obtained by the Afghans before 1978.[32] Exploitation of the country's other natural resources will also be difficult without Soviet participation in projects.

The US seems to be taking a relaxed attitude toward Soviet diplomacy, quite a contrast with the past when any discussions by Moscow with the mujahideen would have been looked upon with great suspicion. The strongest possibility of superpower friction would be in a total breakdown of the country in armed political struggles, or if Moscow acted to Sovietize northern Afghanistan as a means to insulate Soviet Central Asian states from Islamic influences crossing the border.[33] A renewed military solution by the Soviet Union is very doubtful as it would run counter to efforts to demonstrate that force no longer drives Moscow's foreign policy.[34] Any exercise of a reversal in Soviet political policy in Afghanistan would wholly derail cooperation with the US and undermine the political gains in the Third World with the Soviet military pullout of February 1989.

Aside from the Geneva agreement, cooperation between the US and Soviet Union has been evidenced in various understandings involving the Soviet withdrawal. Washington encouraged the mujahideen to allow the Soviets an unimpeded movement of troops to the border in recognition of the Soviet desire not to be left militarily exposed or politically humiliated. When the US closed its Kabul embassy in February 1989 in anticipation of heavy fighting in the capital with the Soviet army's withdrawal, the Soviet Union provided fighter plane coverage for the exiting flight by US diplomats. In the aftermath of the Soviet military withdrawal, it became official policy in Moscow to stress that the Soviet Union and the United States can serve 'as mediators and official guarantors in the settlement of the

Afghan problem,' and that the superpowers 'have set a precedent for the constructive collaboration which is extremely necessary for the improvement of international relations as a whole.'[35] The motive behind this view has been to induce responsibility in Washington to join with Moscow in finding a non-military solution that preserves communist influence in Kabul. Yet the larger implications of establishing a model of behavior is the recognition that the superpowers can sound one another out on the feasibility of defusing regional conflicts where they threaten to impede progress in broader US–Soviet relations.

CONCLUSION

This chapter has raised the question whether revolutionary Iran and a post-communist Afghanistan, so recently arenas of superpower competition, will become prominent settings for cooperative policies. The changing global character of relations between the US and the Soviet Union, in which countries of Southwest Asia are expected to become less directly critical to the superpowers' strategic interests, have apparently improved the possibilities of cooperation. US and Soviet policies must be understood in terms of their risks, costs and benefits in the Third World, and more specifically in Southwest Asia. The realities on which such calculations are based have changed as a result of forces outside the reach of the superpowers as well as developments over which the United States and Soviet Union have had some control.

Future Soviet policies toward Iran and Afghanistan are expected to be in harmony with the gradual disengagement from expensive and troublesome commitments in the Third World. Leaders in Moscow appear to have greater incentive in strengthening relations with those affluent and influential non-communist countries that can be profitable for the Soviet Union in its own economic reform programs. Less attention to the developing countries of Asia and Africa could leave new economic and development assistance to international organizations in which the Soviets are, to be sure, playing an increasingly active role. Over the long run, a less ambitious, active policy in the Third World may pay greater political dividends as the Soviets are able to create mutually beneficial relations with important countries, including the more conservative regimes of the Middle East, that have previously shunned them. In particular, Soviet decisions in

Afghanistan have lifted a heavy weight off the Soviets in their overtures to the Third World.

The Soviet Union in the postwar period in Iran and Afghanistan has twin monkeys off its back, one the awkward position of supporting Iraq against Iran, the other the embarrassment of killing Muslims in Afghanistan. But the Soviet approach will not be the familiar search for parties to sign pacts of mutual security. It will be more inclined to contribute to solving the region's conflicts and to assisting its economic development. Initially the efforts are aimed at rebuilding the prestige of the Soviets in the region. Moscow will be less interested than in the past in driving a wedge between the US and its traditional friends in the region. Even the commitment to continued competition with the US in the Indian Ocean could diminish, especially if the US reduces its presence.[36] Above all, the Soviets want to be a player. They have something to bring to the region, something far more constructive than the provocateur or spoiler roles they assumed in the past. They do not expect to replace the US in a potential broker role, but to join it, even if as junior partner for the present. If new Soviet moves come at the expense of the United States this is likely only because Washington fails to demonstrate similar energy and creativity in its foreign policies.

After the wars in Vietnam and Afghanistan, the superpowers are chastened in similar ways, making them reassess their presence in the Third World and, more particularly, re-estimate the limits of their military power, specifically the potential for victory by conventional military forces against dedicated guerrilla armies. For both the Soviets and the US, competitive political involvement has also been demonstrated as too costly, the rewards too few. The Soviets obviously failed to create in Afghanistan the kind of legitimate government for which they strived. Meanwhile, the US may have cultivated an Afghan resistance that, in power, would be neither capable of governing nor particularly Western in its political orientation. Both superpowers have had their hands burned in Iran. The US could not prevent the Shah's monarchy from falling and was unable to exert any influence on the kind of regime that emerged in its place. Supporters of Moscow were notably unsuccessful in sustaining their influence in ruling circles in Tehran. Neither superpower can presently be confident of the outcome of internal struggles in Iran or Afghanistan. A certain degree of benign neglect may look increasingly attractive. But this can occur only if the two superpowers are prepared to exercise self-restraint and entertain even more active forms of cooperation at the regional level. Only then is it possible for one power to believe that the other is not quietly trying to take advantage of a policy of limited involvement. The superpowers will, then, take their cues from one another. Flexible policies will be bolstered by a *mutuality* in lowering the stakes, retrenching on involvement. Above all, there is a willingness to question whether gains for one superpower necessarily imply a loss to the other. The Soviets' apparent willingness to live with a regime in Kabul containing non-communist elements reduces the sense of threat to the US and its allies in the region. With less ideological regimes in both Moscow and Washington, there can be expected fewer missions to accomplish, less posturing. There was a tendency earlier toward overreaction by the superpowers. Genuine non-alignment for Iran and Afghanistan may be more palatable than it has been in recent years. Indeed, this neutralism can lessen circumstances where the US and Soviet Union become hostages to a third country's interests, limiting Moscow and Washington's freedom of action.

Much of the potential for influence by the superpowers over domestic and foreign policy in Tehran and Kabul will come from the degree to which they are willing to play a part in the economic reconstruction of Iran and Afghanistan. The US and Soviet Union ha.:: some immediate ways in which they can collaborate, as in the reconstruction of Afghanistan. There are tangible areas of cooperation, particularly in resettlement of refugees and rebuilding of the country's infrastructure. Opportunities for joint efforts, certainly of an open kind, are less obvious in Iran.

Because Soviet and US relations are in transition from a bipolar world to a multipolar one, a situation no longer exists where a Third World country feeling the need for assistance must choose between East and West. Economic and even military aid can be found elsewhere. The Japanese, the Saudis, the Chinese, the Indians, and the various international agencies can function fairly independently of older alignments. Important non-government channels exist to meet military needs; the US and the Soviet Union no longer have the same monopoly or pre-eminence they once enjoyed in several countries.

Iran and Afghanistan, both sharing borders with the Soviet Union, are not, of course, of equal strategic importance to the superpowers. A stable Iran and Afghanistan have direct bearing on Soviet Central Asia. (Until now what has occurred in Iran has actually had far less influence on the Islamization of Soviet Central Asia than has the war in Afghanistan.) The Soviet Union also has a direct economic stake in the two countries' energy resources. Of the two, Afghanistan can be expected to recede more quickly in its significance. Iran is too important economically and politically to fade away, and both the West and the Soviet Union will want to bring Iran out of its not so splendid revolutionary isolation. An essentially non-aligned Iran, one willing to do business with the Soviets and the West, will be acceptable by all parties.

An issue on which both the US and the Soviet Union have direct common interests is the export of Islamic radicalism from Iran. Moscow and Washington are anxious to prevent its dominance in a postwar Afghanistan. The US also sees the need to restrain militant fundamentalism as a way of securing friendly states in the Arab world; and the Soviets are concerned about Islamic consciousness in their Muslim republics. There is bound to be a convergence of views on a political status quo in the area of the Persian Gulf. What form the cooperation will take remains uncertain. It may involve joint assistance to littoral states in their defense build-ups. But because of the sensitivity born of history that the big powers may be carving up the region, assistance to the states is bound to be bilateral and cooperation between Washington and Moscow more informal than formal.

With much of the threat of the Soviet Union seemingly removed, similar political dynamics apply across the entire northern tier of the Middle East. Turkish governments, which have until now prospered handsomely from American fears of Soviet capabilities in the region, may find their leverage with the US greatly diminished. At the same time, lowered fears of Soviet influence and domination could increase the possibility of agreements between Ankara and Moscow. 'The notion of a neutral nonaligned buffer zone across the northern tier of the Middle East and Southwest Asia would be increasingly attractive for the Turks.'[37] The Soviets in their new thinking can be expected to cultivate friendships with Turkish authorities, and Washington may have to be content with a government in Ankara pursuing more independent policies and relinquishing its deterrent role against the Soviets in a revised NATO.

The possibilities are stronger that the Soviets can assume a more non-adversarial approach along the northern tier than in the more complicated relations between Arabs and Israelis. Soviet policy and its regional coordination with the US will, however, hinge to some extent on what progress is made in the Middle East's most protracted conflict. A prominent Soviet role in an Arab–Israeli peace process would make any efforts toward joint policies or understandings in Iran and Afghanistan that much easier. The other side of the coin carries regional effects from Soviet military disengagement in Afghanistan on Moscow's relations with Iran and Pakistan, China, the Gulf Emirates, and Saudi Arabia where diplomatic ties are increasingly possible. The interrelatedness of policies within the region was underscored by the apparent use by Moscow of improved economic ties with Iran after the Iraq war to gain Tehran's willingness to press Iranian-backed mujahideen to reach a compromise settlement in Afghanistan.

A critical question is, of course, whether a new era of *détente*, one that is perhaps more explicitly cooperative in policies, will do anything to restrain or contain, or even prevent future conflicts among states in the region. The evidence to date seem to be that the superpowers have a useful role to play, restraining their clients and providing their good offices for the resolution of differences. Less directly, the US and Soviet roles have already helped, if very obliquely, to dampen regional conflicts, notably in Iran's conflict with Iraq. More openly, the Soviets, for their own specific purposes, have sought to arrange a compromise in Afghanistan through a broad-based government that would include the communists in order to end hostilities as well as protect their protégés.

The dangers of misunderstanding in the superpowers' bilateral relations with countries in the region may actually grow in an era of increased cooperation. Importantly, it may matter less. The US and Soviet Union can probably accept policies adopted by Iran and Afghanistan once thought to be intolerable so long as these policies do not threaten to spill over beyond the region. Moscow and Washington will have learned to live with more independent-minded regimes that will themselves appreciate that not all policies can be acquiesced in by one or both of the superpowers. Generally, because fewer demands will be put on these countries, there will be less reason for disappointments and apprehension. With Cold War issues in recess, regional disagreements will be left to the local states to deal with, for better or worse. The better is likely to witness increased regionalism, the worse a settling of old debts. In either case, the states of Southwest Asia will be less inclined to find their security in their major power alignments and more in regional security arrangements, an outcome that the US and Soviet Union can encourage.

POSTSCRIPT

Iraq's military invasion of Kuwait in August 1990, together with regional and international reactions that it evoked, corroborates expectations in this chapter and is also at some variance with it. The discussion concludes with the observation that, with the disengagement of the US and the Soviet Union, countries in the region might choose to settle old debts rather than agree on new security arrangements. Implied as well is the fact that, where the conflict threatens to spill over and superpowers have strong stakes in the outcome, they will have an incentive to act cooperatively. The Iraqi attack that sought to bring the oil production and reserves of Kuwait under Baghdad's control and that could intimidate or threaten the territorial integrity of Saudi Arabia is this kind of concern. Less anticipated was the clear formalization of the US's long-held tacit alliance with Saudi Arabia and the broad international support for the US-led trade sanctions and military deployment. If Soviet policies have been more cautious than those in the West, they were predictable in light of extensive ties with Iraq, Moscow's domestic preoccupations, and a public reluctance, after Afghanistan, to see military forces committed beyond Soviet borders.

Unclear is the extent to which the pre-eminent US role in confronting Iraqi aggression is a harbinger of a new world order in which Washington assumes the role of global policeman and the international community provides mechanisms for collective security. Much depends on the effectiveness of multilateral policies to restore stability and address underlying injustices in the region. With global dependence on Persian Gulf oil and associations with the Arab–Israeli conflict, there may be something unique about this crisis as a post-cold war test in resolving regional conflicts. As the chapter suggests, the US, its allies, and others may be less inclined to pursue interventionary actions in future cases where a breakdown in regional security occurs.

NOTES

1. Richard W. Cottam, *Iran and the United States* (Pittsburgh: University of Pittsburgh Press, 1988), pp. 66, 68.
2. J. C. Hurowitz, 'Iran in World and Regional Affairs', in Ehsan Yar-Sharter (ed.), *Iran Faces the Seventies* (New York: Praeger, 1971), p. 134.

3. Rouhallah K. Ramazani, *Iran's Foreign Policy, 1941–1973* (Charlottes-ville: University Press of Virginia, 1975), p. 317.
4. Ramazani, op. cit., pp. 320, 325.
5. Cottam, op. cit., p. 144.
6. Ramazani, op. cit., pp. 369–70.
7. Cottom, op. cit., p. 142.
8. Marvin G. Weinbaum, 'Soviet Policy and the Constraints of National-ism in Iran and Afghanistan', in Ya'acov Ro'i (ed.), *The USSR and the Muslim World* (London: George Allen & Unwin, 1984), p. 240.
9. Cottom, op. cit., pp. 202–3.
10. Louis Dupree, 'Afghanistan: 1966', *American Universities Field Staff*, South Asia Series, vol. X, no. 4 (July 1966), pp. 20–1.
11. Louis Dupree, 'Afghanistan's Big Gamble: Part I', *AUFS*, South Asia Series, vol. IV, no. 3 (29 April 1960), pp. 14, 16. For brief accounts of the several stages of US–Soviet relations see Alam Payind, 'Soviet–Afghan Relations from Cooperation to Occupation', *International Journal of Middle East Studies*, vol. 21, no. 1 (February 1989), pp. 105–28.
12. Between 1952 and 1965, the Soviet Union had given $414 million in loans and $68.5 million in grants, and the US $12 million in loans and $131 million in grants. The remaining sources of international aid included West Germany ($60 million), China, ($28 million), Czechos-lovakia ($12 million), World Bank ($4 million), UK, ($6 million): Dupree, 'Afghanistan: 1966', op. cit., p. 16. By the time of the April 1978 coup, the Soviets, mainly in the form of loans, had committed $1.2 billion in economic assistance. Henry Bradsher, *Afghanistan and the Soviet Union* (Durham, NC: Duke University Press, 1983), p. 24.
13. Ibid., pp. 23–35.
14. Dupree, 'Afghanistan's Big Gamble, Part II', *AUFS*, South Asia Series, vol. IV, no. 4 (9 May 1960), p. 3.
15. Dupree, 'Afghanistan: 1966', op. cit., p. 20.
16. See fuller discussion in Marvin G. Weinbaum, 'The Soviets in Afgha-nistan: Risks, Costs, and Opportunities', in Edward Kolodziej and Roger Kanet (eds), *The Limits of Soviet Power in the Developing World* (London: Macmillan, 1989), pp. 232–5.
17. Bhabani Sen Gupta, *Afghanistan, Politics, Economics and Society* (Boulder, CO: Rynne Rienner, 1986), p. 23.
18. Ibid., p. 94.
19. See Harold H. Saunders, 'Regulating Soviet–US Competition and Cooperation in the Arab–Israeli Arena, 1967–86', in Alexander L. George, Philip J. Farley, and Alexander Dallin (eds), *US–Soviet Security Cooperation: Achievements, Failures, Lessons* (New York: Oxford University Press, 1988), p. 540.
20. Sen Gupta, op. cit., p. 100.
21. Ramazani, op. cit., p. 340, observes that in April 1974 when military maneuvers involving thousands of American military personnel took place, the Soviets mounted press criticism but otherwise acted in a very restrained way. Absent was the kind of rigorous attack on US–Iranian military cooperation that occurred during the 1950s.

22. These observations are stimulated by remarks by Gary Sick that were addressed to US errors in Iran in a talk on 'Iran and American Decisionmakers', at a conference on 'The Iranian Revolution Ten Years Later: What Has Been Its Global Impact?' at the School of Advanced International Studies, Johns Hopkins University, Washington, DC, 4 February 1989.

23. These questions are inspired by ones raised by William B. Quandt, in 'The Superpowers and Middle East Crises', a paper delivered at the annual meeting of the Middle East Studies Association, Los Angeles, 3 November 1988.

24. This idea was reportedly to be broached by Secretary of State James A. Baker during a trip to Moscow, *The New York Times*, in an article by Thomas Friedman, 21 April 1989.

25. Eqbal Ahmad and Nasim Zehra, 'Pakistan after Zia', *Middle East Report* (November–December 1988), p. 31.

26. See John T. Haldane, 'Thawing Relations with Tehran', in the *Christian Science Monitor*, 10 February 1989.

27. It is probably true that there remains a preference in Iran for American goods and technical know-how. In 1988, trade between the USA and Iran amounted to only $54 million. This compared with $230 million by Canada. At the same time, trade with the Soviets was expected to reach $350 million for 1988: ibid. In 1972 the USA had exported $480 million in non-military goods and technical services.

28. Ibid.

29. *The New York Times*, 6 February 1989.

30. Richard S. Newell, 'Prospects for State Building in Afghanistan', in Ali Banuazizi and Myron Weiner (eds), *The State, Religion, and Ethnic Politics in Afghanistan, Iran, and Pakistan* (Syracuse, NY: Syracuse University Press, 1986), p. 120.

31. See editorials in the *Christian Science Monitor*, 2 April 1989, and *The New York Times*, 3 April 1989.

32. For a discussion of probable economic ties with the Soviet Union see Marvin G. Weinbaum, 'The Politics of Afghan Resettlement and Rehabilitation', *Asian Survey*, vol. XXVIX, no. 3 (March 1989).

33. Joseph Newman, Jr, 'The Future of Northern Afghanistan', *Asian Survey* vol. XXVII, no. 7 (July 1988), p. 735.

34. Marshall D. Shulman, in *The New York Times*, 5 February 1989.

35. *Izvestia*, 22 April 1988, p. 5, as quoted in Melvin A. Goodman and Caroly Ekedahl, 'Gorbachev's "New Directions" in the Middle East', *The Middle East Journal*, vol. 42, no. 4 (Autumn 1988), p. 586.

36. For a different prediction see Milan Hauner, 'The Soviet Geostrategic Dilemma', in Milan Hauner and Robert L. Canfield (eds), *Afghanistan and the Soviet Union* (Boulder, CO: Westview Press, 1989), p. 177.

37. Bruce R. Kuniholm, 'A Strategy for the Gulf and Southwest Asia', in S. Wells, Jr and M. Bruzonsky, *Security in the Middle East* (Boulder, CO: Westview Press, 1987), p. 332.

13 Superpower Cooperation in Southeast Asia*
Sheldon W. Simon

INTRODUCTION

Overt superpower cooperation has been rare in post-World War II Southeast Asia. Although the global code of conduct for United States–Soviet relations has applied to this region, it has been employed more to limit potential conflict than to promote jointly agreed goals. Both Washington and Moscow have consistently advanced nuclear non-proliferation goals in Southeast Asia. They have also ensured that there has been little opportunity for direct military confrontation between themselves. This latter objective is facilitated by Southeast Asia's maritime environment in which US naval prowess dominates over essentially land-based Soviet military power.

Unlike South Asia, where the United States and Soviet Union have run parallel though competitive aid programs in India, with the exception of Indonesia during the Sukarno era (1949–66), each superpower has had separate clients with mutually exclusive aid programs. Until the end of the Second Indochina War (1963–75), Moscow's assistance was confined primarily to North Vietnam and its communist allies in South Vietnam, Laos, and Cambodia. Moreover, the Soviet Union also had to compete with China for influence in this subregion. Thus, the USSR has had to cope with both communist and capitalist competitors in Southeast Asia.

Southeast Asia's strategic importance for both superpowers is inherent in its location – a maritime region adjacent to Northeast Asia and the northwest Pacific where vital interests and important allies of each great power reside. The interdiction of Southeast Asian sea lanes could threaten Japan's and South Korea's economic viability or Siberian development. Freedom of movement for international commerce through these busy ocean arteries is an important condi-

* Research for the chapter was supported by travel grants from The Earhart Foundation (Ann Arbor) and the US Information Agency.

tion for the superpowers as well as the trading states of both Northeast and Southeast Asia.

Initial Soviet–American interaction in post-World War II Southeast Asia can be traced to the beginnings of the Cold War in the late 1940s. Since the 1930s, the United States had deployed air and naval forces from the Philippine bases to monitor Southeast Asian waters.[1] The decision to keep these bases grew from a series of complex postwar developments which included Cominform-directed uprisings in Indonesia and Malaya in 1948–9; America's decision to aid the French in Indochina and the Dutch in Indonesia because Washington wanted their support for US policies in Europe; and finally the victory of the Chinese communists in 1949 and subsequent outbreak of the Korean war in 1950. Taken together, these events were seen in Washington as part of a global challenge directed from Moscow.

The United States responded by building up Japan as a counterweight to what was perceived to be a Sino–Soviet monolith intent on dominating the Asian balance of power. Southeast Asia's importance for Japan's new role consisted of the region's raw materials and markets.

One of the rare instances of direct Soviet–American cooperation occurred at the 1954 Geneva Conference which legitimated the Vietnamese communist (Vietminh) military victory in North Vietnam. Both the Soviet Union and China were interested in promoting peaceful coexistence at this time, the former in order to forestall the creation of a European Defense Community and the latter in hopes of convincing the Americans not to replace the French in Indochina. Thus, the United States, the Soviet Union, and China collaborated to force Vietminh acceptance of the division of Vietnam at the 17th parallel (pending national elections) and the neutralization of Laos and Cambodia. Despite the successful compromise, the United States soon moved to subvert the provision for Vietnamese elections and instead supported a separate non-communist state in South Vietnam which, under the newly negotiated Manila Pact, became a protocol protected state alongside Laos and Cambodia. The Manila Pact represented a considerable escalation of the US commitment to Southeast Asia and negated the cooperation with Moscow and Beijing which had been achieved a few months earlier at Geneva. Once again, Washington's policy was based on the belief that the communist challenge was global and monolithic and had to be restricted wherever and whenever it appeared.

A second major example of direct Soviet–American cooperation did not occur until 1962 at another Geneva Conference, this time over Laos. Backing right-wing Lao forces against Vietminh-supported Pathet Lao advances, the Kennedy administration feared the possibility of superpower escalation, thus violating the implicit code of conduct. The 1961–2 Geneva Conference was convened to create a tripartite government for Laos composed of communist, neutralist, and right-wing elements. While the outcome led to an arrangement whereby the great powers disengaged from Laos, US military involvement in Southeast Asia actually increased. In order to assuage Thailand's fear over an ultimate Pathet Lao victory, the United States acceded to a bilateral executive agreement (the Rusk-Thanat accord) which committed it to the defense of Thailand in the event of external aggression.

The Cold War era in Southeast Asia from the mid-1950s to the 1980s created a tripartite division among most of its members: (a) those aligned with the United States (Thailand and the Philippines); (b) those aligned with the Soviet Union (the communist movements and subsequent regimes in Vietnam, Laos, and Cambodia); and (c) non-aligned states which, in fact, leaned toward the West, fearing China more than the Soviet Union (Malaysia, Indonesia, and Singapore).[2] The 1975 US defeat in Indochina appeared to weaken the first and third groups, especially as the United States withdrew all its military personnel from mainland Southeast Asia. However, the apparent weakening of the US position in Southeast Asia also led to a coalescence of the first and third groups into a new organization – the Association of Southeast Asian Nations (ASEAN) – whose purpose was to protect its members' independence and promote their econo-mic development within the capitalist world economy. Although Soviet clients won the Second Indochina War, installing communist regimes in all three Indochinese states, the net effect was actually to increase the region's polarization and to further isolate the Soviet Union as mentor to a predatory power which was threatening to subvert its ASEAN neighbors from Hanoi.

In sum, through the mid-1980s, although Southeast Asian conflicts did not interfere with more important global cooperative Soviet–US actions – such as Prime Minister Alexei Kosygin's visit and the SALT 1 during President Richard Nixon's 1972 bombing of Haiphong harbor – within the region itself cooperation was infrequent. The Soviet Union did not hesitate to provide Hanoi with the arms it required to emerge victorious. Moreover, after the war, Moscow continued to underwrite Vietnamese occupation forces in Laos and its 1978–89 intervention in Cambodia.

General Secretary Leonid Brezhnev believed that America's defeat in Indochina had shifted the 'correlation of forces' in the USSR's favor. The Soviet–Vietnam alliance, formalized in November 1978, would lead to Soviet dominance in Indochina that could be employed both to contain China and to further weaken the American position along the Soviet Union's Asian periphery.

Since the end of the Second Indochina War, the United States has been concerned about three Southeast Asian threat environments:

(a) a spillover of the 1980s Cambodian conflict into Thailand which could entail American involvement under the Manila Pact (1954) reconfirmed during the Reagan administration. The 1987 Thai–US agreement to create an American weapons stockpile in Thailand is designed to insure that Thailand will have the equipment on hand for its own defense in the event of an Indochina war spillover;

(b) local insurgencies against regimes friendly to the United States which might appeal for American assistance. In 1956, these concerns led to direct US military involvement in Indochina. By 1990, with the exceptions of the Philippines and the unresolved Cambodian conflict, no Southeast Asia government faced a significant insurgent challenge;

(c) the 1980s build-up of the Soviet Pacific Fleet and the deployment of 20–25 of its ships to Cam Ranh Bay. Washington views a permanent regional Soviet naval presence as a threat to the Southeast Asian straits in a crisis situation. This naval presence also provides Moscow with an ability to challenge US maritime assistance to countries engaged in fighting local communist regimes.

Finally, the United States has focused its Southeast Asian hopes on the success of the Association of Southeast Asian Nations (ASEAN), a group of six international market-oriented anti-communist states which actively seek international trade and investment (Malaysia, Indonesia, Thailand, Singapore, the Philippines and Brunei). For the most part, ASEAN has welcomed the American air and naval presence in Southeast Asia as a guarantee against external threats to their political and economic growth. As long as the United States is primarily responsible for regional defense, the ASEAN states need not divert large portions of their own resources from civilian purposes to build their militaries.

In contrast to the United States, the Soviet Union is a relative latecomer to Southeast Asian politics. Until the Second Indochina War, Moscow had only one important relationship – with Sukarno's Indonesia in the 1950s and early 1960s to which it supplied military hardware. With the abortive Indonesian communist party coup in 1965, Moscow's Jakarta connection abruptly ended, although, unlike China, the USSR was not accused of direct involvement. Indeed, Southeast Asian communist parties and insurgent movements looked to Beijing for guidance rather than Moscow in the 1960s. This was to prove a serendipitous advantage in later years as a Soviet regional presence was seen as more politically acceptable than a Chinese.

From the Second Indochina War to the present, the Soviet Union's most important Southeast Asian relationship has been with Vietnam. Moscow's decision in the late 1970s to underwrite Hanoi's regional ambitions provided it with a formidable regional client whose military power exceeded that of all the ASEAN states combined. The relationship has, however, proved a mixed blessing. While providing the USSR with a strategic location along South China Sea trade routes and opposite America's foremost regional naval base, Vietnam has also proved to be an economic burden, costing between $2 and $3 billion annually to maintain its economy and military dominance in Indochina. The USSR and other Warsaw Pact countries provided the military hardware, petroleum, and even the uniforms for the Vietnam Peoples Army (PAVN). The COMECON states also served as Vietnam's major export market and its international creditor, mortgaging much of the country's current and future exports for the repayment of cumulated debt.[3]

The Soviet decision to adopt Vietnam as a client and back its interventions in Cambodia and Laos had the effect, however, of isolating Moscow from Southeast Asia's most dynamic regional association, ASEAN. These market-oriented, export growth-led economies burgeoned in the 1970s and 1980s, creating strong trade and investment links with such major OECD countries as the United States, Japan, and members of the European Economic Community (EEC). By the late 1980s, trade among these partners had exceeded $3 trillion annually. Neither the Soviet Union or Indochina has participated in this synergistic economic network. Consequently, their economic performance has fallen far behind that of the dominant Pacific Basin economies.

In effect, the Soviet Union has discovered that its political and strategic objectives in Southeast Asia are not fully compatible. Strategically, the Soviet–Vietnam alliance provides the USSR with naval and air bases in Vietnam sufficient for the projection of force into the South China Sea and Indian Ocean. These deployments complicate American naval and air missions in the region and demonstrate that the USSR can operate throughout Asia, not merely in its northwest quadrant. This Soviet naval and air presence is the ticket by which the USSR gains admission to decisions about the region's strategic future. Evidence for this proposition may be found in Soviet President Gorbachev's 1988 Krasnoyarsk address where he posited the possibility of a tradeoff between Soviet and US bases in Southeast Asia through his proposals for regional disarmament. Abandonment of Cam Ranh Bay could be used to obtain Southeast Asian backing for Moscow's efforts to reduce American naval dominance by eliminating the more important Subic Bay base at the same time.

Nevertheless, Moscow's support for Hanoi's Cambodian occupation has isolated the USSR from ASEAN and served to strengthen political ties among the Association, the United States, Japan, and even China. (The latter has become an important political ally of Thailand in its opposition to Vietnam and, since 1988, a significant weapons supplier for the Thai armed services.) Soviet political hopes of reducing the US role in Southeast Asia and inhibiting the development of Chinese and Japanese ties to the region have foundered because Moscow has been so closely identified with Hanoi's regional ambitions. Moreover, until the late 1980s, the Soviet Union feared that if it pressured Vietnam to withdraw its forces from Cambodia, accept a coalition government for that country, or reduce its military and economic assistance, Hanoi might unilaterally close down the base at Cam Ranh Bay, thus undermining Moscow's regional strategic position.

For the past decade, the Soviet–Vietnam relationship has constituted an example of exchange theory in international politics: each side possesses a resource needed by the other. To Vietnam, Soviet assistance has been essential for both its domestic economy and its military deployments in Laos and Cambodia. For the USSR, use of Cam Ranh Bay is crucial for the permanent deployment of Soviet forces in the region and their projection into the Indian Ocean.

In concluding this brief overview of American and Soviet perspectives and policies toward Southeast Asia, it is worth noting that certain commonalities in their positions have evolved, commonalities that could form the basis for future cooperation.

(a) Both the Soviet Union and the United States see their air and naval presences in Southeast Asia as a long-term commitment.

(b) Each is probably concerned more with maintaining open sea lines of communication (SLOCs) than denying them to the other. Indeed, the Soviet Pacific Fleet contingent operating from Cam Ranh Bay depends on a peaceful environment to sustain its presence. In the event of war, the base could be eliminated in a matter of hours. Although Moscow withdrew most of its aircraft from Cam Ranh Bay in December 1989, Soviet ships remain.

(c) Both a Soviet and American military presence may continue to be acceptable if Southeast Asian states foresee Japan and China deploying their navies and airforces to the region around the end of the century. Jurisdictional conflicts over the Spratly Islands in the South China Sea have already led to a Chinese deployment, while Japan might well extend its naval reach to protect its SLOCs to the south.

SUPERPOWER RULES OF CONDUCT IN SOUTHEAST ASIA

The Brezhnev legacy

The Soviet military position in Southeast Asia is part of the Brezhnev legacy which emphasized the fungibility between military power and political influence. An emphasis on acquiring clients with revolutionary goals by extending military aid directly challenged the American security policy of supporting status quo regimes. This zero-sum superpower relationship meant that the Brezhnev era witnessed little open cooperation.

Flying Bear-D long-range reconnaissance aircraft and Badger anti-submarine warfare planes from Cam Ranh Bay until late 1989, Soviet operational and intelligence gathering activities cover maritime Southeast Asia. From Vietnam, the Soviets are able to shadow the US Seventh Fleet and monitor US air force activity originating from Clark Air Base in the Philippines. These forces also demonstrate that, like the Americans, Soviet political interests in the region must be taken into consideration by its members.

The USSR is particularly concerned that the Philippine bases provide the United States with a *surge capacity* to send naval and air reinforcements north to the Sea of Japan in the event of a Soviet–US crisis. The US maritime strategy during the Reagan years threatened the possibility of American naval and air attacks on Vladivostok in the event of a Soviet–American confrontation elsewhere (perhaps the Persian Gulf) under the rubric of *horizontal escalation*. This strategy's success depends on the use of the Philippine bases to reinforce rapidly US air and naval assets stationed in Japan. The loss of the Philippine facilities could, therefore, undermine the viability of the maritime strategy.[4] At the same time, as long as the Americans maintain bases in the Philippines, Soviet facilities in Vietnam are an important asset, demonstrating to the region that the Americans are not the only great power able to sustain a permanent air and naval presence.

During the Brezhnev era, however, the Soviet bases in Vietnam were directed as much at China as at the United States. Indeed, the Soviet relationship with Vietnam served two ends: to surround and pressure China toward greater accommodation in Sino–Soviet relations and to force the United States to maintain a portion of its Pacific air and naval forces in Southeast Asia near Cam Ranh Bay and therefore, away from the North Pacific where they could be a direct threat to Vladivostok, home of the Soviet Pacific Fleet.

The first Reagan legacy (1981–5)

During the first Reagan administration, the United States tilted heavily toward China in its Southeast Asia strategy, moving to create a broad united front against the USSR consisting of the United States, the PRC, Japan, and the ASEAN states. This effort reinforced Soviet beliefs that Washington and Moscow were engaged in a zero-sum conflict in the region. Each superpower's efforts to obtain an ally or client would require exclusive claims on that partner's loyalty. This US policy was not entirely successful, however. Although suspicion about Moscow's intentions toward Southeast Asia pervaded ASEAN, deliberations – particularly because Soviet economic and military aid constituted the *sine qua non* for Vietnam's occupation of Cambodia – the Association was divided over the wisdom of involving China in the region's strategic concerns. American attempts to convince the ASEAN states to cooperate with Chinese efforts to isolate both Vietnam and the Soviet Union were interpreted by Indonesia and Malaysia particularly as misguided and, worse, in violation of ASEAN's long-term hopes to deny outside powers significant roles in regional security arrangements. Thus, the Soviet Union (and Vietnam) could exploit these ASEAN divisions to argue the advantages of a Soviet regional presence for offsetting future Chinese action aimed at Southeast Asia.

The United States has also been uneasy over ASEAN's Zone of Peace, Freedom, and Neutrality (ZOPFAN) proposal. Originally tabled in 1971, ZOPFAN served several purposes for the young ASEAN:

(a) to eliminate great power rivalry from Southeast Asia;
(b) to rationalize the containment of Soviet and Chinese influence in the region in anticipation of US withdrawal;
(c) to provide a leadership role for Indonesia whose prominence within the non-aligned movement was transferred to Southeast Asia's regional order via ZOPFAN.

Although Washington has never endorsed ZOPFAN and has privately expressed its disagreement over the provision that all foreign bases in Southeast Asia are temporary and must be eliminated, ASEAN members have reassured US officials that American military forces remain welcome in the region. In sum, there has been a disjunction between ASEAN declaratory long-term policy – the elimination of foreign bases and armed forces – and current practical security needs centered on the maintenance of US forces to balance those of the Soviet Union, Vietnam, and possibly China. As long as ZOPFAN remained a rhetorical device, the United States could ignore its long-term implications for the Philippine bases and Southeast Asia's future role in providing a strategic location for US force projection both west to the Indian Ocean and north to the Sea of Japan.

THE NEW SOUTHEAST ASIA: GORBACHEV, REAGAN II, AND THE BUSH ADMINISTRATION

The ascendency of General Secretary Mikhail Gorbachev brought a change in Soviet global diplomacy which, in due course, affected Southeast Asia as well. Concerned primarily with revitalizing the Soviet economy through the reduction of defense costs and *détente* with the United States and its allies, the Soviet leader has concentrated – since his 1986 Vladivostok address – on creating new political and economic ties to the ASEAN states. He has encouraged neutralist and anti-nuclear sentiment throughout Southeast Asia in order to constrain US military access, while still maintaining the Soviet–Vietnam alliance. The Soviet leadership believes that a foreign policy which reduces ASEAN's perception of the USSR as a military threat and substitutes an image of the Soviet Union as an economic partner will gradually erode the US anti-Soviet coalition in the region. As the new Soviet General Secretary formulated an Asian strategy, the stalemate in Indochina began to resolve, ASEAN's ZOPFAN formula was revived, and the future of foreign bases in the region was called into question for the first time as a near-term issue. New rules for the Soviet–American relationship in Southeast Asia required formulation.

Three new axioms in Gorbachev's security thinking appear applicable to Southeast Asia: (a) security must be mutual – one country's security cannot be enhanced at the expense of other states' security; (b) reasonable sufficiency should be the combat basis for Soviet armed forces; and (c) Soviet strategy should be based on defensive not offensive capabilities.[5] The emphasis on stability provides doctrinal support for politico-diplomatic efforts to reduce regional tension.

Yet, there are risks for the USSR as well. Soviet relations with its important ally, Vietnam, may be jeopardized as Moscow pressures Hanoi to subordinate its security goals in Indochina for broader Soviet objectives in the region as a whole. One interpretation of the doubling of Soviet aid to Vietnam to $2 billion annually for the 1986–90 Five Year Plan is that this so increases Hanoi's dependency that it has no choice but to support Moscow's policy for a negotiated Vietnamese withdrawal from Cambodia.[6] If the Soviets can facilitate a resolution to the Cambodian conflict, prospects for a new relationship with ASEAN are bright. Not only is the Association Southeast Asia's economic dynamo, but a new Soviet connection with it could encourage trends toward multipolarity, weakening US linkages. Gorbachev hopes to change ASEAN's view of the Soviet Union from that of mentor to the region's most disruptive power to one of conciliator of the region's two opposing blocs.

Thus, at the December 1986 Vietnam Communist Party Congress, Soviet delegates urged Vietnam to settle its dispute with China by agreeing to a role for the Cambodian resistance in that country's future government. A month later in Thailand, the Soviet ambassador signaled a major shift in position by stating that a coalition of *all* warring factions in the conflict would be acceptable. And, in March 1987, Gorbachev told the visiting Vietnamese party chief, Nguyen Van Linh, that even the Chinese-backed Khmer Rouge should be included in a peaceful Cambodian settlement. In May 1989, Vietnam promised a complete withdrawal of its forces from Cambodia by the end of September even if a negotiated settlement had not been reached. By mid-1988, the PRC had also moved toward a compromise position as relations with the Soviets warmed. China assured ASEAN that it would not support a return to power by the Khmer Rouge as long as the Cambodian communist faction was kept within the Resistance Coalition.[7]

The main sticking point to complete diplomatic resolution of the Cambodia situation centers on whether the Vietnam-backed Phnom Penh government should remain in control of the country during a transition period. Vietnam and the USSR have not accepted the ASEAN–China demand that the Heng Samrin regime be replaced by an interim coalition of all parties. Rather, Hanoi insists – and the Soviets concur – that the PRK should continue to run the country and administer elections to determine Cambodia's future. In this way, Vietnam believes it can maximize its client's prospects of remaining in control of the country while eliminating the China–ASEAN backed insurgency.[8] (These Vietnamese calculations may be over-optimistic since intelligence estimates indicate that the Khmer Rouge have stocked some two years' worth of war material in Cambodia in the event of an aid cutoff.)[9]

The United States was essentially a bystander as these developments unfolded. Publicly backing the ASEAN position over the past decade, Washington, nevertheless, has been neither a source of major financial support for the Resistance nor an important participant in negotiations to end the Vietnamese occupation. Until 1989 Washington had been content to see the Vietnamese 'bleed' politically and economically because of their Cambodian intervention. The United States did participate, however, with the Soviet Union and others in the Paris conference of that summer convened to prepare the way for a Cambodian successor regime. Prior to the conference, in a diplomatic shift which moved Washington closer to the Soviet–

Vietnamese position (and away from China), the United States declared that it opposed any Khmer Rouge role in a Cambodian coalition government after the Vietnamese military withdrawal. The United States also implicitly accepted the Soviet–Vietnam condition that the Hanoi-Backed Hun Sen government in Phnom Penh would be a component of the successor regime. Moreover, if victorious through a UN-supervised election, the Hun Sen administration might even dominate the coalition. Washington continued to back ASEAN's insistence on a UN-supervised Vietnamese withdrawal and free elections in Cambodia; the US also warned that its support for any successor regime would be inversely related to the strength of the Khmer Rouge within it.[10] The Americans and the Soviets had developed parallel policies on Cambodia's future, both supporting the idea of a communist/non-communist coalition obtained through internationally supervised elections after a Vietnamese troop withdrawal. Only China insisted on a Khmer Rouge role because, as Prince Norodom Sihanouk declared, denied a share of political power, the Khmer Rouge would certainly continue their civil war against any new regime.

There is little doubt that the Soviets would prefer to reduce the economic burden of their Vietnam alliance. Hanoi fears that Soviet largesse will be reduced when the next Five Year Plan begins in 1990. Both Soviet and Vietnamese officials openly complain about the economic policies of the other. The Russians bemoan the fact that many of the projects they have built in Vietnam since 1978 stand idle or operate at less than 50 per cent capacity, while Hanoi complains that the Soviets overcharge for outmoded technology and pay less than world market value for Vietnam's products. The Soviet riposte has been that Vietnam's exports are substandard and could not be sold on the world market anyway.[11]

Noteworthy is the new Thai diplomatic stance enunciated in 1988 by Prime Minister Chatchai Chunhavan. Foreseeing a Vietnamese withdrawal from Cambodia, Thai officials are investigating prospects for economic cooperation with the Indochinese states in fisheries, timber, gem production, tourism, and labor-intensive joint ventures with minimal technological requirements. Looking ahead, Bangkok foresees a new decade in which the burgeoning Thai economy can serve to dominate Indochinese developments as Vietnam strikes out on a new path of economic construction. (The implications of these changes are discussed in the concluding section of this chapter.)

In the last half of the 1980s, the Soviets approached ASEAN in hopes of expanding political and economic relations beyond the Russian position in Indochina. Aware that its strategic position in Vietnam was purchased at the cost of political influence in the rest of the region, General Secretary Gorbachev launched a diplomatic campaign in 1986 to court ASEAN members. The Russians requested 'dialogue partner' status with ASEAN – the first and only communist state to do so. However, ASEAN's disinterest highlighted the disparity between the Soviets' military presence in Southeast Asia and their minimal economic importance – Soviet trade with ASEAN being about four per cent of the Association's trade with the United States.[12]

In the last half of the 1980s, the Soviets worked hard to overcome these deficits. In his July 1986 Vladivostock speech, Gorbachev repudiated earlier Soviet charges that ASEAN was merely a reincarnation of SEATO and declared that 'there is much of positive value in the activity of ASEAN and in bilateral contacts.' Following its political gesture, Moscow has proposed ship repair contracts to Singapore and the Philippines, the purchase of Thai rice after the United States had failed to honor its commitment not to flood the world market with US exports, and expanded trade with Malaysia, Indonesia, and the Philippines. COMECON has also urged ASEAN to develop institutional ties with Eastern Europe.[13] The Soviets have additionally offered to build a coal-fired power plant in the Philippines and even participate in Manila's long-term development plans as a supplement and/or alternative to the Japan–US–EEC 'mini-Marshall Plan'.

Neither the United States nor the ASEAN countries have reacted with any particular enthusiasm or concern to these overtures. Washington does not see the Soviet Union as an economic rival. The ruble is not a convertible currency, and both the quality and follow-up service arrangements for Soviet products are well below world-market standards. Moreover, the ASEAN states are interested primarily in hard currency transactions rather than countertrade.

Along the military dimension, the United States has a long tradition of arms sales, training, and joint exercises with ASEAN members.[14] In the late 1980s, the United States established a joint weapons stockpile with Thailand, the first such US arrangement in Southeast Asia, as a guarantee of rapid supply in the event of future Vietnamese incursions over the Thai border. Annual American joint exercises with Thailand – *Cobra Gold* – in recent years have been designed to repel invaders from the northeast. The United States has also welcomed PRC arms sales at giveaway prices to Thailand. In effect, Washington is supplying high-tech capital-intensive systems such as M-48 tanks and F-16 aircraft, while Beijing is providing lighter, more easily maintainable hardware including armored personnel carriers, light tanks, artillery, and even Chinese frigates and F7 aircraft, the latter to serve as a ground-support fighter. (Since the F7 is comparable to the MiG 21, the Thai air force increases its superiority over its Indochinese neighbors whose air forces are equipped predominantly with MiG 19s.)

The United States is confident that its political and economic position among the ASEAN states will not be challenged by the USSR and that an increase in Soviet economic activity in the region can only add to Southeast Asian stability. Similarly, Soviet officials seem to acknowledge their country's limited influence in Southeast Asia. The Soviet ambassador to the Philippines, Oleg Sokolov, summed up his government's position *vis-à-vis* the United States:

> I think that one essential point insofar as we are not out to push somebody out of the Philippines or from the region or from the traditional kinds of links that [were] quite well establishe 1 for generations. We realize that we are sort of Johnny-come-laᵗ ly in this region and have a lot of things to do to catch up.[15]

The Soviets realize, then, that their future in Southeast Asia after the Indochina–ASEAN relationship is resolved in the early 1990s depends on what they can offer the region as a trade and investment partner – an area in which the USSR is very much a neophyte.

Although the Soviets will remain a minor player in Southeast Asia's economic future, they have offered ASEAN support for the Association's future plans to create a Zone of Peace, Freedom, and Neutrality (ZOPFAN), a concept viewed by the United States as an obstacle to the maintenance of its air and naval presence in the Pacific. The USSR will, therefore, continue to be a major player in political-security affairs. Its influence will be based both on its security relationship with Vietnam and derivative naval and air facilities at Cam Ranh as well as its vocal support for ZOPFAN. While ZOPFAN's realization could ultimately lead to a Soviet exit from the Vietnamese bases, the concept would also require that the Americans close down their much more important facilities at Clark and Subic in the Philippines.

Unlike the Soviet Union, 90 per cent of whose Pacific Fleet remains within 200 miles of Vladivostok, large elements of the US

Seventh Fleet – including carrier battle groups – reguarly ply Southeast Asian waters. These ships carry such nuclear-capable weapons as the Tomahawk cruise missile. Washington justifies its policy of neither confirming nor denying the presence of nuclear weapons on its ships and aircraft in order to complicate Soviet targeting. The US also argues that its forward deployment strategy requires strategic mobility to move its forces throughout the world's oceans. Any efforts to limit those deployments, such as ASEAN's ZOPFAN, presents a direct challenge to American naval strategy.

From an American viewpoint, ZOPFAN took on a particularly worrisome cast at the December 1987 ASEAN Manila summit. Deferring to Indonesia's desire to reassert leadership in the Association's security matters after having backed Thailand for over a decade, ASEAN heads of state agreed to a plan for the creation of a nuclear weapons free zone (NWFZ) for Southeast Asia. The NWFZ would become a first step toward the achievement of ZOPFAN. Washington's fear of the proliferation of such zones had earlier led to its strong opposition to the Treaty of Rarotonga for the South Pacific and its subsequent abrogation of ANZUS ties with New Zealand. By contrast, the USSR signed the Treaty of Rarotonga and endorsed ASEAN's NWFZ. Going further, the Soviets have stated they are prepared to announce the presence or absence of nuclear weapons on their warships entering the ports of other countries.[16]

Washington's adamant opposition to NWFZ emanates from its 1980s naval arms policy. The Reagan administration decided to deploy missile systems such as the Tomahawk, which is dual-capable, on all US surface combatants. Strict adherence to a NWFZ would either prohibit US naval bases and port calls in Southeast Asia for these ships or require the US navy either to remove the dual-capable systems or open them to international inspection. This latter possibility has been suggested by the USSR, but the American navy's traditional secrecy has obstructed even an exploratory response to the Soviet proposal at the time this chapter was written (late 1989).

Although ASEAN has declared its hopes for the creation of a NWFZ, it is also clear that its members do not want to see an abrupt American air and naval exit from the region. Nevertheless, the US refusal to consider any of Gorbachev's arms control initiatives for the Pacific places Washington on the political defensive. A case can be made that the United States could adhere to an arms control arrangement such as the Treaty of Rarotonga without jeopardizing its NCND policy. The Treaty forbids the stationing of nuclear weapons in the territories of the signatories but does not interfere with ship visits or unhampered access to their ports and airfields. Thus, under the Treaty of Rarotonga, US port calls need not differ from its current access procedure in Japanese ports under Tokyo's three non-nuclear principles.

The nuclear weapons issue is important for the future of the Philippine and Vietnam bases in Southeast Asia. The new Philippine constitution, ratified in 1987, contains two provisions which impinge on the future of the bases. The first prohibits the deployment of nuclear weapons on Philippine territory 'consistent with the national interest'. The second requires a new treaty to be negotiated for the future of the bases after 1991 which must be ratified by two-thirds of the Philippine Senate, a body half of whose members in 1988 indicated that they are opposed to a continuation of the bases arrangement. Some Philippine leaders, including Foreign Minister Raul Manglapus, have stated that if the rest of ASEAN wishes to see US forces remain in Southeast Asia, then they should share the burdens of hosting them. (Interestingly, in 1989, Singapore offered to provide some limited facilities for US air and naval forces. Moscow's reaction was predictably negative.)

Although the United States is investigating alternatives to the Philippine bases which include other Southeast Asian locations (Singapore, Thailand), Australia, Japan, and the mid-Pacific (Guam and the Marianas), US planners agree that there would be no single substitute for the Philippines given America's forward deployment maritime strategy. Although in peacetime, the bases would not be essential to maintain US patrols in Southeast Asia, in a conflict with the USSR, they would play a key role in keeping the sea lanes open and reinforcing US positions to the north and west.

ASEAN's primary concern about the closure of US facilities in Southeast Asia is that a regional imbalance could occur to the immediate political advantage of the Soviet Union and Vietnam.[17] A secondary apprehension foresees both China and Japan gradually moving their forces into the region – countries whose intentions are less trusted than those of the United States. Finally, there are fears that the termination of Philippine base facilities would discourage foreign investment from the United States, Japan, Taiwan and the EEC. Political risks in the region would increase. In the Philippine case, capital flight could occur, just as Manila had begun to attract new domestic and foreign investment.

Despite these reasons for maintaining the status quo with respect to the Philippine bases, there are formidable forces for change. The tide of Philippine nationalism will not be stemmed. Signs already exist that the Philippine Senate may attach conditions to a new treaty which would make a continued American presence impossible. In 1988, the Senate passed a bill that would bar nuclear-armed ships and aircraft from the Philippines. US Secretary of State George Shultz responded that if such a bill became law, 'then we have to part company.' In effect, there would be no future for US forces in the Philippines.

There is little official Filipino sentiment for an abrupt termination of the bases. The economic upheaval of a sudden withdrawal would be enormous, particularly since 78,000 Filipinos are directly employed at Clark and Subic. Philippine officials are beginning to speak of a gradual phase-out of the bases by the end of the century as the country's economic situation improves and regional security arrangements evolve.[18]

Soviet facilities at Cam Ranh Bay are less important for Moscow's Pacific strategy than are the Philippine bases for the United States. Moscow can use its Southeast Asia bases, therefore, for political and diplomatic bargaining more than the Americans. Indeed, a major Soviet goal for the Asian Pacific appears to be to reduce the perception of Soviet threat sufficiently to undermine the United States' military position in the region.

Soviet naval and air forces at Cam Ranh Bay have not increased since the mid-1980s. Official US sources put them at 20–25 warships; three to five submarines; 14 MiG-23s; 16 TU-16 Badgers; two TU-142 anti-submarine aircraft; and 400 Soviet marines. There are seven piers plus facilities for petroleum, ammunition, and communications. In sum, an important peacetime facility which permits the Soviet Pacific Fleet to double its time in the South China Sea/Indian Ocean region compared to deploying the ships from Vladivostok.

Under Gorbachev's direction, Soviet diplomacy on the bases issue has been subtle. Foreign Minister Eduard Shevardnadze has assured Manila that the USSR has no intention of interfering in Philippine–US negotiations over the future of the American bases. In a December 1988 joint communiqué, the Philippines and the Soviet Union proposed the gradual phase-out of both superpowers' bases from the region as tension abated.[19] Moscow has even acknowledged that the Vietnamese are exploring alternative uses for Cam Ranh Bay, opening up the port to vessels from other countries.[20] In December 1989 the Soviets unilaterally withdrew most of their combat aircraft from the base.

Vietnam's growing concerns about Soviet reliability were probably

exacerbated by Moscow's refusal to back Vietnamese claims to the
Spratly Islands and the fact that the USSR did nothing special either
to support or rapidly resupply the Vietnamese navy after its March
1988 clash with Chinese forces in the South China Sea in the Spratlys
chain. Soviet unwillingness to become involved in the PRC–Vietnam
Spratly conflict sharply contrasts with its behavior after the February–
March 1979 Chinese invasion of northern Vietnam. At that time,
Soviet intelligence kept Hanoi informed of China's military plans,
and Soviet supplies were rushed to both the Vietnamese military and
civilian sectors. The more recent Spratly clashes demonstrate the
limits of the Soviet role as guarantor and can only encourage Vietnam
to make its peace with China and ASEAN over Southeast Asia's
future. Reduced dependence on the USSR may also motivate Hanoi
to look toward US diplomatic ties as a way of expanding its political
and economic options.

PROSPECTS FOR SUPERPOWER COOPERATION

Until the Gorbachev era, superpower cooperation in Southeast Asia
was inhibited by the spillover of global competition in three Indochina Wars, a strong non-aligned orientation by two important regional
actors (Indonesia and Malaysia), and the polarization of other major
players with Thailand, Singapore and the Philippines either formally
or informally linked to the United States and the Indochinese states
tied to the Soviet Union. In the 40 years after World War II, then,
superpower relations in Southeast Asia were essentially zero-sum.
Each side vied for the allegiance of the region's members through
competitive security arrangements. In the case of Indochina, one
superpower – the United States – fought a major war in a futile effort
to prevent a shift in allegiance.

The military victory of Vietnamese communist forces and their
then Khmer Rouge allies in the mid-1970s proved somewhat pyrrhic
for the USSR, however. Instead of precipitating a shift in regional
political orientations to accommodate Moscow, the ASEAN states
pulled together against Soviet-backed Vietnamese efforts to consolidate Hanoi's military dominance in Indochina. ASEAN encouraged
the maintenance of US air and naval forces in the region while
simultaneously insisting that Southeast Asia's long-term goal would
be the exclusion of all external military forces. In so far as Vietnam
hopes to become a participant in this ASEAN vision, Hanoi, too,

must plan for a reduction of the Soviet Military presence.

At the beginning of the 1990s, then, political power in Southeast Asia has become essentially decentralized as alliance arrangements forged between the 1950s and 1970s weaken. Neither superpower can dominate its allies. Interestingly, this situation may actually facilitate superpower cooperation. On the other hand, this low tension level probably inhibits bold initiatives toward conflict reduction. Since the future of Indochina and the Philippine and Vietnam bases as well as ASEAN's orientation toward the superpowers all appear to emerge from local dynamics, there is little incentive for the superpowers to take the lead in bringing these issues to closure.

Soviet diplomacy under Gorbachev has been more active than its American counterpart. Seeking to ease Asian apprehensions about Soviet intentions, Soviet officials pressed Vietnam to withdraw from Cambodia, offered to trade away naval facilities in Vietnam for those in the Philippines, and proposed new economic and political relations with ASEAN. These policies are designed to make the USSR an acceptable participant in Southeast Asia's future. If successful, they will provide a Southeast Asia framework for the Soviet view of *comprehensive security* throughout the Asian Pacific rim. By agreeing to limit Soviet naval force deployments in the region, for example, Moscow establishes its bona fides as an honest broker and participant in Asia's 'web of interdependence'.[21]

Some Soviet proposals are clearly mischievous, designed to weaken the American position. Support for Southeast Asian and South Pacific nuclear weapons free zones fall into this category. However, Soviet rhetoric should not be construed as a serious problem by Washington. ASEAN leaders are well aware of the fact that the US navy is a nuclear navy; and they are prepared to accept the Seventh Fleet's ships and aircraft throughout the region regardless of declarations such as ZOPFAN and SEANWFZ. In sum, Gorbachev's denial strategy toward US deployments in Southeast Asia will probably not succeed.

As Edward Kolodziej suggests, a Soviet Thermidor presents the United States with a more serious challenge for it puts the USSR in the forefront of seeking arms reductions in various world regions.[22] The United States will have to respond to these prospects or risk being out of step where regional trends point to tension reduction. Moreover, American participation in the search for regional compromises is good policy. It contributes to such longer-range US goals as continued access to important states containing both economic and military resources and to insuring that an anti-Western grouping does not form. Both superpowers are developing a different mix of bilateral relations for developing world regions defined by the mutual interests of the regional state and the superpower. Neither Washington nor Moscow need view these developments as threatening. But, unless Washington is prepared to respond with its own program when the Soviets offer concessions in Southeast Asia, it risks being seen as obstructionist.

The United States could begin by taking up the Soviet call for confidence-building measures in the Pacific. In Southeast Asia, the superpowers could notify each other of naval maneuvers, cease encroaching on the other's air identification zones over the Philippines and Vietnam, and develop measures to prevent incidents on the open seas and the airspace above them. The superpowers might even consider cooperation in keeping the SLOCs open to peaceful international commerce. (There is a danger inherent in this cooperation, however. If it appears too successful, regional states might fear the establishment of a superpower condominium!)

THE BASES ISSUE

Are the Southeast Asian bases a source of conflict, or do they contribute to regional stability? The answer appears to be both. For ASEAN, the US bases assure security against external threats. For Vietnam, the Soviet bases protect against China and serve to tie Moscow's security interests to the Vietnamese economy via military and economic assistance. For both the Philippines and Vietnam, however, the bases also bruise nationalist sensibilities and serve as a constant reminder of their countries' weakness and vulnerability.

A major obstacle to a tradeoff between the bases is their asymmetrical importance. For Washington, Subic Bay constitutes the largest multi-purpose naval base outside the continental United States. It can service and repair virtually any ship in the Navy's inventory. From Subic and Clark, ships and aircraft can rapidly deploy north of the Sea of Japan and west into the South China Sea and Indian Ocean toward the US base at Diego Garcia. Maintenance of the Philippine bases guarantees a continuous US presence in the Southwest Pacific. By contrast, the Soviet facilities in Vietnam are used primarily for bunkering and supplying a detached task force from the Pacific Fleet, 80 per cent of which remains in the Sea of Okhotsk and northern Sea of Japan. In a crisis, Soviet ships and planes in Vietnam would be cut off from the protection of their home bases.

The US presence in the Philippines symbolizes Washington's commitment to the region and helps to guarantee that a sufficient balance of naval and air forces will be present to offset the Soviet Pacific Fleet. An even trade of the facilities would be perceived as an American abandonment of Southeast Asia unless it was accompanied by a naval arms limitation agreement covering *both* Northeast and Southeast Asia. This agreement would have to reduce significantly the number of Soviet surface combatants and submarines in exchange, perhaps, for a modification of the US maritime strategy of forward deployment. However, even if the United States and the Soviet Union reached such an agreement, it may not be seen as desirable to Southeast Asians for it could open the region to Chinese, Japanese, and possibly Indian naval deployments.

Rather than an abrupt termination of either the Soviet and American facilities which would call into question the reliability of both superpowers, create a naval vacuum, and probably lead to a reduction of foreign investment in the Philippines, a mutual phase-out of forces from both countries, providing time for the build-up of local forces to supplement a reduced superpower presence may yield the most stable outcome. Washington could turn Clark Field over to the Philippines while maintaining Subic Bay over a 10–15 year period. The United States could also encourage an opening of the bases to ASEAN forces in addition to those of the USA. Such a development would have the combined effects of mitigating the allegation of exclusive American control and also helping to train friendly naval and air forces to undertake their own regional security responsibilities. Indeed, over the long term, the dispersal of aircraft and ship repair facilities to other Pacific locations could be an asset to US forces. Dependence on any single nation and its particular political concerns would diminish.

The two most troubling outcomes would be unilateral closures of the bases in either Vietnam or the Philippines. If the Philippine Senate refused to ratify a new treaty, an abrupt termination of US deployments would enhance the Soviet position in Southeast Asia and probably reduce foreign investor confidence, at least in the Philippines. It could also accelerate Chinese plans to develop a Southeast Asian naval presence. If the Soviets left Cam Ranh Bay precipitously, nationalist pressures in the Philippines and some ASEAN sentiment for an early realization of ZOPFAN could also increase pressures on the Americans to leave as well.

Complicating these calculations was a tentative offer by Singapore in August 1989 to host some of the US forces currently in the Philippines.[23] Arguing that the US military presence in Southeast Asia has both permitted the ASEAN states to concentrate on commercial activities and also protected trade routes, Singapore hoped that its proposal would smooth the way politically for the Philippines to renew its bases arrangement with the United States after the current agreement expires in 1991. In effect, Singapore was offering to share the burden of the bases so that the Philippines would no longer be the sole ASEAN member with a major foreign military presence.

The Singapore offer has split ASEAN along predictable lines: Thailand has welcomed it, but Malaysia openly opposed it and Indonesia indirectly expressed disagreement. The Philippines maintained an official silence. For Kuala Lumpur and Jakarta, the prospect of new American facilities in Singapore contradicts plans for both ZOPFAN and SEANWFZ. For Indonesia, particularly, Singapore's gambit would appear to postpone Jakarta's hopes to emerge as the dominant actor in regional security affairs. Jakarta had even been considering new ASEAN military cooperation presumably after the superpowers left their Southeast Asian bases. Singapore's proposal would nullify that prospect.[24]

INDOCHINA'S FUTURE

Strategically, Soviet and US goals for mainland Southeast Asia should be compatible. Each wishes to ensure its ally (Thailand for the United States and Vietnam for the USSR) is protected against a potential adversarial neighbor (Vietnam for Thailand and China for Vietnam). Each also hopes to participate in the region's economic prosperity. And each would prefer to retain its military facilities. The Soviets desire a successor regime in Cambodia acceptable to both Vietnam and ASEAN so that Moscow can go about the important task of establishing commercial ties with the latter. The United States is prepared to establish diplomatic relations with Vietnam (and perhaps commence limited economic aid) once Vietnamese forces withdrew from Cambodia and an acceptable successor government takes office. The Vietnamese exit has vindicated the isolation policy toward Vietnam followed over the past decade by ASEAN, the West, and China.

At a minimum, Hanoi wants a secure western border, while Bangkok insists on a government in Phnom Penh which will neither threaten Thailand's east nor send new waves of refugees over the Thai frontier. Both of these outcomes require either the suppression of the Khmer Rouge or its subordination within a successor regime composed of the anti-communist elements of the Resistance (the Sihanouk ANS and Son Sann's Kampuchean People's National Liberation Front) plus Hanoi's client in the capital. Supervision and/or subordination of the Khmer Rouge requires, in turn, China's agreement to halt its military aid to Pol Pot's army.

With Vietnam's October 1989 withdrawal, the United States and ASEAN have pressed for a reconciliation government under Prince Sihanouk. This government would provide a role for the current Phnom Penh regime within a pluralistic environment which would allow the non-communists to survive and prosper. These developments would also be favorable for the USSR. They would help to cement Sino–Soviet relations, improve Soviet ties with ASEAN, and buttress Gorbachev's overall claim that the Soviet Union is de-emphasizing the role of military force as a foreign policy instrument. A Vietnamese exit from Cambodia would also reduce the Soviet annual aid bill of $2 to $3 billion.

Despite Soviet and American interest in peaceful change for Cambodia, the Vietnamese exit has led to renewed civil war between a Vietnam-supplied Hun Sen military which will control eastern Cambodia and the major population centers and the Khmer Rouge which have stockpiled arms in the west for up to two years of renewed hostilities. Chinese analysts told the author in the summer and fall of 1988 that unless the Khmer Rouge were provided with a significant role in a successor regime, they would fight to create an area under Khmer Rouge control from which to overthrow whichever government emerged in Phnom Penh. If this scenario develops and a Hanoi client-dominated successor regime army contains the Khmer Rouge, then the long-term prospect for Cambodia is one of a Vietnamese-dominated regime led nominally by Prince Sihanouk. This administration could well prevail over the Khmer Rouge if it was supplied by the West and ASEAN, Thailand closed Khmer Rouge supply routes, and Khmer Rouge popularity eroded with the Vietnamese exit from Cambodia.

If China agrees to stop backing the Khmer Rouge, perhaps after some kind of electoral exercise demonstrates its lack of popular support, then prospects are open for the Cambodian successor government along with Laos and Vietnam to affiliate with ASEAN. (The stalemated summer 1989 Paris conference on Cambodia's future called for internationally supervised elections to determine a new government within three months after a Vietnamese withdrawal. Both the Soviet Union and the United States supported the proposal, though many observers were skeptical whether such an election could be held if the Khmer Rouge continued to fight.) Initially the Indochinese states could adhere to the 1976 Southeast Asia Treaty of Amity and Cooperation. This could form the basis for new commercial and investment ties between ASEAN and Indochina as well as signaling the political acceptability of Western aid and investment for Indochina.

American aid to Vietnam might further be proffered on condition that Hanoi reduce the size of its military and locates it in a defensive posture away from the Cambodian frontier. The Soviets, in turn, could agree to limit the level of new military technology given to the Vietnam army, by not going beyond the currently supplied MiG-23s and *Petya II*-class frigates. A big factor for the success of this scenario is, of course, its acceptability to China. Beijing's interest in a long-term relationship with ASEAN, including Thailand, and the PRC's own desire for a tranquil international environment suggest that it may be willing to sacrifice the Khmer Rouge after some face-saving exercise in Cambodian self-determination.

Finally, both the United States and the Soviet Union could benefit from a more encompassing regionalism, incorporating Indochina into an expanded Southeast Asian order. If successful, this could reduce Vietnam's dependence on the USSR and serve to balance China's growing regional presence. An Indochinese linkage to ASEAN would also encourage foreign investment for the former and accelerate its integration into the world market economy. Thailand already foresees its future role to be a bridge for private trade and investment to its long-term adversary.

The 1990s portend Asian tension reduction ranging from Sino–Soviet relations to Sino–Indian affairs. Southeast Asia's contribution depends on transcending the ASEAN–Indochina conflict through the creation of a new Cambodian reconciliation government. Soviet and American efforts to support a regime acceptable to the rival Cambodian factions could create the groundwork for a more peaceful regional order, encompassing virtually all of Southeast Asia for the first time in history.

NOTES

1. For an elaboration of US security interests in Southeast Asia, see Sheldon W. Simon, 'Explaining US Security Interests in Southeast Asia', in T. B. Millar (ed.), *Southeast Asia and the Southwest Pacific* (St Lucia: University of Queensland Press, 1983).
2. Burma does not fit this division, preferring to remain a non-participant in any international group as the best way of ensuring its security.
3. Soviet security interests in Southeast Asia are discussed by Sheldon W. Simon, 'The Soviet Union and Southeast Asia: The Vietnam Connection', in Edward Kolodziej and Roger Kanet (eds), *The Limits of Soviet Power in the Developing World* (London: Macmillan, 1989), pp. 149–70.
4. For an Asia-wide discussion of the US maritime strategy, see Sheldon W. Simon, 'Pacific Rim Reactions to US Military Strategy', in Young Whan Kihl and Lawrence E. Grinter, (eds), *Security, Strategy, and Policy Responses in the Pacific Rim* (Boulder, CO: Lynne Rienner Publishers, 1989), pp. 81–101.
5. These are elaborated in Stephen M. Meyer, 'The Source and Prospects of Gorbachev's New Political Thinking on Security', *International Security*, vol. 13, no. 2 (Fall 1988), pp. 134 ff. Also see Robert A. Manning, 'Moscow's Pacific Future', *World Policy Journal*, vol. 5, no. 1 (Winter 1987–88).
6. Hiroshi Kimura, 'Gorbachev's Agenda For Asia', *The Pacific Review*, vol. 1, no. 3 (1988), p. 220.
7. These developments are traced in Chang Pao-min, 'Kampuchean Conflict: The Diplomatic Breakthrough', *The Pacific Review*, vol. 1, no. 4 (1988), pp. 430–1, 435.
8. In September 1990, the UN Security Council and the ASEAN states agreed to a new plan which would provide roles for the Phnom Penh government and the Resistance in a Supreme National Council. This Council would operate under United Nations auspices during an interim period of perhaps two years while the antagonists were disarmed and Cambodia-wide elections held to establish a new non-aligned government.
9. Sukhumbhand Paribatra, 'The Road to Peace in Cambodia', *Far Eastern Economic Review*, 2 February 1989, p. 24.
10. The shift in US diplomacy toward the Soviet–Vietnamese of a Cambodian successor regime may be found in Vice President J. Danforth Quayle's address to the Heritage Foundation, *For the US Continued Commitment to Asia* (Washington: The Heritage Foundation, 22 June 1989). See also Robert Pear, 'Now the US looks at Cambodia Differently', *New York Times*, 16 July 1989.
11. *Far Eastern Economic Review*, 10 Novermber 1988, p. 23.

12. Robyn Lim, 'Implications for Southeast Asia', in Ramesh Thakur and Carlyle Thayer (eds), *The Soviet Union as an Asian Pacific Power* (Boulder, CO: Westview Press, 1987), p. 82.

13. Bilveer Singh, 'Gorbachev and a "Pacific Community"', *The Pacific Review*, vol. 1, no. 3 (1988), p. 231.

14. These are detailed in Sheldon W. Simon, *The ASEAN States and Regional Security* (Stanford: The Hoover Institution Press, 1982).

15. Interview with the Soviet ambassador as telecast by Quezon City People's Television 4, 26 January 1989, in FBIS, *Daily Report, East Asia*, 31 January 1989, p. 53.

16. *Merkeka* (Jakarta) 21 July 1988, in FBIS, *Daily Report, East Asia*, 4 August 1988, pp. 4–7.

17. Author's discussion with Noordin Soipee and Jusuf Wanandi, directors respectively of the most prominent strategic studies research institutes in Malaysia and Indonesia, at the National Defense University Pacific Security Symposium, Honolulu, 2–3 March 1989.

18. Philippine Defense Secretary Fidel Ramos favors a ten-year phase-out arrangement. See the *Philippine Daily Gobe*, 27 February 1989, in FBIS, *Daily Report, East Asia*, 27 February 1989, p. 55.

19. *Philippine Daily Globe* quoting Shevardnadze, 23 December 1988, in FBIS, *Daily Report, East Asia*, 23 December 1988, p. 40. The joint communiqué was reported by *Agence France Presse* (Hong Kong) in English, 22 December 1988, in FBIS, *Daily Report, East Asia*, 22 December 1988, p. 47.

20. *Izvestiya*, 29 November 1988, in FBIS, *Daily Report, Soviet Union*, 30 November 1988, p. 16.

21. A good discussion of this strategy is found in Elizabeth Wishnick, 'Soviet Asian Collective Security Policy From Brezhnev to Gorbachev', *Journal of Northeast Asian Studies*, vol. 7, no. 3 (Fall 1988), especially pp. 3, 4, 11, 24.

22. Edward Kolodziej, 'Soviet Prospects in the Developing World: Implications for US Policy', in Kolodziej and Kanet (eds), op. cit., p. 441.

23. A good review of the implications of the Singapore offer is found in 'Singapore Offer Complicates Discussion Over Future of US Bases in Philippines', *The Asian Wall Street Journal Weekly*, 14 August 1989, p. 20. Also see *The Straits Times* (Singapore), 11 August 1989.

24. See *The Jakarta Post* editorial, 8 August 1989, in FBIS, *Daily Report, East Asia*, 11 August 1989, p. 35.

14 Superpower Cooperation in Northeast Asia
Samuel S. Kim*

Northeast Asia is at the vortex of the Asia–Pacific Basin where four of the world's five centers of power – the United States, the Soviet Union, China, and Japan – meet and interact. This is the only region in the world where such a mixture of two-power (superpower), three-power (strategic triangle), and four-power games are played out on multiple chessboards with all their complexities and configurations. Like great tectonic plates of the earth's crust, any collision or collusion between and among the Big Four tends to restructure the alignment patterns not only of the region but globally as well. Northeast Asia also seems to be the only region where superpower conflict persists contrary to the more synchronized rhythms and the expanding virtuous circle of Soviet–American *détente* elsewhere.

At the same time, there are certain endemic regional characteristics that could hinder more than help superpower cooperation in the region. The powerful presence of the world's second largest economic power and the largest economic credit power (Japan since 1985) and the world's third largest nuclear power with irredentist claims (China), and the festering fratricidal politics of divided but assertively nationalistic countries (China–Taiwan and North–South Korea), which severely limits the ability of either or both superpowers to shape the strategic and economic structure of the region, creates the necessary, if not sufficient, condition for superpower tacit cooperation to accept and live with less than the ideal situation.

Given its geostrategic and geoeconomic impotance, however, it is hardly surprising that Northeast Asia is fertile soil for great-power rivalry. Historically, too, for almost a century now, the region has remained one of the bloodiest zones of great-power conflict, con-

* I would like to thank Henry Bienen and William Feeney for their valuable comments and suggestions on an earlier version of the chapter. I wish also to acknowledge the support of much of the research and writing of this paper by the Peter B. Lewis Fund of the Center of International Studies, Princeton University.

frontation and war. Northeast Asia still remains the only region in the world where nuclear weapons have been used in war, during the last days of World War II, and their use was threatened repeatedly over the Korean peninsula and the Taiwan Strait.

Studies on the origins of the Cold War have concentrated on the Soviet–American conflict over Europe, the Middle East and the atomic bomb, as if the Cold War in Asia were but a corollary of its lateral escalation from elsewhere or as if it were the later unfortunate but inevitable outcome of the Chinese Civil War. Faced with the imminent fall of the Japanese empire in 1945 and with a clear and present threat of the Soviet Red Army pushing its way into Northeast Asia, American policy-makers had already defined Japan as the linchpin of a postwar *Pax Americana* in the region and had decided that the United States had to play a decisive leadership role in determining the future of Korea, China, and to a lesser degree, Indochina. By the end of 1945, a *de facto* Cold War in Asia had already begun with the United States adopting many of the features that would characterize its Cold War foreign policy: minimizing local causes of the spreading revolutionary struggles in the region; perceiving nearly all leftist revolutions as Soviet-inspired and controlled; dismissing negotiations and compromise as a sign of weakness; and providing military assistance to Nationalist China and South Korea.[1]

Contrary to widely held opinion, the division of Korea at the 38th parallel was neither a secret deal made at wartime conferences nor an inevitable outcome of Cold War rivalry. As early as the autumn of 1943, State Department planners had defined Soviet control of the Korean peninsula as a threat to the security of the postwar Pacific.[2] The Cairo Declaration (December 1943) merely noted that 'in due course Korea shall become free and independent.' The Yalta Agreement makes no reference to Korea, although the Korean question was tangentially discussed. Roosevelt proposed a Soviet–American–Chinese trusteeship of 20 to 30 years; Stalin merely noted that the period of trusteeship should be as short as possible and that the British should be invited to join the trusteeship. Both leaders agreed that foreign troops should not be stationed in Korea.[3]

The seeming confusion and contradiction in US Korean policy in the period 1945–50 is accounted for by its commitment/capability gap. The State Department wished to define Korea as important to US security, but its military planners sensed the limits of American military power and wondered if this peninsula were all that important in the context of global US security concerns. Thus, the origins of the

Korean War can be situated in the five-year period preceding the war, when Korea was dominated by widespread demands for revolutionary change. Pre-emptive American policies had more to do with creating a bulwark against revolution in the South and communism in the North than at checking Soviet expansionism at the 38th parallel.[4] Nonetheless, North Korea's invasion made it possible for the implementation of the NSC-68, including the instant tripling of military spending to $38.5 billion. One Cold War alliance pact after another was established in the Asian–Pacific region (APR). Korea was once again placed – and this time apparently for good – on America's global geopolitical chessboard to be defended at any cost. The image of the enemy – and the Wilsonian Second Image of War – was confirmed on the battlefield of Korea, and the zero-sum of foreign policy thinking – the Cold War syndrome – was legitimized. Above all, the Korean War served to freeze the pattern of Soviet–American conflict in the region into a rigid geopolitical construct, resisting adaptation to the changing geopolitical changes and realignments in the region in the following years.

Today, the dialectics of war and peace – and conflict and cooperation – in Northeast Asia can be examined at two levels of generalization. At the most visible level, at the tip of the iceberg one sees the region emerging in the 1980s as the most dynamic exporting region of the world with seemingly ever-expanding concentric waves of regional economic development: Japan led the way with its first big developmental wave (with a large dosage of neomercantilism), the Asian newly industrialized countries (NICs – South Korea, Taiwan, Hong Kong, and Singapore) initiated a second, and Thailand, Malaysia, Indonesia and China produced a third – a repetitive cycle all within the growing networks of the global political economy.

The bottom line of Gorbachev's Asian–Pacific overtures is 'double integration' of the political economy of the Soviet Far East (SFE), a mixture of national, regional, and international developmental and linkage strategies, calling for greater horizontal integration of the SFE with the center at home and fuller vertical integration into the political economy of the APR. At the deeper level (the iceberg) the two competing Cold War alliance systems have been reduced in size and severity with the collapse of the Sino–Soviet alliance but still persist in Korea and Japan. The APR remained, as of 1987, the region where half of the present world military conflicts persist.[5] Still, the recent Sino–Soviet *détente* has both reflected and effected a gradual reduction of military tensions in the region – indeed, a *de facto* arms control agreement – as well as a marked shift in regional trend from military conflict to economic cooperation.

The United States made its debut as an aspiring hegemon in Northeast Asia at the turn of the century only to downplay its role until severely challenged by Japan toward the end of the interwar period. In the postwar period the United States returned to the region – this time the Cold War with its Soviet and Chinese revisionist challengers turned into a hot war which played a key role in fostering the regional Cold War alliance system. If America won this war, however, it may well have proved to be a pyrrhic victory, for that very success seemed to undermine the economic foundation of American hegemony. The heavy costs of American hegemony throughout the world – disproportionally so in the maintenance of the Cold War system in East Asia – have eroded the economic and ideological foundations of American hegemony in the international system. There is now growing evidence that the United States is already on the downward trajectory in the long cycles of hegemonic rise and fall following the well-trodden path: rising external burdens of leadership (hegemony); internal tendencies toward rising consumption; and the international diffusion of technology.[6]

Ironically, President Reagan's strategy of hegemonic restoration accelerated the world historical process of gradual hegemonic decline that first became visible in the course of America's second costly Asian war in the postwar era. Reagan's instigation of the largest military expansion in American peacetime history simply worked to undercut the economic and technological bases of US hegemony. By 1985, the United States had become a net debtor – and today the world's largest debtor nation – for the first time since 1914 and Japan the world's largest credit power. By the mid-1980s Japan, replacing West Germany as America's principal economic ally, could only mask America's epochal decline and help such a role reversal by subsidizing its hegemony.[7] In the short run, the anomaly is likely to continue because of mutual assured dependency, something akin to what Maoist China had once likened the Trilateralists' concept of 'interdependence' to that between 'a horseman and his mount'.

In short, American Cold War allies in Northeast Asia, especially Japan, whose political economies have experienced spectacular growth due in no small part to American geopolitical payoffs (e.g. a free ride on defense, access to American markets, and preferential treatment in US-dominated major international economic institutions) have become more indispensable than ever in determining the longevity of American hegemony in the world economy and its economic health. Thus, America's plea for burden-sharing has forced Japan to bridge, to a certain extent, the widening gaps between American military commitments and American economic capabilities. In the meantime, the Soviet threat can still function to sustain the present anomalous relationship, whereby the United States maintains its regional military alliance system while Japan underwrites some of the costs.

The Soviet Union emerged from the ashes of World War II a crippled giant, a proud victor only by dint of its enormous human sacrifice in the defeat of Nazi Germany. The Great Patriotic War had destroyed well over a quarter of Russia's national wealth. From Potsdam on, it was open to atomic threat. And it was encountering massive problems of empire building in Eastern Europe. This may explain why Stalin was telling Mao to switch to a coalition government strategy rather than to fight Chiang Kai-shek in the Chinese Civil War. And yet, in a few years Moscow found itself presiding over the vast socialist camp in East Asia, with a Chinese alliance and an ideological commitment against American hegemony. Still, China proved to be an extremely elusive ally which both demanded and resented Soviet aid (including nuclear assistance). As late as 1954, Nikita Khrushchev resisted Chinese pressures for more aid with the plea that the Soviet Union was still 'hungry and poverty-ridden from the war' and that its economy was 'in shambles'.[8]

Revolutionary and nationalist objectives inspired Mao to seek nothing less than the overthrow of the US-dominated East Asian international order. With China thus positioned in opposition to the United States, Moscow could safely view Northeast Asia, at least until the mid-1960s, as a region of secondary importance in its hierarchy of foreign policy priorities. With the progessive deterioration of the Sino–Soviet relationship and escalating border incidents in the mid-1960s, however, Soviet attention began to shift toward the Far East. Much of the Soviet military build-up in the region from 1965 to the mid-1980s occurred in response to the Chinese threat, first as a result of escalating Sino–Soviet tensions in the late 1960s and then to the clear and continuing possibility of an anti-Soviet trilateral Sino–American–Japanese geostrategic coalition in the late 1970s. The latest round of Soviet military build-up (from the late 1970s to the mid-1980s), accompanied by the Soviet invasion of Afghanistan and a new strategy of greater reliance on nuclear submarines in the Sea of Okhotsk, seemed sufficiently menacing for Japan to launch a major military expansion of its naval and air forces to protect its strategic lines of commerce and communication.

Mikhail Gorbachev's Vladivostok Speech of 28 July 1986 represents a turning point. On the one hand, Gorbachev specifically addressed two of China's Three Obstacles and added a teasing bait. In the process, Gorbachev succeeded, to a greater extent than most analysts had anticipated, in bringing about a Chinese reappraisal of Soviet foreign policy. The Soviet Union under the leadership of Gorbachev is seen by the Chinese as having redefined the limits and possibilities of its foreign policy 'with extraordinary accuracy' and as having become 'self-restrained and responsible' in the conduct of foreign policy.[9] The much touted demobilization of one million troops and the relative decline of the defense budget as a percentage of total state budget (from 17.5 per cent in 1979 to 7.49 per cent in 1988) constitute a strategy of making a normative virtue of an economic necessity, to be sure, but such a move would not have been possible without a prior positive reappraisal of the Soviet threat.

On the other hand, Gorbachev's Asian push envisioned the SFE gradually becoming a critical link for not only domestic economic development of the USSR as a whole but also for external integration into the political economy of the APR. The SFE has been redefined as well as an integral component of the 'comprehensive system of global security'. Today, the SFE is said to provide two-thirds of Soviet oil and gas, more than 40 per cent of the coal, 20 per cent of the electrical power, and 37 per cent of commercial timber shipments. The Soviet Union, Gorbachev flatly admitted, 'cannot survive without what Siberia and the Far East provide.'[10] In 1987, the Soviet Union adopted a 'Long-Term State Programme for Complex Development of Productive Forces in the Far Eastern Economic Area, Buryatia and the Chita Region until the Year 2000' followed up by the establishment of the Soviet National Committee for Asia–Pacific Economic Cooperation in 1988. The logic of the SFE's external linkage is based on the Soviet redefinition of the international situation of the APR – that such linkage would 'create prerequisites for our economy's integration into the structure of the rapidly developing Asia–Pacific world, in the direction of which the center of the world economy, and possibly politics, is moving.'[11]

PRINCIPAL FORMS OF SUPERPOWER INTERACTION

Over the years Northeast Asia has become a region of direct interest and vital importance to both superpowers. Despite, or perhaps more precisely because of, the persistence of Soviet–American conflict and alliance relationships accompanied by an arms race and frequent war games and military exercises in the region, Northeast Asia has not played host to international fora allowing discussion of underlying regional issues or encouraging confidence-building measures. Both superpowers either have ignored local and regional issues and conflicts, or have globalized them as part of a zero-sum game. In such an aggregating process, local or regional conflicts take on a transcendental importance, symbolic of the superpowers' abiding concerns regarding leadership, status, prestige, and reputation for meeting alliance commitments. The irony is that the reduction of East–West tensions in Europe, coupled with the move in the center of gravity of the global political economy from the Atlantic to the Asia–Pacific Basin in the late 1970s, has simply shifted the locus of Cold War confrontation from Europe to East Asia.

This is not to say that conflict-management mechanisms are totally absent from superpower behavior in the region. Superpower relations come close to approximating what Charles Lindblom has called 'partisan mutual adjustment'. There are no coordinators, and any coordination obtained is a by-product of decisions 'not specifically intended to coordinate'. The parties in conflict can still coordinate with each other 'without a common purpose and without rules that fully prescribe their relations to each other.'[12] The tacit rules of the superpower game are supposed to provide the informal mechanisms by which conflict can still take place without the coordination of an impartial referee and without leading to the destruction of either competitor or of the arena within which they compete.[13]

In order to discover the tacit rules of the game on this regional chessboard, we have to focus on actual moves each superpower makes toward the other, rather than on the Northeast Asian international system itself. But such an approach is potentially misleading for several reasons. Such tacit rules are not easily ascertained. Neither party can be sure that the other has agreed to follow the rules. Moreover, one is never sure what issue areas have been included or excluded in the game, or how long the game will last. And a special regional geostrategic factor further complicates the progressive development and codification of such tacit rules of cooperation. The most important game in this particular region has not been the bilateral superpower game but rather the three-power strategic triangle with its dominant configuration shifting in response to the changing nature of Sino–Soviet, Sino–American, and Soviet–American relations.

Superpower conflict and cooperation are not mutually exclusive; they are two sides of the same coin. The very existence of superpower conflict demands some degree of cooperation so that the conflict may be controlled. Likewise, every cooperative relationship has an element of conflict lurking in the background. This dialectical relationship between conflict and cooperation produces a continuum of conflict and cooperative behavior, giving rise to the ups and downs of superpower relations. A three-image typology – confrontation, competition, and collaboration – is suggested here as a way of depicting the principal norms of superpower interaction in Northeast Asia in the postwar period.

At one pole of the continuum is the confrontational image. On the American side this is the image of Cold War fundamentalists who define the Soviet threat in terms of the very existence of the Soviet system itself, not what it does abroad. This deterministic image proceeds from the premise that the Soviet Union, being inherently authoritarian, is inherently aggressive both to justify and to ensure the survival of its regime. The very existence of a communist regime poses a clear and continuing danger to the stability of the 'free world'. The fundamentalist strategy is liberationist. Not surprisingly, it acquired its strongest support during the McCarthy and early Reagan eras in the United States. Containment is condemned as both too passive and too immoral. A rollback of the Soviet empire is required.[14] In the current debate (1988–9) about ending the Cold War, fundamentalists, now posing themselves as 'pessimistic skeptics', first dismiss Soviet words ('new thinking') and then discount Soviet unilateral acts as public relations gimmicks in the service of a hegemonic global role, demanding nothing less than a domestic system transformation as a true measure of proof for a revolution in Soviet foreign policy.[15]

The Soviet counterpart of Cold War fundamentalism is based on the Leninist concept of the subordination of the United States to the capitalist monopolies and on the bipolarized view of the world (the rationale articulated by Andrei Zhdanov in 1947). Its strategy is what Franklyn Griffiths calls 'coercive isolationism'. The Soviet Union will isolate itself 'from all but those it was able to subordinate, thereby reproducing an acute Cold War setting conducive to the reimposition of Stalinist totalitarianism within the USSR and Eastern Europe.'[16]

In the middle of the two extreme poles of Cold War liberationists and liberal internationalists is containment realism, supported by large sections of the British foreign policy establishment and such influential realist figures as George F. Kennan and Walter Lippman in the United States. The distance between Cold War fundamentalists and containment realists seems less than that between containment realists and Rooseveltian internationalists. While eschewing liberal internationalism as utopian, the realists rejected frontal military confrontation with and total isolation from the Soviet Union as counterproductive. Such an approach would only reinforce the division of Europe. Containment realism was a compromise position, pleasing neither Right nor Left, but allowing enough room for broad bipartisan foreign policy in the 1950s and early 1960s. True to form, containment realists are more concerned with Soviet behavior than with Soviet ideology. The Soviet threat is perceived as geopolitical rather than ideological. As such, it must be checked with superior American strength. The expansion of American power and influence is the answer.

The Soviet counterpart of containment realism starts from the premise that there is a division within the American monopoly bourgeoisie, giving rise to conflicting tendencies and strategies in their orientation toward the Soviet Union. Such a division allows the Soviet Union an alternative to confrontational global expansion, producing a setting of *détente* and limited cooperation with Washington. Like containment realism, this image too is more geopolitical than ideological; its basic line is the expectation of continuing Soviet–American political and military competition and rivalry in the context of the changing world correlation of forces.[17]

Liberal internationalism has a more benign and ambitious interpretation of Soviet–American relations – a strategy of 'cooperation' to enmesh the Soviet Union in multilateral economic ties that would tame its revolutionary or hegemonic impulses. In the process the Soviet Union would be co-opted into a kind of condominial world order with the United States serving as a *de facto*, if not *de jure*, hegemon in the management of global economic, security, and colonial problems through multilateral institutions including the United Nations. Indeed, this is a strategy of containment by other means – containment idealism as it were. Such a cooperative image of one-worldism died with the passing of President Roosevelt, although some elements of this condominial image of world order were revived by Nixon and Kissinger during the early 1970s only to vanish once again with the collapse of *Détente* II.

Until recently, there seems to be no Soviet counterpart of the liberal cooperative model of one-worldism. With Mikhail Gorbachev's rise to power in 1985 comes a breakaway from traditional Soviet foreign policy thinking. What is distinctive about Gorbachev's push for a new comprehensive global security system – and his Asian–Pacific overtures from Vladivostok in July 1986 to Krasnoyarsk in September 1988 is part and parcel of his vision of one-worldism in a nuclear and ecological age – is that he proceeds from the concepts of global interdependence and common security. In short, Gorbachevism creates new possibilities and opportunities for peace and development in Northeast Asia. Also, the Soviet Union has become a remarkably forthcoming member of the United Nations, breathing a renewed sense of relevance into it.[18]

In practice, Soviet–American relations have always consisted of a mixture of varying properties of confrontation, competition and cooperation. Still, it is analytically useful to examine superpower interaction in the region over time, in different contexts, across different issues, in terms of the three principal norms of foreign policy behavior.

Confrontation

Despite the persistence of Russo–American and Soviet–American conflict since the turn of the century, the two countries have never been at war against each other. Instead, confrontation has taken the form of using military forces but stopping short of war, or of waging war by proxy, as was the case in Korea. When the United States turned its containment intervention into liberationist rollback in September 1950, taking advantage of its decisive military advantage, it was met by Chinese, not Soviet, containment intervention. The hot war turned back to Cold War in 1953 with a status quo ante bellum equilibrium and a new demilitarized zone (DMZ) serving a tripwire function for confrontation short of war. After numerous incidents and crises in the following three and a half decades, the Korean peninsula still remains volatile, with the confrontation game now acted out at a higher level of weapons technology including US nuclear forces.

Central to American geopolitical behavior in the region has been the forward confrontational posture it has maintained to give credibility and integrity to its alliance (deterrence) system. Jinmen (Quemoy) and Mazu (Matsu), two small offshore islands whose value is more symbolic than strategic, became a test of the US resolve to counter 'aggression', evoking US nuclear diplomacy. Nothing illustrates more clearly how fighting fire with fire can backfire. The resort to nuclear threats during the first Jinmen-Mazu crisis of 1955 merely strengthened and legitimized China's national resolve to go nuclear.[19]

Even during the immediate post-Vietnam retrenchment/ readjustment period, South Korea acquired the dubious distinction of being the frontline domino. As the then Secretary of Defense James Schlesinger put it, 'the forward defense areas must continue to be Western Europe and Korea, and indirectly Japan.'[20] President Carter's 1977 troop withdrawal promise collapsed allegedly because of a new intelligence report about North Korea's military strength. Actually the Carter administration realized rather quickly that the issue was not South Korea's security but its critical link in Japan's defense and in containing the Soviet Union in Northeast Asia. In American Asia policy, Korea never mattered except as part of some larger regional and global strategic concern. Symbolically and strategically, Korea has been viewed since the Korean War as a frontline country in Asia in the defense of America's global alliance network in Asia.

The Korean conflict was an early incident of the globalization of superpower conflict. Every local or indigenous conflict is in clear danger of escalation because almost any regime – and at times even a political party – can exploit East–West rivalry to some degree to elicit material and military supplies at early stages of domestic social and political conflict. There is a sense, therefore, in which warfare is being continuously fought in the modern form of structural intervention. This form of war lacks formal acknowledgement (declaration of war) and direct visibility (body count), but, like traditional war, it uses or threatens to use force for political objectives. In a major study of US military intervention between 1946 and 1975, 215 incidents were identified (compared to 115 for the Soviet Union) in which the United States utilized its armed forces for political objectives.

Central to Soviet geopolitical behavior in Northeast Asia has been prudential realism and opportunism, coupled with a condominial desire to act as a self-styled co-guardian of the postwar international order with the United States, and failing this, at least to secure recognition of its hegemonic role within its own alliance network embracing North Korea, China, and Mongolia. With the breaking away of China, however, Soviet behavior became predominantly reactive to China's posturing in the strategic triangle. In ever crisis situation starting with the Chinese Civil War through the Korean War to the present time, however, the determination to avoid direct confrontation with the United States has become the unstated objective of the code of conduct in Soviet policy. In the wake of the 1954 US–Taiwan Mutual Security Treaty, Moscow in effect drew its containment lines through the Taiwan Strait. If the United States threatened China's mainland, Moscow was obliged in theory to come to Beijing's defense; if Beijing tried to invade Taiwan or even Jinmen and Mazu islands, it was on its own. In the second Jinmen–Mazu crisis of 1958, for example, Moscow belatedly came to China's defense only after the crisis had passed. As early as 1954, Khrushchev told his colleagues in Moscow after an official visit to Beijing that 'conflict with China is inevitable.'[22] By 1959 this prophecy was taking a life of its own, becoming almost self-fulfilling. The Sino–Soviet split was beyond repair, leading Khrushchev to push vigorously for what the Chinese regard as *Détente* I with the United States.

Both in the Korean peninsula and the Taiwan Strait, then, Soviet–American confrontation was more apparent than real during the 1950s and 1960s. In reality there was one hegemon, not two, in the postwar international relations of Northeast Asia. The Soviet threat was more like a geopolitical thermostat that could be calibrated in the service of mobilizing bipartisan foreign policy consensus at home and intra-bloc cohesion in the region. The United States has routinely acted as if the Eurasian periphery of the Soviet Union constituted a new domain of the Monroe Doctrine. That Gorbachev felt compelled to publicly assert in his 1986 Vladivostok speech that 'the Soviet Union is also an Asian and Pacific country'[23] merely confirms Moscow's marginal economic role and the limits of translating its military presence into political influence in the region.

In the Soviet perception, US policy during the 1970s gradually shifted from a relatively evenhanded triangular diplomacy to active alignment with China on an anti-Soviet united global front. As if to heighten the Soviet siege mentality, this American shift in the strategic triangle both reflected and effected a rapid deterioration of Soviet–American *détente* of the early 1970s (*Détente* II). In the process superpower relations moved away from collaboration/ competition to confrontation. The Soviet Union responded by beefing up its nuclear forces in the Far East. The build-up began with a public visit by Brezhnev and Defense Minister Ustinov to the commands at Khaborovsk and Vladivostok in April 1978. In December 1978 General of the Army Vasily I. Petrov was appointed to command a new Theater of Military Operations in the Far East, involving the Far Eastern, Transbaikal, and Siberian military districts and the Pacific Ocean Fleet, the first such consolidated regional command in the region since the end of the Korean War in 1953. In October 1981, the Soviet Union established an Air Command Center on Sakhalin to coordinate all air and aeronaval operations in the Far East. Such military build-up and reorganization formalized a shift from the feasibility of the 'swing' strategy of massive transfers from West to East in a time of crisis to a self-sufficient military presence in the Far East.

The Reagan administration's approach departed from the adjustment policies of previous administrations to bridge the gap between overseas commitments and emerging limits of American economic and military power. Rejecting the policy of *détente* and the strategy of adjustment as being too passive, the new administration was set on the strategy of hegemonic restoration – the strategy of liberationist rollback anchored in the tripod of the Reagan Doctrine *vis-à-vis* the Third World, accelerated and unprecedented peacetime military spending, and Reaganomics. Each element of the 1970s strategy of adjustment was rejected including the conception of Soviet–American mutual interest.[24]

One component of the strategy of restoration was the formation of Tokyo–Seoul–Manila links in American global strategy, confronting Moscow with another war in the East should the Soviet Union attack in the West. Such a strategy required a 600-ship navy, much of which was slated for the northern Pacific to carry out a new forward naval strategy to pin down and destroy Soviet forces in their Pacific bases. This strategy rested on the twin pillars of the Lehman Doctrine of Maritime Supremacy to achieve 'a frank maritime superiority over any other power or group of powers' and the Weinberger Doctrine of Horizontal Escalation to 'launch counteroffensives in other regions and exploit the aggressor's weaknesses wherever we find them,' if the Soviet Union were to attack US interests at one of its weak points.[25]

In this way the grand strategy was designed to demonstrate credibility for a projected Washington–Seoul–Tokyo axis against the Soviet Union.

In such a grand strategy of restoration, the China card matters less than the Japan card. Financially, strategically, and technologically, Japan is beyond compare. Situated close to Soviet Far Eastern naval choke points and with superior technological capabilities and the world's dominant credit power, Japan is irreplaceable for the implementation of this pre-eminently naval strategy based on control of sea lanes, maneuverable forward postures, and high-tech war-fighting capability. From the geopolitical perspective of Japan and South Korea, this kind of global linkage makes a lot of geopolitical and geoeconomic sense, provided, of course, the US continues to bear the risks and burdens of its hegemony in the region.

The tragedy of KAL 007 – the Korean Airlines Boeing 747 that was shot down by a Soviet fighter and plunged into the Sea of Japan with the loss of all its 269 passengers and crew on 1 September 1983 – underlines the deep structure of Soviet–American conflict in the region. In fact, a crisis of this kind was just waiting to happen, as the incident occurred against the backdrop of an intensified arms race and a series of military exercises. Moreover, the Soviet Far Eastern military facilities were subject to massive and continuous US spy flights and ringed with an extensive US network of electronic reconnaissance posts, with ground facilities in China, Japan, South Korea, Australia, Guam, Diego Garcia, the Philippines, the Aleutians, and the Marshall and Marianas Islands. This was the regional military context within which the last flight of KAL 007 took place.[26] Murphy's Law could not have asked for a more congenial setting.

Each country responded to the tragedy with a zero-sum style of conflict management. At the top of the American rank order of priorities was damage maximization – branding the Soviet Union as criminally guilty of mass murder (and to the surprise of most people in the West, China abstained on a UN Security Council draft resolution 'deploring' Soviet behavior). At the top of the Soviet rank order of priorities was counter-accusation and damage minimization – maintaining the regime's credibility with its domestic audience.[27] For the Reagan administration the incident seemed made to order for its moral crusade against the Evil Empire. For the Soviet Union the incident underscored once again its abiding siege mentality. As one senior Soviet official replied privately to the question as to why the Soviet Union did not save itself a lot of trouble by admitting its mistake, 'To have done so would, in effect, have legalized flights by American spy planes over our territory. Our borders would no longer be inviolate.'[28]

The incident dramatizes the absence of tacit rules of the game for crisis prevention and management. Taking the necessary steps to prevent a possible recurrence of such an incident was at the lowest end of the American and Soviet order of priorities.[29] If Gorbachev made a series of proposals to break away from this pattern of military confrontation in the region in 1986–8, there has occurred no discernible reciprocation by the American side. A recent US–Japan joint military exercise called 'Orient Shield 89' in November 1988 was only the latest in a series of unrelenting exercises ensuring that the military forces of the two Pacific allies will be prepared to fight together.[30]

Finally, the KAL crisis serves as a telling reminder of the extent to which the two war systems buttressed by great nuclear air and sea armadas confront one another, simultaneously constrained and compelled by the norms of mutual deterrence. The logic of a credible, effective deterrence requires a never-ending, infinitely escalating demonstration of the deterrer's capability as well as the latter's intention to use force. Deterrence is an autistic, self-executing regime, generating its own imperatives and momentum for both extensive war preparation to enhance credible capability and constant brinkmanship to emphasize credible intent. There is a behavioral paradox at work here. Each expression of intent to use force in order to enhance works to undermine the inhibition to engagement. Confrontation becomes a functional equivalent of war.

Competition

Superpower interaction can be conditioned and shaped by tacit rules of competition. Such rules are seldom formal and explicit. Instead, they both reflect and affect the patterns of mutual restraint and adjustment that the two parties find useful to observe in new situations. The key operative assumption is that such a competitive game can be played without an umpire or explicit rules of the game but still in an orderly and mutually advantageous way. Thus, the more one plays such a game the better sense one has about how the rules establish the limits of the possible and permissible. Rules of competition may be said to perform three functions: they permit the superpowers to compete for power, influence, and advantage in areas that are not of vital interest to them; they delineate the zone of influence in which the other superpower must not trespass because of the latter's marginal interest; and they define the means of competition that do not contain a high potential for violence escalation. Unlike formal agreements of a legal character, such norms of competition are supposed to grow out of a mixture of custom, precedent, and mutual interest analogous to customary law that develops through usage. Thus they are said to offer useful 'precedents or benchmarks'.[31]

If such conceptualization is accurate, the rules of superpower competition in the context of Northeast Asia raise several problems of legitimacy and applicability. First, such rules would not be able to escape the main problem of international customary law. By definition, an international custom must satisfy the requirements of long duration, consistent pattern of practice, and wide acceptance, all of which are difficult to reconcile with the fast pace and heavy demands of a rapidly changing and increasingly interdependent and technological world. This explains in part the relative decline of customary international law during the postwar period. At the same time, the so-called 'instant customary law' is a legal axymoron.[32]

Such a consistent pattern of superpower behavior, especially in the domain of global high politics, is difficult to sustain. Second, rules of competition, in the absence of a compliance regime, are difficult to define, let alone monitor and enforce. Each player would find it difficult to resist a self-serving interpretation of such rules. Third, if rules of competition are to perform the boundary function of delineating a safe arena of competition, an area of secondary importance to both parties, then the development of competitive rules of the game in Northeast Asia is made even more problematic because of the vital importance Northeast Asia holds for both superpowers. In short, rules of competition are easier to evolve in a non-zero-sum game setting. And finally, as mentioned earlier, Northeast Asia is the region where four great powers, not two, meet and interact. It is not always possible for the superpowers to exclude the other players, especially China, from the game.

The rise and fall of *Détente* II in the 1970s suggest the limits and possibilities of the superpower competitive game. *Détente* II was designed to shift superpower interaction from confrontation to a mixture of competition and collaboration. Although each superpower had different motives, expectations, and set of priorities, *Détente* II worked well in 1972–5 in easing tensions in Northeast Asia when the United States maintained an evenhanded approach toward Moscow and Beijing. It produced immediate positive ('shocking') effects upon the politics of the two Koreas and of the Sino–Soviet–Japanese relationship. At the same time, Soviet–American competition in the region continued in such a way to avoid direct military confrontation. Superpower confrontation at the Taiwan Strait disappeared. Neither superpower trespassed the Cold War divide in the Korean peninsula.

Détente II represents the first serious attempt to formalize rules of superpower competition. The twin objectives were to legitimize such competition, while at the same time defining the 'rules of play' needed to limit the risks of the competitive game. Nixon and Brezhnev signed the Basic Principles Agreement (BPA) at their first summit in Moscow in May 1972, providing rules of conduct by which their global competition would be regulated.Thus the BPA embodied growing recognition of the common shared interest in preventing superpower competition from escalating into uncontrolled confrontation. And yet, the BPA masked the unpleasant fact that Moscow and Washington could not agree upon specific rules, or even a common standard, for regulating their global competition.

From 1975 onward, the Soviet Union, in large part as a response to increasing Chinese activism in Southern Africa, started shifting toward a more competitive/confrontational direction in troubled spots of the Third World (e.g. Angola, Ethiopia, South Yemen, and Indochina). Moscow interpreted the norms of *détente* narrowly in terms of avoidance of direct superpower confrontation, not constraining superpower competition in the Third World. Hence, the use of direct military and political involvement as well as reliance on East German, Cuban, and Vietnamese proxies designed to produce a more decisive and lasting Soviet Presence in the Third World did not defy the BPA. In reality several events intruded into Moscow's strategic calculus to change the balance of interests and incentives for Soviet initiatives in the Third World: foremost, the strategic 'loss' of China; Kissinger's exclusionary diplomacy in the Middle East, and rising opportunities in Africa and Indochina.

In Washington's eye, however, Soviet fingerprints were to be found in all of the world's troubled spots, marking their defiance of the BPA. From the beginning, the United States gave a broad interpretation to the BPA in terms of an all embracing linkage with Soviet behavior at home and abroad. As Raymond Garthoff put it, 'the unilateral application of the constraints and restraints of *détente* only to the actions of the other side constituted a rather large blind spot in the vision of the Americans who designed *détente*.'[33] In the end, *détente* collapsed because each side tried to define the norms of *détente* in a self-serving way – the United States broadly and the Soviet Union narrowly – geared more toward maximizing its own unilateral advantages than toward expanding the terms of reciprocity and mutual interest. At the same time, the United States had been unable or unwilling to offer much in the way of positive incentives to influence Soviet behavior. For its part, China, always suspecting a Soviet–American condominium, vigorously played the role of *agent provocateur* to subvert *Détente* II.

Because of the growing pressures of combat/competition fatigue and the internal and external burdens of imperial extension, both Moscow and Washington since 1986 have arrived at a more realistic reassessment of each other, as well as of themselves, ushering in *Détente* III. Three restructuring – and multipolarizing – developments have brought about another *détente*, one that promises to be more enduring than previous ones. The first is Japan's replacement of the United States as the world's leading credit power. The second development is Gorbachev's 'new thinking' in foreign policy and its corollary, the new Soviet concept of security or what Robert Legvold aptly calls 'the revolution in Soviet foreign policy'.[34] And the third is what we may call a second revolution in Chinese foreign policy. If the Sino–American *rapprochement* of 1971–2 can be called a first revolution in Chinese foreign policy with its restructuring impact of the Asian geopolitical landscape, the Sino–Soviet renormalization process of 1982–9 is even more revolutionary in its unprecedented 'dual cooperative policy' *vis-à-vis* both superpowers through the globalization of the Five Principles of Peaceful Coexistence. This means that for the first time in modern history, China is redefining itself as part of the solution in superpower relations, offering a clear and continuing possibility of a *ménage à trois*. One major military consequence of this Sino–Soviet *détente* is a *de facto* arms reduction agreement of halving Soviet troops along the Sino–Soviet border and a one-fourth reduction of the Chinese troops with instant second-order ripple effects on the geoeconomic landscape of the region.

In the latest (pre-Tiananmen) Chinese definition of the international situation, a new scientific and technological revolution is sweeping over the world. This gives rise to a peaceful competition for 'overall national strength', a neo-Darwinian competition devoid of warfare yet of life-and-death importance. The rules of superpower competition have been transformed and winning the scientific and technological race is now the name of the game. Domestically, a new wave of reform and restructuring has been generated. Internationally, an irresistible tendency toward competition, interdependence, and coordination has developed in the context of one world market.[35]

The superpowers have always remained central to China's assessment of the constraints and opportunities facing its foreign policy. Its shift from an *entente* period (May 1978 to mid-1981), when China and the United States moved on a parallel anti-Soviet track, to an independent foreign policy has coincided with a subtle but significant reassessment in China's perception of both superpowers. In China's revised perception, the influence of the Soviet Union peaked in the mid-to-late 1970s and began its decline in the early 1980s. Even before the rise of Gorbachev, the image of the Soviet Union as the more irrational, more aggressive, and more threatening superpower began to wane. During the early Reagan years, China seemed to have finally awakened from its anti-Soviet obsession to find that in many ways the Soviet entanglements in troubled spots of the Third World may have actually enhanced its own security through multiple effects of the growing difficulties the Soviet Union encountered at home and abroad. The Soviet Union, in China's eyes, increasingly resembled a swollen military superstate, gradually exhausting itself financially and morally on the path to overall decline in national strength.

Clearly, competing and even contradictory forces are at work in the Chinese perception of the United States. Geostrategically, China can hardly afford to express disdain for the United States as another superpower on the downward trajectory, given the fact that the United States no longer poses any military threat to China, while the Soviet Union still confronts China with a formidable military presence in Northeast Asia. Geoeconomically, the United States is the only superpower that can greatly help or hinder China's modernization drive. Hegemonic decline or not, the United States still has – and often exercises – its veto power in the keystone multilateral economic institutions (e.g. the World Bank, the International Monetary Fund, the General Agreement on Tariffs and Trade, and the Asian Development Bank). It still holds what post-Mao China calls the master key to its modernization drive – science and technology – and it still enforces its will through substantial penalties and payoffs. China can hardly ignore the fact that none of the Asian NICs achieved an economic miracle without first capturing its share of the American market.[36]

While China's redefinition of the international situation bears traces of wish-fulfillment, it does capture the China factor as an essential and elusive aspect of the changing rules of superpower competition in Northeast Asia. The Chinese practice of geopolitics in the region over the years has carefully cultivated the expectation that China is both capable and willing to play a decisive role of 'balancer' in the central strategic equilibrium between the two superpowers. Indeed, China can be said to have succeeded in assuming such a strategic role, inasmuch as both Washington and Moscow acted as if China had already become a key factor in their respective strategic calculus. By acknowledging China as a great power in the region and beyond, both Washington and Moscow have accepted the limits of their influence in the international relations of Northeast Asia. In superpower conflict or cooperation, China cannot be taken for granted.

Collaboration

Collaboration generally requires a set of rules, norms, and procedures for communicating and coordinating policies and actions on issues of common concern or interest on a joint and reciprocal basis. In theory, superpower collaboration may address a wide range of economic, functional, and strategic issues, resulting in formal (explicit) cooperation or informal (tacit) cooperation. However, superpower collaboration in the international relations of Northeast Asia encounters serious practical and normative problems because of the constant intrusion of East–West, North–South, and even East–East (Sino–Soviet) cleavages. The legitimation of superpower collaboration, as George Breslauer suggests, must meet two criteria of reciprocity, at two levels of superpower relationship. At the general level, it calls for 'diffuse support for the relationship by affirming the equal status of the two powers.' At the more specific level, 'the norm of reciprocity requires a mutual commitment to equivalent exchange.'[37]

As explained earlier, superpower interaction in Northeast Asia has been more confrontational and competitive than collaborative during much of the postwar era. In the Korean peninsula, North Korea first attacked South Korea with Soviet support and the United States only tried its rollback strategy during the second phase of the Korean War, inviting Chinese intervention. The Soviet Union could have intervened in the war for its retreating client state but did not. Still, both superpowers can be said to have carried out informal cooperation by first recognizing the limits of their power to prevail in Korea without unacceptable or costly consequences and then by successfully negotiating a truce agreement. Although the Soviet Union was not a direct party in the conflict or in the protracted negotiations leading to the end of the Korean War, it would be inconceivable to imagine such an outcome without Soviet approval. Robert C. Tucker argues that 'negotiations for a formal Korean armistice, stalled at the start of 1953, proceeded after Stalin's death to the successful conclusion that had been impossible to reach while he yet lived.'[38] Since the armistice, both superpowers can also be said to have carried out tacit cooperation by non-action in the preservation of the postwar status quo, as each superpower refrained from military attack on the ally of the other superpower. Both superpowers followed tacit rules of cooperation not to trespass into the other side of the DMZ except through periodic joint military exercises. When the United States introduced nuclear weapons into South Korea and Taiwan in 1957, based on the assumption of continuing Sino–Soviet nuclear collaboration, there was no equivalent response owing to the growing Sino–Soviet differences over the implications of nuclear weapons for war and peace. These differences brought about the initial (still secret) Soviet decision in early 1958 to renege its agreement to provide China with a prototype atomic bomb and missiles as well as related data and became a major cause of the Sino–Soviet split.

If *Détente* I of the late 1950s and the early 1960s was largely limited to passive 'peaceful coexistence' and symbolic summit diplomacy lacking substance (the 1963 Partial Nuclear Test Ban Treaty is an exception), *Détente* II witnessed during its heyday a series of bilateral agreements on arms control issues, East–West trade, and functional cooperation in scientific, cultural, and educational fields. The Non-Proliferation Treaty (NPT) – signed in 1968 and put into force in 1970 – stands out as a product of the most active superpower formal cooperation in the postwar era, with both the United States and the Soviet Union submitting (on 14 March 1968) the same draft treaty to the UN General Assembly.

Détente III opens up new ideas and paths for multilateral cooperation in the APR. There is now tacit superpower cooperation to prevent the two Koreas from going nuclear. South Korea finally gave up under US pressures and with assurances that it would remain under the American nuclear umbrella. After learning of a nuclear reactor in Yongbyon, North Korea, the United States is reported to have approached Moscow, with the result that the Soviets pressured Pyongyang into ratifying the NPT on 12 December 1985.[39] For the 1988 Seoul Olympics, both superpowers again carried out informal cooperation not only to bring about universal participation but also to make the Games terrorism-free. The United States officially thanked the Soviet Union for Moscow's constructive and stabilizing role during the Olympic period. The 1088 Seoul Olympiad may also be remembered as a benchmark event in accelerating cross-bloc functional cooperation between Seoul and Moscow as well as between Seoul and Beijing. Cross-recognition is not the only way to regional cooperation. The Soviet interest in Korea shifted from a desire to avoid an unwanted confrontation to soliciting South Korea as another way of becoming involved in regional economic integration.

That not a single major incident or crisis occurred over Japan is also a demonstration of superpower informal cooperation by non-action. On the question of the so-called Northern Territories – the four Kurile islands taken by the Soviet Union as part of postwar territorial settlement – the Soviet Union has remained a defender of the status quo while Japan with US support has become a revisionist challenger. Here the Soviet Union failed to implement an Asian version of the Conference on Security and Cooperation in Europe (CSCE), which has lent legitimacy to the postwar boundary settlements in Europe and its attendant series of confidence-building measures.

In the Gorbachev years, however, Soviet officials and scholars have advanced a number of suggestions and proposals to bridge the gap between the Soviet and Japanese positions.[40] If Gorbachev can clear away China's Three Obstacles through unilateral concessions in his successful push for the 1989 Beijing summit, it is hard to believe that he will not bring some major concessions to clear away Japan's One obstacle in his current push for the 1991 Tokyo summit. Still, Japan has remained remarkably unresponsive to Gorbachev's big Asian push. The problem, it seems, is not in the insufficiency or insincerity of Gorbachev's pacific overtures but in the reactive character of the Japanese political system.[41] Gorbachev's proactive foreign policy, which is compelled by the challenge of restructuring the domestic economy, cannot amount to an internal shock or an external pressure (note the Nixon Shocks of 1971–3) that the reactive nature of the Japanese state is conditioned to respond to.

Regarding the China factor, superpower interaction has been most complicated, involved, and volatile, with a great impact upon the geopolitical configuration of the region and beyond. Remarkably in the postwar years, China is the only nation that has participated in both an *entente* and a war with both superpowers at different times. China is also the only nation to have been threatened at different times with nuclear attack by the United States and the Soviet Union in the 1960s by both superpowers.[42] Ostensibly, there was a super-power confrontation by proxy in the 1950s – the Korean War and a series of crises in the Taiwan Strait – but in reality the Soviet Union never fully joined the fray. In the 1960s and 1970s the chief goal of Soviet Far Eastern policy was to contain and isolate China, whether through Brezhnev's Asian Collective Security System (a broad anti-Chinese Eurasian united front), through specific Soviet–American collusion against Chinese nuclear facilities, or through the establishment of an American–Soviet condominial order in East Asia.

All of this is changing rapidly in the Gorbachev years. Judged by vision, agenda, and performance, Soviet Asian–Pacific overtures from Vladivostok (28 July 1986) to Krasnoyarsk (16 September 1988) to New York (8 December 1988) to Beijing (mid-May 1989) together represent a sharp break from the zero-sum game style of thinking and behavior of the past, creating breathing space for cross-bloc multi-lateral economic cooperation in the region.[43] He has issued a series of calls and proposals for reducing military, particularly naval, deploy-ments and exercises as a way of easing tensions and of establishing confidence-building measures around the Korean peninsula, in the Seas of Japan and Okhotsk and also as a way of integrating the Soviet Far East into the political economy of the APR. Indeed, the Soviet Union under Gorbachev is talking less and less like a superpower and becoming in significant ways what Richard Ullman calls 'an ordinary state'.[44] Gorbachev persists in his drive to join the emerging Asian–Pacific community as a regular member state: 'I would like to state with full responsibility once more: The Soviet Union does not seek privileges or benefits for itself to the detriment of others and does not expect advantages at the expense of others.'[45] Not only has Gor-bachev accepted observer status in the Pacific Economic Cooperation Conference (PECC) but has also expressed his willingness to join 'in this international organization's work *in any form* its members consider acceptable.'[46] Only the United States and Japan now stand in the way of full Soviet participation in the PECC.

At the same time, Gorbachev concedes that the United States is a genuine Pacific power with legitimate interests in the region. The Soviet Union is 'in favor of full US participation in the affairs of the Asia–Pacific region, as befits its status and its political and economic potential.'[47] Unlike all previous attempts and proposals for anti-Chinese superpower collaboration, Gorbachev's Asian–Pacific cooperation initiatives are part and parcel of the comprehensive system of global security.[48]

Gorbachev's Asian–Pacific overtures are not just lip service. He has initiated a series of unilateral measures as if following American psychologist Charles E. Osgood's 1962 peace proposal called 'Graduated Reciprocation in Tension Reduction' (GRIT). The essence of the GRIT approach proceeds from the premise that the tension/arms race spiral is a dynamic of the Cold War mentality and provides the model for its own reversal through unilateral actions that meet four requirements: they should not reduce a nation's retaliatory capacity; they should be graduated in risk potential according to the degree of reciprocation obtained; they should be diversified so as not to weaken a nation's capacity in any one sphere; and they should be unpredictable by an opponent as to their nature, locus, and time of execution.[49]

Gorbachev's unilateral initiatives include: (a) the nuclear testing moratorium in 1985–7; (b) the withdrawal from Afghanistan in 1988–9; (c) the acceptance of a global double-zero option for the INF Treaty, which required the Soviet Union to give up its one hundred SS-20 intermediate-range nuclear missiles stations in its Asian territory without linking them to the Chinese intermediate missiles or to the US nuclear presence in South Korea, the Philippines, and the island of Diego Garcia; (d) the announcement at Krasnoyarsk in September 1988 that 'the Soviet Union will not be increasing, as indeed has been the case for some time now, the number of any type of nuclear weapons in the region';[50] (e) the withdrawal of approximately 20 per cent of Soviet combat fighters from the Far Eastern military region in 1987–8; (f) the reduction of the Soviet troops by 500,000 announced in December 1988; (g) the announcement in January 1989 that Soviet ground forces in Mongolia will be cut by 75 per cent and the air group there removed altogether, that 200,000 of the 500,000 Soviet troops cut in the next two years would come from the SFE, and that chemical weapons would be scrapped; and (h) the meeting in San Francisco in June 1990 with President Roh of South Korea.[51]

Most of the above-mentioned initiatives triggered skeptical reaction or no response from the United States. For the seven-point proposal Gorbachev made in his Krasnoyarsk speech, for example, the US did not even submit a reasoned and diplomatic rejection. The American response came in the rather unusual form of an article in *The New York Times* by two high-ranking officials – Gaston J. Sigur, Assistant Secretary of State for East Asian Pacific Affairs, and Richard L. Armitage, Assistant Secretary for International Security Affairs. Ignoring all the unilateral actions and focusing largely on the fourth point of possible mutual elimination of American military bases in the Philippines and the Soviet naval base at Cam Ranh Bay, Sigur and Armitage rejected Gorbachev's seven-point plan as if it were a kamikaze-style assault on the integrity of the American Cold War alliance system in East Asia, dismissing it as 'entirely one-sided'.[52] The essential concept guiding US security policy in the region is still anchored in the premise that the Cold War alliance system is working well and that now is not the time to tamper with the system – as an old American saying goes, 'If it ain't broke, don't fix it.' Another part of the problem lies in American politics. In the absence of hot war in the region, coupled with a clear and continuing economic challenge from Japan and Asian NICs, Northeast Asia remains detached from the debate about ending the Cold War.

Central to Gorbachev's Asian–Pacific peace initiatives is the proposition that it is high time to establish an international regime of cooperation in the region. 'Why do we not have mutual understanding here,' asks Gorbachev, 'in contrast to other important spheres of world politics? Our state interests appear not to clash. We are not encroaching on the ramified US economic ties. Like everywhere else, we have apparently already demonstrated that we can face up to realities. So what is the problem?'[53] The seven-point proposal in his Krasnoyarsk speech calls for multilateral negotiations for the establishment of the rules of formal cooperation on a number of issues including the non-build-up of nuclear and naval forces, the reduction of military confrontation in areas where the USSR, China, Japan, North and South Korea intersect, the joint elaboration of measures to prevent incidents in the open sea and in the airspace, and the establishment of a peace zone in the Indian Ocean.[54] Gorbachev's Russia has thus redefined the central challenge of its foreign policy in terms of making the world safe for domestic economic reform and restructuring.

RETROSPECT AND PROSPECTS

Today, Northeast Asia stands at a crossroads of system transition where the contradictory forces of creativity and destruction – nationalism and transnationalism, hegemony and anti-hegemony, fragmentation and integration, neo-mercantilism and global inter-dependence – are pulling and pushing the major players in different directions. It is in Asia, not in Europe or any other region in the world, where both the United States and the Soviet Union were made aware of the multipolarizing trends and the limits of their military power – that military power, unlike financial power, is neither easily usable nor readily fungible. Vietnam and Afghanistan, instead of being conquered by massive military power, left 'bleeding wounds' on both superpowers. It is this region as well where both superpowers encounter, albeit in different ways and degrees, the widening gap between their military and economic power. It is in this region where we can see most clearly that the world economic balances already have begun to shift away from the superpowers to Japan, South Korea, and China.

The turbulent history of postwar geopolitics in the region serves as a warning of the hazards in predicting the shape of things to come in the region over the coming decade. Still, it is worth speculating on the basis of the preceding analysis of the dominant strategic behaviors of the three great strategic powers in the region in an effort to extrapolate several possible scenarios of regional cooperation.

America's strategic culture thrives on a Manichaean vision of bipolarity and the Soviet threat. And the Cold War system worked well in the establishment and maintenance of American hegemony in the region until the turn of the 1970s. But in the end, the American hegemon could not arrest, any more successfully than the previous ones, the cycles of the rise and fall of great power. The law of imperial extension turns today's dividends into tomorrow's debts with compound interests. The Reagan Doctrine and the Brezhnev Doctrine have merely telescoped the decline of both superpowers. Hegemons cannot survive by imperial will alone. The only question that remains now for the United States is how long Japan will be able and willing to subsidize American hegemony in the name of 'burden sharing' without 'power-sharing' or refrain from the military super-power temptation itself.

Until recently, Soviet strategic culture has also thrived on the Cold War system. The simplicity of a stark bipolarized world-view provided an indispensable counterpoint for the elusive quest for national identity and security in the region dominated by American hegemony. Soviet geopolitical conduct seems to make no sense at all except when viewed as the drive to assume a superpower role and acquire equal status with the United States as a way of compensating for its siege (insecurity) mentality and legitimizing its authoritarian iron hand at home. A conceptual focus on the Soviet national identity/status crisis seems a promising way of exploring long-term continuities amid historical flux in Soviet foreign policy. Although Soviet national identity is a varied configuration of national experience, values and interests, the invisible hand guiding Soviet international conduct seems to have been the reality of American hegemony and the Leninist/Stalinist notion of the capitalist encirclement chimera.

Indeed, the United States has been the Soviets 'most significant other', the dominant international reference actor, to be envied, emulated, cajoled at times for condominial collaboration, but seldom to be directly challenged let alone threatened. This overriding drive for equal superpower status provides a basis for explaining Soviet conduct under Stalin, Khrushchev, and Brezhnev and in various configurations of the strategic triangle in the region and beyond. The Soviet Union has attempted to resolve its national status/identity crisis through the appropriate adjustment of specific policies ranging from alliance formation and consolidation, Soviet–American condominial collaboration, competitive intervention in the Third World, and competitive/confrontational arms racing. In retrospect, it seems that Soviet influence was at its peak during the 'short decade' of Sino–Soviet marriage in the strategic triangle (1949–58) and began to decline in tandem with the deterioration of Sino–Soviet relations.

In the Gorbachev years there has been a dramatic rise in global learning,[55] with an accompanying public admission that none of the former policies really worked and some were even illegal. The nine-year Soviet involvement in Afghanistan had violated Soviet law and international norms of behavior, we are told, just as the Krasnoyarsk radar station was an open violation of the Anti-Ballistic Missile Treaty with the United States.[56] Underway is a momentous process of redefining national security and identity. 'At the root of the problem,' concedes Alexei Arbatov, department head at the Institute of World Economy and International Relations of the USSR Academy of Sciences, 'is the fact that in the situation that has been taking shape in recent decades the Soviet Union has, drawing primarily on its own resources, to take part in military confrontation simultaneously with many opponents (which include all the other major world powers situated near or far from Soviet borders), and in the entire range of armed forces and armaments.'[57] The Soviet Union has been talking as if it would now be willing to downsize its national role conception as a way of entering the emerging Asian-Pacific Basin community as a normal member state. This change of Soviet role conception, if sustained, would entail more normal relations with the United States.

The geopolitical track record of China in the region from 1949 to the present shows the widest range of options adopted by any major power in international relations. One thing emerges clear and consistent – China's strategic position and value can never be taken for granted by any external power, for it has the will and power to change its geopolitical color and course and to reshape the geostrategic landscape in phase with its changing definition of the domestic and international situation. Gorbachev has gone a long way to ease China's own identity and security crises by publicly recognizing China's status 'as a great socialist power', and engaging her in periodic consultation on global arms control, disarmament and UN peacekeeping issues. He has taken the sting out of the festering ideological and geopolitical conflict by replacing the Brezhnev Doctrine (a Soviet-style domino theory) with China's Five Principles of Peaceful Coexistence. Above all, Gorbachev has drawn back substantially from some of his predecessor's military reinforcements along China's security perimeter.

The 1989 Sino–Soviet summit marks a turning point of regional and global significance. Symbolically, it put an end to three decades of Sino–Soviet conflict and confrontation. Strategically, it underscores a new diffusion and realignment of power that has already taken place. Unlike the 1972 Nixon–Zhou summit, however, this one may well move beyond geopolitical restructuring to open up new possibilities for functional multilateral cooperation in the region. The Sino–Soviet renormalization is a complex linkage process in which domestic and foreign policy, and international systemic factors interact in a synergistic manner. There is a sense in which China's open-door policy has served as a vanguard model for Gorbachev's *perestroika*: concentrating on economic development as a better way of building broad and solid foundations for national security in the largest sense; cutting troop strength and the defense budget; attracting direct foreign investment through a variety of forms including joint ventures; and seeking to join key international economic institutions for greater integration into the world economy. The Sino–Soviet border trade on a barter basis linking contiguous regions of both countries expanded into 'international labor cooperation' in 1988, allowing ten thousand Chinese workers to work in Siberian timber projects.

Since 1984 China has expressed a positive view of the concept of the Asian-Pacific Basin community, which, two years earlier it had dismissed as a mask for the North–South exchange of unequal values (exploitation). As in Gorbachev's Soviet Union, then, there is a strong craving in post-Mao China for a stable external environment. Indeed, the central challenge of Chinese foreign policy has been redefined in terms of making the Asian-Pacific region safe for and receptive to China's modernization drive. Herein lies the logic of China's cross-bloc economic and functional relations with South Korea. How long – and to what extent – the Tiananmen Massacre will affect the contours of the international politics of Northeast Asia remains unclear, but China's peace/development line, at least until mid-1989, presented another historical opportunity to shift the center of political gravity in the region from geostrategic competition to geoeconomic multilateral cooperation.

Against this backdrop, several scenarios of superpower cooperation can be sketched. First of all, maximal collaboration in the form of a superpower condominium can be ruled out as the least likely option. There is no postwar precedent for superpower condominium in the region. During the heyday of *Détente* II in the early 1970s Brezhnev persisted in his repeated appeals for Soviet–American collaboration against China – and his attempts to translate *détente* into *entente* – only to succeed in the end to bring about Cold War II and Sino–American collaboration against the Soviet Union. There are no requisite domestic support bases in Moscow and Washington nor the power symmetry needed to get a superpower condominium off the ground. The United States, as the senior hegemon, has always preferred unilateral action, while the Soviet Union as an aspiring hegemon preferred condominium. Such power and preference differentials make it difficult to establish a requisite organic link between power and the rules of the superpower game. In an age of multipolarization and hegemonic decline, China, Japan, and the two Koreas have all gained greater independence, standing in the way of legitimizing any condominial world order. Any quest for a superpower condominial order in Northeast Asia seems doomed.

A *ménage à trois* in the strategic triangle presents another possible scenario. Of the four triangular configurations,[58] this option provides, in theory, equal security to all three participants and a maximum advantage at minimal cost, as it is in each player's interest to satisfy the other two that no threat is intended. The recent Sino–Soviet renormalization process, engaged in without threatening Sino–American and Soviet–American relations, represents a significant step toward a new security regime. At the same time, it might provide welcome relief from the heavy military burdens of the superpowers, while initiating low-risk adjustment strategies in bridging the spirit/flesh gap through domestic reform and restructuring. And yet, the *ménage à trois* is among the most ambiguous of the four possible triangular configurations. The absence of historical precedent (notice the quick miscarriage of Khrushchev's troika plan in the United Nations in the early 1960s), an enemy, and the requisite leadership all require new thinking and new collective leadership to formulate and execute a common security agenda for the authoritative allocation of equal status, equal stakes, and equal payoffs. This is easier promised than performed even in the most ideal of circumstances. Above all, a *ménage à trois* without Japan is a sure recipe for the revival of Japanese militarism.

A third scenario is the establishment of a multilateral cooperation regime involving all the states including of course both superpowers in the Asian-Pacific Basin region. This is a broadly based functional regime engaging the participation of all, regardless of their different social and political systems, designed to provide institutional mechanisms for multilateral regional cooperation on a wide spectrum of issues ranging from arms control and disarmament to trade to environmental protection. At the very least it would provide a common framework for discussing tension-reducing, confidence-building, and cooperation-expanding measures.

Since the mid-1980s, money, trade, and investment are transforming the topography of national and ideological conflict in the region. Japan's rise as the world's leading credit power, China's open-door policy, the impressive performances of the Asian NICs as trading states, and the initiatives of Gorbachev have been the catalysts for pushing all the players into complex regional – and global – networks of economic interdependence. What is lacking in the translation of these criss-crossing functional and economic ties across ideological and geostrategic divides into an institutional reality is American support. To date, the Bush administration, joined by many of influential mainstream geostrategists, seem more nostalgic about *la belle époque* of the containment strategy than about ending the Cold War, at least in Northeast Asia. Practically all of Bush's principal foreign policy players (Scowcroft, Cheney, Baker, and Eagleburger) were badly burned during *Détente* II – once burned, twice cautious. 'But the signs are,' conceded even such a mainstream realist observer as Paul Kreisberg, 'that the same old threats and the same old arguments for force levels and facilities are being laid on the interagency bargaining table.'[59] The Bush administration seems both unable and unwilling to expand the limits of the possible and the permissible defined by the Right in the Republican Party. The multipolarizing trends in the region, together with the US determination to remain as a Pacific (naval) power, stand in the way of establishing any formal multilateral cooperation regime involving the Soviet Union.

Of course, the three scenarios mentioned do not exhaust all possible permutations and configurations of superpower interaction in the region. One lesson emerges clearly from the successes and failures of superpower interaction in the past four and a half decades. Superpower cooperation, whatever forms it takes, requires for its legitimation and endurance the shared perception of equal status, equal exchange (reciprocity), equal share of power and responsibility, anchored in a broad range of issues. Adhocracy will not do; such cooperation demands a common institutional framework for the management of common security. The Helsinki/Stockholm model provides the European institutional framework. A comparable Northeast Asian framework is needed but not on the cards. The irony is that in a more multipolar and less ideological system that seems almost destined to emerge in the region China, Japan, and the two Koreas will become increasingly more assertive and less amenable to superpower influence.

The prospect of a more peaceful regional order depends, in large part, on where we look. The unrelenting nuclear arms race in the region is a source of concern, to be sure, but the growing globalization of capital, knowledge, production, and markets is shifting the center of gravity in world politics from the domain of high politics to the domain of low politics. Indeed, today low politics is and becomes high politics in the international relations of Northeast Asia. Such a transformation expands the possibilities of international cooperation, moving slowly but steadily, as Edward Kolodziej and Roger Kanet suggest, 'from cooperation arising from conflict and mutual bargaining to possibly enlarged domains of cooperation understood as

co-valuation.' Regarding this transformation Moscow has already
pronounced its stand, but the challenge of moving beyond geopoli-
tics-as-usual toward a new international order in Northeast Asia has
yet to enter the now-on and now-off search for a new ideology of
foreign policy in the United States.

NOTES

1. See Marc S. Gallichio, *The Cold War Begins in Asia: American East
   Asian Policy and the Fall of the Japanese Empire* (New York:
   Columbia University Press, 1988).
2. Bruce Cumings, 'Introduction: The Course of Korean–American
   Relations, 1943–1953', in Bruce Cumings (ed.), *Child of Conflict: The
   Korean–American Relationship, 1943–1953* (Seattle: University of
   Washington Press, 1983), p. 3.
3. For detailed accounts of this and related events, see Soon Sung Cho,
   *Korea in World Politics 1940–1950: An Evaluation of American
   Responsibility* (Berkeley: University of California, 1967); and Gregory
   Henderson, 'Korea', in Gregory Henderson, Richard Ned Lebow, and
   John G. Stoessinger, *Divided Nations in a Divided World* (New York:
   David McKay, 1974), pp. 43–96.
4. Bruce Cumings, *The Origins of the Korean War: Liberation and the
   Emergence of Separate Regimes, 1945–1947* (Princeton: Princeton
   University Press, 1981).
5. See *World Armaments and Disarmament 1987* (New York: Oxford
   University Press, 1987), pp. 310–17.
6. See Rober Gilpin, *War and Change in World Politics* (New York:
   Cambridge University Press, 1981). For a similar line of argument, see
   Paul Kennedy, *The Rise and Fall of the Great Powers: Economic
   Change and Military Conflict from 1500 to 2000* (New York: Random
   House, 1987).
7. Robert Gilpin, *The Political Economy of International Relations*
   (Princeton: Princeton University Press, 1987), pp. 328–36.
8. *Khrushchev Remembers*, trans. and ed. by Strobe Talbott (Boston:
   Little, Brown, 1970), pp. 465–6; *Khrushchev Remembers: The Last
   Testament*, trans. and ed. by Strobe Talbott (Boston: Little, Brown,
   1974), pp. 247–8.
9. Samuel S. Kim, 'Foreign Relations', in John S. Major and Anthony J.
   Kane (eds), *China Briefing, 1987* (Boulder, CO: Westview Press,
   1987), pp. 69–97.
10. Gorbachev's Speech at Krasnoyarsk in FBIS-Sov (hereafter cited as
    the Krasnoyarsk Speech), 20 September 1988, p. 29.
11. Mikhail G. Nossov, 'The USSR and the Security of the Asia-Pacific
    Region: From Vladivostok to Krasnoyarsk', *Asian Survey*, vol. 29, no.
    3 (March 1989), p. 262; see also Henry Trofimenko, 'Long-Term

Trends in the Asia-Pacific Region: A Soviet Evaluation', ibid.,
pp. 227–51.
12. Charles E. Lindblom, *The Intelligence of Democracy* (New York: The
Free Press, 1965), pp. 3, 9, 28–9.
13. For full discussion about various rules of the superpower game, see
Alexander L. George *et al.*, *Managing US–Soviet Rivalry: Problems of
Crisis Prevention* (Boulder, CO: Westview Press, 1983).
14. As James Burnham put it: 'At most, containment can be a temporary
expedient, a transition. As the transition is completed, containment
must move towards one or the other of the two major poles, towards
appeasement or liberation.' See James Burnham, *Containment or
Liberation?* (New York: John Day, 1953, p. 31.
15. For an elegant summation of the believer v. the skeptic debate about
ending the Cold War, see Robert W. Tucker, 'On Ending the Cold
War', *The National Interest*, no. 16 (Summer 1989), pp. 117–22.
16. Franklyn Griffiths, 'The Sources of American Conduct: Soviet Perspectives and Their Policy Implications', *International Security*, vol. 9,
no. 2 (Fall 1984), pp. 29–30.
17. Ibid., pp. 30–4.
18. Mikhail Gorbachev, *Realities and Guarantees for a Secure World*
(Moscow: Novosti Press, 1987).
19. As early as 25 April 1956, Mao, in his secret speech, 'The Ten Major
Relationships', declared 'If we are not to be bullied in the present-day
world, we cannot do without the bomb.' See *Selected Works of Mao
Tsetung*, Vol. 5 (Peking: Foreign Languages Press, 1977), p. 288. For a
more detailed treatment, see John Wilson Lewis and Xue Litai, *China
Builds the Bomb* (Stanford: Stanford University Press, 1988).
20. For partial text of this press conference statement, see Se-Jin Kim
(ed.), *Documents on Korean–American Relations 1943–1976* (Seoul:
Research Center for Peace and Unification, 1976), p. 486. For a more
detailed analysis, see Samuel S. Kim, 'United States Korean Policy and
World Order', *Alternatives: A Journal of World Policy*, vol. 6, no. 3
(Winter 1980–1), pp. 419–52.
21. Barry M. Blechman, Stephen S. Kaplan *et al.*, *Force Without War: US
Armed Forces as a Political Instrument* (Washington, DC: The Brookings Institute, 1978).
22. *Khrushchev Remembers*, op. cit., p. 466.
23. Mikhail Gorbachev's Vladivostok Speech in FBIS-Sov (hereafter cited
as the Vladivostok Speech), 29 July 1986, p. R12.
24. See Kenneth A. Oye, 'International Systems Structure and American
Foreign Policy', in Kenneth A. Oye, Robert J. Lieber, and Donald
Rothchild (eds), *Eagle Defiant: United States Foreign Policy in the
1980s* (Boston: Little, Brown, 1983), pp. 3–31.
25. See R. W. Johnson, *Shootdown: The Verdict on KAL 007* (London:
Chatto & Windus, 1986), p. 53; see also William M. Arkin, 'The
Nuclear Arms Race at Sea', *Neptune Papers*, no. 1 (Greenpeace
Institute for Policy Studies, Washington, DC, October 1987), pp. 13–
14.
26. For a more detailed account, see Johnson, op. cit., pp. 54–61.

27.	Alexander Dallin, *Black Box: KAL 007 and the Superpowers* (Berkeley: University of California Press, 1985), pp. 88–9.
28.	Quoted in ibid., p. 91.
29.	Ibid., p. L88–9.
30.	*Christian Science Monitor*, 28 November 1988, p. 12.
31.	Alexander George, 'US–Soviet Global Rivalry: Norms of Competition', *Journal of Peace Research*, vol. 23, no. 3 (1986), p. 249.
32.	For further discussion on this problem, see Samuel S. Kim, 'The United Nations, Lawmaking, and World Order', *Alternatives: A Journal of World Policy*, vol. 10, no. 4 (1985) pp. 643–75.
33.	Raymond L. Garthoff, *Detente and Confrontation: American–Soviet Relations from Nixon to Reagan* (Washington, DC: The Brookings Institution, 1985), p. 34.
34.	Robert Legvold, 'The Revolution in Soviet Foreign Policy', *Foreeign Affairs*, vol. 68, no. 1 (1989), pp. 82–98.
35.	See Song Yimin, 'The Relaxation of US–Soviet Tensions and Profound Changes in International Relations', *Guoji Wenti Yanjiu* (Journal of International Studies) (Beijing), no. 1 (1988), pp. 1–5.
36.	See Samuel S. Kim, 'Chinese World Policy in Transition', *World Policy Journal*, vol. 1, no. 3 (Spring 1984), pp. 603–33, and *The Third World in Chinese World Policy* (Center of International Studies, Princeton University, January 1989).
37.	George Breslauer, 'Why Detente Failed: An Interpretation', in George *et al.*, op. cit., p. 331; emphasis in original.
38.	Robert C. Tucker, 'The Prehistory of the First Detente: Stalin and the Soviet Controversy over Foreign Policy, 1949–1953' (a paper prepared for the US–USSR Seminar on US–Soviet Relations, 1950–1955, at Columbus, Ohio, October 1988), p. 1.
39.	John McBeth, Nayan Chanda, and Shada Islam, 'Nuclear Jitters', *Far Eastern Economic Review* (2 February 1989), p. 15.
40.	See Nossov, op. cit., p. 260.
41.	See Kent E. Calder, 'Japanese Foreign Economic Policy Formation: Explaining the Reactive State', *World Politics*, vol. 40, no. 4 (July 1988), pp. 517–41.
42.	Raymond Garthoff writes: 'In the mid-1960s the US government had, as the Chinese probably knew, considered unilateral action, and even possible tacit collusive action with the Soviet Union, to eliminate Chinese nuclear weapons facilities. I was involved in these internal deliberations.' See Garthoff, op. cit., p. 984.
43.	For English texts of these groundbreaking speeches, see FBIS-Sov, 29 July 1986, pp. R1–R19; 20 September 1988, pp. 29–41; and 8 December 1988, pp. 11–19.
44.	Richard H. Ullman, 'Ending the Cold War', *Foreign Policy*, no. 72 (Fall 1988), p. 132.
45.	The Krasnoyarsk Speech, p. 37.
46.	Ibid., p. 40; emphasis added.
47.	Ibid., p. 38.
48.	Gorbachev declared: 'We propose a discussion at any level and involving any number of participants of the question of establishing a

negotiating mechanism to examine our and any other proposals relating to the security of the Asia–Pacific region. The USSR, the PRC, and the United States, as permanent members of the UN Security Council might initiate the discussion.' See ibid., p. 39.

49. Charles E. Osgood, 'Graduated Unilateral Initiatives for Peace', in Quincy Wright, William M. Evans, and Morton Deutsch (eds), *Preventing World War III: Some Proposals* (New York: Simon and Schuster, 1962), pp. 161–77.

50. The Krasnoyarsk Speech, p. 39.

51. Tai Ming Cheung, 'A Bad Year at Home, But Better Abroad', *Far Eastern Economic Review* (2 March 1989), p. 65.

52. Gaston J. Sigur and Richard L. Armitage, 'To Play in Asia, Moscow Has to Pay', *The New York Times*, 2 October, 1988.

53. The Krasnoyarsk Speech, p. 38.

54. Ibid., p. 39.

55. For the concept of 'global learning' and its ability in the study of foreign policy, see Samuel S. Kim, 'Thinking Globally in Post-Mao China', *Journal of Peace Research*, vol. 27, no. 2 (1990), pp. 191–209.

56. *The New York Times*, 24 October 1989, pp. A1, A14.

57. Alexei Arbatov, 'Parity and Reasonable Sufficiency', *International Affairs* (Moscow), no. 10 (1988), p. 80.

58. For an excellent discussion about the four triangular configurations, see Lowell Dittmer, *Sino–Soviet Normalization* (Seattle: University of Washington Press, forthcoming), chapter 4.

59. Paul H. Kreisberg, 'Containment's Last Gasp', *Foreign Policy*, no. 75 (Summer 1989), p. 163.

Part III
Conclusions

15 The Shadow of the Future in Light of the Past

Edward A. Kolodziej

The Cold War is rapidly nearing a close. Progress in reaching nuclear, conventional and chemical arms control accords between Washington and Moscow signals the mutual desire of both sides to surmount their titanic conflict and heretofore irreconcilable differences. Real disarmament and a discernible slowdown in the arms race as well as genuine success in resolving their regional differences – in Europe, southern Africa, southeast Asia, and Central America – prompt expectations that superpower relations are evolving toward a new, broader and advanced level of cooperation beyond the Cold War. New forces are driving international politics. Among the most powerful, with which this volume has been primarily concerned, is the rise of new centers of power whose national and socio-economic interests can neither be contained nor satisfied by the superpower struggle and by the Cold War. These forces conspire with compelling internal demands within the domestic societies of the superpowers, especially strong within the Soviet Union, for a break with the Cold War regime.

How can this epochal transformation be explained when only a little while ago the Cold War appeared to be a permanent part of the international universe? In emphasizing the power and influence of third states, this volume supplies a partial answer. A key part of the explanation for the demise of the Cold War lies in the very controlled and calibrated regime reluctantly but prudently constructed by the superpowers to regulate their global conflict since the end of World War II. This regime crystallized as the product of the countervailing power of the superpowers and, as this volume underlines, the resistance of third states to superpower blandishishments and threats. As long as the Cold War and its resultant regime served third-state and domestic societal interests it thrived, especially in catalyzing the globalization of the nation-state system and in promoting the principle of national self-determination. Gradually the superpowers were confronted by a rising tide of recalcitrant states and peoples that diluted, deflected, or defeated their efforts to exert regional influence. Third states, regional groupings, and international movements such as the non-aligned states repeatedly frustrated the aims and strategies of Washington and Moscow – often both simultaneously – or re-fashioned superpower designs to serve their own local purposes. Most notable are Israel and the Arab states in the Middle East; Iran, Iraq, and Saudi Arabia in the Persian Gulf; India and Pakistan in South Asia; Cuba and Nicaragua in Central America; and China and Vietnam in Asia. ASEAN, the non-aligned movement, and the Group of 77 exemplify the coordinated efforts of third states to advance shared interests that clashed in different ways with superpower preferences.

The cost of intervention also grew progressively more costly and risky. As the military capabilities and economic strength of these new centers of decision and initiative have expanded, their ability to shape superpower choices to suit local interests has correspondingly enlarged. Defeats in Afghanistan and Vietnam have instructed the Soviet Union and the United States, respectively, that seemingly powerless nations and peoples can prevail over a militarily superior foe. The unswerving dedication of a mobilized population to what is perceived as a just and legitimate cause, whatever its objective merits may be, can triumph over the force of arms and flawed foreign ideological appeals. Meanwhile, clients and allies also chafed under superpower control and demanded a greater say over their internal and external affairs.

Both superpowers learned from bitter experience that clients were often greater liabilities than assets, not to mention doubtful risks – potentially the source of superpower confrontation – if a superpower associated too closely with a regional power. In different ways each superpower exposed itself to the potentially damaging repercussions of unilaterally pursued client interests over which the patron superpower often had only partial control. Cuban intervention in Africa and Central America and Israeli attacks on its Arab opponents illustrate the limited power and risks run by superpowers in their association with regional states. Specifically, the United States, in its efforts to develop an alliance network to contain the Soviet Union and perceived communist expansionism, has been repeatedly embarrassed by the gap between its announced commitment to democratic practice and human rights, on the one hand, and its assistance and support of authoritarian governments, on the other. Some allies and clients were unable to elicit the support of their own populations. Successive Saigon governments in Vietnam, Somoza's Nicaragua, and Ethiopia's Haile Selassie fell into this category. Other allied regimes ruled by force and fiat, like Park's South Korea, Marcos's Philippines, Pinochet's Chile, and the Shah's Iran; eventually, none of these governments was able to withstand popular (if not always liberal-democratically inspired) demands for their overthrow or replacement.

Once seemingly vital interests in Southeast Asia, Central Africa, or the Taiwan Straits were also discounted by US leaders and popular opinion as the overhead and operating costs of maintaining these portfolios of acquired interests exceeded their real or likely long-term returns on investment. The putative damaging repercussions of withdrawal from exposed and vulnerable salients, especially on one's reputation to carry out deterrent threats and to underwrite alliance commitments, were, as often as not, unduly magnified. Contrary to the expectations of strategic analysts, US military disengagement from an area did not automatically produce a falling domino effect in which the installation of a communist government (Cuba or Vietnam) led inevitably to the extension of similar regimes throughout the region.

Assertion was no match for experience in testing the proposition that the reputation of the United States for honoring its commitments or for supporting its nuclear deterrent posture was discernibly weakened, say in Europe, because of its withdrawal from Southeast Asia. Strategists often had more difficulty discriminating between what seemed to be a superpower's central and peripheral interests than superpower opponents actually had in distinguishing what was significant or not in evaluating their own interests and those of its rival and in estimating (not always accurately as the Cuban and Berlin crises indicate) between its own and those of an opponent's commitments. As a general rule, throughout the Cold War, Eastern Europe was central to the Soviet Union; how else then could the Afghan intervention be viewed as an aberration? Similarly, the Caribbean, Western Europe, the Middle East (oil and Israel), and Japan and the Korean peninsula were determinative for the United States. As the preceding chapters suggest, the leadership corps of successive Moscow and Washington administrations confused at different times their ability to project national power with vital national interests. Disillusionment with these overextensions of national power and interest grew in rough proportion to the demands placed on their treasuries and on popular support in sustaining them.

If US bargaining power can be said to have diminished since World War II, it seems that it has lost more ground to its allies than to the Soviet Union over critical economic and political issues. The fixed attention of the superpowers on each other has had the unanticipated and untoward result of weakening their ability to influence third states in desirable ways, including even their nominal clients. Non-engagement, as in North Africa, did not necessarily prompt intervention by the superpower rival. As William Zartman describes, both superpowers have observed a *modus vivendi* of mutual tolerance of each other's presence and interests in North Africa. The regional states, Libya notwithstanding, have artfully balanced one superpower against the other in managing their contentious regional affairs. Where an opponent's intervention did occur, as in Ethiopia or Angola whose putative communist regimes rested for over a decade on Cuban arms, it did not follow that Moscow gained a lasting strategic advantage in its competition with the United States.

The burden of empire has been especially acute for the Soviet Union. In his celebrated Mr 'X' article, George Kennan correctly diagnosed the symbiotic relationship between the Stalinist totalitarian system and the creation of a Soviet empire ruled by one-party regimes.[1] Each depended on the other to survive. The full costs of the Soviet empire are still not known. By the admission of the Gorbachev regime, they were at the expense of the economic and technological development of the Soviet Union and of the nations subjected to communist rule and centralized economic planning. Kennan also foresaw, as Soviet leaders learned only slowly, that the Stalinist model, applied to the Soviet Union and to its sprawling empire, would be unable to keep pace with Western socio-economic and political progress. Eventually, the legitimacy of one-party rule would erode, at a glacial but inexorable pace, although in a direction that could not exclude the possibility of a catastrophic civil or nuclear war – or both – as embattled communist regimes may have felt compelled to struggle for their lives. The example of Ceaucescu's Romania is a sobering case. The inability of communist regimes in Eastern Europe to provide for economic growth, to meet in some instances basic needs for food and shelter, or to guarantee elemental individual and social rights ultimately voided their right to rule and, correspondingly, weakened their determination to use police and armed forces to enforce their will.

The domino effect in Eastern Europe was the reverse of the one expected by those American strategists who focused exclusively on the superpower military balance and remained insensitive to cross-national economic and political pressures for fundamental change. The disenchantment of the ruling coalition within the Soviet leadership class with its own system has paralleled the trends set in train in Eastern Europe. Approximately three-quarters of a century after the October Revolution, the Central Committee of the Soviet Communist party finally abandoned the party's claim to a monopoly of power. Meanwhile, newly elected bodies were slowly being put in place to rival the once dominant position of the party and the state bureaucracy.

On this score Kennan was also basically correct. He envisioned an evolutionary process that would lead future Russian generations to 'mellow' the Soviet regime once the example of Western economic success and political openness had worked their influence on a deprived Soviet elite and populace. The Gorbachev government's call for *glasnost, perestroika*, and democratization are concepts drawn from Western political practice. Contrary to logic, but not political calculation, the reforms embodied in these slogans are expected, ironically, to restore the confidence of the Soviet people in the communist party. Political reform and the reinstitution of private property and market practices are in turn counted on to stimulate economic growth and provide access to Western investment, know-how, and markets.

As this volume underscores, the Soviet break with the Cold War regime was by no means the simple product of Western example. It also required a long learning process by both superpowers of the limitations of their power abroad and of the infirmities of their domestic societal structures, a recognition most pronounced today in the Soviet Union. Third states, including Moscow's own satellites, played a crucial role in convincing Soviet elites that the Soviet Union neither had the power nor a vital interest in imposing its rule abroad. In overshooting the requirements of containment, through its military intervention abroad, the United States similarly had to learn the same lesson as its superpower counterpart, but only after almost a half century of bitter trial and error in its quest to shape the international system in its own image. It has also been forced to examine its domestic environment – education, transportation system, housing, and savings rates – to reassess its global economic competitiveness.

The incentives for superpower cooperation, generated by their countervailing power and the constraints posed by third states, explain much of the behavior of the superpowers prior to the abandonment of the Cold War regime by the Soviet leadership. The Cold War is being gradually supplanted by new forms of cooperation and competition. These are qualitatively different from those arising simply from the grudging toleration of regional outcomes which neither superpower preferred or from the constraints reluctantly observed by Moscow and Washington to regulate their competition. The precondition for a movement toward cooperation as co-valuation is of course continued progress in reforms in Eastern Europe and the Soviet Union. The prospects for rapid and continuing progress should not be exaggerated. The obstacles to rapid convergence are so formidable (except in the case of East German integration into a united German federal republic) that it may be more accurate to speak of East European approximation of Western models rather than of their unqualified application to regional circumstances. What is happening is that, on the one hand, all of these states are moving away at different rates of change from centralized economic direction and, on the other, toward pluralistic political systems, providing for greater mass and wider elite participation in national decision-making as well as greater protection for personal and group liberties against once all-powerful states. These changes imply the progressive association of these European states, including the Soviet Union, with the Western political and economic system and a return to the pattern of relations that characterized the pre-World War II period and the October 1917 revolution.

While historical analogies inevitably limit themselves, it is well to remember that this earlier period was marked by virulent national rivalries and widespread, often violent, internal social and political upheaval throughout Europe and the United States. The communist revolution was purportedly a solution to nation-state conflict and to Europe's imperial struggles,[2] the rising welfare demands of populations everywhere, and a new basis for the legitimation of political power based on socialist principles. The Stalinist perversion of these solutions, which deepened the domestic and international crises that it was supposed to address, should not obscure the very real and profound structural weaknesses of the capitalist system, evidenced by the chronic global depression of the interwar years. In the first half of this century, the liberal democracies also failed to respond to the same global challenges as the communist movement and to withstand internally the ideological and armed attacks from the Right and Left on open political systems.

The failure of the Soviet system to realize its own political and economic aims and, what few Soviet leaders expected, its inability to sustain the technological arms race with the West puts in relief the relative success of Western models. What such satisfying comparisons do not ensure, however, is that the structural weakness of the global political and socio-economic system will necessarily be overcome solely by relying on Western solutions, even if one optimistically assumes continuing Western cohesion in applying them. The world, if freed from the Cold War, will not be liberated from conflict. The weakening of the international regulatory functions of the superpowers on local rivalries may even engender the release of hitherto pent up local hostilities. Other forces, until now muted by the Cold War, are again driving international conflict: the gap between rich and poor nations; communal, ethnic, racial and national animosities; and an incipiently anarchical nation-state system still impels regional strife with little prospect that these structural features of the international environment will be corrected in the near future.

THE COLD WAR AS COOPERATION: SYSTEMIC RETROSPECTIVE

The Cold War served at least two critical systemic functions. First, it preserved a shaky peace between the two revolutionary powers, each bent on shaping the international system to suit its interests and designs, with enough nuclear striking power to destroy not only themselves but large segments of the globe and its population. The restraint and prudence exercised by successive leadership cohorts in Washington and Moscow in their national and universal struggle kept the future open for both and for other peoples and states. Most Big Power contests in the past resulted in a major clash to test the relative power and resolve of the principals or, as Clausewitz suggested, to settle accounts through an exchange of arms. Except perhaps for the early period of the nuclear era when the United States enjoyed a fleeting nuclear monopoly, that option was never realistically available to either superpower at a level of risk that either was willing to run to impose its will in a regional conflict if the superpower partner-rival would have become actively engaged in the fray. Even the Cuban missile and Berlin crises, as limiting cases, testify to the argument that the superpowers exercised painstaking restraint to avoid a nuclear confrontation.

Second, the competition held both states to a higher standard of international performance than might have otherwise proven to be the case. As a consequence of their adversarial relationship, much like contesting lawyers in a civil trial, both had compelling incentive to censure each other's behavior. In attempting to win allies and support abroad and to hold political coalitions together at home, the latter an especially acute problem for the United States, both superpowers were led to array themselves on the side of decolonization and national self-determination. Both had to couch their self-interested national claims as contributions to universal peace, global economic betterment, and social justice.

The gap between superpower principles and performance exposed them, correspondingly, to the reproach of third states which held Washington and Moscow to the regimen of their professed aims. Home populations, first within Eastern Europe (with countless setbacks along the way) and finally within the Soviet Union itself, joined the chorus of protesters and reformers incensed by lagging economic growth, by repressive political practices, by a burdensome and increasingly pointless arms race and by doubtful interventions abroad as a consequence of the Cold War struggle. As long as nuclear war could be avoided and the superpower rivalry kept cold, then opponents of the Cold War regime could organize and work within each system, East and West, to demand a relaxation of tensions and of war fears, greater economic development over military preparedness and investment, and enlarged personal and social freedoms.

As Victor Kremenyuk's analysis of the Cold War suggests, the Cold War, understood in the context of this volume as an ordered, albeit provisional, structure of superpower cooperation, was a precondition for the nurturing and enlarging of shared values across national frontiers and ideologically prescribed barriers by otherwise historically determined diverse peoples. Even the most resolute and uncompromising attempts to staunch and stymie the public expression of these values – embodied in demands for greater material comfort and wealth, for expanded individual and social freedoms, and for societal protections against monopolistic centers of party or state power – have ultimately failed. It may well be that Western military might and claims of superior political and economic practice are a necessary part of any explanation for the revolutionary changes sweeping Eastern Europe and the Soviet Union. What is not satisfactorily explained is how they could have survived and thrived within these societies despite what appeared to be crushing hardship and overwhelming handicaps.

The end of the Cold War will hardly ensure that the forces pressing for reform through the Soviet Union and Eastern Europe and for redress of grievances within the West will succeed. Nor will the end of the Cold War ensure that the global nation-state will resolve the environmental and ecological problems that have been subordinated until now to global and regional strife. The Cold War did not resolve the chronic and endemic crises of order, welfare, and legitimacy. Its impending demise does not promise solution, either. The structural flaws of the international system are being redefined by the emergence of a new international system in which national self-assertion, pluralist parties and popularly elected institutions, and market practices are gaining ground, respectively, over imperial domination, dictatorial one-party, police, or military rule, and the indifference of governments to the material plight of their national populations. From a systemic perspective, the rise and demise of the Cold War can be most broadly understood as a provisional response to these imperatives.

The Cold War has served its time, neither very well nor wisely, as an instrument of human design to comprise differences between states and peoples and to define opportunities for enlarged cooperation. The leadership of both superpowers gradually learned that limited cooperation could be relied upon to stabilize and moderate the East–West and superpower conflict to mutual advantage. In the absence of this structure of largely tacit and sometimes explicit accords that formed the Cold War regime, it is difficult to see how the breakthrough to a multipolar and decentralized international system, arguably better adapted to cope with the system's structural faults, could have been possible. Certainly, a global political and socio-economic system, resting on increasing cooperation between the United States and the Soviet Union, is a precondition for overcoming some of the structural defects of the global system.

The Cold War, viewed as a cooperative process between competing Big Powers, has propelled the international system to its present level of development and has contributed to the gradual enlargement of the possibilities of mutual cooperation between states and peoples. If measured by the untold damage and staggering deaths of two world wars (not to mention those of previous centuries), the Cold War was certainly an advance over these traditional approaches to resolving international conflict between great powers. There is some basis for the proposition that what we are witnessing, as Paul Schroeder has intriguingly argued,[3] is a ratchet effect in international relations in which each successive epoch is plunged into crisis and war only to emerge after the trauma of wholesale and merciless violence as well as vast human and material destruction possessed of greater international understanding about the sources of global conflict and how to avoid them, and bolstered by new knowledge and institutional mechanisms to cope with global security and with political and socio-economic problems that previous ages were unable to address.

We may be escaping, as Thornton Wilder reminds us, just by the skin of our teeth. Piercing reason and greater prescience might have been sufficient to have avoided not only the Cold War but all past conflagrations. Easy hindsight, earned only by harsh experience, makes that now plain. As a matter of record, the United States and the Soviet Union have learned to compromise their differences even before Soviet *glasnost*, *perestroika*, and democratization pushed cooperation to previously unimagined levels. If the future is unclear, a careful look at the past suggests possible avenues for strengthening and deepening cooperation. Such a look can at least dispel some of the shadows that the future casts.

NOTES

1. George F. Kennan, 'The Sources of Soviet Conduct', *Foreign Affairs*, vol. XXV, no. 4 (July 1947), pp. 566–82.
2. V. I. Lenin, *Imperialism: The Highest State of Capitalism* (New York: International Publications, 1939).
3. Paul W. Schroeder, 'The Nineteenth Century System: Balance of Power or Political Equilibrium?' *Review of International Studies*, vol. XV, (1989), pp. 135–53, and 'The 19th Century International System: Changes in the Structure', *World Politics*, vol. XXXIX, no. 1 (October 1986), pp. 1–26.

Index of Cases of Superpower Cooperation
James M. Finlay

CHAPTER 5: MIDDLE EAST

CHAPTER 6: NORTH AFRICA

Index

Eastern Europe – *cont.*
movement in, 16–17, 66, 80, 82,
93, 104–5, 107, 110–17, 408–9; and
stable European security regime,
95–105; superpower interest in,
90–5; and superpower rules of
behavior, 105–10; US interest in,
91, 93–5
East Germany. *See* German
Democratic Republic (GDR)
Economic systems, legitimacy of, 12
Economy of force, 255, 257
Ecuador, superpower conflict in, 264
Egypt: as mediator in Arab–Israeli
conflict, 142; Soviet influence in,
7, 9, 42, 51, 123, 127, 130, 134,
135, 136, 137, 174; US interest in,
129, 130, 141, 163
Eisenhower, Dwight D., 34, 35, 41,
94, 104, 132
Eisenhower Doctrine (1957), 39
El Salvador: civil war in, 227, 228;
Cuban involvement in, 236;
invasion of Honduras, 228;
revolution in, 268, 269; Soviet
involvement in, 230, 237, 238, 240,
241, 259, 261, 273; superpower
conflict in, 264, 275; US aid to,
234; US involvement in, 225, 226,
230, 238, 242, 256
England. *See* Great Britain
Environment, superpower
cooperation to preserve, 166–7,
321
Equatorial Guinea, tyranny in, 171
Ethiopia: Cuban troops in, 161;
denied membership in CMEA,
181; Soviet influence in, 157, 158,
159, 160, 161, 162, 163, 165, 187;
US influence in, 156–8, 159, 160,
161–2, 163, 165
Europe: post-World War II military
strategies in, 5–6; reduction of
conventional forces in, 3. *See also*
Eastern Europe; Western Europe
European Advisory Commission
(EAC), 67, 68
European Community (EC): as
challenger to US economic power,

82; Common Agricultural Policy
(CAP) of, 78; and economic
reforms, 85–6; Gaullist opposition
to British entry in, 78, 79;
involvement in Central Africa, 191
European Defense Community
(EDC), 68, 342
European Economic Community
(EEC), 345
European Recovery Program
(Marshall Plan), 68, 77, 95

F-4 (Phantom) aircraft, 137
F7 aircraft, 354
F-16 aircraft, 354
F-111 fighter-bomber, 72
Fahd (king of Saudi Arabia), 165
Falklands War, 255
Farabundo Martí National
Liberation Movement (FMLN),
225, 241, 246
Finland: neutrality of, 7; Soviet
relations with, 120n.27; Soviet
withdrawal from, 98
Foco theory, 259, 260
Ford, Gerald, 44, 132, 319
France: Algerian relations with, 151;
national unity in, 11; and
resistance to US leadership in
Western Europe, 13; rivalry for
dominance in Europe, 11; and
Suez crisis, 127; support for Israel
from, 124
French Revolution, 13

Gabon: French military presence in,
184; oil exports from, 173, 174
Gaddis, John, 104
Game theory: and cooperation, 6, 9;
and methodology, 20–1. *See also*
Cold War, as a zero-sum game
Gandhi, Indira, 286, 291, 298
Garang, John, 160
Garthoff, Raymond, 383
General Agreement on Tariffs and
Trade (GATT), 14, 76, 77, 78, 385
Geneva (Switzerland): conference in
1962 in, 343; conference in 1977
in, 50; conferences in 1953 and